Between 1936 and 1938, the French alliance system in East Central Europe collapsed. The resulting dramatic expansion of German power led directly to the Second World War. This illuminating study investigates the implications of French military, economic and diplomatic policies in Central Europe from Versailles until the fall of France, establishing the proper context for the policy options of Léon Blum's Popular Front. It focusses on the clash between the French military and French radical politics in 1936–7 under Blum's government, loyal to the defence of Czechoslovakia. The figure of Blum illustrates the insights and the dilemmas of a democratic Socialist caught up in the imbrication of foreign and domestic politics which increasingly characterised the 1930s.

Using the vast resources of the French archives, key private papers, and diaries, as well as the debates of current historiography, Nicole Jordan re-interprets the central international crises of the 1930s to show how France's options were reduced from the unencumbered eastern terrain to the narrow confines of Belgium, where one mistake would expose the sacred patrimony to another invasion.

In her study of the failure of French democracy successfully to defend itself and its eastern allies in 1938–40, Dr Jordan's wider themes include the effect of the search for détente on alliance systems, the politics of arms limitation, the role of ideology in foreign policy formulation, and the place of ethics in external affairs. The book's impressive scope is underpinned by the most seriously documented analysis of the subject yet produced.

THE POPULAR FRONT AND CENTRAL EUROPE

Cartoon by Soupault in the far right-wing weekly, *Je suis partout*, 11 November 1938, the Armistice Day after Munich. The caption reads 'No thank you… I would rather "Live for France!"'

THE POPULAR FRONT
AND CENTRAL EUROPE:
THE DILEMMAS OF
FRENCH IMPOTENCE,
1918–1940

NICOLE JORDAN

CAMBRIDGE
UNIVERSITY PRESS

Published by the Press Syndicate of the University of Cambridge
The Pitt Building, Trumpington Street, Cambridge CB2 IRP
40 West 20th Street, New York, NY 10011–4211, USA
10 Stamford Road, Oakleigh, Melbourne 3166, Australia

First published 1992

Printed in Great Britain at the University Press, Cambridge

A catalogue record for this book is available from the British Library

Library of Congress cataloguing in publication data

Jordan, Nicole.
The Popular Front & Central Europe: the dilemmas of French
impotence, 1918–1940 / Nicole Jordan.
p.   cm.
Includes bibliographical references and index.
ISBN 0-521-41077-0
1. France–Foreign relations–1914–1940.   2. Blum, Léon.
1872–1950 – Influence.   3. Front populaire.   4. Europe – Politics and
government – 1918–1945.   5. World War, 1939–1945 – Causes.   I. Title.
II. Title: Popular Front and Central Europe.
DC369.J57   1992
327.44043092041 – dc20   91–2622 CIP

ISBN 0 521 41077 0 hardback

For two friends who shared a love of Prague

Noémi Hubert Ripka
1896–1983
and
Robyn Marsack

Contents

Contents

Maps

Acknowledgements

Few studies of this duration are completed without the help of many people. My first debt is to my parents for financial and other support far beyond the call of parental duty. For generous fellowships, I am grateful to the National Endowment for the Humanities; the Campus Research Board and the Humanities Institute of the University of Illinois at Chicago; the American Association of University Women; and Wellesley College. My colleagues at the University of Illinois also made possible release time for writing.

Without Maurice Degros, Conservateur en chef honoraire des Archives du Ministère des Affaires étrangères, who was unfailingly helpful both in the Quai d'Orsay's archives and in facilitating archival access elsewhere, this study would not have been possible. I am indebted as well to M. Degros's distinguished colleagues on the Commission de publication des documents diplomatiques, Yvon Lacaze, the late Jacques Monicat and the late Georges Taboulet; to Monique Constant, also of the Quai d'Orsay; to Marie-Geneviève Chevignard of the Fondation des Sciences Politiques; and to the staffs of the Archives Nationales; the Assemblée Nationale; the Bibliothèque Nationale; the Bodleian Library; the British Library; Churchill College, Cambridge; the Hoover Institution; the Ministère des Finances; the Public Records Office; Regenstein Library, University of Chicago; the Services historiques de l'armée de l'air and de l'armée de terre; and Widener Library, Harvard University.

I have received valuable advice from many French, British, and American historians whom it is a great pleasure to thank here, beginning with three pioneers of monographs on French policy in the 1930s, P. C. F. Bankwitz, Anthony Adamthwaite, and Robert Young. My thanks are also due to: Martin S. Alexander, François Bédarida, Rohan Butler, Jean-Baptiste Duroselle, René Girault, Jean-Noël Jeanneney, Douglas Johnson, Bernard Michel, Nicholas

Rostow, Stephen Schuker, Georges Soutou, Paul Stafford, and Maurice Vaïsse. Professor Donald Cameron Watt of the London School of Economics originally suggested a variant of the present study, while the late Esmonde Robertson showed exemplary patience during my doctoral research. For important criticisms of the draft in its various forms, I am indebted to Maury Feld, George Huppert, Bradford Lee, Marion Miller, R. A. C. Parker, and Henry Rollet. Sir William Deakin, who accompanied Winston Churchill to Paris after the reoccupation of the Rhineland in 1936, has been generous with both criticism and encouragement. The vigilance of their criticism notwithstanding, the errors, like the conclusions reached, are my own. I am grateful to Robyn Marsack who provided much valued editorial help. I should also thank Bonnie Menes for her editorial pains, Amy Goodman for help with the bibliography, and Burton Bledstein for computer programming. Marie-Helène Gold, Jean Laloy, Raimonda Modiano, Henry Rollet, and Michaela Tomaschewsky offset my linguistic deficiencies with polished translations.

I have found the study of Léon Blum a humanising experience. It has been enriched by meetings with Blum's fine biographers, James Joll and Joel Colton, as well as by conversations and correspondence on France in the 1930s with various of Blum's contemporaries: Armand Bérard, the late Hubert Beuve-Méry, Renée Robert Blum, Etienne de Crouy-Chanel, Jean Daridan, Roger Glachant, Jean Laloy, René Massigli, the late Pierre Mendès France, Renée Maly, Eliane and the late Jules Moch, the late Léon Noël, Jean Pasquier, the late Noémi Hubert Ripka, Noël and Marie Rist, Henry Rollet, and the late Louise Weiss.

One last acknowledgement. For shelter in various stages of writing, I would especially like to thank Jenifer and Herbert Hart, Zipporah and Frederick Wiseman, Shirley Katz, Christina von Nolcken, and Kostas Kazazis.

Abbreviations

Assemblée Nationale, Commission	Assemblée Nationale, Commission des Affaires étrangères
CE Témoignages	*Rapport fait au nom de la Commission chargée d'enquêter sur les événements survenus en France de 1933 à 1945. Annexes (Dépositions). Témoignages et documents recueillis par la commission d'enquête parlementaire*
CHEDN	Collège des hautes études de la Défense nationale
CPDN	Comité permanent de la Défense nationale
Czech T-120	Captured Czechoslovak documents in T-120, National Archives classification, Washington DC
DBFP	*Documents on British Foreign Policy*
DDB	*Documents diplomatiques belges*
DDF	*Documents diplomatiques français*
DGFP	*Documents on German Foreign Policy*
EMA	Etat-major de l'armée
Finances	Ministère des Finances

FNSP	Fondation Nationale des Sciences Politiques
FO	Foreign Office
FRUS	*Foreign Relations of the United States*
HCM	Haut Comité militaire
JCH	*Journal of Contemporary History*
JMH	*Journal of Modern History*
L'oeuvre	*L'oeuvre de Léon Blum*
MAE	Ministère des Affaires étrangères
PRO	Public Records Office
RDM	*Revue des deux Mondes*
Schw.	Papiers Schweisguth
SFIO	Section français de l'internationale ouvrière
SHA	Service historique de l'armée de terre
SHAA	Service historique de l'armée de l'air

So we go on searching for *real* causes, with all the emphasis on the word 'real'. And soon we learn that there is nothing easier than to find *real* causes. Anything which makes a situation meaningful can be turned into a cause either in isolation or in conjunction with other elements…One causal sequence will probably look slightly more probable than the other, but plausibility is not a ready criterion for judgement when the situation is extremely complex and many elements are available for different combinations.

Historians, one must admit, were not created by God to search for causes. Any search for causes in history, if it is persistent…becomes comic, such is the abundance of causes discovered…What we want is to understand change by analysing it and giving their due to conscious decisions, deep-seated urges and the interplay of disparate events…[For this] we must have a mental picture…of the whole situation as a term of reference.

Arnaldo Momigliano
Annale della Scuola Normale Superiore di Pisa
Serie III, vol. VIII, Pisa, 1978

Introduction

Traditionally, study of French foreign policy between the world wars has been bounded by two, interlocking perceptions. French diplomats and military are said to have been obsessed with Great Britain and with taking no real initiative without British backing, while French strategy is said to have been almost exclusively concerned with sheltering behind an impregnable Maginot line in the absence of a strong alliance with Great Britain. This book begins by questioning both these propositions in their more absolute forms, and, in so doing, it reinterprets such diplomatic landmarks of the 1930s as the Hoare-Laval Plan and the Rhineland crisis. It also argues for a broad consistency in French strategy in the inter-war period, obsessed not with being pinioned behind the Maginot line (although certainly fortifications were important to French defence), but with carrying a war outside of French territory. This leads to a linkage between earlier French strategy towards the eastern allies and Italy and the reckless French dash to Holland in 1940, which until now has been regarded as contradictory and aberrant. In the picture it draws of French external policy between 1919 and 1940, this book seeks to refocus on the topography of the Danube and the Vistula in the landscape of the 1930s, in order to analyse how the conditions of possible diplomatic and military disaster emerged.

The primacy previously assigned to Great Britain is at the heart of current debate amongst French and British scholars over the role of 'la gouvernante anglaise', the British governess.[1] Whatever its broad constraints, and there were many, French policy had its own internal logic, which, as French archival sources show, was sometimes concealed from British policy-makers. Chapter 1, which examines

---

[1] The phrase was coined by François Bédarida to describe British tutelage of France in the 1930s. F. Bédarida, 'La "gouvernante anglaise"', in René Rémond and Janine Bourdin (eds.), *Edouard Daladier chef du gouvernement* (Paris, 1977), pp. 228–40.

the diplomacy of Louis Barthou and Pierre Laval and the response of the French General Staff to the Ethiopan crisis of 1935, uses internal military and diplomatic memoranda to show that in the mid 1930s the French hoped for benevolent British neutrality, while relying upon a military entente with Italy as an all-purpose bridge to its allies in East Central Europe. (In this context, it is significant that economic data on the implications of a flagging commercial performance for France's ability to arm its allies can be linked back to an Italophile tendency in French diplomacy and strategy, thus composing a previously ignored unity of high policy in the early and mid 1930s.) The key importance attached to Italy well after the Ethiopian crisis of 1935 was inseparable from the importance the General Staff attached to a strategy of distant fronts, a strategy in which eastern allies would bear the brunt of German force. Britain, whatever its strengths, could never altogether supplant the Italian factor in French military planning for a war of coalition.

The prolonged Italophile agony of the General Staff as well as the suppositions with which the French military supported the eastern alliances from the 1920s suggest the strength of military attachment to fighting a war elsewhere by means of allies who would channel and divert German force. The Italian, Polish, and Czech ties thus came to represent an even more defensive strategy than the Maginot line. Their importance actually increased for the French General Staff in the critical period after the Rhineland reoccupation in March 1936. Some of the conclusions drawn from the military archives may surprise. Without knowledge of the military's presuppositions for wars of coalition, they may even appear counter-intuitive. But then few events in modern history have been more surprising or more counter-intuitive than the fall of France.

If the relationship between France's eventual betrayal of its eastern allies and the fall of France itself is critical to the book's argument, its core is those chapters which concern the year-long government of the Socialist Léon Blum. Blum's foreign policy, notably his abiding concern with the defence of Czechoslovakia, is usually neglected on the assumption that his external concerns were limited to the Spanish Civil War and occasional conversations with Hjalmar Schacht, the head of the Reichsbank. In fact the Front populaire was unusually active in negotiations with its Central European allies: Poland, and the three countries of the Petite Entente, Czechoslovakia, Roumania and Yugoslavia.

Histories of the Third Republic justly set great store on governmental instability to explain French impotence in the face of the Hitlerian threat. While it is true that many official decision-makers were figures of legendary permanence, such as Alexis Léger, Maurice Gamelin, and Philippe Pétain, the evanescence and instability of individual ministries certainly created destructive impressions abroad. The analysis here, however, concentrates on the impact of ideology on French diplomacy and strategy during the Blum Government, and includes suppressed testimony from the Riom trials, the political trials organised by the Pétain Government at German behest which were intended to inculpate France's leaders from 1936 for the defeat in 1940. The impact of ideology in external affairs can more readily be seen on the military than on Blum himself. The core chapters trace the impact of ideology on the military's response to the divergent claims for support of Poland, Czechoslovakia, and the USSR. A case study of the Franco-Polish arms accord of 1936 reveals the Front populaire's attempts to remedy the negligence of its predecessors in arming its allies, against the backdrop of the determination of the General Staff and the French Embassy in Warsaw to cultivate Poland and Italy as counterweights to pressures within Blum's Government for a Soviet military entente. Direct Soviet influence on the Franco-Petite Entente negotiations of 1936–7 and Soviet pressures for bilateral staff talks with France set in still sharper relief the ideological constraints which isolated the Blum Government and its Czechoslovak ally.

Blum's brief Government is of particular interest for several reasons: first, the way in which internal struggle for control of the government's foreign policy in East Central Europe reflected aspects of the acute domestic social crisis in 1936–7; and secondly, the way in which the Spanish war narrowed French perceptions of the plight of Czechoslovakia once Blum fell from power. Perhaps most significantly, in the period after the Rhineland reoccupation Hitler began his diplomatic revolution in Europe by a process of ideological selection. Ideology distorted power perceptions in Europe and allowed Hitler the enormous psychological advantage of disarming his potential adversaries one by one. The ideological turbulence surrounding the Popular Front period is essential to an understanding of the French abandonment of Czechoslovakia and thereby of the defeat in 1940. Chapter 7 then surveys the process whereby

war on the cheap – that is, on the peripheries – was lost, as French
strategic options were reduced from the relatively unencumbered
eastern terrain to the confines of Belgium, where one mistake would
expose the sacred patrimony to another invasion.

Among various interwoven themes, military, economic, diplomatic,
and ideological, the realities and the illusions of power politics are
probed, in order to question conventional divisions between the
survival of great and the survival of small powers in a century in
which no single power has been great enough to sustain the human
and financial costs of total war. For this over-arching reason,
attention is given in the pages which follow to the psychology of
individuals as different as General Maurice Gamelin and Premier
Léon Blum. Marc Bloch, a veteran of both the world wars, reflected
that the course of human events is governed in the last analysis by
human psychology.[2] The chief psychological fact of Bloch's book, as
in some sense of this one, is a tragic reluctance to shed French blood
again in self-defence. Gamelin's policy of interposing allies and
diverting German force elsewhere, his fixation on an Italy even less
willing to fight than France; Léon Blum's deep shame at the
temptation, snare and delusion of pseudo-negotiation at Munich:
these were distinct manifestations of a national mentality so
compelling as to appropriate many texts of the decade. Response in
the 1930s ranged from the moral distress of Léon Blum and Marc
Bloch, to the brooding inaction of General Gamelin, to the hideous
retort of *Je suis partout* seen in the frontispiece. Part of the continuing
hold of this painful decade comes from the psychological tension
inherent in this gradation of response, with its terrible suggestion
that there are few clear-cut answers and no easily drawn boundaries
between the particular and the universal. Certainly these years can
only discomfit armchair moralists.

---

[2] M. Bloch, *L'étrange défaite* (Paris, 1946), p. 189.

CHAPTER I

The diplomats, the formation of the eastern alliance system and arms limitation, 1918–1935

FORMATION

Jules Cambon, President of the post-war Conference of Ambassadors, confided to a younger diplomatic colleague in 1921: 'Young man, remember this: in the immediate future the difficulty will be to slide France reasonably smoothly into the ranks of the second-rate powers to which she belongs.'[1] The avuncular dictum of Cambon, who had been France's Ambassador in Berlin before the First World War and President of the Commissions on Czechoslovakia and Poland at the Peace Conference, reflected the acute sense of limitation and vulnerability which underlay French external policy-making from the first days of the peace.

The Ruhr and the treaties with Poland and Czechoslovakia

With the defeat of Clemenceau's ardent hopes for unbroken continuation of wartime inter-allied collaboration, the moderate Right governments of the immediate post-war period, the so-called Bloc National, fell back on a clutch of expedients. They fitfully pursued a policy of settlement with Germany backed by Anglo-Saxon financial power, but at the same time they were reluctant to renounce the recurrent dream of French diplomacy since the Congress of Vienna: a commanding position in the Rhineland. Important recent work on the 1920s by French and American historians suggests the consistent attachment of the Quai d'Orsay, the French Ministry of Foreign Affairs, to Germany's involvement in a revitalised, pacified Europe on which French national fortunes were held to depend.[2] The most striking elements of this historical

---

[1] J. Chastenet, *Quatre fois vingt ans* (Paris, 1974), p. 121.
[2] D. Artaud, *La question des dettes interalliées et la reconstruction de l'Europe, 1917–1929*, 2 vols. (Lille, 1978); J. Bariéty, *Les relations franco-allemandes après la première guerre mondiale* (Paris,

5

revisionism, those which concern the Ruhr crisis, reveal the way in which these hopes for European reintegration were confounded with the ambitious French projects for an autonomous Rhineland.

The reparations crisis had led to the French occupation of the Ruhr in 1923. At that time, reparations were unabashedly seen in some quarters as providing a stirrup for a revival of the Rhenish ambitions which Clemenceau had forfeited at Versailles in 1919. Amidst the effervescence of 1922–3, Rhineland options discussed in Paris ranged from on-the-spot fomentation of violent Rhenish separatism, to far-reaching internationalisation of the Rhineland problem, which would end the French occupation in return for establishment of permanent League control over the zone's demilitarisation, and general security discussions. While his ultimate intentions remain a focus of revisionist debate, it is plain that Raymond Poincaré, the political figure of ram-rod patriotism who headed the Bloc National, negotiated in a narrowly legalistic sense. He deployed the threat of Rhenish separatism to force German resumption of reparations payments under the aegis of what became the Dawes Committee. The point of consensus in the work of the 1920s revisionists, in almost every other respect rich in controversy, is that the Ruhr crisis of 1923 marked the bitter end for Paris of an adventurous Rhineland course. Unilateral French coerciveness in the Rhineland had been definitively discredited.

In the same years, slightly in advance of the acute phase of Franco-German discord over reparations, Paris embarked on a series of continental friendships. While Poincaré was not in office at the conclusion of the treaties with Poland in 1921, the elaboration of the eastern treaties became closely associated with his strong-armed diplomacy. In 1922–3, he oversaw the fledgling steps of Franco-Polish economic and military coordination, as well as the negotiations for a second, eastern treaty with Czechoslovakia.[3]

1977); C. S. Maier, *Recasting Bourgeois Europe* (Princeton, 1975); S. Marks, 'Reparations Reconsidered', *Central European History*, vol. 2, 1969 and 'The myths of reparations', *Central European History*, vol. 11, September 1978; S. A. Schuker, *The End of French Predominance in Europe* (Chapel Hill, 1976); G. Soutou, 'Problèmes concernant le rétablissement des relations économiques franco-allemandes après la première guerre mondiale', *Francia*, vol. 2, 1974 and 'Die deutschen Reparationen und das Seydoux-Projekt 1920–21', *Viertel jahrsheft für Zeitgeschichte*, vol. 23, 1975; M. Trachtenberg, *Reparation in World Politics* (New York, 1980). For concise illustration of the argumentative range of this new scholarship, see Trachtenberg's 'Reparations at the Paris Peace Conference', *JMH*, vol. 51, no. 1, March 1979, p. 43.
[3] As Premier in 1921, Aristide Briand subordinated implementation of the Polish political and military accords to the success of difficult bilateral economic negotiations. By delaying

France concluded its treaties of 1921 and 1924 with Poland and Czechoslovakia in a context marked by an obsessive fear, fanned by the Treaty of Rapallo (1922), of German-Soviet collusion against the peace settlement.[4] In 1921, Millerand, the fiercely anti-Bolshevik French president, and General Buat, the Chief of Staff, rode roughshod over opposition to simultaneous French commitments to Poland against Germany and the USSR from Marshal Foch, as well as from leading diplomats. Foch supported a policy of an eastern counterweight resting on the newly independent states between Germany and Russia, but he questioned the wisdom of precise engagements to the obstreperous and unsettled new Polish state.[5]

The most particularised of Paris's inter-war alliance treaties, the 1921 Franco-Polish military agreement defined the scope of common concern: Soviet menace and German mobilisation. The Poles early saw an interest in integral defence of the Rhineland demilitarisation and arms limitation statutes, causes which would bring confrontation with Germany in the west. They thus accepted that the 1921 military agreement explicitly state that French troops would not be sent to reinforce the Polish war effort. In the case of a German attack in the east, France agreed only to dispatch technicians and war machinery and to secure communication lines with Poland.

In the midst of the Ruhr crisis of 1923, Marshal Foch attempted to consolidate the Polish treaties by a Czech military alliance. The French overtures met with Czech evasiveness. The Czechs disapproved of Poincaré's coercive policy in the Ruhr. The looser 1924 political treaty with Czechoslovakia represented a compromise solution, by which Czechoslovakia also assented to an exchange of military letters providing for staff contacts, rather than the military pact desired by Foch and Poincaré during the Ruhr interlude.[6]

the force of the political and military accords with Warsaw, Briand wooed the British, who were averse to French commitments in Central Europe, and whom he hoped to persuade to revive their defunct 1919 guarantee of France. On assuming the premiership in 1922, Poincaré immediately signed the economic accords with Poland and so activated the alliance. Franco-Polish military talks followed, to London's displeasure. H. Rollet, *La Pologne au XXe siècle* (Paris, 1984), pp. 182–6; G. Soutou, 'L'alliance franco-polonaise (1925–1933) ou comment s'en débarrasser?', *Revue d'histoire diplomatique*, nos. 2–4, 1981, p. 297.

[4] SHA, 'EMA/2 Tchécoslovaquie', revised conclusion, 2e Bureau Note, 1 May 1922.

[5] J. Laroche, *La Pologne de Piłsudski* (Paris, 1953), pp. 13–15; P. Wandycz, *France and her Eastern Allies, 1919–1925* (Minneapolis, 1962), pp. 22, 169–70, 213–19; Rollet, *La Pologne*, p. 181.

[6] Rollet, *La Pologne*, pp. 272, 279, 297–306; J. Laroche, *Au Quai d'Orsay avec Briand et Poincaré* (Paris, 1957), pp. 185–6.

From its earliest involvement with the new eastern states, the Quai d'Orsay and the General Staff had dreamt of a Polish-Czech front. They raised the subject repeatedly in conversations with the Poles, who were given the impression that the Bloc National intended to avoid precise conversations on Germany until Polish-Czech rapprochement occurred.[7] The French dream of cooperation between its two allies was imperilled by a Polish-Czech enmity stubbornly resistant to attempts at mediation. The dislike between Poles and Czechs was rooted in centuries of divergent political and social development, culture and religion. Its post-war virulence dated from the period of competing territorial and minority claims for the border area of Teschen, awarded to Czechoslovakia in 1920, and from the Czechs' obstructionist attitude during the Polish-Soviet conflict over Poland's eastern borders when Czech neutrality impeded French supplies to Poland. Slavophile by inheritance, although distrustful of the new Bolshevik régime, the Czechs envisaged themselves as a bridge between Russia and Western Europe. These Czech security aspirations warred with those of successive Polish régimes. After the 1920 campaign against the Soviets, Piłsudski as Minister of War in 1921 conceived of the alliance with France as a means of protection against German aggression should Poland again become involved in conflict with the USSR, while his successors sought a fully automatic convention with France which would provide security against the USSR and Germany.[8]

The obsession with German-Soviet collusion, which fed the Bloc National's staunchly anti-revisionist diplomacy *vis-à-vis* Poland and Czechoslovakia, faded with Poincaré's fall from power and the general pacification accomplished by the 1924 London Conference. In that year, Herriot's moderate Left government, the *Cartel des gauches*, recognised the Soviet Union, and in 1926 Germany entered the League of Nations.

Briandism and Locarno

Germany's entry into the League of Nations in 1926 was the product of the Locarno negotiations of 1925. The work of European integration, whose self-proclaimed architect was Aristide Briand,

---

[7] Rollet, *La Pologne*, pp. 186, 194.
[8] Wandycz, *France*, pp. 257, 306, 318; 'La Pologne face à la politique locarnienne de Briand', *Revue d'histoire diplomatique*, nos. 2–4, 1981, p. 239; G. Soutou, 'L'alliance franco-polonaise...', pp. 298–9, and 'L'impérialisme du pauvre', *Relations internationales*, vol. 7 (1976), p. 229.

finally appeared to be underway.[9] For Briand, Locarno brought the first fragile successes of his and Herriot's abortive diplomacy over the Geneva Protocol, by which states would agree to submit their disputes to international arbitration. The task of French diplomacy under Briand was the suppression of Germany's natural hegemony by integrating it voluntarily into a Europe whose reorganisation would be instigated by France. Briand's Geneva Protocol and Locarno diplomacy were of one piece with his subsequent project for European union, analysed by Sally Marks as 'an effort to enmesh Germany so deeply in all-European economic, political and diplomatic arrangements that she could never make war on France again'.[10]

In the golden haze of the Locarno era, Briand cast himself as *le pèlerin de la paix*. In his adroit hands, judged a well-placed contemporary, 'Difficulties diminished if not to the point of solution at least until they became transparent... he loved peace and he made it loved'.[11] Briand as a Bloc National Minister in the early twenties had espoused a different diplomacy, sending French troops to occupy three cities in the Ruhr in 1921. The resulting threat of isolation, however, moved him to adopt an openly conciliatory policy towards Germany by 1922, and he vehemently opposed Poincaré's hard-line diplomacy in the Ruhr.[12] This shift in Briand's policies met with steady encouragement from the senior permanent official at the Quai d'Orsay, Philippe Berthelot. Temporarily exiled from the Quai d'Orsay by Poincaré in 1922–3, after allegations of his improper use of influence, Berthelot wrote privately to Briand during the Ruhr crisis, to argue passionately for Franco-German conciliation:

---

[9] Jon Jacobson's *Locarno Diplomacy: Germany and the West 1925–1929* (Princeton, 1972) is an indispensable source on great power relations in this period.

[10] M. Vaïsse, *Sécurité d'abord: la politique française en matière de désarmement* (Paris, 1981), pp. 32–4; S. Marks, *The Illusion of Peace: International Relations in Europe 1918–1933* (London, 1976), p. 65.

[11] P. Claudel, *Oeuvres en prose* (Paris, 1965), pp. 1272–3. Briand's historical reputation has been more dappled. Jacques Néré points to his 'gift for toning down too sharp distinctions, for creating the half-light conducive to harmony', but implicitly also to future misunderstandings. A. J. P. Taylor writes of him as a rhetorician cloaked in 'a cloud of benevolent phrases to make the Germans forget their grievances'. More sharply, Georges Soutou dissects Briand's technique as directed above all to producing a psychological effect, supposing that the Germans chastened by their defeat in 1918 would not dare to compromise their new 'respectability' in opposing Briandist projects like that for European union. J. Néré, *The Foreign Policy of France from 1914 to 1945* (London, 1975), p. 71; A. J. P. Taylor, *The Origins of the Second World War* (New York, 1983), p. 57; Soutou, 'L'alliance franco-polonaise...', p. 343.　　[12] Néré, *Foreign Policy of France*, p. 70.

It should not be forgotten that, although we are the strongest today, and will remain so for a further dozen years, in a twenty to fifty years' time seventy million organised, hard-working men will end up weighing heavier than thirty-eight million Frenchmen. So if we do not try to create a German republic hostile to war, we are doomed. Instead of gaining ground with German democratic opinion, we haven't ceased to stir up its hatred. Even admitting that we will succeed in making Germany yield by our pressure on the Ruhr, the policy immediately afterwards must be very generous, and very probably sacrifice even the objectives of our action...

This was of course the logic of Locarno *avant la lettre*.[13] Restored to grace by Edouard Herriot in 1925, Berthelot resumed his role as the flamboyant *éminence grise* of the Quai d'Orsay. The Locarno negotiations on the French side were a product of the Briand–Berthelot tandem, with Briand as the eloquent public spokesman for European conciliation and Berthelot as the omnicompetent diplomatic technician.[14]

The son of an internationally known chemist and Foreign Minister of the early Third Republic, Berthelot enjoyed renown in diplomatic circles for an imperturbable temperament which allied cynicism and generosity; and an encyclopaedic memory, which ranged freely over politics, diplomacy, horseracing, and avant-garde culture. A coolly impertinent *fils de la Maison*, Berthelot decorated the staid bureaux of the Quai d'Orsay with Gauguins and fascinated younger diplomats with his gift for aphorism. He mordantly consoled a junior colleague on the disappointments of French diplomacy in 1919, 'Tout s'arrange, mais mal, mal' ('Everything works out, but badly, badly'). For his protégés, Berthelot was 'the anti-Talleyrand... he created the sort of diplomat who spoke all his thought'.[15] Within the Quai d'Orsay, he cultivated a literary stable, Paul Claudel, Jean Giraudoux, Paul Morand, and the poet of exoticism who would eventually intrigue his way into Berthelot's post as Secretary-General, Alexis Léger.

---

[13] Berthelot added that the drama of the Ruhr affair was that the slightest retreat would isolate France. If she did not emerge completely victorious from the Ruhr affair, he believed that the crisis would be settled in a fashion as financially ruinous as it was destructive of France's prestige. G. Suarez, *Briand, sa vie, son oeuvre* (Paris, 1941), vol. V, p. 429. These last fears paved the way for Briand's Thoiry meeting with Stresemann in 1926.

[14] R. Challener, 'The French Foreign Office: the Era of Philippe Berthelot', in G. Craig, F. Gilbert, *The Diplomats*, I (New York, 1974), pp. 78–9; Jacobson, *Locarno Diplomacy*, pp. 102, 157; and Jean-Luc Barré's lively, full-scale biography, *Le seigneur-chat: Philippe Berthelot 1866–1934* (Paris, 1988). For Berthelot's later disillusionment with Geneva and the Briandist proposal for a European Union, the work of the ambitious Alexis Léger, ibid., pp. 406–7.   [15] P. Morand, *Journal d'un attaché d'ambassade* (Paris, 1963), p. 120.

Berthelot's role in the wartime and post-war negotiations which resulted in the creation of new states from the debris of the Habsburg empire had been decisive. At Versailles, he guided the committee which drew the borders of the new states, a service for which he was venerated in Prague. His part in engendering France's eastern friendships provides the opening theme of Jean Giraudoux's novel, *Bella*, whose protagonist, René Dubardeau, was modelled on Berthelot:

My father was, excepting Wilson, the only plenipotentiary at Versailles who would have recreated Europe with generosity, and the only one, without exception, with competence. He believed in treaties, in their virtue, in their force. Nephew of the man who brought about chemical synthesis, he judged it possible, especially at this heat, to create new states. Westphalia had produced Switzerland, Vienna, Belgium, states which owed to the very artifice of their birth a natural spirit of neutrality and peace. Versailles was thus duty-bound to give birth to the nations with which Europe was then pregnant, and which were developing to no advantage at its centre. My father helped Wilson at this task, and he did better, he gave movement to Central Europe. Rather than being rounded off, all the young nations advanced, towards the north or towards the south, east or west; they were all poised for a departure. In his youth, to support himself as a student, my father had written for the *Grande Encyclopédie* the entries on vanished and enslaved peoples. At the Conference, without anyone noticing it, he amused himself by repairing the injustices of millennia, by restoring to a Czech town the properties which an overlord had stolen from it in 1300, by returning the use of a river to towns which had been forbidden for centuries the right to fish there...[16]

Given his close association with the new states from their diplomatic inception, Berthelot has sometimes been seen as their protector in the Locarno negotiations.[17] At Locarno, Poland and Czechoslovakia signed arbitration agreements with Germany, and Berthelot insisted that these arbitration agreements be guaranteed by separate, bilateral arrangements between France and its eastern allies. Unlike the treaties with France and Belgium which Germany signed at Locarno, the German arbitration treaties in the east did not include territorial guarantees. Locarno thus created a juridical distinction between the eastern and western territorial settlements. And, as such, it represented one in a series of afterthoughts on the part of Berthelot, whose 1919 involvement in the drawing of borders had left

---

[16] J. Giraudoux, *Bella* (Paris, 1926), pp. 7–8.
[17] See, e.g., Challener, 'French Foreign Office', pp. 75–6.

the new states vulnerable to territorial disputes on all sides. In Giraudoux's colourful geography, 'Rather than being rounded off, all the young nations advanced, towards the north or towards the south, east or west; they were all poised for a departure.' Off-the-record statements by Briand and Berthelot that in the long run Poland and Germany would have to work out their differences, a procedure which France would not obstruct, implied that Locarno would direct Weimar revisionism against Poland. After Locarno, despite flagrant German rearmament violations, Briand agreed to the first phase of allied evacuation of the Rhineland. In unofficial conversations before and after his private meeting at Thoiry with Stresemann in September 1926, Briand and his emissaries went farther, envisioning complete evacuation of the zone, the suspension of allied arms control, and Polish territorial revision.[18]

In situating the shifting position of the eastern alliances within Briandism, the issues of early evacuation of the Rhineland and territorial revisionism are linked.[19] Eclipse of the Rhineland factor jeopardised the ideal terrain for a preventive operation against illegal German rearmament or armed revisionism in the east. The Briandist slogan 'Arbitration – Security – Disarmament' raised the prospect of reparations and eventually arms limitation settlements at the expense of Polish territorial integrity.

By attaching its guarantee to the eastern arbitration treaties signed at Locarno, the Quai d'Orsay assumed an ambiguous diplomatic posture, one which did not preclude limited, peaceable

---

[18] On Thoiry and Berthelot's early (November 1925) support for complete evacuation of the Rhineland in return for German financial concessions, see Jacobson, *Locarno Diplomacy*, pp. 83–90; Soutou, 'L'alliance', pp. 305–11, is excellent on the diplomacy surrounding the Briand-Stresemann meeting. Wandycz's valuable new study, *The Twilight of France's Eastern Alliances* (Princeton, 1988) surveys the problem of territorial revisionism more generally, pp. 3–191.
  The hope of facilitating revisionism by amiable negotiation led Briand to support Poland's bid for a semi-permanent seat on the League Council in 1926. In this period, Briand and Berthelot sought to encourage an economic/territorial settlement between Germany and Piłsudski, whom they rightly believed to be drawn by accommodation with Germany. They were however mistaken in the view that Piłsudski's Government or its successors would tolerate an inch of territorial revision. On the hopes entertained in Paris for Polish-German accommodation, Rollet, *La Pologne*, pp. 239, 246, 249.

[19] It should be noted that Poincaré stood by the territorial status quo after Locarno, while separating it from the issue of early evacuation of the Rhineland of which he privately approved under certain military and financial conditions. Wandycz, *Twilight*, pp. 66–7. Jacobson's *Locarno Diplomacy* discusses Poincaré's virtual repudiation by the end of the 1920s of many of the tenets associated with Poincarism, pp. 86–7, 102–3, 160–2 and n. 43. The traditional view of Briand and Poincaré as pursuing diametrically opposite policies and of the period itself as the product of left-right alternance is thus problematic.

territorial revision. Nuance is necessary here. Even diplomats known for their hard line towards Germany, such as Jacques Seydoux, acknowledged the desirability of eastern territorial revisions over time. The emergent consensus appears to have been for *révision à froid*, that is, revision which not being effected on the spur of the moment or in a crisis would allow time for the consolidation of the new states. The working distinction for French diplomats, classic in nineteenth-century diplomacy from the Congress of Vienna, was that France should guarantee the independence of its smaller allies, not their boundaries.[20] Briandism thus posed as the defender of the independence of pacific states in conformity with League principles, rather than as an *à priori* adversary of Germany, which by its arbitration treaties with Poland and Czechoslovakia and membership in the League implicitly renounced force in pursuing its eastern territorial claims. France's position would be artificially maintained through its role as *la puissance animatrice* of European reconstruction. The presence of allies, while occasionally bothersome, would soften and obscure its painful transition to the new postwar order foreseen by Jules Cambon. Thus Laroche, the Ambassador to Poland, reminded his colleagues when the 1929 Hague Conference accepted early evacuation of the Rhineland that the eastern allies were so many aces in the hand of France: 'We must not allow the value of these aces to be diminished: they make us stronger in dealing with Germany.'[21]

The Czechs responded favourably to Briand's wager for European integration. Beneš, the Czech Foreign Minister, spoke reasonably and with irrepressible optimism of the sincerity of Weimar diplomacy, and the likelihood that German militarism would disappear with the flowering of Weimar democracy and Germany's inclusion in an effective League of Nations.[22] The Czechs conceived their security as resting on the strengthening of a democratic Germany, without which they would be lost.[23] It was no accident

---

[20] Soutou, 'L'alliance', pp. 310, 335; Rollet, *La Pologne*, pp. 197, 249.

[21] Cited in Soutou, 'L'alliance', p. 333, n. 117; MAE, Papiers Massigli, 'Affaires de l'Europe centrale', Note, 8 July 1936.   [22] Wandycz, *France*, p. 336.

[23] The French Military Mission in Prague reported in 1922 that 'Czech politicians and generals almost all feel that a democratic Germany, militarily impotent and disarmed, is the necessary condition for the very existence of the Czech Republic, but they leave to the Allied powers the task of preventing a resurgence of German militarism and content themselves with helping it along by the parallel political work of breaking apart the forces of reaction in Central Europe.' SHA, 7N2520, 'SAE 1920–1936', Mittelhauser note, 11 March 1922.

that the Czechs' reasoning was entirely congruent with Berthelot's 1923 letter to Briand. Czechoslovakia embodied Berthelot's conception of the ideal new state, in Giraudoux's fanciful phrase, 'states which owed to the very artifice of their birth a natural spirit of neutrality and peace'. A state of sizeable minorities, Czechoslovakia under Thomas Masaryk's leadership dutifully aspired to achieve a democracy of Swiss-like stability.

As the immediate object of Weimar Germany's territorial revisionism, however, Warsaw could only see Locarno as fraught with menace. While reiterating their opposition to territorial revision, Polish governments before and after Piłsudski seized power in 1926 publicly stifled dismay at Locarno, lest the alliance appear a burden to France.[24] With the advent of the fiercely anti-Czech Piłsudski, Polish ill-will flared up at Beneš and Masaryk's tendency privately to channel Weimar revisionism towards the Polish Corridor. The Piłsudskites returned the favour by referring to Czechoslovakia as an artificial state doomed to complete disappearance. These resentments were sharpened by rival desires for accommodation with Germany, the Czechs envisioning direct contacts only within the larger Briandist framework, Piłsudski vainly searching for grounds for entente with Berlin.[25]

The Roumanian and Yugoslav treaties: proposed revision of the 1921 treaties with Poland

In the years immediately after Locarno, Paris added two treaties, with Roumania (1926) and Yugoslavia (1927), to its eastern series. French interest in these states had been fostered by the Czechs, who in 1920–1 formed with them a diplomatic and military organisation directed primarily against Hungary, the Petite Entente. The early negotiations between Paris, Bucharest, and Belgrade envisaged treaties modelled on the Franco-Czech treaties of 1924. But Locarno influences, in the form of the Briandist ambition to elevate to a diplomatic paradigm French-sponsored arbitration arrangements, soon overtook them.

The attachment of Roumania and Yugoslavia, states without

---

[24] From the 1924 discussions of the Geneva Protocol, General Sikorski foresaw a western security pact which would direct the Germans eastward. Wandycz, 'La Pologne', pp. 237, 241, 247–8, 250.

[25] Wandycz, *France*, pp. 337, 350–1; *Twilight*, pp. 115–16; 'La Pologne', p. 262; Rollet, *La Pologne*, pp. 191–2, 240–1.

borders on Germany, to the Polish-Czech nucleus of France's eastern system introduced the complexities of Bucharest's and Belgrade's relations with their inimical great power neighbours – the USSR and Italy. The Quai d'Orsay incorporated in the treaties with Roumania and Yugoslavia arbitration provisions taken from its treaties of guarantee with Poland and Czechoslovakia, intended to dampen regional conflicts. The meagreness of France's obligations under the 1926 and 1927 treaties – consultation at the outbreak of a conflict – also restricted the chance of French embroilment in what internal memoranda, in a reference to the antecedents of the First World War, called 'obscure Balkan quarrels'. During the negotiations, the Quai d'Orsay promoted border pacification and détente between the USSR, Italy, and its new partners. This stress on arbitration was galling to the small powers who sought French friendship as much to ward off Italian and Soviet predatoriness in the Adriatic and Bessarabia, as to parry a distant German menace. The Quai d'Orsay was particularly solicitous of Italian susceptibilities. (Six months before the end of the 1914–18 war, Berthelot had envisaged an 'anti-German barrier', composed of Czechoslovakia, Italy, Poland, Yugoslavia, and Roumania.) The Quai d'Orsay repeatedly offered to enlarge its 1927 treaty with Yugoslavia to include Italy. It subsequently blamed the Yugoslavs for failing to transform their troubled relations with Italy by a treaty of non-aggression or arbitration, which France might guarantee. The Roumanian and Yugoslav treaties demonstrated that the Briandist penchant for arbitration provisions and indirect language could shade imperceptibly into designs to involve regional great powers in the defence of Central Europe against Germany. By implying a diminution of French loyalties, Briandism aroused a deepening distrust of France and fear of abandonment, especially on the part of Poland and Yugoslavia, countries which were to become the nerve centre of Central European neutralism.[26]

Locarno diplomacy also occasioned a steady erosion of the Quai d'Orsay's attachment to the 1921 military pact with Poland,

[26] A. J. Toynbee, *Survey of International Affairs 1924* (Oxford, 1926), pp. 441–51, and *Survey of International Affairs 1927* (Oxford, 1929), pp. 161, 163; SHA, 7N3444, 'Compte-Rendu de la réunion tenue le 29 janvier 1924...'; R. de Dampierre, 'Dix années de politique française à Rome', *Revue des deux Mondes*, November 1953, p. 23; Laroche, *Au Quai d'Orsay*, pp. 219–23; MAE, Papiers Massigli, 'Affaires de l'Europe centrale', Note, 8 July 1936; Barré, *Le seigneur-chat*, p. 330 and n. For Berthelot's apprehension in the face of mounting Yugoslav resentment, ibid., p. 412.

specifically its clauses involving the USSR, and the defence of Danzig, the Corridor, and the Rhineland. In 1927, the French made their first explicit démarche to adjust the 1921 accord to the new conditions created by Locarno in 1927. While the French emissary fastidiously avoided evoking the 1925 negotiations, given the Marshal's vehemently negative sentiments on the subject, Piłsudski promptly saw through the French move to 'locarnize' the treaty. The 1925 Franco-Polish agreement contained no explicit reference to the USSR, which had been absent from Locarno, and it subordinated French intervention on Poland's behalf to League identification of the aggressor in a Polish-German conflict. The French wanted to revise the 1921 accord along these lines. Piłsudski and his followers retained their attachment to the existing 1921 accord, as independent of the League, more automatic than the 1925 guarantee, and protecting Poland to the east as well as the west. The Piłsudskites' loathing of Russia, their traditional adversary, exceeded their fear of Germany, which they did not regard as an immediate menace. From 1925, the Polish General Staff did not prepare a war plan against Germany, but concentrated its fire on the Soviets. Detecting in Franchet d'Espérey's 1927 démarche a move to erase the Soviet clauses of the 1921 convention, Piłsudski declined to discuss the matter.[27]

Subsequent Polish attempts to investigate French intentions with regard to Germany revealed the hollowness of the alliance. In the summer of 1928, Polish declarations that it would mobilise and take the offensive in the event of a German attack on France, presumably including a reoccupation of the Rhineland, were met by equivocation. The French were reluctant to reveal their new mobilisation plans. Plan A *bis* of 1926 cancelled the opening offensive of earlier planning in favour of an initial defensive. The more rigorously defensive Plan B, in the process of elaboration in conjunction with the decision to build the Maginot line and the adoption of one year military service, gave priority to the integral defence of French

[27] Virtually since the conclusion of the 1921 treaties, the Poles had been aware that Paris regretted certain of their provisions. When General Haller, the Polish Chief of Staff, visited Paris in 1924, the year of Herriot's recognition of the USSR, he warned his compatriots that the validity of the military convention would in the near future be restricted to Germany. In the same year, a visit by General Sikorski to Paris revealed the Quai d'Orsay's intention of subordinating the Polish alliance to an arbitration system incorporated in the Geneva Protocol, then under discussion. J. Lipski, *Diplomat in Berlin: the Papers of Joseph Lipski*, ed. W. Jędrzjewicz, (New York, 1968), pp. 7, 12; Soutou, 'L'alliance', p. 300; A. Cienciala, 'The Significance of the Declaration of Non-Aggression of January 26, 1934', *East European Quarterly* I, 1 (1967), p. 7; Rollet, *La Pologne*, p. 256; Wandycz, *Twilight*, pp. 98–100.

territory. The Poles were told only that, in the event of a German attack on Poland, the decision to implement the alliance would fall to the French Government, and much would depend on the attitude of London. Supplementary French assurances that mobilisation conditions would permit a preliminary decision by the League and corroboration of German aggression were less than consoling, given Paris's assent to early evacuation of the Rhineland, in negotiations from which the Poles were systematically excluded.[28]

Juridically inconclusive, the Franco-Polish exchanges of 1927–9 produced mutual disaffection. Since Locarno, the Poles had feared that the French would abandon the Rhineland and buy with Polish territorial integrity Germany's assent to the realisation of the Briandist slogan, 'Arbitration, Security, and Disarmament'. Beneath Paris's attempts to rework the 1921 military agreement lay a desire to dilute its Soviet clauses, and a perhaps even stronger desire to minimise the threat of involvement in a Polish-German quarrel over Danzig or the Corridor. The French were uncertain whether, in the event of a conflict breaking over Danzig or the Corridor, the Polish population would maintain 'the necessary sang-froid'.[29] Within a year of the evacuation of the Rhineland in 1930, during preliminary discussions for the Disarmament Conference, high ranking members of the French Government bruited Polish renunciation of Danzig and the Corridor. Linkage between a disarmament settlement and Polish territorial revision became even more pronounced between 1931 and 1933.[30]

BRIANDISM IN DISARRAY

The Four Power pact negotiations

Always an integral part of Briandism, the issue of arms limitation came to the fore in negotiations from March 1933 on Mussolini's proposal for a Four Power pact (Italy, France, Great Britain, and Germany). Arms limitation would remain a fixture of French diplomacy until after Munich, which may be seen as a variant on the

---

[28] Lipski, *Diplomat in Berlin*, pp. 13–19; Soutou, 'L'alliance', pp. 319–20, 323–34.

[29] SHA, 'EMA/2 Pologne', Note, 17 February 1937; L. Noël, *L'agression allemande contre la Pologne* (Paris, 1946), p. 101.

[30] Cienciala, 'Declaration', pp. 12–13; Vaïsse, *Sécurité*, pp. 360–2, 520. The resurgence of German militarism which followed evacuation of the Rhineland zone in 1930 led a disheartened Briand to criticise Weimar Germany's new truculence, but he did not repudiate his aim of revisionism in an atmosphere of trust. Wandycz, *Twilight*, pp. 167, 171, 179, 187, 189, 205–7.

original Four Power negotiations. Such at least was the view taken by Edouard Daladier, Premier in 1933 and again in 1938. The Four Power pact interlude also showed Briandism in disarray. It was a transitional episode between the death of Briand in 1932 and two events of 1934, the German-Polish Declaration of January and the arrival at the Quai d'Orsay of Louis Barthou, which would banish territorial revisionism from the official vocabulary of French diplomats until the Czech crisis of 1938.

The prologue to the Four Power negotiations was the Herriot Government's theoretical concession of equality of rights to German rearmament within the framework of the Disarmament Conference in December 1932.[31] In the words of J.-B. Duroselle, 'after having conceded almost everything in 1932, France started again from zero in 1933, and henceforth there was Hitler'.[32] As Hitler consolidated domestic power in the spring of 1933, internal memoranda at the Quai d'Orsay argued that, if raised in conjunction with arms limitation, limited territorial revision should not be excluded. A Polish military manoeuvre at the Westerplatte in March 1933 – reinforcement of a garrison in Danzig in violation of the international agreements guaranteeing the Free City – fed readiness in highly placed French circles to dispose of the Polish Corridor before it caused a conflagration.[33] An unsigned report on the new Germany written in this period for Alexis Léger, the new Secretary-General of the Quai d'Orsay, decried the Polish provocation and urged timely revision of Versailles:

We should also advise our friends, more readily given to national over-excitement, to calm their emotions – however legitimate – and control their frayed nerves so that they can reason without illusion, and without passion...The time for initiatives is over: we did not know how to seize them when benevolent initiatives would have been profitable...Now we must simply endure making the inevitable concessions and not hamper [the Nazi] movement which nothing seems to stop.

Referring to Mussolini's proposal several days earlier for a Four

---

[31] By the Five Power declaration of December 1932, Herriot attempted to counter Socialist agitation for disarmament as well as Anglo-Saxon disarmament proposals without new guarantees for arbitration and security. Intended as a statement of principle, the formula recognised German equality of rights in return for German acceptance of a security system, presumably to be elaborated under the auspices of the Disarmament Conference. Vaïsse, *Sécurité*, pp. 324–47; Soutou, 'L'alliance', p. 344.

[32] J.-B. Duroselle, *La décadence* (Paris, 1979), pp. 42–3, 67.

[33] Wandycz, *Twilight*, pp. 264, 267.

Power pact, in which revision of the Polish Corridor was explicitly mentioned, the writer concluded with a Briandist flourish: 'In peace and dignity, let us attempt to bring our good will, our sense of the present to constructive solutions which a group of interested powers should study, propose and apply. This front, with or without Germany, is alone capable of moderating national passions and preventing a conflict.'[34]

The *Briandistes* had long seen Italy as a possible partner in Central Europe. As early as 1922, Briand had spoken of the desirability of substituting Italy for the reticent British as a co-protector of the independence of the new states.[35] From 1928 Danubian and colonial problems were the topics of bilateral political and economic conversations, in which French recognition of Italian colonial interests was the *quid pro quo* for Italian partnership in Danubia, where Rome was assiduously cultivating Austria and the most truculent of the small ex-enemy states, Hungary. After Paris vetoed the Austro-German proposals of 1931 for an Anschluss or customs union, it proposed economic action through a series of League-sponsored conferences. The period of international discussion which ended in four power adoption of an economic plan at the Stresa conference of 1932 actively fostered France's reliance on Italy in Danubia.

Regarding Austria's near-bankruptcy and the related problem of preventing Anschluss as only the most intractable of a host of severe structural economic problems with political complications, the Quai d'Orsay took the view that only a 'solution d'ensemble' would provide the basis for regional recovery. In Berthelot's view, France should play the role of catalyst in negotiations to restore the inter-Danubian complementarity disrupted by the First World War, and so neutralise the attractions of the German market for Danubian agricultural produce. He advocated a Danubian economic organisation composed of three powers, Czechoslovakia, and Italy's client states, Austria and Hungary, to which Roumania and Yugoslavia might later adhere.[36] Italy's help would resolve the

---

[34] MAE, Papiers Léger, unsigned 'Note sur la politique intérieure et extérieure de l'Allemagne', 18 March 1933. This note is sometimes erroneously attributed to Léger.

[35] Wandycz, *France*, pp. 254–5.

[36] Berthelot's willingness to bypass the Petite Entente as such illustrates the way he saw France as balanced between the dual perils of Anschluss and a German-dominated Mitteleuropa: 'Our Austrian policy for the last thirteen years has tended to aid [Austria] in order to dissuade it from union with Germany. To reattach it economically to other members of the

crucial problem of an absence of trade complementarity between France and its allies. Berthelot saw every advantage in showing deference to Italy in economic negotiations on Central Europe, which he regarded as a seedbed of Franco-Italian entente: 'There is in my opinion advantage in allowing [Italian] diplomatic activity to direct itself to Central Europe; any clashes with German activities there can only be favourable to [Italy's] relations with France, and Franco-Italian quarrels in Danubia would doubtless lose their acuteness.' Reluctance in certain French quarters to compromise the Petite Entente meant that the Danubian economic organisation eventually put forward by Paris, the Plan Tardieu, included Roumania and Yugoslavia. The five power base of the Plan Tardieu entailed a larger margin of agricultural surpluses for the projected organisation and, by thus increasing its attraction for Germany, magnified Italy's importance in French planning as a check on German economic penetration in Danubia. After the Plan Tardieu collapsed, an international conference held at Stresa agreed that great power aid to the stricken Danubian states should take the form of financial contributions from France and Britain, and unilateral customs preferences from Germany and Italy, bordering states with traditionally high Danubian trade. With a narrow sense of self-interest, France stepped aside at the 1932 Stresa conference, again leaving Italy to dispute the German place in the commercial field.[37]

By 1933, French attempts to foment Italo-German rivalry were seen as equally essential in the context of the Disarmament Conference. The Quai d'Orsay was anxious to break up an Italo-German front on German rearmament.[38] Mussolini's proposal for a four power community of action on arms limitations and territorial revision thus fell on fertile ground in Paris.

Having intended to pursue bilateral entente with Rome, the moderate left-wing Foreign Minister, Paul-Boncour, was easily persuaded when Mussolini proposed widening the discussion to a four power entente. He later recalled that one source of his attraction to Mussolini's original proposal was its provision for a four power arms limitation convention in the likely event that the Geneva

former Austro-Hungarian empire would be the culmination of this policy. To constitute a five power Danubian base to aid it, on the other hand, would risk the most serious setback to this policy. In order to avoid an Anschluss, it would foster the creation of a Mitteleuropa.' MAE, Papiers Massigli, 'Affaires de l'Europe centrale', 22 February 1932.
[37] Ibid., and 17, 27 February 1932; Note, 20 July 1936; MAE, Papiers Tardieu, carton 693, 'Question danubienne', Note, 11 May 1932.   [38] DDF I, 3, no. 363.

disarmament talks failed.[39] Mussolini made clear that, if France did not accede to some form of the Four Power pact, Italy would draw closer to Germany amidst the ruins of the Disarmament Conference. On the nettlesome question of territorial revision, Paul-Boncour was not without sympathy for the Italian proposals, which would be much amended by the end of negotiations to ensconce them within a League context.[40] He was also susceptible to the argument of his special emissary, Henry de Jouvenal, that territorial revision should not, in the interests of peace, be undertaken without salvaging some measure of arms limitation from the deadlocked disarmament proceedings. Jouvenal applauded Mussolini's revisionism, convinced that Mussolini could easily be persuaded to oppose German designs in Austria, while an arrangement over the Corridor would avert European war. In a formulation current in Warsaw, Jouvenal took up the Danzig rather than the Vienna solution.[41]

While Paul-Boncour did attempt to take some distance from free-wheeling conversations in which Mussolini expounded the virtues of territorial revision to an approving Jouvenal, his efforts left Poland and the Petite Entente dissatisfied and distrustful. The Poles, again singled out by the revisionists, and the Czechs, alarmed by Mussolini's vaguer talk of Danubian revision to profit Hungary, considered making common cause. Piłsudski and Jósef Beck, his recently appointed Foreign Minister, talked of Beck's visiting Prague to demonstrate their collective displeasure, a project which came to nothing. Instead, the Poles rapped the knuckles of the French by following the Westerplatte incident with soundings in Berlin, while Beneš eventually settled to furthering Italian economic participation in Danubia on Czech terms.[42]

Vocal allied discontent created a dilemma for the Quai d'Orsay in producing its counter-proposal for Rome. It was the old dilemma inherent in Briandism's vision of a 'rôle conducteur en Europe', in which France's great power status would be artificially maintained by a host of small powers who amplified its voice in international

---

[39] Ibid., and 295.

[40] J. Paul-Boncour, *Entre deux guerres* (Paris, 1946), II, pp. 341–2; P. Reynaud, *Au coeur de la mêlée* (Paris, 1951), p. 64.

[41] DDF I, 2, no. 382. Jouvenal made his point thus: 'France herself has not guaranteed Poland's frontiers. She has guaranteed Poland peace... The solution advocated by M. Mussolini today, if England will join in and if Germany will accept it, could increase the guarantees of peace to Poland at not too high a price.'

[42] The failed Czech-Polish rapprochement of 1933 is exhaustively analysed by Wandycz in *Twilight*, pp. 278–93.

debate. Jouvenal brushed aside the ambiguities inherent in Briand's vision of France's role: 'Instead of defending the great powers to the small powers, and the small powers to the great, we seem to be embracing the cause of opposition to the great powers, of which France is, after all, one.' And in a phrase which would haunt Paul-Boncour: 'Are we sure that our allies themselves will not reproach us one day for having exposed them to more risks than they can bear, and which we are not able to help them to meet?'[43]

The Quai d'Orsay's response was to transform the Italian proposals, as it had done with Stresemann's proposals for Locarno.[44] The result was a draft inspired by Briandism. The Political Directorate hoped to provide a fillip to the ailing Disarmament Conference by amendments involving the League Council, to which action on Herriot's December 1932 concession on equality of rights for German rearmament was to be consigned.[45] Territorial revision would also take place within the League Council, on which Poland held a semi-permanent seat, and thus with its participation – an old Briandist dream, Briand having agreed to a Polish seat on the Council for this purpose.[46] And, by multiplying the pact's references to the League Covenant, the great/small power distinction problematic for French policy was downplayed.

The finished Four Power pact, almost comma by comma that of the amended French draft, was signed but never ratified. Commentators seized on the fact that it contained no provision not already in force by virtue of some other diplomatic document. When Hitler took Germany out of the League of Nations and the Disarmament

---

[43] On the great/small power dilemma facing French policy, Jouvenal drove home the value of Italian cooperation in the disarmament talks: 'This is not a matter of imposing the will of the strong on the weak, but of setting up a kind of insurance against the risks of revision and of failure at the disarmament conference, in order to avoid any form of European war.' DDF I, 3, nos. 44, 112.   [44] Ibid., no. 7.

[45] Ibid. Tortuous Franco-Italian negotiations pertaining to German equality of rights are recounted in H. Lagardelle's partisan *Mission à Rome* (Paris, 1955), pp. 33–4, 44–8.

[46] Paul-Boncour defended this position: 'France, which had not for a moment forgotten her allies in the negotiations, and kept in touch with them every day, at the same time as she served her own legitimate interests by drawing closer to Italy, did she not also serve theirs by obtaining from Italy, and from Germany via Italy...an agreement to submit adjustments and modifications to peaceful procedures, in which [the allies] would have a part, and which could not take place without them?' Paul-Boncour, *Entre deux guerres*, II, p. 347; MAE, Papiers Fouques-Duparc 1940, carton 37, 'Politique extérieure générale: Le pacte à quatre', Note, 24 April 1936. The League Council framework allowed Paris to assure its allies that territorial revision would only be possible by unanimous vote including the interested parties, in effect article 19 of the League Covenant grafted to the promise of a hearing. Wandycz, *Twilight*, p. 288.

Conference in October 1933, its League framework splintered.[47] Louis Barthou, a politician of the Nationalist Right and a stern opponent of the Four Power pact, not the internationalist Paul-Boncour, would pursue the chimera of Italy's partnership in reaching an arms limitation agreement with Germany and in constructing Danubian stability.[48] In the immediate, the Four Power pact was the seedbed not of the Franco-Italian entente long sought by the Quai d'Orsay, but of the German-Polish Non-Aggression Declaration, the first public breach in the French alliance system.

The German-Polish declaration, January 1934

In late January 1934, Polish signature of a non-aggression declaration with Hitler stunned the French. For Piłsudski, the 'immediate and determining cause' of negotiations with Germany was the disarmament question and intertwined fears of territorial revision. A succession of episodes related to the Disarmament Conference, Paris's failure to consult Poland before conceding equality of rights to Germany in December 1932, and its platonic flirtation with anti-Polish revisionism during the Four Power pact negotiations, fuelled the Poles' association of arms limitation with the likelihood of French treachery. A French military commentator looking back on this period observed that Franco-Polish friendship suffered such blows that the abandonment of the alliance was 'if not official, at least inevitable and acknowledged by all'.[49]

Shortly after the dramatic reinforcement of the Polish garrison on the Westerplatte in 1933, Beck observed menacingly to the French Ambassador that any revision of the Polish borders would lead to war. He added that it might be preferable to reach an understanding

[47] Arnold Toynbee, cited in R. Binion, *Defeated Leaders* (New York, 1960), p. 185. Paul-Boncour's eagerness for a Franco-Italian entente on arms limitation persisted after the pact's signature in June 1933, but he had become wary of Italian pressures for 'an alteration of the [disarmament] negotiations along the lines of the Four Power pact', i.e., an atmosphere in which France would be seduced into further arms concessions by an Italy pursuing a policy of equidistance from the other great powers. In a countervailing move, he turned to the Soviets, with whom in July 1933 he raised the possibility of membership at Geneva. DDF, I, 4, no. 376. *International Affairs* (Moscow, 1963), 'The Struggle of the USSR for Collective Security in Europe during 1933–1935', Part I, p. 109.
[48] Paul-Boncour, *Entre deux guerres*, II, pp. 343, 346, 350.
[49] Cienciala, 'Declaration', p. 17; Vaïsse, *Sécurité*, pp. 409–11, and the same author's 'La mission de Jouvenal à Rome', in J.-B. Duroselle and E. Serra (eds.), *Italia è Francia dal 1919 al 1939* (Milan, 1981), pp. 85–9; SHA, 'EMA 2/ Pologne', Note, 17 February 1937.

with Hitler.[50] By implication, the threat for Beck lay less with Hitler's Germany than with Poland's friends. Despite initial apprehension, Piłsudski and his circle welcomed the Austrian Hitler, whom they expected to move south into Austria and Czechoslovakia, rather than east, in pursuit of the traditional Prussian revisionism advocated by Hitler's predecessor, von Schleicher, and encouraged by Mussolini during the negotiations for the Four Power pact.[51] During the Four Power pact episode, Beck deployed the rumours of Polish desire for a preventive war which circulated after the Westerplatte incident to open negotiations with Germany.[52]

German-Polish conversations were carried on in fits and starts from May 1933 through January 1934. In the winter of 1934, the French themselves were in contact with Berlin on the issue of disarmament, a simultaneity which at once 'covered' the Poles' negotiations with Germany, and intensified their desire for an independent agreement with the Reich.[53]

At news of the diplomatic coup of 26 January 1934, the Quai d'Orsay anticipated that the Polish paradigm of balance between Germany and the USSR – Beck followed the German declaration with a trip to Moscow – would in fact slant noticeably towards Germany. It thought that Czechoslovakia would react by gravitating in reaction towards the USSR. Paris was hardly in a position to object to non-aggression provisions as such, but Polish secrecy in the last phase of the negotiations aroused suspicions of more extensive, secret commitments compromising Polish opposition to an Anschluss, and involving it in putative German machinations against Czechoslovakia and the Ukraine.[54] Although these fears were unfounded in any textual sense, many of the Piłsudskites were willing to believe in tacit German recognition of Poland's western frontier. They congratulated themselves on neutralising the menace of western diplomatic projects by deflecting German revisionism

[50] Laroche, *La Pologne*, p. 123.
[51] Beck, Piłsudski's Foreign Minister, believed that Hitler's advent furnished Poland with 'a unique occasion for redressing our situation in the European balance'. J. Beck, *Dernier rapport* (Neuchâtel, 1951), pp. 28–9.
[52] The literature on the alleged Polish desire for a preventive war in 1933 is vast; see especially DDF I, 3, no. 238n; Z. Gasiorowski, 'Did Piłsudski Attempt to Initiate a Preventive War in 1933?', *JMH*, vol. 27, no. 2, June 1955; G. Weinberg, *The Foreign Policy of Hitler's Germany*, I (Chicago, 1970), p. 60; Wandycz, *Twilight*, pp. 268–73; and H. Rollet's brief but trenchant 'Deux mythes des relations franco-polonaises entre les deux guerres', *Revue d'histoire diplomatique*, nos. 3–4, July–December 1982.
[53] Cienciala, 'Declaration', pp. 15–16; Wandycz, *Twilight*, pp. 305, 328; Laroche, *La Pologne*, pp. 137–45.   [54] DDF I, 6, no. 17.

southwards.[55] By taking their destiny in their own hands, however rashly, the Poles modified the problem of the direction of the initial German attack: Czechoslovakia soon became the most menaced of France's allies.[56]

Under the chastening influence of the German-Polish declaration, the cavalierness on the issue of territorial revisionism which had characterised Briandism disappeared virtually overnight. The Quai d'Orsay's new Minister, Barthou, pointedly consulted Poland and the Petite Entente on the multilateral pacts which he elaborated under the auspices of the French disarmament note of 17 April 1934.

ARMS LIMITATION: LOUIS BARTHOU AND THE APRIL 1934
NOTE

Barthou's advent

A septuagenarian in the early 1930s, Louis Barthou had an impressive parliamentary career which went back to the 1880s. Seven times a minister before 1914, he had been Premier (1912–13), *rapporteur* for the passage of the Treaty of Versailles by the *Chambre des députés*, and a minister again in the 1920s. A *petit bourgeois* who married well, he lost his only son in the early months of the First World War. His reputation was for patriotism rather than social conscience, ardent republicanism allied to personal ambition, and opportunism which he manifested with wit and verve. A contemporary of Poincaré and Briand, he enjoyed more than they the flash of rhetorical steel, the play of sheer insolence. A bibliophile of note, Barthou was a cultivated man, but he was dogged by sexual scandal, allegations of personal corruption, and political disloyalty.[57] Previously known for a sparkling malice, his formidable physical and intellectual energies were thought to be flagging by the late 1920s, and many believed that his political career would be permanently

[55] Laroche, *La Pologne*, pp. 141, 192.
[56] For German military planning against Czechoslovakia, triggered by serious discussion of a bilateral Franco-Soviet pact in March 1935, E. M. Robertson, *Hitler's Pre-War Policy and Military Plans* (London, 1963), pp. 89–91.
[57] Philippe Berthelot, a gifted observer of human foible, captured Barthou *sur le vif* in a letter of 1914: 'J'ai dîné hier soir avec…M. Barthou…j'ai éprouvé la même déception que m'inspirent chaque fois son abord et sa conversation un peu prolongé, tant au point de vue du fond que du caractère. Il a parlé dans des termes peu flatteurs de tous ses anciens collaborateurs…' Cited in Barré, *Le seigneur-chat*, p. 267.

relegated to the mausoleum of the Senate. But injections of sheep hormones in the early thirties rejuvenated Barthou physically, restoring his enormous energy, if not quite his former intellectual acuity. When Gaston Doumergue drew up an illustrious cabinet of former prime ministers after the bitterly divisive riots of February 1934, Barthou figured prominently as Minister of Foreign Affairs. His colleagues were optimistic that his renewed dynamism would revive France's fortunes. But he was more fragile than he appeared, a fragility which escaped both his contemporaries and Barthou himself, with tragic consequences on the Canebière in Marseilles, when Croat terrorists taking aim at the visiting Yugoslav monarch also shot Barthou. His death was due not to the seriousness of his gunwounds but to his failure to obtain prompt medical care.[58]

Under Barthou, the course of French arms limitation diplomacy from the spring of 1934 resembled a hair-pin bend. Early in the year, Hitler simultaneously issued an ambitious arms budget and accepted a British plan restricting the *Reichswehr* to 300,000 men. The French Cabinet was at first paralysed. The Premier, Doumergue, and his abrasive *éminence grise*, André Tardieu, opposed accepting the German offer to restrict the *Reichswehr*. The spirited Minister of Foreign Affairs and Pierre Laval, soon to be his canny, unpolished successor, pleaded for acceptance of Hitler's offer. Barthou used ammunition from the French Ambassador in Berlin, François-Poncet, to argue that limited, supervised rearmament by the Reich was preferable to uncontrollable German rearmament and an arms race. None the less, believing the collapse of the Hitlerian régime to be imminent, Tardieu and Doumergue prevailed on Barthou to refuse the German offer in a trenchant note of 17 April 1934. Drafted with the cooperation of Barthou and Weygand, the Chief of Staff, the note proclaimed that France would henceforth give priority to its own security, which was inseparable from that of other interested powers. This stilted phrase, a sensation in its day, implied both France's severance from the Disarmament Conference and an audacious allied diplomacy.[59] But, as René Massigli of the Quai

<hr/>

[58] Duroselle, *La décadence*, pp. 88–92; L. Noël, *La Tchécoslovaquie d'avant Munich* (Paris, 1982), pp. 61–2; conversation with E. de Crouy-Chanel, 7 February 1979.

[59] The genesis of the 17 April note is analysed in Maurice Vaïsse, *Sécurité d'abord: la politique française en matière de désarmement* (Paris, 1981), pp. 529–94. An uncharacteristically supple note of 8 March by General Weygand pointed in the direction of an arms limitation convention in return for mutual aid guarantees to serve as sanctions against rearmament

d'Orsay's Political Directorate shrewdly observed, in itself the 17 April note settled nothing – neither German rearmament nor the French attitude.[60]

Fragmentary documentary evidence renders elusive definitive assessment of Barthou's motivation in accepting the 17 April note. It can be argued that the collective diplomacy *vis-à-vis* Italy and the USSR with which Barthou followed the April note, impelled by his fear of an arms race, represented for him an indirect means to reach an arms agreement with Germany. His allied diplomacy would thus have been intended in important respects to minimise the risks of the April note, which he had originally opposed.

Barthou's overtures to Rome

During the governmental discussions preceding the April note, Barthou, drawn by its 'rough-hewn line between refusal and resignation', personally took the Italian line of no French disarmament, combined with limited, legalised German rearmament.[61] Again in May, French disarmament experts mapped out a tentative new course which broadly conformed to the Italian plan: no reduction in French arms, the concession of moderate rearmament to Germany.[62] Barthou, who met afterwards with the Chief of the Italian delegation in Geneva, Aloisi, made overtures to visit Rome in the autumn of 1934. To facilitate Barthou's road to Rome, Aloisi busied himself with behind-the-scenes diplomacy on the future of the Saar, to be settled by plebescite in the winter of 1935 – a diplomacy which, his diary indicates, he intended to be sympathetic to French interests. In preparation for his visit, Barthou sent word to Mussolini that he would adopt the Italian disarmament memorandum which entailed consideration of the legalisation of German rearmament, provided the German demands could be met outside the disarmament conference, presumably in security negotiations. This was the as yet undefined 'third way' of which Barthou spoke to Aloisi in mid May: French partisanship neither of Britain's willingness to

---

violations. Weygand rejected outright legalisation of German rearmament by abrogating Part V of Versailles; he also urged a German commitment to renounce territorial revisionism for the duration of the arms limitation accord. SHA, 2N19, 8 March 1934.

[60] Vaïsse, *Sécurité*, p. 578; for the French disarmament delegation's quest for a policy on German rearmament in April and May 1934, DDF I, 6, nos. 110, 191.

[61] Vaïsse, *Sécurité*, p. 540; F. Piétri, 'Souvenir de Barthou', *Revue des deux Mondes*, 1 March 1961, p. 67. [62] Vaïsse, *Sécurité*, p. 579.

recognise German rearmament nor of an Italian position which left inexplicit security guarantees for France.[63] While the Italians fervently desired the legalisation of German rearmament, Barthou appears to have aspired to build a bridge back to arms negotiations by the conclusion of a security convention with Italy. Barthou's overtures to Rome in April, May, and June 1934 thus were meant to advance actively the cause of arms limitation by security negotiations involving Germany, rather than by the outright legalisation of German rearmament.[64]

Events in the summer of 1934 outdistanced Barthou's diplomacy: the July murder of the Austrian Chancellor Dollfuss, particularly provocative to his protector Mussolini, and the consolidation of Hitler's control over the *Reichswehr* on Hindenburg's death in August 1934. Given the debate within the French Cabinet over the German arms limitation offer of early 1934, it is unsurprising that Barthou personally reacted more strongly to the prospect of Hitler's remaining in power than to the tragedy of Dollfuss's assassination. He announced to the American Ambassador that the situation in Germany had 'grown definitely worse but...clearer'.[65]

In the last weeks of his own life, Barthou rapidly distanced himself from earlier discussions with Aloisi of disarmament negotiations before his visit to Rome in the autumn. In a September dispatch, full of the verve for which he was celebrated, Barthou castigated the Italian disarmament position in language which played on the fact that Dollfuss's death had temporarily prepared Mussolini to set to one side flexibility on German rearmament.[66] At the September Geneva session, much taken up with the French-sponsored entry of the USSR into the League of Nations, Barthou wooed the Italians, posing for a photograph in which he gave the Fascist salute. He also held out the lure of a new Danubian organisation for the political and economic protection of Austria, to be centred on the states of the Rome Protocols, Italy, Austria, and Hungary, rather than the Petite Entente.[67] In these September 1934 negotiations with the Italians,

[63] P. Aloisi, *Journal 1932–1936* (Paris, 1957), pp. 189–90, 193–4, 196; DDF I, 6, nos. 177, 213.
[64] DDF I, 6, no. 116. This was also the point of Barthou's conversations with the British in July 1934, thus his repeated denials in Warsaw and elsewhere that he intended simply to legalise German rearmament. DBFP, II, 6, nos. 454, 487–9; Wandycz, *Twilight*, p. 342, 347–8. Cf. p. 26, n. 59.
[65] DDF I, 6, no. 509; 7, no. 29; FRUS I (1934), pp. 572–3; Noël, *La Tchécoslovaquie*, pp. 159–60.   [66] DDF I, 7, nos. 233, 265.
[67] Barthou insisted only that a Franco-Italian sponsored merger of the two rival economic blocs be along the lines of unilateral preference advocated by the 1932 Stresa economic conference and that it be accompanied by Italo-Yugoslav political entente, a task at which

Barthou returned to earlier aims pursued by the Quai d'Orsay during the negotiations for the Four Power pact. His tactic was to break apart the Italo-German disarmament front and replace it with a Franco-Italian front in preparation for the next round of arms limitation negotiations, which he expected once the *Reichswehr* accomplished its current rearmament programme.[68] Barthou's stress on a Franco-Italian front for all eventualities reappeared after his death at Marseilles when the Quai d'Orsay circulated a transitional memorandum, in fact a blueprint for future conversations in Rome, under the name of the new Foreign Minister, Pierre Laval. While leaving the door open for future arms limitation negotiations, it covered all eventualities: Franco-Italian solidarity in the event of more negotiations; in the event of unilateral German denunciation of the Versailles arms clauses, Franco-Italian consultation and mutual aid.[69] Under Laval, however, the pendulum would swing back, and more recklessly, to arms limitation.

Barthou's overtures to the USSR

Barthou is better known for his Soviet diplomacy which produced more dramatic results before his death: the *Conseil des ministres'* approval of his ambitious project for an Eastern Locarno to include Germany and the USSR, and Soviet admission to the League, the signal for the Soviets' momentous entry into European politics. The depiction of Barthou as a proponent of a classical alliance system, and for this reason, the great lost hope of French diplomacy, is widespread in the historical literature. It draws much of its force from the argument that Barthou conceived the Eastern pact to screen an alliance with the Soviets, who were deeply alarmed by German rearmament. In fact, Barthou's undertakings to the Soviets for a bilateral pact independent of the Eastern pact were decidedly vague, while his threats in London and Warsaw on the subject were recognised in Moscow as diplomatic manoeuvres.[70]

Even before the 17 April note, the Political Directorate had

he had laboured since the preceding June. DDF I, 7, nos. 220, 290, 316, 352; MAE, SDN 806, 21 September 1934; Aloisi, *Journal*, p. 216.
[68] DDF I, 7, no. 233. The hardening of Barthou's position in September 1934 was also in line with the recommendation of French disarmament experts immediately after the 17 April note that Paris ought not to release its own arms limitation plan until it could realise an international front against Germany, and clear itself of German charges to have sabotaged disarmament negotiations.   [69] Ibid., no. 566.
[70] 'The Struggle of the USSR for Collective Security in Europe during 1933–1935', *International Affairs*, 6 (Moscow, 1963), pp. 113–14, 116; 7, p. 123.

pressed for the inclusion of Germany in Franco-Soviet arrangements with Poland.[71] It was all the more anxious to assure Polish adherence to an Eastern Locarno after the German-Polish non-aggression declaration. According to Barthou's confidante and the diplomatic correspondent of *Le Temps*, Wladimir d'Ormesson, the pacifying effect of German inclusion in an Eastern pact was particularly significant for Barthou. Accelerated German rearmament combined with uncertainty as to Hitler's future action in the east made for extreme instability. D'Ormesson placed Barthou's conception of an Eastern Locarno solidly in the context of his original willingness to accept Hitler's 1934 arms limitation offer and his obsessive desire to avert an arms race. In the opinion of French disarmament experts, the security guarantees afforded by Barthou's project for an Eastern Locarno – the inclusion of Germany not least – presented the surest way to remove the arms clauses of Versailles. Speaking personally to the British Ambassador in June 1934, soon after his conditional acceptance of the Italian disarmament thesis, Barthou held out the prospect of legalised German rearmament in return for its assent to the Eastern pact.[72]

In September 1934, the first negative German and Polish responses to the Eastern pact virtually coincided with Soviet entry into the League. Despite his hardening line on arms limitation, it is by no means clear that, had he lived, Barthou would have concluded a bilateral political pact with the Soviets. Nor did the Soviet Politburo desire this. Litvinov was instructed in September 1934 to take no initiative for a pact without Germany and Poland. Stalin himself reportedly was pessimistic about the prospects for a multilateral mutual aid pact, the original French design for the Eastern pact, and envisaged in its place some more restrictive arrangement to create the balance of force 'necessary to cajole the reluctant to acquiesce even unwillingly in a real policy of European pacification which

---

[71] In autumn 1933 when Paul-Boncour approached the Soviets after Germany's withdrawal from the League of Nations and the Disarmament Conference, the Political Directorate favoured an industrial/technical agreement over the stronger, political accord desired by its Minister. In its view, an industrial accord would tie Poland to Russia as a source of war matériels for Polish defence. DDF I, 5, nos. 28, 84, 120; 6, no. 17; Cienciala, 'Declaration', pp. 15–16.

[72] W. d'Ormesson, *France* (London, 1939), pp. 126–9; DDF I, 6, no. 180; DBFP II, 6, no. 454. In subsequent conversations with Simon, the British Foreign Secretary, Barthou was more cautious, a caution attributable to the Soviet position and to domestic pressures of Russophile politicians such as Herriot. Ibid., nos. 487–9; DDF I, 6, no. 457.

Europe, but above all Russia needs, in anticipation of a conflict with Japan'.[73]

The inclusion of Germany remained for many more months an indispensable part of the Quai d'Orsay's definition of collective security. The legacy of Barthou's Soviet policy lay in the inherently flawed aspiration to use a wary Stalin as the 'hard option' (an option of a different kind than the Italian conduit, made ductile by Mussolini's pretensions to be the Great Conciliator) for a French diplomacy consistently determined to coax Hitler into a broad European settlement including arms limitation.

Barthou's diplomacy with regard to Italy and the USSR was thus nuanced. While he was solicitous of Poland and the countries of the Petite Entente, visiting Central Europe in the spring and summer of 1934, he was not, as is often believed, a proponent of a strong eastern alliance system. His energetic diplomacy was not a willingness to increase commitments to France's eastern allies of the 1920s. Indeed, much of the drama of France's foreign policy from 1934 on sprang from the distrust and fear of abandonment rife within the allied camp in response to French benevolence towards the USSR and amiability to Italy, benevolence meant to abet the cause of arms limitation, not war with an intransigent Germany.

For Warsaw, the Eastern pact negotiations scarcely concealed another campaign to revise the 1921 military accord and so diminish France's obligations to Poland by interposing Soviet aid. Barthou had been less than candid when he visited Warsaw in April 1934. The recent Germano-Polish Non-Aggression Declaration and Polish dismay at the February 1934 riots in Paris meant that he walked on eggshells in Warsaw, neglecting even to mention the Eastern pact. Indulging in empty flattery of the Poles, Barthou left serious discussion to a military visitor, General Debeney, to whom he entrusted the futile mission of convincing Piłsudski to accept revision of the 1921 accord, by deleting its anti-Soviet clauses.[74] The Poles also justifiably feared that the French and British would seek to

[73] J. Haslam, *The Soviet Union and the Struggle for Collective Security in Europe 1933–1939* (London, 1984), pp. 41, 43.

[74] DDF I, nos. 7, 17, 133, 139, 299; SHAA, 2B97, 2e Bureau, 12 June 1934; SHA, 'EMA: Pologne', 'Rapport du général Debeney sur sa mission … du 24 à 28 juin 1934'. Debeney's mission 'made [Piłsudski] lose the remaining illusions about the object of Barthou's trip and about the foreign policy of the Doumergue cabinet'. Laroche, *La Pologne*, p. 200. The Poles subsequently suspended exchanges with French intelligence. Schw. 1SC2 Dr4, 14 May 1935.

entice the Germans into the Eastern pact with arms limitation concessions.[75]

For its part, Belgrade regarded the Italo-Yugoslav entente ardently desired by the French as a snare allowing them to withdraw behind their frontiers, whilst abetting Italian designs to succeed France as the dominant power in the region.[76] Only Czechoslovakia, ever the amenable ally, followed Barthou's lead in all respects, accepting Franco-Italian entente, encouraging the Soviets to enter the League, and consulting with Litvinov on a weakened Eastern pact, in the vain hope of softening Polish objections.[77]

ARMS LIMITATION: PIERRE LAVAL AND THE GERMAN RESURGENCE

Laval's diplomacy in London and Rome

In March 1935, Hitler announced German conscription. By unilaterally invalidating the disarmament clauses of Versailles, the German conscription announcement pre-empted recent Franco-British planning for arms limitation as part of a general settlement. In February 1935, Laval and the Premier, Pierre-Etienne Flandin, had journeyed to London for talks. Laval, in a critical concession on arms limitation, agreed to consider it simultaneously with security arrangements in Eastern Europe and Danubia. In return, the British agreed to sponsor a Western Air pact made up of the five Locarno powers.[78] Laval's concession compromised Barthou's position on negotiating arms limitation only after the successful conclusion of regional security pacts.[79]

Laval's diplomacy in Rome manifested the same determined adherence to the cause of arms limitation. From Laval's arrival at

[75] Wandycz sympathetically develops the Polish objections to the Eastern pact in *Twilight*, p. 363.
[76] On the ground that it would offend Italy, Barthou blocked efforts by Weygand and Gamelin shortly after the 17 April note to institute peacetime staff collaboration with Roumania and Yugoslavia. Barthou's response to a mission by General Victor Pétin to Bucharest demonstrated, as had the Debeney mission to Warsaw, the limits of his willingness to strengthen the traditional alliances. SHAA, 2B93, 'Rapport du général Pétin', 8 April; SHA, 'Roumanie', Barthou-Pétain correspondence, 12, 28 May, 25 July; MAE, 'Etudes militaires', 17 May 1934.
[77] DDF I, 7, nos. 225, 264, 335, 406; 8, no. 134.
[78] Ibid., 9, nos. 142, 144; Czech T-120, 1041/1809/414122, 414126.
[79] Laval justified his action in advance to his colleagues and the military: 'the big effort to be made in London is to ensure that England does nothing with Germany as long as Germany remains outside the [collective] pacts'. DDF I, 9, no. 57.

the Quai d'Orsay in November 1934, Mussolini had displayed a keen sense of the new Foreign Minister's readiness for agreement with Germany, an alacrity which impressed all with whom Laval spoke in these months. Mussolini immediately consented to Laval's desiderata on the arms limitation question (consultation should Germany publicly denounce the arms clauses of Versailles; Italian support of French claims for a margin of arms superiority should Germany negotiate for its equality of rights). Laval's attachment to the Italian negotiations was thus ensured, for a Franco-Italian disarmament front would greatly increase his manoeuvrability *vis-à-vis* Germany in the discussions which he anticipated would follow the Saar plebescite.[80]

When Laval journeyed to Rome in early 1935 for wide-ranging conversations with Mussolini on Danubia and colonial issues including Italian designs on Ethiopia, their joint arms limitation stance was reiterated.[81] Mussolini told Laval: 'Either we make war with Germany or we negotiate with her.' Although Rome was shortly to make overtures for bilateral military talks on Austria, Mussolini and Laval in effect agreed on certain conditions to legalise German rearmament, as well as to obtain German participation in a Danubian pact for the security of Austria, to supplant the Rome Accords. Laval, in Mussolini's presence, met with the German Ambassador, to whom he announced that 'after the settlement of the Saar question and the conclusion of the Rome Agreements, the disarmament question could be tackled...a settlement must be found'.[82] Even after the German declaration of conscription in March 1935 prompted the creation of a porous Anglo-Italo-French front at Stresa, the determination to include Germany remained a factor in Franco-Italian relations. As a Quai d'Orsay memorandum reflected in the early summer of 1935:

a German refusal to participate [in a Central European pact] would entirely modify the general conception of the Rome Accords. Perhaps the attitude of Germany will one day induce us to construct and organise a unilateral chain of resistance to its ambitions. For the moment at least, we can hardly refrain from entirely exhausting the possibilities of collective security, in Central as in Eastern Europe.[83]

[80] R. de Dampierre, 'Dix années de politique française à Rome', Pt. II, *Revue des deux Mondes*, December 1953, p. 279.   [81] DDF I, 8, no. 420.
[82] DGFP, C, III, no. 413.
[83] MAE, Papiers Massigli, 'L'Europe centrale', 10 June 1935. In part because he was reluctant to compromise future German negotiations by too marked an Italian orientation,

Laval having also coordinated the Eastern pact negotiations in late 1934 and 1935, with hopes for Franco-German entente and arms limitation within a collective context, his chagrin at Hitler's *fait accompli* of 16 March 1935 can easily be surmised. When Mussolini opened the conference held at Stresa in April 1935 to condemn the unilateral German action, the Italian dictator observed portentously that 'the entire world places its hope in this conference'. In fact, in private discussions at Stresa, Mussolini was genially non-committal on the topic of German rearmament, saying little while Laval and Ramsay MacDonald, the British Prime Minister, sulked over the suspension of negotiations with Germany, without closing the door to their resumption. Sir John Simon, the British Foreign Secretary, recently returned from talks with Hitler in Berlin, openly favoured resuming arms limitation talks. The conference's communication to the League of Nations thus opportunely reiterated the key points of the February Anglo-French overture to Berlin, amid passages on the impropriety of Germany's disruption of the orderly settlement of outstanding European problems and its own return to the League of Nations. The conference's final communiqué stated outright the participants' desire for arms limitation negotiations.[84] Not even a façade, the Stresa front was vitiated by Britain's June naval accord with Germany, and then by the international destabilisation brought about by Mussolini's war against Ethiopia from October 1935.

Ethiopia and the Hoare-Laval pact revisited

When the Ethiopian crisis broke, Laval gave himself over to a tortuous diplomacy: support only for innocuous sanctions against Italy, and the promotion of a compromise peace. His efforts were intensified by strong resentment at the conclusion of the Anglo-German naval pact. He was loath to break with Italy when Britain had broken ranks in a violation of the Versailles naval clauses and created new difficulties for France *vis-à-vis* Germany.[85] As Laval explained his policy to the *Chambre des députés'* Foreign Policy

---

Laval at first cautiously received the Italian military offer. The Franco-Italian staff talks of June 1935 are analysed in chapter 2.

[84] DDF I, 10, nos. 128, 173, 180, 186, 190.

[85] The official French position in the Ethiopian affair was crisply put by René Massigli of the Quai d'Orsay's Political Directorate to Lord Robert Cecil, the President of the League of Nations Union. MAE, Papiers Massigli, 'Correspondance personnelle', Massigli-Cecil correspondence, 8, 18 July 1935.

Commission in October 1935 amid allusions to the suspension of Danubian negotiations, the rupture of Stresa and the menace of Italo-German entente: 'Think only of this... Tell yourself that if, by sanctions, by conciliation, by no matter what means, we can arrive at a rapid end to the Italo-Ethiopian quarrel, it is peace...'[86]

When the British demanded unconditional French commitments against Italy in October and November 1935, Laval asked for compensatory security guarantees covering an Anschluss and a Rhineland reoccupation. (The French War Ministry had warned before the conflict's outbreak that Germany might profit from British bad humour to denounce the treaties relating to the demilitarised zone.)[87] When they predictably refused, he accepted only limited staff contacts with London (not without strong opposition to petrol sanctions and countervailing assurances to the Italians) in return for its assent to another attempt to conciliate Mussolini.[88] The results – the so-called Hoare-Laval plan – were unveiled after the British elections.

For its namesakes, Laval and Sir Samuel Hoare, the British Foreign Secretary, the December 1935 peace offer to Mussolini was intended to restore the Stresa peace front and, its less conspicuous corollary, the salvaging of arms limitation negotiations with Hitler. The Hoare-Laval interlude had then a four rather than three power design. Shortly after leakage of the Franco-British proposals in the French press forced his resignation, Hoare justified to a confidante his negotiations with Laval by the closeness of entente with Germany:

It is true that when I made the agreement in Paris with Laval, the country was unprepared for the changeover [in British policy, from Hoare's very pro-League stance of September 1935]. But bear in mind the importance of Germany. I had an assurance from Laval that in return for my helping France over Abyssinia, he would go all out with me to make peace with Germany.

Hoare boasted that Hitler had sent him a personal letter approving his course. But, in the hubris of fall from office, he exaggerated his influence on Laval, who reminisced after the war about telling Hoare in December 1935: 'Now we have finished with Italy.

[86] Assemblée Nationale, Commission des Affaires étrangères, 23 October 1935, pp. 81–2.
[87] SHA, Papiers Fabry, 'Journal de marche', 19 August 1935.
[88] R. A. C. Parker, 'Great Britain, France and the Ethiopian Crisis', *English Historical Review*, April 1974, pp. 293–332.

Together we are going to approach Germany.'[89] As has been seen, Laval had been burning for months for arms negotiations with Germany.

Before an *Haut Comité militaire* meeting in late November 1935, Laval addressed the need to suspend the arms race by direct talks with Germany. To Marshal Pétain's objection that France could only speak with firmness to Germany when it had made the necessary financial and rearmament effort, Laval retorted by assailing the April 1934 note: 'We must do the maximum for national defence, but it is not wise to neglect all direct conversations with Germany: the note of 17 April 1934 was perhaps not opportune. Germany continued to rearm and England concluded the Anglo-German Naval Accord.'[90]

Laval's determination to carry on arms negotiations with Berlin, like his characteristic disparagement of the April 1934 note to which he had never been reconciled ('elle est négative et on ne peut pas vivre dans la négation...'), represented a sequel in mid Ethiopian war to his diplomacy in early 1935 *vis-à-vis* Italy and the British. The urgency of Laval's remarks in November 1935 derived, however, from fear of Hitler's reaction to the pending ratification of the Franco-Soviet pact.

Laval's Soviet diplomacy

The course of Laval's Soviet diplomacy had been chequered, to say the least. An outspoken opponent of any rapprochement with the Soviets during the constructive phase of Barthou's diplomacy after the circulation of the April note, Laval gave his assent to a bilateral Franco-Soviet pact in late March 1935, shortly after the German conscription announcement. A Quai d'Orsay memorandum written for Laval shortly before a critical conversation with the Soviet Ambassador suggests that he may have been drawn into the Soviet *engrenage*, as Barthou had been, by a desire to avert an arms race: 'The policy of collective security, to the very extent that it permits a pooling of the forces of the states associated with it, on the other

[89] Privately printed diary of Thomas Jones, 28 June 1936; *Procès du maréchal Pétain: compte-rendu officiel in extenso des audiences de la Haute Cour de Justice* (Paris, 1976), 3 August 1945, p. 233.

[90] SHAA, 2B188, *Haut Comité militaire*, 21 November 1935; cf. Maurice Gamelin's retouched accounts in *Servir* II, pp. 177–81, and in an earlier manuscript note published in P. Le Goyet, *Le mystère Gamelin* (Paris, 1976), pp. 109–13. For Laval's sarcastic denunciation of the 17 April note in the immediate aftermath of the Anglo-German accord, see Assemblée Nationale, Commission des Affaires étrangères, 19 June 1935, pp. 35–7.

hand permits – and alone permits – limitation of the rearmament effort. An arms race would be the first consequence of its abandonment.' The surest way to accelerate European rearmament, it was argued, would be to leave Germany and the USSR to an internecine quarrel.[91]

On the subject of Soviet ideological contagion, on which Laval's personal sensitivities were notorious, the Quai d'Orsay in March 1935 viewed Hitler's anti-Bolshevism as a cover for pan-Germanism, and the dynamism of the USSR as a form of pan-Slavism. The diplomatic pressures of the Petite Entente and the year-old Balkan Entente for progress in the Franco-Soviet negotiations after Laval's voyage to Rome, pressures especially strong at a Petite Entente meeting at Ljubljana in Yugoslavia, were explained in pan-Slav terms.[92]

The Quai d'Orsay disastrously misgauged the strength of Petite Entente Russophilia, notably that of the Yugoslavs, who were volatile after the murder of their sovereign at Marseilles by Oustachis Croat terrorists. Laval's role at Geneva in arranging the judicial cover-up of probable Italian complicity in training the Oustachis murderers of Alexander and Barthou, and his willingness to go to Rome without firm Italian assent to a political accord with Yugoslavia, made the Petite Entente attentive to a Soviet whispering campaign that unalloyed French reliance on Italy would encourage the Italians to revive their revisionist Four Power pact.[93]

The possibility of German-Soviet conflict (in March 1935 viewed largely in terms of the old pan-German-pan-Slav antagonism), and the threat of a return to the German-Soviet cooperation of Rapallo constituted the two poles of the Quai d'Orsay's definition of the Russian question. The Political Directorate argued that France could forestall both perils – and an ideological polarisation of

---

[91] MAE, Papiers Massigli, 'Pacte franco-soviétique', Note, 29 March 1935.
[92] Dov Lungu, *Romania and the Great Powers* (Durham, N.C., 1989), pp. 58–9. The Balkan Entente, formed in February 1934, was composed of two members of the Petite Entente, Yugoslavia and Roumania, plus Turkey and Greece. A fact later to be of moment, Czechoslovakia was not a member. The Balkan Entente had no formal connection with France, although Paris recognised that the Entente might influence Greece to grant French troops transit through Salonika in a conflict. (Greek opposition to allied troop transit in 1915 had gravely compromised the allied position in the east.)
[93] Litvinov expressed concern that 'in the event of England's adherence [to the Rome Accords, to which the British gave approval in February 1935] Mussolini might, under the talk of a new agreement, attempt to resurrect the Four Power pact'. Litvinov to Potemkine, the Soviet Ambassador in Paris, 17 January 1935, cited in Haslam, *Soviet Union*, p. 45.

Europe – by interposing itself between Germany and the USSR. The Quai d'Orsay thus succumbed to the tempting belief that it could moderate the Soviets' 'régime en pleine évolution'.

As its argumentation on arms limitation implied, the Political Directorate's pressures after German conscription for a French commitment to the USSR were not directed towards a separate bilateral agreement.[94] Its March memorandum, in preparation for the Stresa conference, amalgamated Barthou's various diplomatic projects to exalt the preservation of European peace by a Franco-Italian-Soviet entente supported by three-quarters of continental Europe and a benevolently neutral England.[95]

Laval, however, found himself confronted a week later by Soviet threats to terminate the negotiations if he did not agree to a bilateral pact. Actuated by domestic pressures from Edouard Herriot of the Radical party, and against the advice of Léger, Laval accepted Soviet proposals for a free-standing bilateral pact.[96] During a visit to Moscow after the pact's signature, Laval himself suggested military conversations, a plunge which doubtless facilitated his approach to Stalin to end Comintern agitation against the French defence effort.[97]

Immediately after his obeisance to Moscow, Laval ostentatiously took up a British plan for a general non-aggression pact, a project to which the Reich briefly pretended to lend an ear.[98] In Warsaw en route to Moscow, Laval sought to rally the Poles by proposing that a general non-aggression pact including Germany and Poland might replace the Franco-Soviet pact. On the same occasion, Léger confided that his government was loath to be left alone with the Soviets (alone save for the Czech-Soviet mutual aid pact signed the following month).[99] Laval's manoeuvrings strengthened the hand of those inside the Soviet Politburo who wished to revive Rapallo, by economic and then political means, in opposition to the policy of

[94] In the phrase of Paul Bargeton, the Quai d'Orsay's Political Director, the dissociation of a Franco-Soviet pact from large-scale multilateral arrangements in Eastern Europe was 'a last resort'. DDF, II, 9, no. 97.

[95] MAE, Papiers Massigli, 'Pacte franco-soviétique', 29 March 1935; for similar Czech views in this period, Czech T-120, 1041/1809/414154.

[96] 'Struggle...for Collective Security', 10, pp. 112–14; see also ibid., 7, pp. 119–20, 122.

[97] PRO, FO 371, 19880, C7262/92/62. For Stalin's subsequent, dismissive attitude to his statement of support for French national defence at the close of the communiqué on Laval's visit, see Haslam, *Soviet Union*, p. 51.

[98] For Czech reports of continuing French and Soviet desire for a general non-aggression pact to include Germany and Poland, Czech T-120, 1041/1809/414154.

[99] J. Szembek, *Journal 1933–1939* (Paris, 1952), pp. 70–6.

collective security pursued by Litvinov.[100] The tortuous negotiations for the Eastern pact, Laval's clear preference for the Rome Accords, and the Soviet exclusion from Stresa, so galling to Moscow that Litvinov was originally instructed to abstain from the French motion at Geneva censuring Hitler's unilateral declaration of conscription – all of these episodes intensified the mutual distrust which vitiated the Franco-Soviet mutual aid pact from its inception. While Laval spoke to the Poles of a general non-aggression pact to replace the Franco-Soviet pact, Litvinov was reduced to proposing to the German Ambassador a bilateral non-aggression pact on similar grounds (to 'lessen the significance of the Franco-Soviet pact'), if only to quieten his critics in the Politburo by demonstrating that Berlin had no intention of signing a political agreement with the Soviets. By November 1935, Litvinov wrote bitterly to the Soviet Ambassador in Paris that 'Laval has decided, in so far as it depends on him, that whatever happens he will wreck Franco-Soviet cooperation and join a German anti-Soviet bloc'.[101]

The Ethiopian *débâcle* only intensified the anxieties about being left in close quarters with the USSR of which Laval and Léger had spoken in Warsaw. Fearful that Hitler would seize on the Franco-Soviet ratification to reoccupy the Rhineland before the Ethiopian imbroglio could be liquidated and arms limitation achieved, Laval spoke to the 21 November HCM of the danger of being dragged into war by the Soviets. To pacify the Reich before Franco-Soviet ratification, he wanted to conclude a Franco-German non-aggression pact, preceded by a démarche which would extract from Hitler a repudiation of the extremism of *Mein Kampf* and a non-aggression undertaking *vis-à-vis* the Soviets. These conditions being met, he thought of proceeding to bilateral arms limitation discussions and a Western Air pact including Britain and Italy. He remarked that the Germans should be told: 'France will not negotiate its foreign policy without England's knowing.'[102] Such was the arms

---

[100] Preoccupied by events in the Far East, Stalin was lured by the prospect of cooperation with Germany to counter the increasing possibility of Germano-Japanese *rapprochement*. Haslam's excellent analysis also makes clear that the Soviets believed that they could exploit the Reich's economic difficulties to begin cooperation with Berlin. Haslam, *Soviet Union*, pp. 51, 80, 93, 95. For economic conversations between the Soviet emissary, David Kandelaki, and Hjalmar Schacht in July 1935, prompted also by Laval's procrastination in seeking ratification of the Franco-Soviet pact, ibid., pp. 85–6.

[101] Ibid., pp. 49, 82, 90.

[102] SHAA, 2B188; HCM, 21 November 1935; 'Struggle...for Collective Security', 10, pp. 119–20; DGFP, C, IV, nos. 415, 425.

limitation diplomacy *vis-à-vis* Germany which Laval championed as coming out of a compromise peace settlement over Ethiopia.

THE CENTRAL EUROPEAN RESPONSE

The Polish Foreign Minister's disdain of economic sanctions against Italy was a natural result of his scepticism concerning collective security in any guise. Beck thus sometimes seconded Laval's diplomacy, as when he opposed the extension of sanctions in the League's Committee of Five; he was particularly proud of having reached a private agreement with Eden which protected Polish coal exports to Italy.[103] The Hoare-Laval interlude, however, brought to the surface Polish fears of a Four Power pact. The semi-official Polish press, which regarded Laval's policy with cynicism, joined Petite Entente press and diplomats in again decrying the threat of a great power directorate.[104]

Titulesco, the Roumanian Foreign Minister, despite his country's position as an exporter of petrol to Italy, was the most vehement supporter of sanctions against Italy at Geneva. He complained in the autumn of 1935 that Laval's oscillations made him 'seasick'. The French Foreign Minister 'zig-zagged over Ethiopia, spoke of an accord with Germany, admitted to uncertainty as to whether to ratify the Franco-Soviet pact, and then reversed himself declaring that it would be ratified, then took no action', and so forth. In attempting to chart his own foreign policy amid turbulent domestic waters, Titulesco opted for an audacious Russophile line, with the ballast of offers to the Reich for a mutual aid pact in July 1935. Roumanian diplomatic initiative was deadlocked, however, by Litvinov's reluctance to commit himself until Laval ratified the Franco-Soviet mutual aid pact.[105]

---

[103] MAE, Papiers Noël, 4 December 1935; Beck, *Dernier rapport*, pp. 105–6.
[104] MAE, Papiers Noël, 16 December 1935.
[105] MAE, SDN 770, 16 July 1935; Papiers Massigli, 'Pacte franco-soviétique', 20 September 1935; I. M. Oprea, *Nicolae Titulesco's Diplomatic Activity* (Bucharest, 1968), pp. 98–101; PRO, FO 371, 19572, R6781/6781/37.
   At Ljubljana in January 1935, Titulesco, qualifying the Danubian pact as subservient to Italy, had taken the lead in pressing for rapid progress in the Franco-Soviet negotiations. (The Quai d'Orsay attributed his priorities to Roumania's peripheral place in its own collective pacts and to Titulesco's desire for compensation for what he called the Polish betrayal of January 1934.) He also waxed enthusiastic over the prospect of Franco-German rapprochement, which he described as 'the final and crowning phase in the Petite Entente political program'. Ibid., 19500, R3447/302/67. Titulesco's manoeuvring amidst the great powers was choppy, particularly when Paris emitted few consistent signals.

The course of Czech diplomacy was, at least outwardly, more placid. In May 1935 the Czechs had concluded a mutual pact with the USSR, its operation by mutual consent dependent on the implementation of the French pact. Bitter that they had been unable to settle their perennial quarrel with Poland before the conclusion of a Soviet pact, the Czechs were anxious not to be forced into an exclusive reliance on Moscow, dispensing assurances to this effect in Berlin and elsewhere.[106] None the less, in the first months after the pact's conclusion, Beneš enjoyed good relations with the Czech Communist party which defied the Comintern actively to support both his election to the Presidency of Czechoslovakia, and the national defence effort of which he was an ardent champion.[107]

Alongside his involuted Soviet diplomacy, Beneš attempted to coordinate his policy with Laval's in the Danubian negotiations.[108] Throughout the summer of 1935, Beneš raced to realise progress on the Danubian pact before Italy launched its colonial campaign in the autumn.[109] He had reluctantly accepted the Quai d'Orsay's decision to dilute the pact's force from mutual aid to non-aggression, a decision meant to facilitate German and Italian adherence. Observers attributed this flexibility to the victory of Henlein's Sudetendeutsch Partei in the Czech municipal elections of spring 1935, and to the virulence of German propaganda against the Czech-Soviet link. Ominously this propaganda had been taken up by Jósef Beck, the Polish Foreign Minister, who returned from one of his periodic visits to Berlin convinced that Czechoslovakia was a Red Army base and Beneš completely under Soviet influence.[110]

---

[106] The Czech Foreign Ministry considered that its earlier willingness to sign a general non-aggression pact including Germany indicated the good faith of its bilateral pact with the USSR. Beneš expected allied Roumania and Yugoslavia to conclude pacts on the Czech-Soviet model. As for Polish hostility to the pact, while Beneš sought to reassure Warsaw, he considered that it 'sent up in smoke' the Poles' anticipation that the fate of Czechoslovakia would one day be delivered to them. Czech T-120, 1041/1809/41351, 414131, 414146, 414166. Wandycz, *Twilight*, pp. 388, 398–400.

[107] Haslam, *Soviet Union*, p. 88.

[108] The genuine Czech desire to cooperate with Italy was related in part to Czech euphoria over the Stresa conference, seen, for all its shortcomings, as a demonstration of great power unity against the threat of war, Czech T-120, 1041/1809/413451–2, 414146–8.

[109] Beneš lectured the Italian Minister in Prague on Italy's foolhardiness in delaying Danubian negotiations at the time it was undertaking, as he put it, an effort of some scale in Ethiopia: 'it risks jeopardising everything on both counts simultaneously'. MAE, SDN 806, 7 June 1935.

[110] MAE, SDN 806, 27, 28 June; Papiers Noël, 21 June, 10, 11 July; 'Tchécoslovaquie', 13 July. A Laval letter to the Minister of War, ibid., 25 July 1935, warned of German diplomatic insistence that in the event that complications arose as a result of the Czech-Soviet pact, 'and these were to be expected since it was a question of the Russians',

In the weeks before the Hoare-Laval fiasco, Beneš privately admitted that, while French efforts at conciliation were in themselves praiseworthy, he was disquieted at the crystallisation of French public opinion in favour of *de facto* neutrality in the Ethiopian conflict. The Czech public felt profoundly threatened by the precedent of Italian impunity. A celebrated article in the Czech press discredited the principal arguments which a segment of the French press had borrowed from Fascist propaganda by substituting 'Czechoslovakia' for 'Ethiopia' and 'Hitler' for 'Mussolini'. Beneš's diplomacy in the autumn of 1935 consisted of fruitless overtures to Hoare, the British Foreign Secretary, whom Beneš hoped to persuade to realise the promise of his much acclaimed September 1935 Geneva speech by creating a Franco-British front in Central Europe. In a widely distributed speech to the Czech Parliament in early November, Beneš extolled Hoare's speech as exemplary, and carefully elaborated a distinction between Czechoslovakia's League duties, and its friendship for Italy and hopes for the resumption of the Danubian negotiations.[111]

Material captured by the Germans in 1939 from the archives of the Czech Foreign Ministry demonstrates that the Czechs sheltered behind the League and the action of the great powers in Geneva, refusing to take leadership in formulating a strong public position against Italy. Kamil Krofta, the Czech Minister of Foreign Affairs and an historian by formation, resembled Beneš in his almost obtuse optimism. In briefing fellow officials at the Czech Foreign Ministry, Krofta showed sympathy for Laval's attempts to end the conflict. The briefings, crudely translated and abridged by the Germans, make clear that this sympathy rested on Krofta's estimation that an Italy satisfied in Ethiopia might return to Central European politics in the ranks of the status quo powers, a calculation shared by the Quai d'Orsay. As a result, the Hoare-Laval plan received what he called 'a quiet reception' in Prague.[112] Hoare-Laval was an

---

Germany would make its first retaliation against Czechoslovakia as the aircraft-carrier of its adversaries.

[111] MAE, Papiers Léger, Naggiar-Léger letter, 23 October; 'Tchécoslovaquie', 20 October, 5 November 1935; Czech T-120, 1041/1809/414170, 414171, 414172. Czech identification with Ethiopia as a blameless victim of aggression none the less extended to sending arms to Addis Ababa, a manifestation of League loyalty which rankled Mussolini. Ibid., 414089.

[112] Ibid., 414171–3, 414179–81. Krofta was aware in this period of Laval's soundings *vis-à-vis* the Germans, and, while he did not see their relation to a compromise peace over Ethiopia, he spoke of the interest for Czechoslovakia in obtaining guarantees from across-the-board

'unlovable precedent' but the prudent Czechs considered that its viability depended on Ethiopia's acceptance of it, as well as on the position of the great powers and the League as a whole. Czechoslovakia, in Krofta's phrase, would not step up on the stage to attack Italy.[113]

To complete this picture of small power diplomacy amidst the international destabilisation of the Ethiopian crisis: Yugoslavia, the small state most fearful of Italian designs, vacillated between dread that an Italy victorious in Ethiopia would turn on Yugoslavia, and wild hope that the Ethiopian venture would make the Italians more accommodating. After the Hoare-Laval interlude, the French military attaché in Belgrade reported that France's situation there was unusually difficult. Yugoslav distrust of Hoare-Laval had been compounded by the desultory trial in Aix of the accomplices in the murder of Alexander, according to Béthouart, an event more damaging to French reputation than the Yugoslav monarch's assassination; and by unsatisfactory negotiations in Paris for compensation for losses caused by Yugoslav participation in sanctions against Italy. Of the Petite Entente states, Yugoslavia was most at the mercy of the economic dislocation of Italian trade, a dislocation which imperilled its internal consolidation and intensified the fears of the Regent Paul of military menace from Italy. In such a contingency, the operation of French aid to Yugoslavia, blurred by the Franco-Italian staff talks of June 1935, was far from certain. Béthouart wrote that, until the Ethiopian crisis, the Yugoslavs had relied upon the smooth operation of the Geneva mechanism to bring them French aid in a crisis. The malaise of the collective security system, for which the Yugoslavs blamed Laval, greatly worsened their long-standing insecurity *vis-à-vis* Italy. Béthouart warned that, if Yugoslavia could no longer be sure of receiving support from France, it would modify its policy.[114] German commercial and propaganda inroads in Yugoslavia were such that no one in Paris could doubt that this modification would be to Berlin's benefit. Yugoslavia's apparent Russophilia at the beginning of 1935 had been a diplomatic mirage. Belgrade persisted in its refusal to

Franco-German negotiations. Ibid., 414176; for earlier Franco-Czech discussion of French soundings in Berlin, MAE, 'Tchécoslovaquie', 11, 17 November 1935.

[113] The mildness of the Czech response may have prompted bumbling Italian attempts made in January 1936 to cajole the Czechs into action in Geneva to liquidate the conflict in a manner to satisfy Rome's interests, Czech T-120, 1041/1809/414082.

[114] SHA, 'Yougoslavie', 11, 19 December 1935.

recognise the USSR, a refusal on which Laval saw fit to congratulate the Yugoslav Minister in Paris, remarking in August 1935 that Yugoslavia had 'remained an oasis in a world which has recognised the Soviets'.[115]

The prospects at the close of 1935 was that, as Czechoslovakia and Roumania gravitated towards the USSR, Yugoslavia would drift into the German orbit, a state of affairs which underscored the incoherence and facile opportunism of Laval's diplomacy. While Hoare and Laval fancied that a Franco-British approach to Hitler arising from their plan would have altered the course of events, the reality was chastening. Hoare fell from office when the French press prematurely leaked the plan. Laval fell in his turn in January 1936, as the Communist-backed Front populaire political alliance drew up its battalions for national elections in April and May 1936. The inglorious end of the Hoare-Laval episode left French diplomacy in complete disarray. Italy was receptive to the suit of the non-sanctionist Reich; the Petite Entente states were consumed with anxiety over a neutralist evolution of French opinion, while the Poles joined Germany in virulently anti-Czech propaganda.

To summarise, the discordant eastern treaty system was imperilled from the mid 1920s, first by French diplomatic willingness to contemplate territorial revision, and then by the Quai d'Orsay's fixation on arms limitation. Visible in the negotiations for a Four Power pact, arms limitation underwrote Barthou's ambitious diplomacy from April 1934, although it was most conspicuous under Pierre Laval. For both Barthou and Laval, the security linkages with Italy and the USSR were associated with the desire to halt the arms race by cajoling Hitler into negotiations. In the face of greater provocation, Laval found it as difficult as Barthou to divorce security from arms limitation. Confronted with the *fait accompli* of the unilateral German announcement of conscription, Laval joined Mussolini and the British in the Stresa front, whose censure of the German move only half-concealed an invitation to resume arms limitation negotiations among the four great powers. The Stresa front broke apart under the strains of Mussolini's Ethiopian enterprise. The failure of the Hoare-Laval agreement, designed by its authors to revive four power arms limitation negotiations by a compromise peace in Ethiopia, opened the way for Hitler to

[115] PRO, FO 371, 19500, R5404/232/67; Lungu, *Romania*, p. 62.

reoccupy the Rhineland. Struck by the disarray of the great powers at the close of 1935, the Czechs concluded that the Reich would base its imminent decision as to the future of the demilitarised zone on France's willingness to act outside its national territory, in the interests of collective security.[116]

[116] DDF II, 1, no. 76.

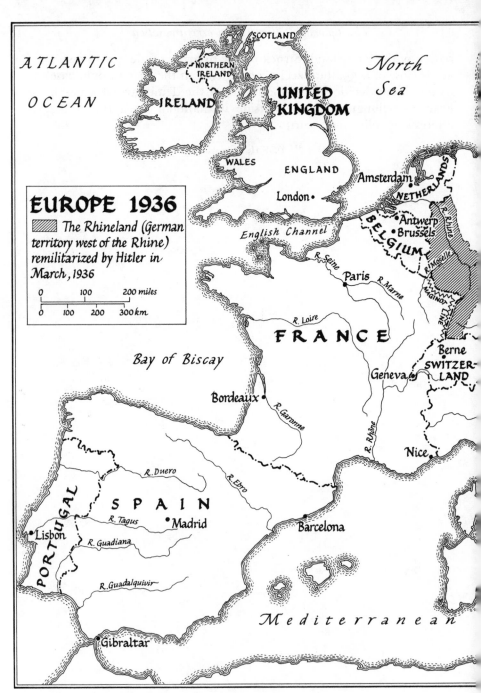

Map 1   Europe 1936

CHAPTER 2

The military, the Rhineland and the eastern alliances, 1918–1936

After the 1939–45 war, the former head of the Quai d'Orsay, the poet-diplomat Alexis Léger, remarked about the ill-fated eastern system: 'It was not the diplomats but the military in France who held most tightly to the Eastern alliances. Treaty obligations which the diplomats had come to regard as "charges", both "morally and juridically embarrassing", the military still looked upon as assets.'[1]

It is a truism for historians of France from 1890 to 1945 that French security rested on alliances. For historians of inter-war France, this has meant first and foremost the Franco-British entente of 1939–40, the not-so-happy ending to France's chequered diplomacy of the 1930s. It is true that important recent work has examined the French military's infatuation with Italy in the mid thirties. But placed above all in the traditional context of the Stresa front, and so said to represent a lost opportunity to construct a solid West European front against Germany, this Italian infatuation has not radically altered our picture of France's reliance on allies.[2] In a historiography dominated by the assumption that the French Commander in Chief, Maurice Gamelin, was preparing for a German attack in the west, so that the eastern alliances as well as the omnibus Italian entente had a chiefly western referent, the role and efficacy of the eastern system has been enigmatic. Given our knowledge of Gamelin's brooding inaction during the Czech and Polish crises in 1938–9, Léger's lonely reflection seems startling, even paradoxical.

---

1 E. Cameron, 'Alexis Saint-Léger Léger', in G. A. Craig, F. Gilbert, *The Diplomats* (New York, 1974), vol. 2, p. 393. For independent historical assessment that it was the military, not the diplomats, who remained attached to the eastern allies, Soutou, 'L'alliance franco-polonaise...', pp. 321, 335, 339–40, and especially 347.

2 W. I. Shorrock, *From Ally to Enemy: the Enigma of Fascist Italy in French Diplomacy, 1920–1940* (Kent, Ohio, 1988); R. J. Young, 'Soldiers and Diplomats: the French Embassy and Franco-Italian Relations, 1935–6', *The Journal of Strategic Studies*, 7, 1984; and 'French Military Intelligence and the Franco-Italian Alliance 1933–9', *The Historical Journal*, 28, 1985.

This chapter will explore Gamelin's lengthy anticipation of an imminent Rhineland reoccupation, an event which he sought to parry by elaborating an anticipatory strategy for a war elsewhere, a war in the east predicated on Italy. In so doing, it will challenge the view of French defence policy in the mid 1930s as based on preparation for a war in the west, arguing instead that Gamelin sought from the early 1930s to construct an eastern strategy to channel the German flood. Chapters 3–7 of the book will consider the ideological disintegration of this Italophile strategy during the Socialist-led Front populaire of 1936–7, and Gamelin's response to the eastern crises of 1938–9 which, it will be argued, redounded with full force against France itself in 1940.

THE EMA AND THE CONSTRUCTION OF THE PEACE

The immediate rationale for a French presence in Central Europe originated in wartime experience – in 1918, French troops were present over much of Central Europe – and in the strategic concerns of the General Staff in the construction of the peace. With the cessation of hostilities in 1918, the French military pressed for the pinioning of Germany in the west by a permanent Rhineland occupation, and in the east by the attachment of Danzig and Upper Silesia to Poland and of Bohemia to Czechoslovakia. With French troops permanently in the Rhineland, military operations *on German soil* could subdue Germany in aid of an eastern ally or prevent an attack on France itself. In 1919, however, Clemenceau exchanged the military's Rhineland demands for the stillborn Anglo-American guarantee.[3] To the military's dismay, while the zone was theoretically to be demilitarised in perpetuity, the duration of the military occupation was highly uncertain. (It was slated to last until 1935, with a proviso for extension of the occupation should the reparations clauses of Versailles go unfulfilled.)

After Clemenceau's concessions, the French military could have little confidence in a Rhineland buffer zone, and they restively searched for *espaces de manoeuvre* in Belgium, betwixt France and Germany, and in Poland and Czechoslovakia, which ringed Germany in the east.[4] For the Quai d'Orsay, the eight treaties

---

[3] For the origins of Clemenceau's compromise, Berthelot's hopes that French good grace in the Rhineland would predispose Britain to French claims on Syria, Barré, *Le seigneur-chat*, pp. 335–6.

[4] H. Dutailly, *Les problèmes de l'armée de terre française (1935–9)* (Paris, 1980), pp. 18–19. When the treaty with Czechoslovakia was added in 1924, Marshal Foch extolled the new political

concluded with Belgium, Poland, and the Petite Entente between 1920 and 1927 represented a ragbag of diplomatic interest. Elements of its estrangement were already visible by Locarno in 1925. But, for the French General Staff, interest in the eastern alliances developed along highly rational lines. This outwardly Cartesian development was inseparable from diplomatic concessions over the Rhineland and German rearmament.[5]

To the Polish-Czech-Belgian nucleus of 1920–4, the later treaties with Roumania and Yugoslavia added concentric states, among whose military attractions was communications: Roumania's position on the Black Sea, Yugoslavia's connections with the Adriatic and with Salonika, the site of the major French amphibious operation in the First World War. Roumania and Yugoslavia also possessed natural resources and vast reservoirs of peasant soldiery, which drew a General Staff preoccupied by the weakness of its own industrial and demographic base. This French military interest was fostered by Czechoslovakia, which in 1920–1 had formed with Roumania and Yugoslavia a diplomatic and military organisation directed primarily against Hungarian revisionism, the Petite Entente. In the early and mid 1920s, the General Staff consolidated its Polish, Yugoslav, and Roumanian ties with substantial arms loans and cessions, while one of its members, Eugène Mittelhauser, commanded the Czech Army until 1926.[6] For the French military, the alliance treaties were shaped by geographical imperatives, whose defensive trajectory was towards a conflict on the peripheries.

The long-term strategic function of the eastern and Belgian treaties was to enable France to fight outside her frontiers. This became the central imperative of French military planning between the wars. Blisteringly aware of the slaughter of the First World War, the General Staff shied away from a repetition of the Franco-German stalemate of 1914–18 along France's north-eastern frontier. It is essential to understand the societal consensus on which this planning rested. The military tenet of integral defence of the

and military treaties with states bordering on Germany, seeing in Belgium, Czechoslovakia, and Poland 'a single front which constitutes the best safeguard of peace'. SHA, 'EMA/2 Tchécoslovaquie', 19 March 1924. For Foch's attachment to the Polish alliance after initial scepticism, Soutou, 'L'alliance franco-polonaise...', pp. 297, 300–1, 315; Wandycz, 'La Pologne', pp. 250, 254.   [5] Cf. Soutou, 'L'alliance franco-polonaise...', p. 298.
[6] Laroche, *Au Quai d'Orsay*, p. 137; Soutou, 'L'impérialisme du pauvre', pp. 221–2, 230–1; SHA, 7N2520, 1 June 1935; A. Marès, 'La faillite des relations franco-tchécoslovaques: la mission militaire française à Prague', *Revue d'histoire de la deuxième guerre mondiale*, 28, 111 (1978).

frontiers commanded early and virtually automatic assent in a society with a debilitating awareness of its industrial and demographic inferiority, an abhorrence of war from which no segment of opinion was exempt, and an overwhelming sentiment of exhaustion. The interactions of such profound factors produced a defensive strategy impervious to real innovation. Eventually symbolised in the popular imagination by the Maginot line, the military's determination to shield France from war also induced a less conspicuous fixation on a war elsewhere.[7]

The disaster of the Ruhr occupation in 1923–4 having definitively discredited unilateral French coerciveness in the Rhineland, Briand's diplomacy sought to elaborate a durable European settlement resting on the formula 'Arbitration – Security – Disarmament'. Shortly after Locarno, Briand agreed to the first phase of allied evacuation of the Rhineland, despite German rearmament violations. In private talks at Thoiry, he and Stresemann went farther, discussing complete evacuation of the Rhineland and the suspension of allied arms supervision.

For the General Staff (EMA), Briandism posed divisive challenges: early evacuation of the Rhineland and a dedication to arms limitation. In 1929–30, the French military were not consulted about the principle of an early evacuation of the occupied zone. Immediately after Locarno, Foch, as Commander in Chief of the Allied Armies, had vehemently objected to premature abandonment of the Rhineland bastion. Foch's outspoken letter to his government, however, lacked any trace of resolve to defend the zone's demilitarised status once allied troops were withdrawn. At that point, and he pleaded that it be as late as possible, Foch argued that French security would demand fortifications. In 1926, as in 1919, Foch's advice on the zone was disregarded. The erection of the Maginot line, however, would be decreed as a corollary to early French withdrawal. It was to parry France's demographic weakness, to protect it against surprise attack, and to provide time for the army to mobilise. In this last sense, it would replace the line of the Rhine surrendered by early French evacuation, the Rhine having been unanimously regarded by the General Staff as France's natural

---

[7] The attachment of public opinion and the politicians to fixed fortifications soon surpassed that of the EMA. B. A. Lee, 'Strategy, arms and the collapse of France 1930–1940', R. Langhorne (ed.), *Diplomacy and Intelligence during the Second World War* (Cambridge, 1985), p. 64.

military frontier.[8] Construction of the Maginot line also invited fortifications in the zone after it fell to Germany and indirectly, German attack in the east or through Belgium. Foch, having long justified the scheduled allied occupation for fifteen years as necessary for the consolidation of the new eastern states, could only focus on their vulnerability after early French evacuation of the Rhineland. He thus sounded the alarm that, unable to intervene on their behalf, an impotent France could only witness the collapse of those countries established by the victory of 1918.[9]

GAMELIN'S STRATEGY FOR A WAR OF COALITION IN THE
EAST

Maurice Gamelin

The early evacuation of the Rhineland furnished the backdrop to the sisyphean task Maurice Gamelin adopted on the eve of Hitler's advent to power. He would attempt to salvage France's security by a coalition effort which would gain time by a war in the east, a war in which the bulk of German force would be directed elsewhere. Designated as Deputy Chief of Staff in 1930, Gamelin accepted as given an imminent German reoccupation of the Rhineland – an eventuality which had obsessed the EMA, particularly Pétain, since the early 1920s – as well as more recent civilian pressures for arms limitation.

His attachment to the prospect of a war in the east makes it worthwhile to probe the famous enigma of Gamelin's personality. In an apologia for the 1940 defeat, written at the close of his life, he wistfully signed himself 'General Gamelin, born in Paris, Blvd. St. Germain, across from the Ministry of War, of a Flemish father and

---

[8] Discussion of the construction of the Maginot line, and with it, the larger issue of organisation of frontier defence actually began in the early 1920s. At that time, Foch relied on the allied occupation of the Rhineland, although he was more prepared than his colleagues to risk fighting on French territory. (As he put it, 'If one is victorious, one thus assures preservation of the territory.') Pétain, in contrast, sought to forge into doctrine the absolute inviolability of national territory. Believing French evacuation of the Rhineland imminent, he was anxious from 1920 to organise frontier defence, including massive fortification to compensate for the loss of the Rhineland frontier, a task which he regarded as requiring attention to the diplomatic conjuncture. SHA, 7N3497, 'Projets d'évacuation de la Ruhr', n.d.; J. Doise and M. Vaïsse, *Diplomatie et outil militaire* (Paris, 1987), pp. 276–8 is useful on these 1920–2 discussions and the transformation of the army's mobilisation planning in 1925–6 to ensure integral defence of the frontiers.

[9] Foch letter to the French Government, 8 March 1926 in A. Adamthwaite, *The Lost Peace* (New York, 1981), pp. 79–82.

a mother from Lorraine'.[10] He was born in 1872 into a family with strong military credentials on both sides. His father was a senior military official, his maternal grandfather, the last French military governor of Strasbourg. The young Gamelin had a vocation for soldiering as well as a gift for painting. From his lively youthful interest in painting, he derived a talent for cartography, a skill which in its attentiveness to geography would colour his military planning.[11]

His military record as a cadet and young soldier was impeccable. Academically, he was, in those phrases by which Marc Bloch castigated the upper echelons of a General Staff bureaucratised by the 1930s, 'Too good a student... a creature of exams.'[12] After completing St. Cyr, Gamelin saw action in Algeria and in the 1914–18 war at the end of which he led an infantry division and improvised corps. He was not merely a staff officer, but his experience early in the war as Joffre's *chef du cabinet* made an indelible impression. From his association with Joffre, who was dismissed in 1916, he culled the lesson that a general must cultivate politicians to preserve his position. He became the quintessential political general, with contacts which spanned the republican spectrum from Tardieu to Blum. Soft-spoken, unabrasive, and guarded, Gamelin reassured. His inveterate habit was to tell interlocutors whatever he sensed that they wanted to hear. The diplomat René Massigli remembers Gamelin's manner: 'Systematically, he made the statements, to all and sundry, which he thought they expected.'[13] As the German military attaché in Paris astutely observed, he was 'the exceptional French soldier who was accepted by the politicians because he did not... arouse the belief that he was making himself too powerful'.[14] From 1930 Deputy Chief of Staff, a post to which he was appointed by the right-wing politician André Tardieu, Commander in Chief from 1935, a designation owed to

---

[10] SHA, Fonds Gamelin, 7, 'Les causes de nos revers en 1940'.
[11] Cf. 'His aptitude and liking for cartography bloomed... he dared to illustrate gloomy, austere maps with explanatory plans, and demonstrated how colour could embellish them without any loss of precision. His syntheses of the terrain were so remarkable that often tactical solutions simply emerged from them.' P. Le Goyet, *Le mystère Gamelin* (Paris, 1976), pp. 14, 16. *Le mystère Gamelin* is a hard-hitting and invaluable analysis of Gamelin's career.
[12] Bloch, *L'étrange défaite*, pp. 141–4.
[13] Cited in *Munich 1938, Revue des études slaves*, LII, fascicule 1–2 (1979), p. 234.
[14] Cited in Martin Alexander, 'The French officer corps and leftist government, 1935–7', in M. Alexander and H. Graham, *The French and Spanish Popular Fronts* (Cambridge, 1989), p. 65.

Pierre Laval, Gamelin in the course of the decade in fact amassed considerable power from his position as an entrenched civil servant advising a temporary clientèle of politicians.[15] His own political orientation is finally unclear, ranging from the fire-breathing anti-leftism of an impassioned memorandum which he circulated, but characteristically did not deliver orally, at the Riom trial in 1941, to the burnished liberalism of his tendentious post-war memoirs, *Servir*.[16] The constant underlying his apoliticism in the 1930s and his post-war political statements appears to have been a certain obseqiousness and a desire to retain rank, camouflaged, no doubt even to himself, by devotion to duty.[17]

Legend has it that Gamelin drafted the battle orders for the Marne. Whether or not this was so, the harrowing experience of being at Joffre's side during those critical days appears to have left him with a life-long sublimated fear of not being able again to hold the Germans. Gamelin was known for an outward calm, almost a phlegmatism modelled on Joffre's famous imperturbability.[18] The British would publicly refer to him as 'notre Gamelin', but beneath the general's oblique and taciturn public persona was a man of intense emotion sometimes bordering on panic. As Maurice Vaïsse has pointed out, this oscillation between panic and complacency characterised the entire General Staff, although Gamelin remains an outstanding example of it.[19]

A central issue with regard to Gamelin's personality and influence is the extent to which he was representative of General Staff thinking, as against the role he played in forming it. Marc Bloch recalled the General Staff of 1939–40 as above all a pedagogical outfit; 'Of all the sports played by the army, the pedagogical sport counted among the most fashionable... [the Army] presented the

---

[15] It is worth stressing that Gamelin owed these promotions to Tardieu and Laval, politicians of the right with reservations as to the workability of parliamentarianism in France. Gamelin, always a jealous defender of his own turf, privately castigated parliamentary infighting and influence, a pastime which by 1939 distracted his attention from operational planning. I am indebted to Dr Martin Alexander of the University of Southampton for allowing me to consult his notes on Gamelin's journal in 1939–40.

[16] FNSP, Papiers Blum, 3BL3 Dr1, M. Gamelin, 'La politique étrangère de la France 1930–39 au point de vue militaire'; M. Gamelin, *Servir*, 3 vols. (Paris, 1946–7).

[17] Le Goyet cites in full the statement which Gamelin did deliver at Riom; it is eloquent as to his flight from responsibility and the uses to which he put the concept of duty. Le Goyet, *Le mystère*, pp. 355–7.

[18] So he appeared, a model of calm command and the rewards of teamwork, on the cards sold with American chewing tobacco in 1939. These usually featured baseball players, but with the outbreak of war in Europe, pictured generals, tanks, and guns.

[19] Doise and Vaïsse, *Diplomatie*, p. 316.

image of an immense scholarly hive.' Gamelin retained all of his life
– the British historian Richard Cobb remembers him thus, strolling
in the Bois de Boulogne in the early 1950s – a distinctly professorial
air.[20] Overseeing the various teaching bodies of the General Staff
and the synthesising of its doctrine, a doctrine self-consciously
conceived as the modernisation of the lessons of the last war,
Gamelin fostered an EMA orientation which was one-dimensional,
often confined to what best suited an allied war effort rather than to
what conditions might obtain in reality. These deficiencies were not
glaringly apparent until the war, although significantly, they appear
much earlier in Gamelin's planning for an eastern front. He closely
oversaw relations with the eastern allies, Italy, and the USSR. His
policies were often derived from General Staff studies earmarked for
his approval. They were then institutionalised by organisations like
the *Haut Comité militaire* from 1932 and the *Comité permanent de la
Défense nationale* from 1936, in which the military came to exercise
a preponderant influence, and by his dictate establishing the high
command as the sole arbiter of military doctrine. From 1935, all
articles, letters, and books appearing under the EMA's auspices had
to receive its specific approval before publication.[21] The process of
policy formation was circular and self-reflexive.

A second issue raised by Gamelin's career is whether or not he
possessed a strategy. Many students of the French military in this
period firmly dismiss the possibility. Even so shrewd an historian as
Maurice Vaïsse is inclined to disregard any statement by Gamelin or
for that matter, his military colleagues on any given strategic
problem: 'It is useless to refer to the declarations of the military
leaders: they said everything and its opposite. Skilfully managing
loopholes and alibis, they multiplied warnings while strutting about
when their views were asked.'[22] This book will argue that Gamelin
did evolve a strategy, albeit a strategy of default, which rapidly
degenerated into political buck-passing. In appearance so pliable to
circumstance, Gamelin formulated a static military policy based on
external space for manoeuvre. Again, this characterisation has been

[20] Bloch, *L'étrange défaite*, p. 134; Richard Cobb, Remarks to the Society for French Historical Studies, March 1987.
[21] Doise and Vaïsse, *Diplomatie*, p. 327; Williamson Murray, *The Change in the European Balance of Power, 1938–1939* (Princeton, 1984), p. 104.
[22] Doise and Vaïsse, *Diplomatie*, p. 328. Anyone who has read very much of Gamelin cannot but sympathise with Vaïsse's dismissiveness. In Daladier's phrase, Gamelin's counsel could resemble sand trickling through the fingers. Still, it will be argued here that his various pronouncements evidence clear strategic themes and internal consistency from the early 1930s to the Breda Variant in 1940.

applied to Gamelin's strategy when war submerged Western Europe, but attention to the specifically eastern aspect of Gamelin's planning shows it to have been present much earlier.

Gamelin and Syrový

In late January 1933, during the week Adolf Hitler took power in Germany, Gamelin, the heir-apparent of the French defence establishment, met Syrový, the chief of the Czech General Staff, for unofficial conversations in Paris. In the adverse but highly stimulating circumstances of the disarmament talks, Gamelin turned his hand to the preparation of an allied coalition in the east. Recent French concessions to the German demand for equality of rights at the Geneva disarmament conference signified to Gamelin and Syrový that the Germans intended to remilitarise and fortify the Rhineland.[23] The two agreed that Germany would then attack in the east. Walled in by German fortifications, France would be unable to force the barrier erected against it to aid an unspecified eastern ally.[24]

The rationale for the collapse of the French alliance system – the unopposed Rhineland reoccupation of March 1936 and the French abdication at Munich in 1938 – is arrestingly mapped out in these candid, unofficial conversations between two generals, each destined to preside over the collapse of his nation's military establishment. But for all that he wrote off the Rhineland and renounced unilateral French action on behalf of Poland or Czechoslovakia, Gamelin did not meet with Syrový to pronounce a post-mortem on the eastern system. He was too attentive to the immediate past not to attend to the fact that traditional French strategy *vis-à-vis* Germany required an eastern counterweight in a two-front war. France's pre-1914 alliance system, with its surgically precise Russian accord, had been based on the assumption that France would bear the brunt of

---

[23] The transcript of the Gamelin-Syrový conversations contains no allusion to the governmental change in Germany. From 1932 French intelligence had been attentive to what it deemed the *Reichswehr*'s virtually unopposed power within the collapsing Weimar Republic and it assumed that the *Reichswehr* would retain the upper hand over domestic political events. The explicit political concern in the Gamelin-Syrový talks was Paris's December 1932 recognition of German equality of rights in the disarmament talks, that is, the need to adapt to civilian French concessions likely to affect the Rhineland Zone in an ongoing climate of exacerbated German nationalism and militarism. SHA, 7N2520, 2e Bureau Note, 10 June 1932.

[24] SHAA, 2B98, 'Conversations franco-tchécoslovaques', 28–31 January 1933.

German force. With their shared assumption that the next conflict would begin in the east, the 1933 conversations between Gamelin and Syrový acknowledged that the chronic problem of an eastern counterweight had to be seen in a radically different light.

Official EMA orthodoxy was and remained that the direction of the German attack could not be predicted. Gamelin's conversations with Syrový suggested, however, that the corollary of France's early evacuation of the Rhineland might not be the territorial *révision à froid* mooted for so long, but French acquiescence in a German remilitarisation of the Rhineland which would presage German military movement in the east.

In January 1933, Gamelin's strategic picture was of a two-front war, initially with quasi-autonomous fronts. Since France was not obliged by any of its Central European conventions to send troops, direct French involvement in the Central European theatre at the start of a conflict would be limited to the dispatch of several air squadrons and eventually to the establishment of a land liaison, to prolong the life of the eastern front beyond the Czechs' thirty-day estimate for their resistance. The immediate prospect was that of a static war, in which the largely separate pressures of two fronts would prepare a victorious offensive linking the theatres. Pronouncing the conduct of the war to be a governmental problem, Gamelin declined to consider in advance the coordination between the allied eastern and western blocs; instead he directed his attention to operations in a limited Central European theatre. While allowing for the particular interests of each state, such as Yugoslav and Roumanian concern with Italian and Hungarian animosity, Gamelin counselled broadening the Petite Entente's war plans against Hungary to encompass a general conflict: 'We must not lose sight of our aim: the realisation of a front against Germany.' To this front, Polish-Petite Entente cooperation was indispensable. Since the mid 1920s, the EMA had assumed that the Polish-Czech animosity would conveniently recede once a German resurgence made rapprochement a vital necessity. More disconcerted by the Polish animus against Russia – 'Roumania and Poland, linked by their defence agreement against Russia, have to be convinced of the necessity of building a front against Germany...' – Gamelin urged Syrový to join forces with the Poles to subjugate Upper Silesia.[25]

[25] Ibid.

Gamelin's military diplomacy

Gamelin's various counsels to Syrový in 1933 closely followed a 1932 EMA study which set ground rules for coordination of a Central European campaign. According to the study, the EMA would have more influence over the eastern allies if its action appeared disinterested. Thus Czechoslovakia and Poland should not be asked to act decisively against Germany until France was prepared to do so. In the first instance, 'their action should aim only at pinning down the maximum number of [German] troops and at holding out (tenir)'. Under the same principle of safeguarding its influence, EMA directives were to build on the national interests of each country, defence of vital zones, and common operations to assure borders. This was crucial in the case of Czechoslovakia, whose extensive borders were so drawn as to advance the cause, dear to Gamelin, of a combined Polish-Czech offensive against German Silesia. At Franco-Czech staff conversations shortly after signature of the German-Polish non-aggression declaration, the Czechs, who were discouraged by the uncertainty of Polish dispositions and who had themselves recently received German offers for a non-aggression pact, were dissuaded by Gamelin from renouncing the defence of Bohemia, a renunciation which would have prejudiced his project for Czech-Polish operations in Silesia.[26]

Envisaging a fusion of the forces of Poland and the Petite Entente against Germany, Gamelin said little to the Czechs in 1933–4 of the regional great powers: Italy, presumed to be hostile, and the USSR, although he did indicate to Syrový in 1933 the desirability of Soviet neutrality for the security of the Polish and Roumanian rear lines.[27]

Interministerial studies in 1932–3 of a quasi-autonomous front in Central Europe worked to encourage military support for a more

[26] SHA, 7N3444, Gamelin-Krejči conversations, 11, 12 July 1934. This was the second such decisive intervention by the French. Thomas Masaryk had offered at the Paris Peace Conference to redraw the traditional frontiers of Bohemia so as to cede Germany those areas of the Sudetenland predominantly German in population. Opposed to any move which would increase the German population, the French had dissuaded him. J. W. Wheeler-Bennett, *Knaves, Fools and Heroes* (London, 1974), p. 131.

[27] SHA, 7N2520, 1 June 1934; 7N3444, June 1932; Gamelin-Krejči conversations, 11, 12 July 1934. An expression of the tangled relationships in the region, the Polish-Roumanian treaty of 1922, directed against the USSR, subsisted alongside the allegedly Russophile Petite Entente. In the early 1930s, the treaty fell into disrepair. The Polish and Roumanian Ministers of Foreign Affairs pursued both a personal vendetta towards each other and divergent policies towards the USSR, Beck increasingly hostile, Titulesco increasingly inclined to reach an accommodation with the Soviets.

broadly based war of coalition. French attempts to revise the 1921 pacts had unsuccessfully posed the problem of France's obligation to supply Poland in the event of Germany's gaining control of the Baltic: the option of supplying Poland by developing Central European war industries was impractical during the economic crisis. Deeming material transports indispensable to the longevity of an eastern front, the War Ministry considered vital the study and establishment of workable supply lines. Gamelin, who supervised the study, considered that the most efficient of these would be through Salonika. The studies, however, underscored the extent to which such routes would be at the mercy of the great powers in the area: Italy could block access to Salonika and the eastern Mediterranean, the USSR, to the Straits and Black Sea ports.[28]

The predominance of geographical imperatives in EMA thinking, which gave it a marked quality of diplomatic unreality, appeared already in the proceedings of the 1932–3 interministerial commission on allied purveyance summoned by the *Conseil supérieur de la Défense nationale*. The Commission was dominated by a juridical expert from the Quai d'Orsay, who successfully opposed the practice of elaborating the most pessimistic appreciation of alignments in a conflict in favour of the maximalist French position systematically being advanced in the disarmament negotiations.[29] The EMA, itself sensitive to the fluidity of the international situation, was in effect asked to present in an apparent vacuum the technical advantages of potential alignments. Gamelin was careful always to present himself as a mere technician, modestly labelling his strategic desiderata as 'questions de métier'. He emphasised prepared installations, the precise uses – or workability – of which might only be determined in a crisis.[30] To the diplomats went the task of securing and maintaining the necessary alignments. The resulting division of labour between military and diplomats produced a static allied planning, increasingly isolated from considerations of diplomatic probability. This diplomatic–military division of labour did not prevent Gamelin from seeking to influence successive governments, in order to secure the

---

[28] SHA, 7N3444, Notes, June 1932, 21 January 1933; Rollet, *La Pologne*, p. 195; Cienciala, 'Declaration', pp. 9–10; MAE, 'Tchécoslovaquie-Petite Entente: Etudes militaires/Ravitaillement', Gamelin-Paul-Boncour letter, 20 January 1933; 20 December 1932.
[29] MAE, 'Tchécoslovaquie-Petite Entente: Etudes militaires/Ravitaillement', Political Directorate Notes, 2, 3, November 1933.
[30] See, e.g., SHAA, 2B98, passim, for the bilateral air planning which followed Gamelin's conversation with Syrový.

requisite configurations. As he had remarked to Syrový, it was necessary to ginger up governments on these subjects: 'Russian neutrality is a question over which governments have jurisdiction, but which the military chiefs have a duty to broach.'[31]

The Czechs were the chief channel for Gamelin's military diplomacy in the east. EMA information about Petite Entente military deliberations came primarily from the French Military Mission in Prague, which, through the exertions of its chiefs, Pellé and Faucher, was completely integrated into the Czech defensive system. The Poles' summary dismissal of their French Military Mission in 1932 intensified this reliance on Prague, which was all the stronger as, at Quai d'Orsay insistence, the General Staff found itself compelled to refuse sporadic Roumanian and Yugoslav requests in the 1930s for peacetime staff collaboration. The Czechs proved undemanding partners in yearly exchanges with the EMA, a state of affairs which had its attractions for Paris, but provoked this reflection from Faucher:

> The Czech General Staff has no doubt asked itself if the French military effort responded to circumstances and to the spirit of our commitments...The very general information as to our means and plans with which the Czech General Staff contents itself constitutes sufficient proof of its trust. I add that in my opinion, it shows itself too discreet; but it is plainly not up to the head of mission to suggest that it be more demanding.[32]

Arms limitation and military entente with Italy and the USSR

In January 1934, a year after he first mentioned a Rhineland reoccupation to Syrový in the context of the disarmament conference, conversations with the French disarmament delegation in Geneva induced Gamelin to postulate Soviet and Italian

---

[31] SHAA, 2B98, Conversations, 28–31 January 1933.

[32] SHA, 'MMF Prague', Faucher dispatch, 30 October 1934; A. Marès, 'La faillite des relations franco-tchécoslovaques', *Revue d'histoire de la deuxième guerre mondiale*, no. 111, July 1978, pp. 49–58.

French military and diplomatic personnel in Prague traced Czech reticence with regard to Germany to Thomas Masaryk's pacifism and determination not to disrupt good relations with Germany; to internal considerations, notably the presence within successive governments of ministers from the German minority; and to the vulnerability created by its extensive borders. SHA, 7N2520, 'SAE 1920–1936', Mittelhauser note, 11 March 1922; 7N3444, 'Relations militaires entre la France et les pays de la Petite Entente', Charles-Roux dispatch, 19 April 1928.

integration into an eastern coalition. The possibility of arms limitation in itself spurred a search for great power allies to maintain security in the face of arms cuts, but, for Gamelin, the aspiration to integrate the USSR and Italy into the French system had a decidedly eastern referent. After a Rhineland reoccupation, an eastern counterweight could only be held together by great power allies who would act as conduits for French involvement in a Central European conflict. In a January 1934 memorandum, Gamelin reiterated the point he had made to Syrový about the desirability of Soviet benevolent neutrality to safeguard the Polish and Roumanian rear lines, and went on to indicate the advantage of Soviet air action against the Reich. The memorandum also contains his earliest documented reference to the possibility of Soviet purveyance of the Central European states, henceforth the central tenet of his planning *vis-à-vis* the USSR, ideologically suspect and geographically remote. This was acceptable to the Quai d'Orsay, which, since the last phase of the Salonika study in late 1933, had espoused industrial collaboration with the USSR not going beyond benevolent neutrality.

Gamelin's January 1934 observations on Italy demonstrated the transitional nature of his appreciations. While envisaging an Italo-German attack on France and French aid to Yugoslavia should it be attacked, Gamelin included a passage on the desirability of Italian neutrality and an Italian guarantee for Austria, and he added: 'Franco-Italian cooperation against Germany on Austrian territory would also be very interesting, but at a distant date.' Mussolini's show of force at the Austrian frontier in July 1934, in protest against the assassination of the Austrian Chancellor Dollfuss by Austrian Nazis, allowed him to shelve the hypothesis of Italian hostility.[33] The perspective of Italian cooperation against Germany in the defence of Austria and Czechoslovakia rapidly conditioned Gamelin's allegiances to France's traditional allies.

Under consideration by Gamelin for months as a corollary to arms limitation, the collective diplomacy of 1934–5 *vis-à-vis* Italy and the USSR was in the event launched by the diplomatic note of April

---

[33] SHA, 'Cabinet du ministre', Gamelin note, January 1934; DDF I, 4, nos. 3, 35; 5, nos. 28, 84, 120. An unsigned November 1934 memorandum by Gamelin's *cabinet* credited recent Italian military solicitude for France (at the moment Laval undertook wide-ranging negotiations including colonial issues with Rome) to Mussolini's unshakeable attachment to Austrian independence. SHA, 1N43, 'Note pour le ministre', November 1934.

1934, in which France ostensibly took its leave from the disarmament conference. The preceding chapter argued that Barthou's Italian and Soviet diplomacy – Danubian and Eastern pacts to include Germany, and French sponsorship of Soviet entry into the League – should be placed in the context of his disquiet at the refusal of a recent arms offer by Hitler and his obsessive desire to avert an arms race. For the French military, the most significant fact about the April 1934 note was the lack of substantial French rearmament at a time it believed that German rearmament was massively accelerating.[34] From May 1934, the chief military deliberating body, the *Conseil supérieur de la Guerre*, warned that France was in danger of losing its military edge over Germany.[35] Pessimistic EMA estimates of the Franco-German balance reflected not only the enormous reservoir of rapidly mobilisable German paramilitary forces and police housed in barracks, but also slashes in French strength between 1931 and 1934. Faced with the world economic crisis, successive governments of the centre-right and centre-left alike cut defence expenditure in an attempt to balance the country's budget and avoid the currency devaluation repugnant to French political opinion. The pacifism of opinion also lent itself to deep defence cuts.

In these years, Gamelin's superior in the military hierarchy, Maxime Weygand, abrasively lobbied for the army's restoration to its 1931 strength. In contrast, Gamelin's nimble advancement amid the mine field of French civil–military relations in the early 1930s testified to his readiness to adapt the Command's requirements to the domestic political climate. Gamelin, like Barthou, had initially favoured acceptance of Hitler's early 1934 arms limitation offer. His resigned justification, that civilian financial stringency would gravely handicap the already diminished French army in a arms race with Germany, revealed his pervasive sense of France's inferiority.

On the politically sensitive topic of disarmament, Gamelin considered that 'there are currents which one cannot resist

---

[34] Vaïsse points out that the Doumergue Government, while making heavy defence cuts in April 1934 in the name of deflation, also established important supplementary defence credits. Vaïsse, *Sécurité*, pp. 590–2. But as Martin Alexander has shown, the predictable fate of these supplementary credits under the succeeding Laval Government – considerable reductions, particularly in new arms allocations, much to the detriment of French arms productivity, and the extension of remaining funds over several years – did not reassure the EMA. M. S. Alexander, 'Maurice Gamelin and the Defence of France', Diss. University of Oxford, 1982, pp. 27–33.

[35] 'Faute de réalisations immédiates, l'Armée française ne pourrait être en état de faire face aux dangers que constituent pour le pays, les possibilités militaires actuelles de l'Allemagne.' Cited in Dutailly, *Les problèmes de l'armée*, p. 119.

directly... I saw it not as a matter of formulating principles in this area, but of resolving "particular cases".'[36] An obvious case was a Rhineland reoccupation, when arms cuts and the civilians' refusal to extend military service to compensate for the *années creuses*, the lean years of French demographic growth, ensured that Gamelin could not tranquilly contemplate an armed contest with Germany in the west. After the April note, he and Barthou were at one on the desirability of a refurbished eastern security system predicated on the support of regional great powers. For the military, these continental ententes would minimise the actual French contribution to an eastern coalition, while ensuring its survival and maintaining French pretensions to lead it, should it become practical politics when Germany turned east after reoccupying the Rhineland.

Gamelin's response to the unresolved problem of arms limitation and the alarming changes in the Franco-German military balance was to intensify reliance on an allied coalition in the east. When Weygand retired in January 1935, disillusioned, he opined that allies could do little for France's security. Gamelin's retort, 'All of this is very interesting, mon Général... But you know, I am a strategist', is often quoted.[37] The self-definition was precise. As a recent writer has put it, 'When one begins to ask *which* wars shall be fought, or *if* war should be fought, one has entered the realm of strategy.'[38]

Immediately after Gamelin succeeded Weygand as Commander in Chief designate in January 1935, a new French mobilisation plan (D *bis*) incorporated the decision not to fight for the Rhineland zone, and carried with it the implication that the French offensive Gamelin deemed necessary for victory would depend on the direction of the German attack.[39] In other words, a French offensive would be difficult unless the bulk of the German forces attacked elsewhere, in the east. The wager implicit in Gamelin's opening stamp on French defence planning was that the Franco-German balance, imperilled by France's *de facto* disarmament, could be redressed by an allied strategy unofficially resting on the eastern calculation voiced in his

[36] Gamelin, *Servir* II, p. 56.
[37] J. Weygand, *Weygand, mon père* (Paris, 1970), p. 239; P. C. F. Bankwitz, *Maxime Weygand and Civil-Military Relations in Modern France* (Cambridge, Mass., 1967), p. 113.
[38] Barry R. Posen, *The Sources of Military Doctrine* (Ithaca, 1984), p. 245, n. 3. Cf. the opening definition under 'Strategy' in the *Larousse* of Gamelin's childhood: 'vast movements aimed at occupying the best line of operation. (Thiers)', an enticing definition for a future general perennially drawn to a war of extended fronts, whether farflung operations to Salonika or the Breda Variant. *Grand dictionnaire universel du XIXe siècle* (Larousse: Paris, 1875), vol. 14, p. 1133. [39] Dutailly, *Les problèmes de l'armée*, pp. 19, 42, 70.

1933 talks with Syrový – that Germany would turn east after reoccupying the Rhineland.[40] Plan D *bis* met the post-Rhineland contingency by its stipulation that France should not remain pinioned behind the Maginot line, although operations at that point would depend entirely upon the functioning of the allied coalition.

GAMELIN, ITALY, AND THE USSR 1935

Gamelin and Italy

While the unimpeded German resurgence of 1935 made arms limitation a burning subject for Pierre Laval and his colleague at the Matignon, Pierre-Etienne Flandin, Gamelin held steady. On receiving the news of German conscription, he told his colleagues: 'If the Germans have not reoccupied the demilitarised zone, it is because they are not ready.'[41] The reoccupation was imminent; the timing was a matter of German choosing and would signify German preparedness for a larger conflict.

During interministerial exchanges before the Stresa conference on German conscription, Gamelin, in a skilful letter to the Minister of War, turned the government's consideration from the Rhineland to a riposte with Italy in a Central European theatre. Having been asked by Laval whether France could respond militarily at a reoccupation and at an Anschluss, Gamelin in his letter to Maurin argued that the time for a 'preventive war' – a reprisal operation in the Rhineland to force Germany to conform to the peace treaties – was over. Amidst ritual allusions to the danger of a sudden German attack which guarded against further arms cuts, and reiterations of the EMA's orthodoxy that Germany could attack in any direction, Gamelin's bent was plain. He preferred a war in Central Europe:

It is certain that the interest for us is in a conflict beginning in Central Europe, so that we could act as a secondary force against a Germany whose principal forces were already engaged in that region. Naturally, the

---

[40] The arms limitation-strategy linkage appeared implicitly in a January 1935 interchange between Gamelin and the Premier, P.-E. Flandin. Enticed by British schemes to incorporate arms limitation into a general European settlement, Flandin pressed for figures of the Franco-German balance. Gamelin quietly insisted that such figures were less important than the German aim, action in the east. DDF I, 9, no. 57.

[41] Schw., 1SC2 Dr1, 'Notes générales'; 1SC2 Dr3, 'Rapport', 16 April 1935.

condition of effective action in Central Europe is the collaboration of the Petite Entente and *entails the possibility of using Austrian territory.*[42]

Gamelin's letter to Maurin showed a striking determination to view a reoccupation not as an event putting at stake France's security, but from the more distant perspective of a war of coalition beginning elsewhere. On the immediate issue of France's parrying German moves into the Rhineland and Austria, he advocated reiterating a readiness he knew to be critically flawed. Discretion for Gamelin had become the better part of valour.

While he did not rule out a more independent French retort to German truculence, Gamelin implied that time was elastic and might only prolong the Franco-German stalemate. His approach was soothingly oblique: foreground melted reassuringly into background. Confirming his long-standing wish, the Italian offers of staff talks made after Laval's January 1935 visit to Rome had reinforced a natural willingness on Gamelin's part to choose the terrain and most favourable moment of engagement. A Central European operation with Italy would allow a more effective response to German bellicosity, and with minimum French losses, especially as Gamelin assumed that Germany would not reoccupy the zone in order to wage war in the west.

By his letter to Maurin and cool suasion in governmental meetings, Gamelin in early spring 1935 prodded a hesitant Laval into accepting Italian offers of peacetime staff conversations. In Rome in January 1935 Laval and Mussolini had agreed on certain conditions to legalise German rearmament, and Laval even after the announcement of German conscription remained reluctant to compromise future German negotiations by too marked an Italian orientation.[43] He also hesitated to take up the pressing Italian offers because he was belatedly attempting to placate Yugoslav fury at Italy's alleged complicity in the Marseilles murders by making Italo-Yugoslav entente a precondition of Franco-Italian staff talks. Gamelin brushed aside the smoldering Italo-Yugoslav hostility, pointing out that it would make the two sides more dependent on French military liaison. He appears to have supposed that the

[42] DDF I, 10, no. 155; Gamelin's italics.
[43] DDF I, 9, nos. 247, 495; MAE, 26 January 1935. Laval approached the talks from the cautionary angle of aviation, authorising General Denain to journey to Rome some weeks before Gamelin's visit in June 1935. He saw bilateral air talks as an anticipation of the bilateral technical pacts slated to accompany a West European air pact. Schw., 2SC2 Dr2, 'Rapport du commandant Petibon'.

German resurgence, symbolised by a Rhineland reoccupation, would be sufficient to dampen Central European animosities and call forth a front predicated on Italy.[44]

Avid to conquer Ethiopia, Mussolini had no real interest in a war with Germany over Austria. Indeed, from the first stages of planning for his Ethiopian venture in 1932, Mussolini privately acknowledged the inescapability of Anschluss.[45] In the spring of 1935, as Stresa coincided with blatant Italian military preparations, insistent overtures to France were an essential part of his diplomatic preparation for the Ethiopian enterprise.

The exorbitantly generous Italian military offers shrewdly promised the French a cut-price war on the peripheries. Marshal Badoglio offered to commit his army to action in Austria, or to send nine divisions to France, but asked in return only two French divisions for the Central European front. The manpower for this French force would in itself be a neat by-product of acceptance of the Italian overtures. French alpine units released from guarding the Italian frontier could be reconstituted as an expeditionary force for action in Central Europe. The French contribution would be political liaison and the timely dispatch of expeditionary forces, across Italy and eventually via Salonika to provide heavy-duty *matériel* which could not be obtained from the Soviets. Others – the stalwart Czechs, and the Balkan states rich in peasant soldiery – would do most of the fighting on the Central European front, which Gamelin was eager to designate the principal front of the next war. By ensuring the safe transport of French troops stationed in North Africa, Italian friendship would also make available troops for the Belgian theatre, into which Gamelin intended to move when the Germans invaded Central Europe after a reoccupation.[46]

The June 1935 talks conferred on the Italian entente a paramount place in French strategy. Gamelin's penchant for Italy met the necessity of having a staff plan giving latitude for a broad variety of manoeuvres, including the search for an arms limitation accord, while avoiding the impression that France contemplated making war on its own soil. Italian friendship increased France's potential

---

[44] DDF, I, 10, nos. 247, 495; MAE, 'Autriche', 1 August 1935.
[45] Aloisi, cited in E. M. Robertson, *Mussolini as Empire Builder* (London, 1977), pp. 42, 66.
[46] DDF, I, 10, no. 155; 11, no. 179; and R. J. Young's detailed account of Franco-Italian planning in 'French Military Intelligence and the Franco-Italian Alliance', *The Historical Journal*, 28, 1985. 3e Bureau studies of this expeditionary force to Central Europe counted on sending 300 military trains across Italy within a two week period. Ibid., p. 161.

strength in the Belgian theatre; it was the *sine qua non* of the Austrian operation envisaged by Gamelin since January 1934; and it was a geographical bridge between east and west, allowing the timely dispatch of a French expeditionary force in the conflict to follow the reoccupation. So brilliant were the strategic prospects held out by his June 1935 meeting with Badoglio that Gamelin soon considered Italy indispensable to any French effort on behalf of Czechoslovakia.

Unlike Marshal Badoglio, however, Gamelin was not empowered in June 1935 to sign a military pact, only to initial a *procès-verbal* of the conversations. Governmental decisions were reserved, the staff accords being placed solely on the level of the two commands and avoiding all terms referring to the political premisses of the problem, notably an Anschluss and a Rhineland reoccupation. Aside from these strictures of a sort which consistently hampered EMA planning, Gamelin set special value on the conversations which he had with Mussolini and Badoglio. With consummate diplomacy, Mussolini, ever mindful of Paris's penchant for arms limitation and deterrence by collective security, asked Gamelin whether the French General Staff was optimistic, 'as much with regard to the possibility of avoiding a war as to its eventual outcome'. Gamelin replied that 'logically, we would not have war if we did not present Germany an occasion to make one with chances of success'. To Gamelin's delight, Badoglio, an old acquaintance from his days as head of the French military mission in Brazil, proclaimed that 'Italy will forever be at our side'. With Badoglio as with the Belgian Command and Rydz-Śmigły, the Polish Chief of Staff whom he would meet the following year, Gamelin pursued a systematic policy of trust in the smoothness of his own military diplomacy and in the efficacy of close personal relations with foreign military figures to compensate for the looseness and limitations of the actual military arrangements made with them.[47]

The Ethiopian affair: Britain versus Italy

In Rome, Badoglio introduced the topic of Ethiopia, saying that, whatever happened, continental Italian forces would not be weakened. Mussolini gave similar assurances. The Italian military

---

[47] In a moment of fervour, Badoglio went so far as to promise that he would resign rather than lead the Italian army in a war against France, a private promise as fragile as those which the Belgian and Polish militaries made to Gamelin. DDF I, 11, no. 179; Schw., 1SC2 Dr4, 29 June 1935.

was candid regarding its African projects. The French military attaché in Rome had reported before Gamelin's visit that Mussolini would make war in September; by late June, French estimates of the opening of hostilities for early October were on target.[48]

Given the strength of his reliance on Italy, it is difficult to overestimate Gamelin's consternation at the unfolding Ethiopian crisis. He advised his colleagues that they had every interest in supporting Italy from both European and colonial viewpoints. Gamelin, who had delivered a pale warning against excessive zeal in Ethiopia when Badoglio attended the French manoeuvres in September 1935, cancelled an official trip abroad later in the month in order to remain in Paris and restrain the Quai d'Orsay in the matter of sanctions against Italy. In the view of Fabry, the Minister of War of the day, 'the loss of Italian friendship...would oblige us to rearrange our security planning completely'.[49] The French defence establishment thus championed Laval's diplomacy of promoting peace negotiations while supporting only innocuous sanctions.

The Ethiopian war caught the EMA squarely between Britain and Italy. Before the outbreak of the war, its clear preference was not to be forced to choose between the two states, both of whom were precious to French defence against Germany: 'In any event the chances of an Anglo-Italian conflict are increasing; it is thus advisable to envisage the repercussions that this conflict would entail for France, which wishes above all to remain in the background and enter the scene only at the moment Germany does.'[50] A crucial memorandum of October 1935 spelled out the time factor inherent in the contrasting values of British and Italian aid in the west. It argued that Britain's superior resources, together with those of its empire, would only permit France to finish the war well, while, without Italian aid, France risked succumbing to German superiority in the first battle. While optimally France would not have to choose between Britain and Italy, Italian aid offered the greater advantage.[51]

[48] Schw., 1SC2 Dr4, 25 May; 'Rapport', 25 June 1935.
[49] Schw., 1SC2 Dr5, 6 August, 19, 21 September 1935; SHA, Papiers Fabry, 'Journal de marche du Ministère de la Guerre du 7 juin 1935 au 25 janvier 1936', 29 July, 28 August 1935.   [50] SHA, 5N579, 'Procès-verbal de la réunion du 19 septembre 1935'.
[51] Ibid., 'Etude des repercussions exercées sur la Défense nationale par le conflit italo-éthiopien...', 8 October 1935. The same memorandum suggested that, if for political

French military appraisals of the value of British land aid, deemed to be inferior to that of 1914, were entirely realistic. After Gamelin's visit to Rome in June 1935, he pointedly drew the government's attention to the weakness of the British Army, telling Fabry that its contribution after several months of war would be nugatory.[52] The doctrine of *la guerre de longue durée*, the belief that the next war would be long and so most likely to be won with British staying power, had by no means achieved the prominence in 1935 that it would from late 1937, when the General Staff abandoned hope for the defence of Austria and Czechoslovakia. Indeed, early in 1935, Pétain, the wooden colossus of French inter-war military doctrine, opined in a discussion of British military inadequacies that the next war would be short: 'A war is no longer likely to last four years, for it would involve such an enormous amount of *matériel* and would cause such demoralisation that it can only be a question of several months of conflict.'[53] In 1935 the General Staff still attached great importance to Central Europe. One of its justifications for a position of neutrality in the Ethiopian conflict was that France should devote its attention to the maintenance of peace in Central Europe. As a military note on the attitude of Germany put it: 'Finally, it is not a matter of indifference to Germany that the principal defender of Austrian independence is henceforth heavily engaged outside Europe, and that the centre of gravity of European preoccupations is being displaced from Central Europe to the Mediterranean.'[54] Accelerated by the Spanish war, this Mediterranean shift, over time, would produce the French military's disengagement from the defence of Central Europe with Italian aid and their consequent attachment to *une guerre de longue durée* dependent on British resources.

Gamelin and the USSR

The Ethiopian crisis also brought renewed anxiety over the future of the Rhineland zone. As has been seen, Laval feared that Hitler might seize on the ratification of the Franco-Soviet pact as a pretext

reasons the government opted for the British entente, Britain should be asked to reinstitute conscription and prepare to send twenty divisions to the continent. As this dates from after Hoare's unsatisfactory response to Laval's questions on Britain's willingness to take up continental responsibilities, it can be taken as a rhetorical underscoring of the value of the Italian entente.

[52] SHA, Papiers Fabry, 'Journal de marche', 29 July 1935, 10 January 1936.
[53] DDF I, 9, no. 57.
[54] SHA, 7N2520, 'L'Allemagne en face du conflit italo-éthiopien', 1 October 1935.

to reoccupy the zone. In the course of 1934–5, alongside its advocacy of entente with Italy, the EMA had been called upon to assess the value of a Soviet alliance. It shared the Quai d'Orsay's initial reluctance regarding bilateral dealings with Moscow. Gamelin later insisted that his enthusiastic appreciations of Soviet aid in 1934 had been given strictly in the context of an Eastern pact.[55]

A virtually definitive version of the EMA's reading of the advantages and disadvantages of alliance with the Soviets was expounded in a lengthy note of April 1935. An obvious response to alliance pressures after the German conscription declaration, its themes informed the EMA's reading of a war in the east until September 1939. Much of the memorandum was given over to debate on the value of Polish versus Soviet military entente. The argument ran as follows: Soviet aid would only acquire full military value for France if the USSR and Germany shared a common border, and this would only come about in the disastrous eventuality that Poland joined the German camp. In any other case, the USSR, which could decide not to intervene in a conflict in Central Europe distant from its borders, would always be less at risk than France: 'There would thus be *flagrant inequality between the military obligations of Russia and France*, the latter, on account of its common frontier with Germany, being called upon to commit itself to the hilt from the beginning of a conflict, in any circumstances.'[56]

The writers of the memorandum regarded the Soviets as highly untrustworthy. While acknowledging that foremost among the advantages of a Franco-Soviet alliance was prevention of a renewal of Rapallo, of German-Soviet cooperation, they went on to castigate Russian treachery:

To link ourselves with a government which betrayed us in the midst of war, ruined our small investors, whose doctrine saps our institutions, and in particular our military institution, and whose Francophilia is notoriously opportunistic. This is a dreadful handicap for France in a future conflict... *and all the while we would feel under permanent menace of a new Brest-Litovsk.*

Speculation amplified the threat of a renewal of Rapallo: even if allied to France, the Soviets might reach an agreement with

---

[55] Schw., 1SC2 Dr8, 24 March 1936; for Gamelin's minimalist expectations of the Soviets in 1935, expectations virtually unchanged from his January 1934 memorandum, DDF I, 10, no. 155.

[56] SHA, 7N2520, 'Note sur les avantages et les inconvénients de l'alliance russe', 24 April 1935; italics throughout in the original.

Germany, which might concede the Baltic states to them, in return for their willingness to create a *casus belli* for a conflict into which France would be drawn at the moment most propitious for Germany. The writers also envisioned a conflict in the west in which, the Reich having bought its neutrality, the USSR lent no aid to France. They conceded that at that moment Poland leaned towards Germany, but the Polish Army was depicted, despite Polish-Czech acrimony, as likely to lend immediate and durable aid to France and to cooperate with the Petite Entente. Close entente with Russia would disrupt the situation of trust which would otherwise reign in the French system:

If our alliance bloc remains coherent, all our allies will give the same degree of credence to the ally under attack, and 'common action' will be assured in good conditions. But if we include Russia, in the case of an eastern conflict must we not fear that Poland, at present inclined towards Berlin, would interpret 'aggression' in such a way as to oppose Russia and therefore oppose us?

Giving the Poles ample means for military blackmail, this prospect of a Polish-German alignment against France and the USSR became the recurrent nightmare of French strategists. In April 1935, the EMA staunchly formulated the position it would adopt on the issue of Soviet aid in the spring and summer of 1939: '*The Polish alliance must not in any case be sacrificed to the Russian alliance.* If [the Government] decides on [a Russian alliance], it should only be as a supplement to the Polish alliance, with the full consent of the Warsaw Government.'

Fright at the prospect of a Polish-German bloc was rooted in lessons drawn from 1914, the Schlieffen Plan and the issue of the direction of the German attack. Poland, if definitively rejected into the German camp, would cover Germany against Russia's slow mobilisation. It would then have almost the totality of its forces free for action in the west, against France. In contrast, with Polish aid to France or a French ally, Germany would be pinned down in the east. The writers of the memorandum emphasised that France had no interest in giving up on the complicated eastern game, because a Germany victorious in the east and reinforced by its victories would not renounce its claims in the west. A war in the west on such terms would be much harder than French participation in a war in the east to which the bulk of the German forces were committed. As for the talk of a war between Germany and the USSR current after the German announcement of conscription, while it was not in French interest for Germany to emerge victorious from such a conflict, neither should it enter into a conflict involving Russia, whose object might be foreign to French interests. Evoking Napoleon's failure before the immensity of Russia, the writers did allow, without reference to their earlier aspersions on Soviet trustworthiness: 'our intervention can always take place at the time we choose, when the German army is deeply engaged in the Russian eiderdown'. France then was to retain its freedom of action, to intervene or not when the moment came, and it could do this only by avoiding a military convention. The note concluded that a Soviet alliance was hardly tempting: 'We would certainly bring more than we would receive in a contract concluded with such an uncertain partner, who could drag us into an adventure and then abandon us.'

Like Gamelin's April 1935 letter to Maurin, which dismissed resistance to an imminent Rhineland reoccupation in favour of the Italian entente and an ideal conflict on Austrian soil, this note with its brusque dismissal of a Soviet alliance is revealing as to the nature of the EMA's attachment to a war elsewhere. Time and space were the essential dimensions of the planning whose allied hierarchies were set in the aftermath of German conscription. Alluding to the experience of 1914 and the war machine that France possessed in 1935, Gamelin wrote to Maurin that France had every interest in gaining time, but that, as time worked for Germany at least as much as it did for France, the clear advantage was a war in Central and Eastern Europe. The note on the USSR hinted at the source of this preference: war in the east in close alliance with the Poles rather than the Soviets would forestall war in the west. It would purchase the time for France to mobilise, implement an initial defensive and then a victorious offensive with its best troops outside of French soil.[57]

THE RHINELAND CRISIS

Prelude

In January 1936, amidst the disarray of French diplomacy after the Hoare-Laval fiasco, Gamelin clung to the linkage between a Rhineland reoccupation and a war in the east. Before the *Haut Comité militaire*, he repeated his frayed wager that Germany would attack

[57] DDF I, 10, no. 155.

Central Europe after neutralising France with fortifications, adding, 'The Demilitarised Zone will be reoccupied with this aim as soon as possible'.[58] In the same weeks, the EMA pressed for the implementation of a new arms programme, or in its phraseology, for permanent measures rather than 'gestures without a future'. Fabry had told the EMA in the summer of 1935 that a new arms programme could only be justified by a changed situation. The arms proposals of early 1936 thus carried a fatalistic title: 'Plan for the Reinforcement of the French Army in the event of a Rhineland reoccupation'. The plan styled a reoccupation as a wave of German force beating against the foot of the sea wall, the Maginot line.[59] As the German recrudescence could only be hastened by the Quai d'Orsay's growing preference for negotiating away the zone, Gamelin favoured leaving the water to rise, inexorably, albeit as gradually as possible until the tide of its own accord ran eastwards.

Ironically, when Hitler reoccupied the Rhineland on 7 March 1936, the exact timing surprised Gamelin, whose strategy had for years taken the event as its point of departure. He had waited so long for the reoccupation that, on 3 March, he wondered aloud whether the next German move would not be against Czechoslovakia after all.[60] Gamelin's musings illustrate the deadening quality of Hitlerian surprise, which far from doing the totally unexpected, encouraged the potential adversary to indulge in an overkill of anticipation.

French military-diplomatic skirmishing

For the military, the threat posed by the Rhineland crisis arose less from Hitler's long anticipated action than from Italian estrangement over Ethiopia, and from the civilians' deep fear of isolation if France did not respond forcefully. In the weeks before 7 March, the military vantage on the zone had been sharply defined in a series of interchanges with the Quai d'Orsay. Growing nervousness in early 1936 about the wisdom of the Franco-Soviet ratification, coupled

[58] DDF II, 1, no. 83.
[59] Issued under the signature of the Chief of Army Headquarters, Louis Colson, the plan concluded: 'If France wishes to remain "the rampart of Peace", when the German flood beats against the sea wall, it will be necessary to reinforce [the Maginot line] with new props, in addition to those planned for 1936.' SHA 1N36, 'Plan de renforcement de l'armée française en cas de réoccupation de la zone démilitarisée rhénane', 24 January 1936; Schw., 1SC2 Dr7, 21, 27 January; SHA, Papiers Fabry, 'Journal de marche', 8 January 1936.
[60] Schw. 1SC2 Dr8, 'Rapport', 3 March 1936.

with attentiveness in governmental circles to the likelihood of an imminent reoccupation, led the Quai d'Orsay to propose a preventive collective démarche in Berlin, to be followed by negotiations over the zone's status. To lend this collective démarche a coercive edge, the Quai d'Orsay requested military cooperation in the form of simulated planning. Maurin, Gamelin's old colleague from the Ecole de Guerre who was again Minister of War, refused to discuss unilateral French offensive action, even for purposes of diplomacy. (The only unilateral measure Maurin would contemplate was occupation of the Maginot line.) He also opposed negotiations over the zone's status, insisting on the importance of its maintenance for as long as possible, as Gamelin had done since January 1935.[61]

Maurin was visibly concerned to do nothing which would provoke Germany into accompanying a reoccupation with an attack on France itself. At a German *fait accompli*, he blandly counselled an appeal to the League and the association of the Locarno powers with French action. An important internal note of mid February commented that a reoccupation would signify that Hitler had crossed the Rubicon to all intents and purposes. (A true enough supposition in light of the *Wehrmacht*'s actual orders on 7 March to fall back, but not flee, at an armed response.) For the EMA, the primary use of a reoccupation would be political. It would free Britain from the impartiality of Locarno by allowing it to conclude staff accords with France. More importantly, a clear anti-German stand by Britain would cut short the Belgians' flirtation with neutralism. For the EMA, compensation for the loss of the Rhineland 'no man's land' was to be a Franco-British-Belgian front, that is, security guarantees rather than ineffective action.[62]

Balked of its collective démarche in Berlin, the Quai d'Orsay dispensed assurances that France would proceed to 'aucune action isolée', no isolated action, while it reserved the right to take preparatory measures.[63] As Minister of Foreign Affairs, Flandin made last minute approaches on the future of the zone to Hitler and the British. Both were abortive.[64]

[61] DDF II, 1, nos. 25, 91, 105, 141 and note, 155, 170, 186, 196, 203.
[62] Ibid., no. 202.
[63] Ibid., no. 241. The reservation covered a statement made by Flandin at Stresa, to the annoyance of the French military who were not consulted, that France would mobilise at a reoccupation. Schw., 1SC2 Dr1; 1SC2 Dr4, 'Rapport', 7 May 1935.
[64] DDF II, 1, nos. 265, 283.

The *Wehrmacht* reoccupied the Rhineland at daybreak on 7 March. Six weeks from elections and fearful of destroying the franc, the caretaker French cabinet debated a range of collective actions, some of which risked provoking Germany, but all of which were meant to facilitate negotiation. The debate ranged from action under League auspices, the drift of a rhetorically powerful broadcast to the country by Premier Sarraut, to partial mobilisation (along with Poland). This continuing orientation towards negotiation, ideally following a German withdrawal from the zone, was epitomised by the theatrical and evasive Flandin. He engaged the military in a renewed dialogue of the deaf, each side attempting to save face over the demilitarised zone whose violation neither had been determined to prevent. In emergency meetings on 9 March, Flandin, with negotiations in mind, suggested mobilising two divisions to compel the Germans to evacuate the zone. Afraid of unleashing action against France, Maurin gave the impression of knowing nothing of the army's mobilisation plans.[65] The upshot was a decision to confront the Locarno powers with the crisis at a special London meeting. For these discussions, Gamelin went to work on a *modus vivendi* which incorporated many of the points for which the EMA had pressed in the previous weeks.[66]

At the London meetings of the League Council and the Locarno powers, a stunned French delegation found itself confronted by the menace of complete inaction. Italy's role was limited to observation, on account of sanctions, and British opinion – as represented by *The Times* – was disarmed by Hitler's offer that Germany should rejoin the League of Nations. Led by Flandin, who in 1935 had foreseen Franco-British staff talks as a guarantee for a European general settlement, French diplomats rapidly drew the conclusion that honour could best be salvaged by giving priority to staff talks.[67] General Debeney, one of Gamelin's predecessors, gave insouciant expression to the military view that France was correct to await a better occasion to resist Germany. Alluding to Italy's African involvement and Britain's unarmed state, Debeney observed that League procedure and the voyage to London permitted it to save

[65] DDF II, 1, nos. 328, 334; Schw., 1SC2 Dr8, 9, 10 March 1936; BN, Papiers Déat, 'Ière Partie: Le Massacre des Possibles', chapter 16; G. Sakwa, 'The Franco-Polish Alliance and the Remilitarisation of the Rhineland', *The Historical Journal*, 16, 1 (1973), pp. 135–6.
[66] Schw., 'Rapports', 9, 10 March 1936; DDF II, 1, nos. 391, 425.
[67] Schw., 1SC2 Dr8, 17 March; 2SC2 Dr11, 18 March; BN, Papiers Flandin, carton 74, Notes, 29, 31 March, 4 April 1936.

face: the humiliation of the reoccupation no longer affected it directly.[68]

The strategic uses of Britain and Belgium, April 1936

Curiously reminiscent of the Franco-Italian staff talks of June 1935, the Anglo-Franco-Belgian staff talks of April 1936 were completely divorced from the Rhineland issue and reserved all governmental decisions. The sole hypothesis which the British would envision was the dispatch of an expeditionary force of two divisions to France *if* HMG chose to intervene.[69] The question for the historian is: what strategic value had such talks for the EMA, when it had known for months that British land aid would be nugatory for many months into a conflict?

The immediate French priority in the trilateral staff talks of April 1936 was to press for British aid to Belgium and so repair the badly damaged Franco-Belgian entente. In February 1936, the Belgians had finally denounced their 1920 military accord with France. Denunciation of the outmoded accord had been expected in Paris from the early allied evacuation of the Rhineland in 1930. Brussels had worked from 1931–2 to steer its foreign relations towards a safer position, independent of treaty obligations which would make the country one of the battlefields of the next war. Although in 1935 the resounding Nazi victory in the Saar plebescite briefly revived cordial Franco-Belgian military relations, these were overshadowed on the Belgian side by growing domestic debate over the Franco-Soviet pact. To an already flammable controversy between the francophone and Francophile Walloons and the anti-French Flemish over the French military connection, the pending ratification of the Franco-Soviet pact in February 1936 had added the final tinder, in the form of Flemish allegations that France intended to drag Belgium into a war inspired by the Soviets. British aid for Belgium was to disarm the vociferous Flemish opposition to Franco-Belgian entente by transforming it into a trilateral front in which the less adventurous British would be present.[70]

---

[68] Schw., 1SC2 Dr8, 24 March 1936.
[69] DDF II, 2, no. 97; Schw. 1SC2 Dr8, 18 March 1936.
[70] In 1932–5, Gamelin had been disquieted by the risks attendant on the EMA's policy of a 'forward defence' of heavily industrialised northern France by advancing, even without adequate Belgian cooperation, into Belgian territory. From 1936, when the German move into the Rhineland activated Gamelin's planning for a war of coalition in the east, he relied

As the non-commital British were still smarting from Laval's cavalier treatment in the early stages of the Ethiopian war, Gamelin decided not to broach directly French plans involving Italy and the Central European uses of the Belgian front. He relied instead on genuine British protestations of weakness to incline London to the cardinal conclusion, improving the general strategic situation by ending the Ethiopian war.[71] In the long run, the talks could be turned to the better occasion for resisting Germany of which Debeney spoke, an occasion which required Italian friendship. Gamelin also looked to the British to supplement French capability in the Belgian theatre with mechanised forces. He tailored his expectations to reports that London had assigned itself the role of purveyor of *matériel*, not men, in a future conflict.[72]

Gamelin's close attention to the development of German mechanised forces convinced him that the ideal terrains for their operation would be Belgium and Poland. He reckoned that Germany would attack not against an organised position such as the Maginot line but rapidly, over free terrain, in the east against Poland or against Belgium, where the French themselves might race to the encounter.[73] Galvanised by the Rhineland crisis, by September Gamelin had transmuted the January 1936 rearmament plan into a plan with increased expenditure for tanks and mobile artillery to carry a war into the flat terrain of the Low Countries. (The January plan, drawn up by Colson, had stressed fortifications and manpower increases in mobile reserves.)

Gamelin also set out to revise French defence doctrine to meet the challenge of German mechanisation. While static defence of fronts by fortification troops – the celebrated policy of continuous fronts – would ensure that the enemy did not break through to French soil, the battle to defend France would be maintained entirely on Belgian soil by the so-called Grandes Unités, whose forces would incorporate numerous elements of the general reserve. The key point here is that,

---

not only on the British to shore up Franco-Belgian relations, but also on developing his own covert technical contacts with the Belgian General Staff to circumvent deepening Belgian neutralism. SHA, 5N579, 'Compte-rendu par le gal. Weygand d'un voyage à Bruxelles et à Londres 11 mai 1935'; M. S. Alexander, 'Maurice Gamelin and the Defence of France', Diss. University of Oxford 1982, pp. 135–59. I am indebted to Martin Alexander for sharing his extensive knowledge of Franco-Belgian relations.
[71] DDF II, 2, no. 46; Schw., 2SC2 Dr13, undated letter draft, Ministry of War to Foreign Affairs; BN, Papiers Flandin, 74, 29 March 1936.
[72] DDF I, 2, no. 375; Schw. 1SC2 Dr8, 1 April 1936; M. Alexander, 'Gamelin', pp. 207–8, 228–35. [73] SHA, CSG, 29 April 1936.

from spring 1936, Gamelin redefined the strategic reserve. From being an uncommitted force on French soil, ready to be called to any front as needed, it was to become a highly specialised, mobile force to be committed to the Low Countries from the very first days of a conflict: 'One is thus led to abandon the concept of reserves fit for all offensive and defensive tasks on all fronts, in favour of units specifically adapted to their mission in the first days [of a conflict], in a phrase, the specialisation of the Grandes Unités.'

Such a modernisation, it was argued in the months after the Rhineland affair, would be excellent for national morale, crestfallen that France lagged behind the 'constant evolution' of the German army; it could easily be accomplished by reorganisation and regrouping of existing resources. A military writer in June 1936 used circular logic to put the case that specialisation of the strategic reserve would allow the stripping of units charged with static defence of the fronts. In other words, France's security would be so increased by a specialised reserve that units along sectors regarded as static and relegated to the lowest priority by the Command, such as the Ardennes, could be reduced to realise the economies in manpower necessary to reorganise reserve units designated to fight in the Low Countries. This modernisation of the strategic reserve, it was concluded, would offer the Command possibilities of manoeuvre which it had not previously possessed, as well as defensive security which would allow it to loosen the linear fortification system on which French defence had previously rested. For Gamelin, then, a redefined strategic reserve would ensure maximum manoeuvre, and so achieve his increasingly overriding priority of transporting the war outside of French territory.[74] By spring 1936, his personal advocacy of mechanisation transposed the defence of France far into the Belgian quadrant. The writer of the June memorandum spoke of holding the Albert Canal, which was on a line with Antwerp, in the 1940 campaign the embarkation point for the dispatch of Gamelin's strategic reserve to Breda.[75]

---

[74] Doise and Vaïsse, *Diplomatie*, p. 286. Cf. Gamelin's advice to the Czechs in 1934 to model their defensive system on that of France, with fortifications and strategic reserves and motorised units to carry out a Polish-Czech advance into Eastern Silesia, the eastern counterpart of the French advance into Belgium. SHA, 7N3444, Gamelin-Krejči conversations, 12 July 1934. Gamelin's stress on both fronts was on the need to ensure manoeuvre.

[75] SHA, 7N3697, 'Le problème militaire français', 1 June 1936 forcefully presents the lessons drawn from the development of German mechanisation. Within the highest echelons of the EMA, the mechanisation issue revealed real divisions over a French advance into Belgium.

General Schweisguth, as Gamelin's representative to the allied armies at the April staff talks, diffidently attempted to orient the British towards Gamelin's strategic agenda in the Low Countries. Schweisguth told the British that they were wise not to define as yet the exact uses of their continental expeditionary force, as who could foretell whether Germany would attack in the east or in the west. Speaking personally, he hinted that, because of German fortifications, Franco-British operations would be placed in the more open terrain of the Low Countries, where mutual interests had always closely tied them. This military diplomacy met British and Belgian fears of a German irruption through Holland, a contingency for which the British military had already generated a 'paper plan', and which was openly acknowledged by Gamelin and his Belgian counterpart, Van den Bergen, in their bilateral staff talks in May 1936.[76] In a French governmental meeting several months after the reoccupation, Gamelin spoke of a manoeuvre into Belgium and Holland to circumvent anticipated German fortifications in the Rhineland. While in 1936 all of these Belgian conjectures were linked to Gamelin's premise that the main German attack would come in the east, his strategy contained in essence the Breda Variant of 1940, with its reckless dash through Belgium to Holland to head off a German breakthrough.[77]

An entry from Schweisguth's private journal in the period preparatory to the trilateral staff talks suggests a commonality between 1936 and 1940. Since Germany would soon turn eastwards, Schweisguth opined that a Franco-British convention referring only to the French frontier would apply to an inoperative case.[78] In 1936, Gamelin preferred a war beginning in the east to one on French soil; in 1939–40, at the first word of *Wehrmacht* shuttles from east to west, he would rapidly prepare for the movement of British and French troops into Belgium. But at no point did he plan a major Franco-

Gamelin's colleagues, notably General Georges who would command the north-eastern front in 1939–40, were already disquieted at the lengths to which Gamelin wanted to go in committing mechanized divisions in Belgium. Georges, like Colson, championed reinforced fortifications in the face of the escalated threat of sudden German attack in the west after the Rhineland reoccupation, a threat which for Georges meant that the Germans might actually break through the existing French fortifications. Ibid., 1N46, Georges Notes, 29 January 1936, 9 February 1937. He was an early opponent of stripping the French centre of reserves for use in the Low Countries.

[76] Schw. 2SC2 Dr12, 17 April 1936; *Les relations militaires franco-belges mars 1936 – 10 mai 1940: travaux d'un colloque d'historiens belges et français* (Paris, 1968), pp. 56–7; M. Alexander, 'Gamelin', pp. 169–71. [77] SHA, CPDN, 29 July 1936.
[78] Schw., 1SC2 Dr8, 31 March 1936.

British campaign on French soil in defence of France – the one, in Schweisguth's phrase, 'inoperative case'. For precisely this reason, Gamelin from 1936 sought to modernise and mechanise the French army by planning that would commit his mechanised strategic reserve in the Low Countries as soon as the German army appeared to concentrate its attack there. He thus went against a classic doctrinal point: the reserve should not be committed before waiting to see that the direction of the main German thrust had been confirmed. He inferred, however, from his knowledge of the speed and mobility of German mechanisation that a rapid decision as to committing the reserve would be of the essence, especially given his desire to maintain the battle deep in Belgian territory. While it would be misleading to see the race to encounter the German army in 1940, the Breda Variant, as in any iron-clad sense pre-determined from 1936, the possibility existed from that time that Gamelin would commit the bulk of his strategic reserve to the Low Countries *if* the German army appeared to oblige by attacking there. Certainly, from 1936, Gamelin began to alter the concept of the strategic reserve, no longer a force to be kept on French soil for widely undefined purposes, but an élite force to be sent outside France, and as in all of his planning for wars of coalition, whether with the aloof Dutch and Belgians or the quarrelling Italians and Yugoslavs, to act as liaison between less than communicative allies in a coalition soldered together by the very heat of conflict.

Behind closed doors in Paris in the early spring of 1936, Gamelin insisted on the need to solder the French and Belgian frontiers so that the French army could move into Belgium at a German aggression in Central Europe. The Belgian *porte de sortie* would provide the assurance, vital to France's eastern allies, that it would not remain pinioned behind the Maginot line. Elliptical statements to this effect were promptly made to the Central European military attachés, and through successive map exercises in early 1938 Gamelin maintained the theme of French operations in Belgium in the case of a German attack in Central Europe.[79]

---

[79] Schw., 1SC2 Dr8, 'Rapport', 31 March, 1 April 1936; SC4 Dr3, 20 April 1937; SHA, 'MMF Prague', Circular, 13 March; 'Roumanie AM', 1 May 1936; Barclay minute to PRO, FO 371, 20696, C4888/822/17; Dutailly, *Les problèmes de l'armée*, pp. 107–8. The possibility of a manoeuvre in Belgium to aid Czechoslovakia, envisioned by the EMA as early as January 1933 (SHA, 7N3444, 21 January 1933) in conjunction with Gamelin's anticipation of an imminent Rhineland reoccupation, was finally abandoned by Gamelin in April 1938 after Italian acceptance of the Anschluss.

Gamelin after the Rhineland

In March and April 1936, Hitler issued peace proposals including offers of non-aggression pacts to Austria and Czechoslovakia. Legitimately, given the gangrene of panic which spread in Central and Eastern Europe after 7 March, the government voiced fears that Hitler's peace offers and German fortification in the Rhineland would draw France's allies into the German camp, thus leaving France isolated. In response, Gamelin imperturbably guided discussion away from the government's emphasis on preventing the construction of German fortifications to the French position once German fortifications faced the Maginot line.[80]

In early April meetings with the government, he subtly shifted the strategic focus from the violation of the Rhineland to a war of coalition in the east, as he had done in governmental discussions after the announcement of German conscription in March 1935. To banish the civilians' *post hoc* resentment at military reluctance to contemplate an offensive in the Rhineland, he argued that a conflict on the Franco-German frontier would produce stalemate and a war of attrition: 'In a closed battlefield, a confined space, the French and German armies would very soon be able to saturate the terrain. Now the experience of the last war shows that if empty spaces initially allowed manoeuvre, the saturation of fronts rapidly led to a balance of forces, which could only be broken after painful attrition of German power.' Gamelin advocated a coalition, a coalition based not on British support in a long war, but on entente with Italy and Poland in a war of extended fronts over Czechoslovakia: 'Since on land, a conflict limited to France and Germany would hardly allow decisive results, those should be obtained by an extension of fronts, that is, with the aid of alliances. It is in this regard that the question of Italy, in particular, and of Poland arises.' While making no mention of Britain, Gamelin voiced the feeling among the military that the politicians had to be made to understand France's need for allies, and in particular that it ought to be known whether Italy and

---

[80] Gamelin depicted future German fortifications as quickly constructed, concrete field works, rather than a continuous line of Maginot-like solidity. He deduced this from the fact that the Germans need never fear surprise attack. He contrasted the case of France which, obliged to constant preoccupation with sudden German aggression, possessed a system of fortifications, of continuous fronts so solid that it could be manned by reduced forces. SHA, 1N36, 'Note résumant l'exposé fait par le général Gamelin à la réunion du 4 avril 1936'.

Poland could be counted upon before any further consideration of military action.[81] The strategic root of Gamelin's planning was laid bare, when, after outlining governmental measures to be taken at the next crisis, he concluded: 'These are indispensable conditions for carrying the war outside our national territory.'[82]

To the agitated politicians, Gamelin advocated an operation to Salonika, as in the First World War. French military and diplomatic circles believed that the allies' failure to carry out a far-reaching offensive from Salonika in the final months of the First World War had hopelessly botched the peace, by depriving the allies of a decisive blow from the south against Germany itself, at a time that the conflict in Western Europe was still entirely on French soil. In autumn 1918, a Franco-British force under General Franchet d'Espérey, aided by Serbian troops, 'prepared to march on Vienna and Berlin'. It was, in Churchill's famous phrase, to strike a blow against 'the soft underbelly' of the flagging Central Powers. But, in early October 1918, Franchet d'Espérey's offensive was abruptly stopped by Clemenceau at word of the German military's demand for an armistice. Philippe Berthelot had vainly protested that the establishment of a durable peace required 'a victorious and a vanquished [power]', that is, an allied invasion of Germany.[83] After the Rhineland, Gamelin calmed the civilians by evoking the opportuneness of another Salonika operation to offset renewed Franco-German stalemate on the north-eastern frontier. He in effect proposed not only to carry the war outside of French territory, but to achieve the decisive victory over Germany elusive in 1918.

In the next weeks Gamelin proliferated projects, like that to Salonika, dependent on Italian goodwill: the dispatch of a French division to the Brenner in the event of a Nazi putsch in Austria, and the constitution of a French expeditionary force for action in Central Europe.[84] On the desirability of liquidating the Ethiopian crisis and reviving ties with Italy, there was no theoretical disagreement within the government. Nor did the diplomats dispute the emergent linkage in the military's post-reoccupation planning of Italy and Czechoslovakia.[85] In mid April, Flandin began a series of compromise peace

[81] Schw., 1SC2 Dr8, 4 April 1936.   [82] SHA, 1N36, Note, 4 April 1936.
[83] Barré, *Le seigneur-chat*, pp. 287–9, 323–5.   [84] DDF II, 2, no. 23.
[85] That the EMA preached to the converted on the subject of making the Italian alliance the principal element of a reoriented French policy was shown by an unusually candid conversation between Léger's secretary, Croy, and a British diplomat. PRO, FO 371, 19899, C2547/4/18.

overtures in Rome, aimed at inducing Mussolini to assume obligations towards Czechoslovakia as a *quid pro quo* for the ending of sanctions. While decidedly cool at the prospect of taking up such obligations, Mussolini allowed that, once satisfied in Africa, Italy, 'the most conservative of all', would tolerate no change in the status quo either on the Rhine or on the Danube. Italy would defend the line of the Danube, and particularly Austria, with all its forces.[86]

During these inconclusive démarches in Rome, Flandin succumbed to panic that the Austrian affair would come to a head in mid-Ethiopian crisis.[87] At odds with Maurin since February, Flandin in a shoddy manoeuvre tried to foist on to the EMA complete blame for France's disintegrating international prospects. Indicting Maurin's behaviour at the reoccupation for what he called the loss of 'a magnificent occasion' to resist Germany, Flandin insisted that, when he had to inform the Cabinet that the Nazis had occupied Austria, he wanted a French retort to have been prepared.[88] Infuriated, Gamelin and Maurin mooted the immediate dispatch of a French division to the Brenner, a move which had tempted Gamelin for months. He ordered the examination of this and other projects – offensive preparations on the north-eastern frontier and an eventual action in the Saar – all from the point of view of consequences for the government.[89]

[86] DDF II, 1, no. 526; 2, nos. 17, 46, 62, 90; BN, Papiers Flandin, carton 74, 'Conversation Cerruti fin avril 1936'. Mussolini's talk of the 'line of the Danube' neatly excluded Czechoslovakia. The Danube defined a section of the Czech-Hungarian border but did not run through Czechoslovakia. The General Staff pressed for explicit entente with Italy over Czechoslovakia before an Italian victory in Ethiopia. Complete victory in Ethiopia soon led Mussolini to demand the lifting of sanctions in return for even a pledge to defend Austrian independence. Shorrock, *From Ally to Enemy*, pp. 170–80, contains a highly sympathetic view of Italian policy in this period.

[87] For Central European alarm at the possibility of an immediate German attack, DDF II, 1, nos. 256, 270, 308, 424, 476, 495.

[88] Schw., 1SC2 Dr8, 'Compte-rendu d'une conversation entre M. Flandin et le gal. Schweisguth (21 avril 1936)'.

[89] Ibid., 24 March, 22 April 1936; DDF II, 2, no. 113. Personally galled by Flandin's censure, Gamelin asked and was authorised by the Ministry of War to take command at the *couverture* (cover of the frontiers) rather than at general mobilisation, a more serious measure. He also requested that future pressing political and military questions be submitted for civilian-military consideration in the *Haut Comité militaire* before discussion in the Cabinet, so that the military's views would be fully taken into consideration when governmental decisions were made. In 1938 the HCM's replacement, the *Comité permanent de la Défense nationale*, deliberated on the military position to be adopted in the face of Hitler's designs on Czechoslovakia after the Anschluss. Gamelin was even more successful then than he had been at the reoccupation in stifling the government's will to act in circumstances – by 1938, the total estrangement of Italy – which he judged unpropitious. Not only did the Rhineland leave unaltered the pattern of military response to the German

A follow-up conversation at the Quai d'Orsay between Léger's faithful second, Paul Bargeton, and a military deputation revealed both the hollowness of Flandin's assertiveness and the strength of Gamelin's attachment to an expeditionary force to Central Europe. Bargeton disparaged rumours of imminent German attack on Austria and showed a fastidious concern that a French gesture on behalf of Austria would cast it and Italy in the role of aggressors. His dismayed military listeners reported: 'Everything M. Bargeton said left the impression of great uncertainty, even absolute disarray, at the Quai d'Orsay.' Weygand's protégé on the EMA, General Georges, present at the conversation with Bargeton, wondered aloud whether the Salonika project should not be shelved for the time being. Gamelin refused to be dissuaded from his planning for a large-scale Salonika landing, planning which in its dependence on Italian friendship would accommodate the immediate dispatch of a French division to Italy in the event of a Nazi putsch in Austria.[90] In late May, he ordered reorganisation of the Alpine units designated for the expeditionary force. A June period of Italian military alert in protest at the continuance of sanctions demoted his orders from execution to study, but the resultant study was meticulously carried out, down to the testing of boats for Danubian transport.[91]

Gamelin also moved to advance cooperation with Poland. With the promise of important arms aid to Poland in May 1936, he attempted to foster Polish-Czech staff contacts and an eventual Polish front in Eastern Prussia against Germany.[92] For him, as for his colleague Schweisguth, the eastern theatre had characteristics which made it an enticing target for the German offensive machine: immense, sparsely populated spaces and flat terrain, defended by excellent peasant armies such as Poland's. Their enthusiasm for the singularities of the eastern front is worth citing:

resurgence, but Flandin's Austrian tantrum gave the military occasion to close ranks in the matter of governmental procedures for crisis management. Schw., 1SC2 Dr8, 22 April 1936; DDF II, 2, no. 138; 8, no. 446.   [90] DDF II, 2, nos. 113, 138.
[91] Schw., SC4 Dr3, CHEDN lectures, 17, 20 April 1937; documents from SHA, 7N3449 are summarised in Dutailly, *Les problèmes de l'armée*, pp. 51–2. The uncertainty of Franco-Italian relations provides the context for a statement from a 3e Bureau memorandum of 1 June 1936: 'Direct aid to our Central or East European allies is beyond the scope of this study, and has no influence on the future constitution of our army', direct aid being defined here not as a French offensive on behalf of an eastern ally, but as aid delivered to the eastern front. The military writer remarked, tentatively given the state of relations with Italy, that it might be possible to put at the disposition of the eastern allies a specially formed Expeditionary Corps with arms that they lacked. SHA, 7N3697, 1 June 1936.
[92] SHA, 7N3032, d'Arbonneau-Gérodias letter, 13 May 1936.

This terrain has no value in itself. Fighting here or there makes absolutely no difference! One can retreat 50 kilometres without discovering an important road, a town, a factory or a railroad. So there can be rapid and deep withdrawals, necessitating advances of the same order; consequently, it is necessary to have troops able to break or resume contact with the enemy: light infantry, cavalry, tanks.[93]

The traditional view of the Rhineland crisis as nullifying at one stroke France's eastern strategy thus misconstrues the significance of the crisis. For Gamelin, the form of the reoccupation – a symbolic remilitarisation without an attack on France – validated his conception of the most advantageous conflict, a war of coalition in which the brunt of German force would be directed against Central Europe. His calculations emerged starkly from an April 1936 map synthesis, which took as its theme the impact of the Rhineland affair. The exercise was dominated by Gamelin's dictum that German fortifications would make impossible a timely French intervention on behalf of an ally, explicitly identified as Czechoslovakia. As a result, the French offensive would be limited to Belgium. Italy and, above all, Poland would save the Czechs.[94] Like his over-hasty anticipation of finished German fortifications in the west, Gamelin's increased dependence on Italy and Poland made planning for a war of coalition virtually indistinguishable from warnings against a unilateral French intervention on behalf of Czechoslovakia.

THE CENTRAL EUROPEAN RESPONSE

The Central European response to French military inaction on 7 March was less uncontrolled than retrospective accounts sometimes suggest. Appearances were largely preserved. After all, the allies, like Gamelin, had anticipated a German reoccupation since early allied evacuation of the Rhineland in 1930.

Beck, the Polish Foreign Minister, skilfully manipulated Paris's disarray to advance the cause of Polish arms demands, without assuming the additional obligations of which a maladroit French approach of mid February had warned him. In a démarche to the Polish Ambassador, prompted by uncertainty over German action in the wake of ratification of the Franco-Soviet pact, Flandin had broached the question of French financial aid for Polish rearmament, under discussion between the two capitals for weeks; he then had slid

---

[93] Schw., 2SC2 Dr2 sdr a, 'Mission en Roumanie', 'Rapport', 2 October 1935.
[94] Schw., 1SC2 Dr8, 1 April, 'Rapport', 4 April 1936.

in the knife, expressing doubt that Poland would give aid or remain neutral at a German attack on Czechoslovakia or that it would mobilise at a reoccupation, should France mobilise, as Flandin had declared at Stresa that it would do.[95]

When the reoccupation happened, Beck overrode real divisions within the Polish Government over how strong the French retort would be by tactics which combined his government's strong desire for French arms aid and his own conviction that France would not adopt *la manière forte*. Although the Polish Government had discussed a *mobilisation de solidarité*. Beck's version of a gesture of great significance was spontaneously to summon Léon Noël, the French Ambassador, and insist that Poland desired all the exchanges of view to which it was entitled by the alliance.[96] Beck increased the strength of his assurances of loyal bilateralism as French inaction became more and more certain, culminating in his otiose assurance during the London meetings that Poland would mobilise if France did so.[97]

In these confused bilateral conversations after the German repudiation of Locarno had left highly uncertain the fate of the 1925 Franco-Polish accord, he manoeuvred to reassert the controversial 1921 agreements. This diplomacy rallied the Polish military, who were disappointed by the flaccid French response. Beck's stress on the 1921 accords, however, included assurances made several days into the crisis that Poland would fulfil its obligations in the event that France was attacked (an assurance which carefully did not specify the Polish reaction to German action outside of France's borders, in the Rhineland or Czechoslovakia), thus giving the French notice that Poland would not aid another French ally should it be the victim of a German attack. The theme of Poland's strictly bilateral obligations was again rehearsed when the Belgian Premier visited Warsaw several weeks later. As he would do during a visit to Belgrade in May, Beck carried out a neutralist mission, telling his guest that states with limited interests should remain in contact lest they be reduced to following in the wake of these powers with a greater range of action. Van Zeeland had the impression that, in the event of troubles in Central Europe, Poland would limit itself to

[95] G. Sakwa, 'The Franco-Polish Alliance...', pp. 129, 135–6.
[96] Noël was wary of Beck's insistence on exchanges of view. In March 1935, Beck had capitalised on consultations with the French to manoeuvre between the French and German positions at Geneva. L. Noël, *L'agression allemande contre la Pologne* (Paris, 1946), p. 129; DDF II, 1, nos. 303, 331; Szembek, *Journal*, p. 166.
[97] Sakwa, 'The Franco-Polish Alliance', p. 140; P.-E. Flandin, *Politique française 1919–1940* (Paris, 1947), p. 206; DDF II, 1, no. 445.

actions in its own interest, a telling comment on the unlikelihood of détente between Prague and Warsaw.[98]

Beck also threw out ample ballast on the German side. His spontaneous declarations of fidelity to the French were almost immediately countermanded by a communiqué of 8 March from the semi-official press agency, Iskra. The Iskra communiqué placed the reoccupation firmly in the context of the Soviet ratification, implying that the German reaction, although not necessarily its strength, was legitimate. Beck was no doubt pleased to taunt the French and to present Polish policy as motivated by truer principles.[99] Before leaving Warsaw for London, he announced to the German Ambassador that the Polish Government had no unfriendly feelings towards Germany, against whom it would not support sanctions. He dismissed press reports of his assurances to the French by saying that, since Germany did not intend to attack France, they were mere statements of the obvious. Beck's colleague, Szembek, was even more candid: Poland had certain obligations, but he did not see how she could play any part at all in international action against the German violation. The London meetings created further discord between French and Polish diplomacy, when Beck joined several neutral powers in making difficulties for the French-sponsored motion condemning the German action.[100]

The Yugoslav reaction closely resembled that of Poland. Stoyadinovitch, the Prime Minister, tardily assured the French Minister of his country's loyalty, promising on 10 March that, if forced into war, France would have the complete support of the Yugoslav army in its defence. The force of this assurance was diminished by segments of the Yugoslav press, which advocated neutrality on the subject of the Rhineland. Stoyadinovitch himself candidly told the British Minister that Yugoslavia intended to 'lie low and play the modest part of a small power'. If France were the victim of unprovoked aggression, Yugoslavia would stand by it, but in no other case. He was particularly afraid that sanctions against Germany might be

---

[98] DDF II, 1, no. 142; Beck, *Dernier rapport*, pp. 118–21. Cf. François-Poncet's report in this period of the Reich's belief that it could 'manoeuvre a group of states who were only united for negative reasons and out of fear of complications'. DDF II, 2, no. 382.

[99] When Noël divulged Beck's assurances to his British colleague, Beck retaliated by informing the Foreign Office that Poland had little interest in the Demilitarised Zone, which he described as an attempt to place a nation in perpetual servitude. DDF II, 1, nos. 325, 408; 2, no. 71; Noël, *L'agression*, p. 136; PRO, FO 371, 19890, C1717/4/18, Minute by Cranborne.

[100] DGFP, C., V. nos. 61, 173; Szembek, *Journal*, pp. 168, 170; MAE, Papiers Noël, 3 April 1936; Flandin, *Politique française*, p. 206; DDF II, 1, no. 445.

adopted.[101] Yugoslav external commerce had become heavily dependent on Germany during the Ethiopian war, when sanctions against Italy had deprived Yugoslavia of one of its principal clients.

The congruence in the Polish and Yugoslav responses to the Rhineland reoccupation prompted René Massigli of the Quai d'Orsay's Political Directorate to observe by 12 March that, while it was clear that if the European situation deteriorated further France's Central European allies would be at its side, this very measure of support was dangerous given the moderation of the French response. If some facsimile of French victory could not be wrested from the situation, the Germanophiles in every country would be strengthened, and their governments might strike out on a new course with every pretext of having supported France in its hour of need.[102]

The Roumanian response was divided. Partisans of limited French military action like Tataresco, the Premier, called for a French concentration of forces at the Franco-German frontier. Titulesco, the Foreign Minister, at first took a hard line, support of sanctions against Germany, and then emerged in London as an exponent of negotiations. He also worked to prevent the triumph in London of the neutralist theses of his adversary Beck.[103]

Beneš too supported sanctions against Germany and negotiations. Immediately after the reoccupation, the Czech Government repeatedly assured the French Legation that it would take no initiative. The initiative belonged to France, and French policy would be followed in every respect. Like Titulesco, Beneš combined loyalty with warnings that the unhampered success of the German enterprise in the Rhineland would rapidly lead to the collapse of the French security system. Once he accepted the impracticality of sanctions, Beneš accommodated himself to Paris's emphasis on a strong Franco-British front rather than punishment of Germany.[104]

---

[101] DDF II, 1, nos. 360, 422; PRO, FO 371, 19890, C1699/4/18.

[102] Massigli, one of the most substantive French diplomats in this period, concluded his note for Flandin: 'The question at stake at this moment is to know whether Europe will be German or not.' DDF II, 1, no. 407.

[103] Ibid., nos. 309, 326, 432, 444, 454; PRO, FO 371, 19891, C1832/4/18.

[104] Beneš and Titulesco in fact supported sanctions more zealously than Flandin, who used them as a tactical wedge to obtain British assent to staff talks. Flandin concluded beforehand that it was superior politics to press the British for a military accord, although he was quite prepared to exploit London's refusal of sanctions to obtain its assent to staff talks. BN, Papiers Flandin, carton 74, Massigli note, 30 March; Schw., 1SC2 Dr8, 20, 21 March 1936; Czech T-120, 1041/1809/414086, 414087; DDF II, 1, nos. 307, 343, 373, 385, 402, 424, 476, 482.

To the French Chargé d'Affaires, he expatiated on the principles which he hoped would guide the coming negotiations: independent Franco-British military accords; German, Italian, and Czech guarantees of Austria; and a close correlation between German engagements in the east and west.

The German peace proposals, both those accompanying the reoccupation and those of late March, included bilateral non-aggression pacts *à la polonaise* with Czechoslovakia and Austria. In early April, the German Minister in Prague conveyed additional offers for recognition of the Czech-Soviet treaty and the Petite Entente's collective treaties, to be given after agreement had been reached in the west. These offers ensured German impunity in the Rhineland affair, anaesthetising the Czechs during the diplomatic dithering around negotiations for a new Locarno, while the Reich mounted pressure on Austria for a bilateral agreement. They were meant to induce a false sense of security in Prague. Eisenlohr implied that the next target of German expansionism would be Poland.[105]

At the same time, Berlin evidenced a willingness to coerce the Czechs. The German press kept up its campaign against the alleged use of Czech air bases by the Soviets, and rumours of an imminent German attack circulated. Beneš was dismissive of the rumours, although he and other members of the Czech Government considered the Rhineland *fait accompli* a disquieting revelation of acute German internal difficulties, which might prompt Hitler to turn on Czechoslovakia or Austria.[106] Most ominously, after the reoccupation, the Reich gave new importance to Czechoslovakia's treatment of the Sudetendeutsch. A burning domestic issue in Czechoslovakia from the electoral victories of Henlein's pro-Nazi Sudetendeutsch Partei in 1935, the Sudetendeutsch question became after 7 March a key negotiating counter in the Reich's approaches. In conversation with the Czechs, the Germans henceforth assiduously raised the Sudetendeutsch problem, which Beneš had long been eager to treat as a function of the international situation, not as a Czech-German issue. In spring 1936, he had high hopes for a programme of conciliation towards the Sudetendeutsch, entrusted in early May to Kamil Krofta, the Foreign Minister.[107]

---

[105] DDF II, 1, no. 398; 2, nos. 2, 26, 32.
[106] Ibid., 1, nos. 385, 398, 423-4, 465, 482; 2, nos. 3, 26, 42, 46, 96; Czech T-120, 1041/1809/414092.
[107] DDF II, 2, nos. 26, 39, 84, 96, 178, 182, 235, 317, 343; Czech T-120, 1041/1809/414089.

Beneš's acceleration of Czech rearmament in spring 1936 indicates that he was intimidated by the prospect of direct, bilateral contacts with Germany. He hinted to the French that his calm advocacy of parallelism with their policy encompassed a desire for a French lead in improved relations with Germany:

> For sixteen years Franco-Czech intimacy has been unclouded. This is because he [Beneš] has never wanted Czechoslovakia to be a burden on France. He wanted to know what line French policy would take only so that he could take a similar line... especially if the French Government wanted to try to negotiate with Germany, he would make arrangements to coordinate his action with ours.[108]

A new aura surrounded the German menace immediately after the Rhineland reoccupation. Aggressively solicitous of the effect he wished to create – a dynamic tension between the prestige of force and its use – Hitler henceforth stressed not in-depth preparations for combat but the rapid organisation of the German army to overawe its neighbours.[109] A charismatic Reich might then infiltrate German-speaking populations, skilfully deploying an intense propaganda and commercial campaign in Central Europe to collect the benefits of its highly muscular inaction. It could be counted upon not to neglect attempts to turn the resultant neutralist current – and in this Poland provided an example for France's other allies – to its precise uses: control of Austria and the isolation of Czechoslovakia. From the French Embassy in Rome came reports in early June of the crumbling of Italian influence in Vienna and Budapest to Nazi advantage, and of a conjunction of German, Hungarian, Austrian, and Polish antipathies to Czechoslovakia. Recalling Mussolini's coldness towards Czechoslovakia, Chambrun suggested that, by aligning itself with this Czechophobe configuration of powers, Italy might seek to remove the Austrian problem at least temporarily to the background. The implications were far-reaching: with French military prestige at a low ebb, an Italo-German conjunction would exercise great attraction not only on revisionist states, but on all countries susceptible to armed strength.[110]

The exposed nerves of Czech policy were visible in an outburst by the head of the Czech delegation in Geneva in April 1936. While Czechoslovakia had not demanded a French military retort on 7 March, the delayed effect of the Rhineland crisis was an outpouring

---

[108] DDF II, 1, no. 482; 2, no. 255.   [109] DDF II, 2, no. 123.
[110] Ibid., nos. 254, 272.

of the anxiety building up in Central Europe since the international destabilisation of the Ethiopian war. The usually compliant Czechs resented, after the Rhineland reoccupation, French soldiers and diplomats advocating increased dependence on Italy as a bridge for the French expeditionary force to be sent to Central Europe in a conflict. The Czech diplomat in Geneva deplored the growing estrangement of Yugoslavia, paralysed by fear of Italian attack, as organised Ethiopian military resistance to Italy collapsed. He then blasted the 'absence of clarity' in his country's relations with France:

The system of collective security no longer exists; these are words which have no meaning. The League Covenant has bit by bit been destroyed by the Italophile policy of France. The Locarno treaty which protected Czechoslovakia has been repudiated by Germany. No one cares about Czechoslovakia, which is none the less the cornerstone of order and the status quo in Central Europe.

If it was strong enough to struggle against the Nazi movement in Bohemia, Czechoslovakia could not alone confront Germany. It was unsurprising, he concluded, that leading personalities, such as the Premier, Hodža, were said to be ready to accept German offers for a bilateral agreement.[111]

To summarise, this chapter has contended that the General Staff under Maurice Gamelin evolved an eastern strategy of default. His planning sought to ensure that the next war would be carried outside of French territory, thus chanelling irrepressible German force by letting the waters flow eastward of their own accord. His view of the next conflict rested in the first instance on unalterable geographical imperatives which gave importance to alliances with Italy, Belgium, and Poland. Great Britain occupied a less exalted place in the mid 1930s in French military planning than has sometimes been assumed. Its role was to supply war *matériel* and liaison with the recalcitrant Belgians.

Gamelin's defensive attachment to an eastern front in a war commonly supposed to be over Czechoslovakia was also inextricable from domestic constraints. His strategy was originally evolved to

---

[111] SHA, 7N3107, 'SR 1921–1939', 18 April 1936. For the Yugoslavs' acrid discontents, DDF II, 1, nos. 20, 424; 2, nos. 16, 143, 180; PRO, FO 371, 20380, R2656/125/67; for earlier aspirations by Hodža to reach agreement with Germany in the collective context of a Danubian economic federation, DDF II, 1, no. 84 and Wandycz, *Twilight*, pp. 422–4.

compensate for the political pressures generated by the disarmament conference, fiscal cuts, and a diplomacy avid for arms limitation. It mirrored these pressures in its awareness of French weakness and vulnerability, as in his fear of directly provoking a Germany whose strength, he soon believed, had attained parity level with France. The peculiarly debilitating quality of this perception, however, arose less from the particular constraints of the early thirties, which Gamelin after all tolerated, than from the military's long anticipation of impotence caused by the recent history of civilian concessions over the Rhineland zone.

From 1933 Gamelin complacently assumed that, by creating an indisputable German menace in the east, the event of the reoccupation would coalesce the threatened states, notably Poland and Czechoslovakia. But, as the Nazis were demonstrating domestically with resounding success, a blatant threat to a vulnerable segment of a community did not generate solidarity. Gamelin's strategic preference for a war in the east left Hitler with ample leeway to mark out Czechoslovakia with its key strategic position, its treaties with France and the Soviet Union, and its situation as a refuge for political exiles from throughout Europe. He could pit against it other French allies, whom the Reich could leave unthreatened so long as that served German purposes. The weapon for this selection process lay readily to hand: ideology.

Entr'acte: Paris, June 1936

France's diminished prestige after the Rhineland reoccupation and the uncertain terms on which it could hope to reintegrate Italy into the defence of Central Europe presented the controversial Socialist-led government, elected in May 1936, with a Central European conundrum of highly unstable elements. The victorious Front populaire coalition was headed by Léon Blum, the first Socialist and the first Jew to become Premier of France. He took power in June amid social unrest, but also enormous popular hope.

Blum was a humanistic Socialist and conditional pacifist in the tradition of his mentor, Jean Jaurès, the creator of the pre-1914 French Socialist party. James Joll has admiringly defined the Socialism which Jaurès bequeathed to Blum as 'a liberal, ethical humanism and a deep sense of social justice with elements drawn from Marx's analysis of historical development...His Socialism...owed as much to Kant as it did to dialectical materialism.'[1] More influenced by French history than by German or Russian Socialism, it sought to combine with internationalism the revolutionary patriotism of 1789 and 1870. It was also marked by a concern to create a democratic Socialism by educating the working class.

Blum originally confined his political activism to moments in which division menaced the Third Republic or the Socialist camp within it. It began with his passionate involvement in the Dreyfus Affair, which he recounted in a vivid memoir published shortly before he took power. From 1905, the creation of the SFIO, a single Socialist party from various Socialist splinter groups, until 1914, the assassination of Jaurès and the outbreak of war, Blum was not militant in the Socialist cause. He returned to his first love, literary

[1] J. Joll, *Europe Since 1870* (London, 1973), p. 64; idem., *Three Intellectuals in Politics* (New York, 1960), p. 12.

93

and theatre criticism. In 1907, he published *Du mariage*, a combination of fiction and sociology which advocated equal rights for women in sexual experience before marriage. Scandalous in its day, it was still considered so by much of the bourgeoisie in 1936. On the eve of the First World War, he published an illuminating study of Stendhal. He might well have pursued a literary career financed by professional work as a jurist at the *Conseil d'Etat*, the high court of French administrative law, had Jaurès not been murdered in July 1914 by a right-wing fanatic inflamed by the gutter journalism of Maurras, the ideologue of the anti-Dreyfusard *Action française*. As leader of the SFIO in the 1920s, Blum devised complex theoretical constraints for Socialist participation in bourgeois governments. But, after the February 1934 riots, which he considered a threat to republican liberties, he refined the party's doctrine to justify its joining in the Front populaire formation against domestic Fascism.[2]

An intellectual *par excellence*, educated at the Lycée Henri IV, the Ecole Normale, and the Sorbonne, Blum was neither a demogogue nor a hard-core ideologue. His tastes were rarefied, his voice fluted, his manner patrician without being patronising. His discourse consisted of persuasion by rational argument, and he did not abandon it whether he spoke to the Parisian élites or to his wine-growing constituents in the south. Blum's biographer, Joel Colton, has remarked that in Blum's concise, logical speeches, 'the subordinate clauses all began with the word, "but". He carried his audiences with him by his sympathetic insight into the position of his opponents and by the devastating counterlogic of his own syllogisms.'[3] He well understood the sources, if he sometimes underestimated the strength, of the massive obstacles to change within French society but he believed that a united, socially democratic working class might surmount them. His effort was towards persuasion without coercion. The American historian Stuart Hughes, in France as a vacationing college student in the summer of 1936, remembers that, at the large popular rallies of that summer, Blum gave the left-wing salute, the raised fist, but it was 'such a gentle fist'.[4]

Hope was a political as well as a cultural value for Blum. He wrote sentences which might have been his political motto in the Socialist

[2] James Joll's essay on Blum in *Three Intellectuals in Politics* is excellent on Blum's various doctrinal distinctions on the problem of a Socialist exercise of power, as is Julian Jackson's *The Popular Front in France* (Cambridge, 1988), pp. 57–60.
[3] J. Colton, *Léon Blum: Humanist in Politics* (New York, 1966), p. 60.
[4] Conversation with Stuart Hughes, 15 October 1986.

paper, *Le Populaire*, shortly before his death in 1950: 'I hope for it and I believe it. I believe it because I hope for it.'[5] For this almost visionary sense of hope, Blum has often been faulted by historians. J.-B. Duroselle has argued that Blum's espousal of unilateral disarmament in the early 1930s shows him to have been a visionary of unsure judgement, a man who made 'dangerous errors'. Blum's position on many issues in the early thirties was highly doctrinal, but in power he maintained a tension between principle and adaptation to challenge, as his willingness to support intensive French rearmament from September 1936 attests. While his economic policies led to a tardy devaluation of the franc and the disastrous impact of the forty hour week on French rearmament and have been almost universally criticised, he was a man of radically educable perception. Pierre Mendès France, a collaborator at the Ministry of Finance during Blum's second government, pointed to his neo-Keynesian fiscal programme of 1938 to argue: 'His capacity for adaptation, which in no way detracted from his fundamental convictions, constituted one of the most remarkable aspects of Blum's intelligence.'[6]

Even for those historians most sympathetic to him, James Joll and Joel Colton, he remains a brilliant failure. Blum had to an unusual extent the defects of his virtues. He allied to flexibility a noble optimism with regard to social change which in many instances only time could bear out. He also had an excessive belief in the power of rationality and empathy in a period when warring and intransigent ideologies threatened to engulf Europe. As Colton has suggested, Blum's political epitaph is perhaps best taken from Machiavelli: 'A man who wishes to make a profession of goodness in everything must necessarily come to grief among many who are not so good.'[7] The ambiguities inherent in democratic socialism provide an additional, structural dimension to Blum's predicament as a Kantian socialist in the political wilderness.

For almost the length of his active political career, he was the subject of intense polemic and sometimes of hatred. At the Congress of Tours in 1920, the year after he entered the French parliament, he eloquently opposed a Socialism which took its dictates from the newly created Comintern. Blum's vision was of a Socialist party characterised by internal freedom and democratic control, by the

---

[5] Blum's last editorial in the newspaper of the SFIO, *Le Populaire*, 29 March 1950.
[6] Duroselle, *La décadence*, p. 293; P. Mendès France, *La vérité guidait leurs pas* (Paris, 1976), p. 167.   [7] Colton, *Léon Blum*, p. 483.

Jaurèsian fusion of internationalism and national defence, and by rejection of government by terror. This position earned him the loathing of the fledgling French Communist party, with which the Socialists competed electorally until 1934 when Stalin advocated a policy of cooperation with parties to its right, the policy of Popular Fronts. Before the Socialist-Communist-Radical electoral alliance of 1935–6, Blum's competition with the Communists had been direct and visceral. He had lost a bitter legislative race in Paris in 1929 to a Communist candidate.[8]

For the extreme right of Maurras and his disciples who wrote for the scurrilous weekly, *Je suis partout*, and militated in the anti-parliamentary leagues which had taken to the street in February 1934, Blum was hardly human, a figure to be execrated. In February 1936, passing by street demonstrations at the funeral of the right-wing historian, Jacques Bainville, he was manhandled by sympathisers of Maurras who had incited his readers to murder Blum as he had incited them in 1914 to kill Jaurès. He stigmatised Blum as 'Human trash to be treated as such!... a man to shoot, but in the back'.[9]

Even for the *haute bourgeoisie juive*, scandalised like the rest of the bourgeoisie by his betrayal of the social class into which he had been educated and whose way of life he unostentatiously enjoyed, Blum was the most discomfiting of politicians. The *Consistoire*, the official organisation of native-born French Jews (as opposed to those naturalised or non-naturalised immigrants from other parts of Europe), allegedly offered Blum an annuity for life to desist from taking power in June 1936. The *Consistoire* had received letters from native-born Jews denouncing Blum as responsible for the growth of anti-Semitism in France after February 1934 attacks on him in the *Chambre des députés* during the political scandal over the swindler and Jewish immigré Staviski, by Xavier Vallat, later Vichy Com-

---

[8] See Colette Audry, *Léon Blum ou la politique du juste: essai* (Paris, 1955) for a sample of the post-war criticism of Blum by the hard core Left which has argued that Blum neglected the chances for revolution in 1936 from a desire to remain pure to his own, in their view, naive idealism that the means should not betray the nobility of the ends.

[9] Maurras, 9 April 1935, cited in L. Bodin and J. Touchard, *Front populaire 1936* (Paris, 1985), p. 34. After the Front populaire's electoral victory, Maurras significantly qualified his order of execution, writing in May 1936: 'It is as a Jew that one must see, imagine, hear, fight and *fell* "the Blum". This last verb seems to me the result of too much coffee: I hasten to add that it will only be necessary to bring Blum down physically the day when his politics have led us to the unholy war of which he dreams against our Italian companions in arms. On that day, it is true, one must not miss.' Cited in ibid., p. 72.

missioner on Jewish questions.[10] This repudiation of Blum, as David Weinberg has argued, underlined intense strains within the Jewish community between Jews long established in France and newcomers fleeing persecution in Germany and Eastern Europe. In *Souvenirs sur l'affaire*, the memoir of the Dreyfus affair which Blum wrote the year before he became Premier, he reflected on the passivity of the native, organised Jewish community in the face of virulent anti-Semitism, indigenous in the 1890s and European-wide in the 1930s. For Jewish newcomers to France, the completely secular Blum was a hero: a rare assimilated, native-born Jew who did not try to hide his identity, or apologise for it with the upper-class designation, *israélite*. In the effusive words of one Yiddish journalist, 'Blum is not simply a Jew but a real Jew, a Jew with a Jewish heart and a Jewish understanding, a Jew who even cares about the establishment of the Land of Israel as a Jewish homeland, and that such a Jew is...the premier of one of the greatest countries in Europe...is unique in modern history.'[11] Blum in turn minced no words in defending the embattled immigrants and their right to refuge in France to a native-born community fearful that waves of immigrants would increase anti-Semitism and imperil its own position, as in a speech after the Munich conference and Kristallnacht:

I will say everything I think, here, even if I offend other Jews, even if it means protesting against the statements made or published recently by men who, at least from the religious point of view, are considered to be representatives of Jewry. I can think of nothing in the world so painful and so dishonourable as seeing French Jews attempting at this moment to close the doors of France to Jewish refugees from other countries. Let them not delude themselves into believing that they are assuring their security. There has never been a time in history when security has been achieved through cowardice, whether it be nations, human groups or individuals.[12]

Anti-Semitism scarred Blum's political career. In October 1936, the French novelist Marcel Jouhandeau wrote: 'I always instinctively felt myself a thousand times closer...to our former

---

[10] D. H. Weinberg, *A Community on Trial* (Chicago, 1977), p. 98 n. 45; for a recent revival of the misbegotten allegation that Blum's political career and the allegiance of many French Jews to the Left in some sense justified French anti-Semitism, see S. Schuker, 'Origins of the Jewish Problem in the Later Third Republic', in F. Malino and B. Wasserstein, *The Jews in Modern France* (Hanover, 1985), pp. 135–80. As Pierre Birnbaum has remarked, Schuker's argumentation comes very close to adopting the theses of political anti-Semites of the 1930s, notably that of 'reasoned anti-Semitism'. P. Birnbaum, *Un mythe politique: la 'République juive'* (Paris, 1988), p. 323.

[11] Shmuel Jatzkan, cited in Weinberg, *A Community*, pp. 138–9 n. 17; on Blum's conception of the links between his Jewishness and his socialism, Colton, *Léon Blum*, pp. 4–7.

[12] Blum, 26 November 1938, cited in Weinberg, *A Community*, p. 101 n. 85.

German enemies than to all those Jewish riffraff who call themselves French, and although I have no personal sympathy for M. Hitler, I am disgusted by M. Blum.'[13] In a turbulent and degrading climate in which the slogan *Mieux Hitler que Blum* expressed the revulsion of a section of educated opinion, Blum aspired to lead all the nation, in the first instance by rallying an estranged working class to the Third Republic by means of important social reforms already effected in Britain and Germany by 1914.

Despite his absorption in the negotiations for major social reforms into which the government had been plunged by nationwide strikes – *les grèves sur le tas* – in which workers occupied factories and department stores, Blum was able to maintain a closer surveillance over foreign policy than his immediate predecessors. He was aided in this by his close communication with his Minister of Foreign Affairs, Yvon Delbos, his neighbour on the Ile St. Louis, and by a reorganisation of the *présidence du Conseil* under which he held no portfolio and could profit, at least in his first months in office, from the assiduous efforts of his lieutenants, André Blumel and Jules Moch, who deflected inessential calls and visits. He insisted on personally reading much of the diplomatic correspondence during his year as Premier, including that, notoriously lengthy, of André François-Poncet, Ambassador in Berlin. As his appointment of the colourless and relatively inexperienced Delbos indicated, Blum was determined to play a major part in the formulation of his government's foreign policy.[14]

Foreign policy considerations in the first weeks of the new government, before the outbreak of the Spanish conflict on 19 July, were dominated by the need to liquidate the two international crises left by its predecessors: the Rhineland reoccupation and the Ethiopian war which ended with the flight of Haile Selassie in May 1936.

Blum described in 1947 the great impression made on him by the harm the Rhineland reoccupation had done to France's relations with its traditional allies: 'What we tried to do in this period, without altogether being able to appreciate the extent of the damage, was to remedy it to the extent that we could. We felt Europe to be

[13] Cited in J. Sherwood, *Georges Mandel and the Third Republic* (Palo Alto, 1970), p. 213.
[14] *CE Témoignages*, I, 126; *Léon Blum chef du gouvernement* (Paris, 1967), pp. 37, 41–2; J. Moch, *Rencontres avec Léon Blum* (Paris, 1970), pp. 137–9; A. Bérard, *Au temps du danger allemand* (Paris, 1976), p. 321.

fragmented, dislocated. We felt France to be isolated and we tried to put something back together again.'[15] Blum's first concern was to reassure France's allies of its loyalty. He sent personal assurances to Central European governments, and the Ministry's foreign policy declaration was an unusually strong statement of attachment to Poland and the Petite Entente. Nor had the new government only words to offer. With explicit reference to the precariousness of the Petite Entente after the reoccupation, Blum solicited and received the assent of the newly formed *Comité permanent de la Défense nationale* to the dispatch of munitions and replacement parts to Czechoslovakia for the eventual use of the French Air Force.[16] Addressing the League Assembly the following month, Blum stressed that, if France had not reacted militarily to the reoccupation, its desire for peace 'is neither an out and out weakness nor an egotistical withdrawal in on itself'. In the same speech, Blum indicated a willingness to approach Germany directly concerning a new Locarno extended to Eastern Europe. He was said to have been prepared to send Delbos to Berlin if an arrangement was possible.[17]

A revulsion at the horsetrading of Laval's diplomacy towards Mussolini and the British broadly characterised the leaders of the new government, but Blum, commonly viewed as its most Italophobe member, was not an irreconcilable opponent of dealings with Italy. He had supported both the revised Four Power pact of 1933 and, initially, the Rome Accords negotiated by Laval and Mussolini in January 1935.[18] Laval's conduct of the Ethiopian affair had been far more of an issue than the Rhineland in the elections of spring 1936. When the defeat of Ethiopia in May 1936 brought to the fore the problem of raising sanctions, Blum in conversation with Anthony Eden appeared predisposed to believe in an Italo-German entente. This attitude fostered his concern to do nothing out of step with London, but did not signify blind Italophobia.[19] Although Blum's political views made him less open than his predecessors with regard to Italy, he made clear in high quarters in Geneva and elsewhere

---

[15] *CE Témoignages*, I, pp. 126–7.
[16] DDF II, 2, no. 369. Discussion of the dispatch of replacement parts to Prague had been postponed in the immediate aftermath of the reoccupation. DDF II, 1, nos. 83, 393.
[17] DDF II, 2, no. 379; *L'oeuvre*, vol. IV:1, Foreign Policy Declaration of the Blum Government, 23 June, pp. 360–1; speech at the League of Nations, 1 July 1936, pp. 364–70; J. Dreifort, *Yvon Delbos at the Quai d'Orsay* (Kansas, 1973), p. 159.
[18] Colton, *Léon Blum*, pp. 119, 219. On the specific point of Blum's alleged refusal to treat with Mussolini as the murderer of Matteotti, Colton is edifying. Ibid., p. 222 and L. Blum, *L'histoire jugera* (Montreal, 1943), pp. 73–5.
[19] PRO, FO 371, 19880, C3693/92/62.

that he did not intend to behave towards Italy as a doctrinaire anti-Fascist.[20] Later in June, the French Ambassador in Rome delivered guarantees that the Blum Government would not raise questions affecting internal politics or party matters.[21]Blum's initial position, then, was nuanced. The election manifestos of the Front populaire had pledged it to active pursuit of collective security, based on the League of Nations, and Blum and Delbos in the first weeks of the government publicly elaborated principles for its conduct on foreign policy.[22] But, if a more generous spirit seemed to inform French diplomacy, the government's beginnings did not mark a radical departure from the solutions to the Rhineland and Ethiopian crises already advocated by the General Staff and the Quai d'Orsay, which soon showed themselves supple enough to accommodate the new government's slogans and concerns, such as the defence of allied Czechoslovakia. While lines of opposition were already forming within the government, Blum hesitated to impose his misgivings in such a way as to immediately alter the prescribed course of French policy.

During the government's first month, the General Staff and the Quai d'Orsay advanced a series of memoranda adapting their recommendations to the conditions of June 1936. The General Staff's view of France's strategic possibilities represented a codification of the conclusions Gamelin had drawn from the Rhineland reoccupation. The *Conseil supérieur de la Guerre*, when called upon to examine the politically dictated hypothesis of a German aggression in the west, concluded that France still held the military balance against Germany with the vital proviso of allied help. Anxious at the prospect of an Italo-German rapprochement or an Italian withdrawal into neutrality, which would increase the German forces on France's north-eastern frontier and require it again to cover its Mediterranean and Alpine frontiers, the CSG stressed that it was vital solely from the vantage of the balance of land forces to maintain and consolidate France's military ties with Italy and Poland.[23] The theme of Italy's indispensability figured in a subsequent General Staff note extolling a Central European front, constituted with Italian aid, which would realise the encirclement of Germany and

[20] J. Barros, *Betrayal from Within* (New Haven, 1969), p. 120; Shorrock, *From Ally to Enemy*, pp. 180–1.

[21] G. Ciano, *Ciano's Diplomatic Papers*, ed. M. Muggeridge (London, 1948), p. 7.

[22] L. Blum, *Populaire*, 23 September 1935, 11 January 1936.

[23] DDF II, 2, no. 357.

give France the largest possibilities for manoeuvre. The General Staff's awareness of the dangers of immobility behind the Maginot line, conspicuous at the time of the reoccupation, was again visible. The EMA suggested to the new government that French units acting as liaison between Italian and Petite Entente forces, under the Franco-Italian military arrangements of June 1935, would assure the wartime functioning of the Central European front: 'The arrival of French units with minimum delay in Central Europe... would be very advantageous to the rapid organisation of a coherent allied front, and eventually for the salvation of Czechoslovakia.'[24]

The writer noted complacently that the Italian authorities had recently reaffirmed the 1935 military accords. On the eve of the Front populaire's advent, the Italians, protesting against the continuance of sanctions after their victory over Ethiopia, had partially mobilised at the French frontier and threatened to denounce the 1935 accords pertaining to the defence of Austria. The EMA was desperately anxious lest Germany profit from the situation to settle its accounts with Czechoslovakia.[25] The tension ended when Gamelin sent a cordial justification of French sanctions policy to Badoglio, to whom he confirmed the force of the June 1935 accords and declared his optimism for the future of bilateral relations. Gamelin's response had been vetted by Léger, who had insisted on a rapid French response.[26]

Implementation of the military's design to forge an Italo-Polish front to save Czechoslovakia rested with the Quai d'Orsay. Its cluster of specific recommendations for liquidating the Ethiopian conflict – League reform and Italian participation in negotiations for Danubian, Mediterranean, and new Locarno pacts – dated from the abortive compromise peace negotiations carried on by Delbos's predecessor, Flandin, in April and May 1936. Although their multilateral orientation was strengthened, Blum's advent did not substantively alter its recommendations.

The conviction that the Rhineland reoccupation signified the Reich's intention to attack in the east led the Political Directorate to

[24] DDF II, 2, no. 419.
[25] Schw., 1SC2 Dr9, 3 June; the atmosphere in Berlin was said to be reminiscent of that before 7 March. Ibid., 10 June 1936.
[26] FNSP, Papiers Daladier, 1DA7/Dr2/sdr b, Badoglio-Gamelin Correspondence, 10, 15 June; Gamelin-Daladier letter, 15 June 1936; Gamelin, *Servir*, II, pp. 223–4. For additional evidence of the alacrity of Léger (usually depicted as violently anti-Italian) to reassure Rome in this period, Shorrock, *From Ally to Enemy*, pp. 171–2, 180.

consider a Danubian pact the most important of its series of multilateral pacts.[27] It aspired to resuscitate negotiations for a Danubian pact in which Germany would have a place, and in which Italy would assume protection of what Paris saw as its regional interests, as the guarantor of Czechoslovakia as well as of Austria. Since May, the Political Directorate had advocated obtaining Italian support for League reforms very much conditioned by the Ethiopian crisis. Economic sanctions by all League members were to be made an adjunct to, rather than a substitute for, regional military action, which was alone held to be decisive.[28]

It had been argued in Paris since Barthou's day that, if a solution to the Austrian problem was necessary to Central European stability, the destruction of Czechoslovakia, which might well precede an Anschluss, would prove fatal to Austria. Italian guarantees to Czechoslovakia had been prominent among the Central European *quid pro quo* advanced by Flandin in his overtures to Mussolini, and they were again sought by the Political Directorate in mid June: 'It is important for us to know if the Italian government admits in particular that the problem of Czech security equally concerns it, because Germany, by destroying Czechoslovakia, could outflank Austria and gain a foothold on the Danube.' The advice of the Rome Embassy after the reoccupation, to set aside temporarily the delicate matter of Italian undertakings to Czechoslovakia, in order to obtain solid Italian guarantees to Austria, was being disregarded. The Political Directorate did concede Italy's chronic lack of enthusiasm for a Danubian pact, but it hoped that changed conditions since the outbreak of the Ethiopian war, notably the progress of German influence in Yugoslavia and Austria, might encourage Italy to support a Danubian settlement.

After the experience of Flandin's bilateral soundings in Rome, the Political Directorate did not advocate a direct approach to Italy, reckoning that Rome would respond 'by several vague, apparently satisfactory formulae, adding that its position could not be defined until after the end of sanctions...'. Anxious to extract major Italian guarantees in return for the ending of sanctions, the Political Directorate sought a tactical middle way in dealing with the triumphant and notoriously self-regarding Fascist régime: 'we must not give Rome the impression that we absolutely need Italy: this

[27] PRO, FO 371, 19899, C2547/4/18.
[28] DDF II, 2, no. 220; MAE, Papiers Massigli, 'Réforme de la SDN', 13 June 1936.

would be the means of increasing its claims; but it is none the less important that the Italian Government cannot claim that the policy of the French Government minimises the importance of its collaboration in surmounting the present crisis'. The Political Directorate considered that France, having justified its tortuous 'politique de ménagement' towards Italy throughout the Ethiopian conflict by the necessity of preserving possibilities of cooperation between Italy and the League, had to keep Italy present at Geneva and obtain binding assurance of Rome's willingness to join in strengthening the League's authority. It urged that the broad lines of French policy be communicated to Rome before the League met, to indicate the direction of French action in Geneva.[29] Lamb-like Italian behaviour after the early June military flurry made such talk of cooperation not farfetched. According to Ciano, the Italian Foreign Minister, Italy would not ask for recognition of its Ethiopian annexation, but would treat Ethiopia as if it were a country under the mandate of the League of Nations.[30]

In order to ensure a constructive end to sanctions, the Political Directorate looked to a Mediterranean pact, a project originally designed by Barthou, and now presented as almost universally beneficial. To reduce Anglo-Italian tension by assuring Italian security, thus preventing Italy from turning to Germany, the pact would also dissipate the frantic alarm of the small Balkan states, particularly Yugoslavia, without France having to contract obligations in the Mediterranean greater than Britain's. Active Italian support was also sought for the Political Directorate's position in what was described as the unresolved crisis opened by Germany's violation of Locarno, the diplomats being less optimistic than Blum with regard to German intentions.[31]

The Quai d'Orsay then sought a global settlement of the Ethiopian conflict, one which would impinge on virtually all other aspects of the broader European settlement to include Germany desired by the Blum Government. But, as throughout its Ethiopian ordeal, it was hampered by the difficulties of coordinating action with London. In unauthorised remarks on 10 June, which took members of his government by surprise, Neville Chamberlain, the

---

[29] MAE, Papiers Massigli, 'Italo-Ethiopie', 15 June 1936.
[30] Schw., 1SC2 Dr9, 26 June 1936.
[31] MAE, Papiers Massigli, 'Italo-Ethiopie', 15 June 1936; DDF II, 2, no. 461; 3, nos. 278, 314.

Chancellor of the Exchequer, called the demand of the League of Nations Union for increased sanctions 'the very midsummer of madness'.[32] Not only did the brusque initiative by Baldwin's heir-designate signal an important shift in the British attitude, but, on 11 June, Anthony Eden, the Foreign Secretary, refused an invitation to meet with Delbos and Blum.[33] In pleading that Eden reconsider, Léger insisted that everything depended on joint Franco-British action. The Political Directorate was concerned that, once the British Government formally announced its intention to raise sanctions, it would be impossible to settle in advance an Italian *quid pro quo* without revealing a Franco-British divergence, which Rome could exploit. Léger voiced to the British his disquiet over indications of an Italo-German rapprochement – a recurrent theme for French diplomats in the coming weeks – although he still claimed that Italy favoured cooperation with France and Britain.[34]

These exchanges were cut short by Eden's 18 June speech in the House of Commons voicing the government's support for cessation of sanctions, without abrogating the assurances which HMG had given various Mediterranean powers in late 1935. Eden's remarks were interpreted in Rome as indicating the constitution of a durable entente against Italy. To Delbos, they seemed to manifest 'a concern to pursue a policy going directly against the effort of détente [the British Government] seemed to have in mind in advocating the raising of sanctions'. But, lest its silence be interpreted as criticism of the positive part of the British decision, the French Government followed suit a day later in raising sanctions. Behind a public show of good grace, Delbos was indignant at Eden's declaration in the Commons that he had repeatedly tried in vain to learn the French Government's views.[35] Although the way London had signalled an end to sanctions gravely prejudiced the Quai d'Orsay's ability to obtain guarantees from Italy, the Political Directorate's 15 June recommendations on the conditions for liquidation of the crisis were taken up by the new government in its foreign policy declaration, read to the French legislature on 23 June.

With the Quai d'Orsay's policy of regional accords involving Italy in jeopardy, debate on the issue of how best to defend Czechoslovakia emerged in the new *Comité permanent de la Défense nationale*. For

[32] MAE, Papiers Massigli, 'Violation de la Rhénanie', 2 July 1936.
[33] DDF II, 2, no. 289.
[34] PRO, FO 371, 19857, C4355/1/17; DDF II, 2, no. 324.
[35] DDF II, 2, nos. 311, 328, 329.

the first time governmental debate set sharply against an Italo-Polish front the air and military support being offered by the USSR. Visiting Paris on his way to Geneva at the end of June, Litvinov called for bilateral staff talks.[36] Within the government the chief proponent of a Soviet military alliance was the Air Minister, Pierre Cot. Cot developed an ambitious strategy for the air force, which, freed from the tactical apron strings of the army, would operate with the technical and industrial collaboration of a host of friendly states, among whom Czechoslovakia and the USSR were prominent. Cot linked Czechoslovakia – 'the only way of being able to reach Berlin' – and the Soviet air factories, which, out of range of German bombing, could work full throttle in a conflict to supply the Petite Entente.[37]

For the General Staff, Cot and Litvinov's pressures had an explosive domestic charge. Cot's enthusiasm for the USSR was familiar to the military from his 1933 tour of duty at the Air Ministry, but in 1936 Cot had a disturbing new constituency. Blum's governing coalition of Radicals and Socialists depended on Communist backing in the *Chambre des députés*. When the spring 1936 elections had sparked spontaneous strikes, taking the trade unions and French Communist party by surprise, the military and Defence Minister Edouard Daladier saw the hand of the Comintern and predicted the extension of Communist-organised strikes to the French arms factories.[38] Externally as well, the EMA regarded the Franco-Soviet connection as fraught with menace. Fledgling Franco-Soviet association had provided Hitler with a highly effective pretext for reoccupying the Rhineland, and the Belgians with a motive for the repudiation of their domestically divisive treaty with France.

In the post-reoccupation miasma of diminished prestige, an undefined German threat, and internal uncertainty, the military was even more inclined than in the past to keep the USSR at a distance.[39] In keeping with Gamelin's position that the army should

---

[36] Schw., 1SC2 Dr9, 24 June 1936.   [37] DDF II, 2, no. 369.
[38] Schw., 1SC2 Dr9, 25 June. Gamelin does not figure among the vocally anti-Bolshevik generals of Schweisguth's journal. Faced with the social turbulence of early June, his only recorded comment was that his colleagues should give an example of silence in all domains. Ibid., 'Rapport', 9 June 1936. His mannered, post-war account of a June 1936 meeting with Blum (*Servir* II, pp. 222–4) should be contrasted with the private assessment of Blum as a 'bogus intellectual' ('un grand esprit faux') in his journal on the eve of the war, SHA, Fonds Gamelin, 1K224/9, 6 October 1939. At Riom, Gamelin circulated a memorandum which blasted 'the criminal demagoguery of the Front populaire... which dragged us to the bottom of the abyss'. FNSP, Papiers Blum, 3BL3 Dr1, p. 21.
[39] DDF II, 2, no. 369.

play its traditional role as the silent servant of the state (*la grande muette*) *vis-à-vis* its new civilian masters, it did not immediately manifest the full strength of its opposition to Cot's plans for Soviet military entente, to which it believed the government as a whole to be sympathetic. The military relied instead on the diplomats, seeking to disarm Cot and to block substantive exchanges between Delbos, Blum, and Litvinov through the Quai d'Orsay.

Schweisguth, Gamelin's *sous-chef* charged with allied relations, accordingly prepared a note for Delbos's services on the inopportunity of Soviet military conversations, along with a request that Delbos postpone discussion on the subject with Litvinov. Schweisguth's note reiterated the General Staff's belief that their result would be to throw Poland into Germany's arms and give Hitler, under the pretext of encirclement, a motive for aggression. The day before the CPDN meeting at which Cot was to present his plan for inter-allied air cooperation, Schweisguth met with the Quai d'Orsay's Political Director, Bargeton, who equally deplored Cot's partisanship of a Soviet military alliance 'whatever the disadvantages might be'. Bargeton, however, tested the weak spots in the General's arguments. If there was danger of war, should Soviet collaboration not be assured; if this collaboration would be slow and uncertain, should it not be organised in peacetime? Schweisguth's response was unhesitating. Collaboration could not be accelerated, given the backwardness of Central European communications, the impossibility of basing an accord on an a priori violation by the USSR of the countries between it and Germany; and the EMA's certainty that Hitler, alleging encirclement, would destroy even a preparatory accord comprising France, Czechoslovakia, and Poland before it could be realised.[40]

In a meeting of the CPDN on 26 June, Cot not only pressed for the creation of an interallied front, but advocated the dispatch of a French mission to the politically sensitive Soviet autumn manoeuvres, slated to be held close to the Polish border. Soviet invitations to the manoeuvres had been accompanied by pressures for early staff talks. Moreover, the Blum Government's solicitude for Czechoslovakia, as demonstrated by the decision to send aviation materials to Prague, appeared to the military to be tinged with a dangerous level of Sovietophilia when taken in the context of Cot's

[40] Schw., 1SC2 Dr9, 24 June, 2 July 1936.

planning, which would make the infrastructure of Czech aviation immediately available to the Soviets.

In the June meeting of the CPDN, Gamelin confined his opposition to the dispatch of a French military mission to the Soviet manoeuvres to the gruff observation: 'The French problem depends essentially on alliances and... Poland will be able to come to the aid of Czechoslovakia quicker than anyone.' Behind the scenes, the military tirelessly continued to mobilise against a Soviet rapprochement.[41] In the tense summer of 1936, Gamelin redoubled his attachment to Italy and Poland and it was this which prompted Alexis Léger's later observation that the military more than the diplomats had held most tightly to the eastern alliances.

Fierce internal disagreement over the best means to pursue the Front populaire's policy of loyalty to its Central European obligations, notably towards Czechoslovakia, was to dog the government during its year of existence. In this nascent atmosphere of frustration, caused by setbacks in its policy of conciliation towards Italy and military-diplomatic resistance aroused by the designs of Pierre Cot and Litvinov, the Blum Government assessed the ill-effects of a June 1936 voyage through South-Eastern Europe by Schacht, the head of the Reichsbank.

[41] DDF II, 2, no. 369; Schw., 1SC2 Dr9, 27 June, 'Rapport', 30 June, 2 July 1936.

CHAPTER 3

Blum and the quandaries of external economic policy: the Schacht voyage

SCHACHT AND THE GERMAN COMMERCIAL-ARMS THREAT

Hjalmar Schacht toured Austria, Yugoslavia, Bulgaria, and Hungary for ten days in mid June 1936. His voyage caused Paris to take fright at the Third Reich's progress throughout Danubia in making real the traditional German dream of Mitteleuropa, while intensifying its rearmament.

Schacht's sales strategy exalted the natural complementarity between industrial Germany and his agrarian hosts. His hard sell was intended to foster a German commercial monopoly in Danubia, by the 'farming' of national economies through intensive purchasing in sectors related to its own war production, and through its 'payments' for Danubian goods in technicians and machinery further developing these sectors. Schacht enhanced Germany's commercial attractiveness by belittling the Italian markets' capacity for absorption, and by inveighing against 'exploitative' French and British capital. Speaking of the Reich's respect for the political integrity of the small states, he presented the Reich's economic collaboration as more productive than the hold of other foreign capital, which impinged on their independence by depriving national economies of important profits from the exportation of their raw materials. With some success, he turned the unimportance of German investments in Central Europe into a polemical weapon against the more orthodox position of trade with strong currency countries.[1]

The Yugoslavs, on whom Schacht concentrated his efforts, were a

---

[1] DDF II, 2, nos. 300, 302, 317, 404, 418; SHA, 'Yougoslavie', Béthouart dispatch, 26 June 1936; P. Marguerat, *Le IIIe Reich et le pétrole roumain 1938–40* (Leiden/Geneva, 1977), pp. 29–65, 87; A. Teichova, *An Economic Background to Munich* (Cambridge, 1974), pp. 336–77; J. Freymond, *Le IIIe Reich et la réorganisation économique de l'Europe 1940–1942* (Leiden/Geneva, 1974), p. 86.

particularly receptive audience. For some months, Béthouart, the very active French military attaché in Belgrade, had been attentive to a xenophobic press campaign and a governmental policy of nationalisation directed against foreign enterprises, most of which enterprises were dominated by French capital. He saw in this campaign the hand of the Reich, which, having relatively slight investments in Yugoslavia, had an interest in evicting French industry in order to replace it once the Yugoslavs' inability to manage alone became evident.[2] Yugoslavia was gradually adapting its economy to that of Germany, its best commercial client, supplying the Reich with raw materials – copper, iron, chromium, and bauxite – as well as agricultural products. In 1934–6, its bauxite exports to Germany increased five-fold, and in the same period Germany doubled its imports of Yugoslav copper, much of it coming from mines controlled by French capital.[3] The same phenomenon was repeated in Roumania, where the Reich systematically encouraged large-scale soya production, of important military use as an ingredient in glycerine. Under the auspices of March 1935 commercial accords, a domestic firm with strong German participation offered prices more than 33 per cent above those on the world market. Germany, as its only foreign purchaser, enjoyed from the start a monopoly of the glycerine crop.[4]

The mechanism behind the Reich's commercial penetration in Central Europe was fashioned from the combined influences of the world economic crisis and rearmament. The complementarity of German and Danubian markets, which had maintained their trade at a high level before 1929, had been reinforced by the economic crisis which caused Danubian agricultural prices to plummet. As politically sympathetic or allied countries such as France applied their protectionist policies more rapidly, the countries in the region were left little choice in markets. Nazi economic policy capitalised on this opportunity, approaching the stricken agrarian states of South-

---

[2] SHA, Béthouart dispatch, 2 September 1935; E. A. Radice, 'General Characteristics of the Region between the Wars', in M. C. Kaser and E. A. Radice (eds.), *The Economic History of Eastern Europe 1919–1975*, I (Oxford, 1985), p. 64; Weinberg, *Foreign Policy*, I, pp. 325–6. [3] DDF II, 2, no. 418.
[4] SHA, 'Roumanie AE', d'Ormesson dispatches, 21 March, 9 April 1936. The Germans often reserved their purchases for products of military value. They were unwilling, for example, to pay high prices for the bulk of Roumanian cereals, buying instead from Argentina and their preferred partners in the Danubian basin, Hungary and Yugoslavia. Marguerat, *Le IIIe Reich et le pétrole*, pp. 76–80.

East Europe with the novel suggestion that its primary aim was to import the goods it required rather than to maximise its exports. The attractiveness of the German market for the Danubian producers of raw materials was increased by the higher prices it paid, prices which reflected the increased demands of its rearmament sector.

After the failure of the World Economic Conference in the autumn of 1933, expedients which had been forced on Germany by the economic crisis were raised to a system, with a firm bilateral orientation towards regions that it could dominate commercially. Continued disintegration of the German domestic economy meant that the large commercial concessions made in early accords to woo Hungary and Yugoslavia came to be regarded in Berlin as a luxury. When rearmament emptied its currency accounts and necessitated exchange controls, Germany offered payments in merchandise rather than currency to its customer states, themselves forced by the crisis to impose currency restrictions and payment moratoria.

The practice of forced indebtedness, whereby massive purchases were paid for by a system of frozen marks in Berlin, lent to German trade in Danubia a pattern of imports much in excess of exports. Employing what French observers in Central Europe called 'the triangular system', the Reich also speculated on its own currency in the barter of finished products for Danubian raw materials, some of which were re-exported. The Bucharest Legation ventured the opinion that this speculation would eventually allow Germany to finance its own exportation. To entice suppliers despite 'this formidable entanglement', Germany offered large tariff reductions, and showed a willingness to sacrifice immediate profit rarely evident in French dealings in Central Europe. Danubian trade figures were eloquent as to the economic inroads made by the Reich. In the five years from 1931 to 1935, German imports from Czechoslovakia rose from 15 per cent to 22 per cent; those from Hungary from 12 per cent to 26 per cent; those from Greece from 22 per cent to 28 per cent; and those from Bulgaria from 29 per cent to 48 per cent. Schacht's voyage brought home to Paris that the Reich had been able to utilise even its financial difficulties to take first place in trade with all the Danubian countries.[5]

---

[5] DDF II, 2, no. 418; Freymond, *Le IIIe Reich et la réorganisation*, pp. 63–77; Radice, 'General Characteristics', p. 61; Hans-Jürgen Schroeder, 'Les relations économiques franco-allemandes de 1936 à 1939' (15. Deutsch-französisches Historikerkolloquium, Bonn, 1978), pp. 21–3; SHA, 'Roumanie AE', d'Ormesson dispatch, 9 April 1936.

FRENCH PERCEPTIONS OF THE GERMAN COMMERCIAL-ARMS THREAT/CONSTRAINING PATTERNS OF FRENCH ECONOMIC ACTIVITY

Historical debate on the regionalisation of Nazi trade policy has focussed on the domestic constraints which generated it and on the slight place in fact held by the Danubian states in overall German trade.[6] Contemporary French perception included an awareness that the Reich's aggressive external economic policy exaggerated weaknesses rooted in the depression, but a vital aspect of Paris's alarm came from the Reich's skill at turning its paucity of means into a bid for monopoly, its fearsome ingenuity in using commerce to create a magnifying effect from small, unsatisfactory resources.[7] The absence of a profit motive in the Reich's regimented commercial activities abroad gave it an obvious advantage. A substantial portion of its commercial proceeds went not into the limbo of a firm's portfolio, but was ploughed back into further commercial activities in the client states, or, as French legations observed with growing disquiet, into popular agitation and propaganda.

In July 1936, the Quai d'Orsay's Assistant Political Director, René Massigli, produced for Delbos a major memorandum on the consequences of the German economic penetration, with Schacht's voyage as its centrepiece.[8] Massigli's concern was Germany's adroit combination of preparation for war with realisation of its political aims in the east after the Rhineland reoccupation. In his view, the most disconcerting aspect of Schacht's voyage was the link which the President of the Reichsbank extolled between intensified commercial relations and the purveyance of arms.

Since implementation of its rearmament programme in 1935, Germany had offered payment in arms to its creditors. Such payment for raw materials, themselves ear-marked for rearmament, worked to maintain the German war machine. Paris knew that German attempts to establish a commerce–arms nexus had met with

[6] See, e.g., Marguerat, *Le IIIe Reich et le pétrole* and D. Kaiser, *Economic Diplomacy and the Origins of the Second World War* (Princeton, 1980).

[7] See, e.g., a 27 August 1936 report from the French financial attaché in Berlin, Finances B31.483: 'The Reichsbank President has shown himself to be, beyond doubt, a remarkable technician, incredibly flexible, not tied to any doctrine…able to draw on the very weaknesses of the Reich in the best German interests. The mark was collapsing on the external markets: he channelled the losses in currency, and creating several categories of depreciated marks, he used them to facilitate the placement of German goods on foreign markets, thanks to a special fund for dumping.'   [8] DDF II, 2, no. 418.

considerable success with two members of the Balkan Entente, Turkey and Greece, where Schacht's stay resulted in orders for war materials worth three-quarters of the German commercial debt. In Belgrade, Schacht issued a press statement which referred sympathetically to attempts by the South-East European states to develop industries meeting the needs of their rearmament.[9]

The danger of these German proposals was plain. In the terse phrase of the French military attaché in Belgrade: 'One does not buy one's arms from a possible enemy.'[10] Acceptance of the German offers would lead to further contacts, for replenishment and spare parts, and eventually to technical collaboration between staffs. Once on this course, Massigli asked, where would rapprochement with Germany stop? He alerted Delbos thus to the gravity of the threat posed by Schacht's voyage:

Thus the continuity of German policy is affirmed and defined. Following a plan conceived after continuous and powerful effort, the Reich is overturning barriers erected by the treaties and resuming its march eastward. Using its economic power, it is gradually making the Danubian economy complementary to and dependent on its own, and where it sees points of least resistance, it is attempting to break up the cluster of alliances blocking its way.

France's own weak commercial situation in Central Europe had damaging repercussions on the French ability to counteract the new aura of German force and prestige after 7 March.[11] Historically, the pattern of French external economic activity had been a dependence on invisible exports, notably revenues from foreign investments, to offset large commercial deficits. Paris was particularly handicapped by an ostensibly enviable investments' position in Central Europe, which blunted perception of the detrimental effects of its outmoded commercial and industrial structures.

France's inter-war investments in Central Europe were substantial, despite the fact that the structure of its investments had been altered by the 1914–18 war, after which they were primarily directed to London, New York, and the empire. Among foreign investors, France came first in Yugoslavia and Poland (French investors in Russian Poland had been the only ones to escape the revolutionary deluge, as the Poles liked to point out), and second in Roumania and Czechoslovakia. The French also held important

---

[9] Ibid., no. 302; Teichova, *An Economic Background*, p. 214.
[10] SHA, 'Yougoslavie', Béthouart dispatch, 4 June 1936.   [11] See above, p. 90.

investments in Austria.[12] They entrenched themselves by treasury advances for Central European arms purchases and loans on the Paris market related to monetary stabilisation and industrial-isation.[13] Inter-war capital implantation in Central Europe had been directly related to the loss of the Russian market after the Bolshevik Revolution, as well as to appeals in Paris and London by the successor states for funds to dislodge German and Austrian holdings. The most spectacular example of this was Beneš's engineering of the takeover of the Škoda arms works by the French iron and steel combine, Schneider-Creusot, which also acquired interests in Poland, Austria, and Hungary.[14] Before the Herriot Government's capitulation to Anglo-American financial strength after the Ruhr crisis in 1924, successive governments saw in the treaty provisions a means of achieving an economic programme fixed at the end of the war, by which the control of raw materials would play an essential role in maintaining French predominance. Paris overrated the possibilities offered by the 1919 treaties to supplant Austrian and particularly German economic influence. Its 'macro-economic and political preoccupations' were compromised in part because indispensable economic relations with Germany made Poland and Czechoslovakia cautious in the use of their rights under the treaties.[15]

Politically, the most significant fact about this privileged invest-ments position in Central Europe was that the French failed to underwrite the larger economic and political benefits of their investments by enlarging their commerce in Central Europe. Georges Soutou's seminal work on French external investments in the 1920s suggests that this failure cannot be attributed to a lack of awareness of the 'multiplying effect' which investments could produce on commerce by conferring potential control of key economic sectors. The central administration advocated a strategy of concentration in sectors, particularly banking, in order to give French investors 'the role of leader for an entire industrial sector... in

---

[12] Duroselle, *La décadence*, pp. 220, 233, 238; Teichova, *An Economic Background*, pp. 14–29; Soutou, 'L'impérialisme', pp. 229–33, 238.

[13] Soutou, 'L'impérialisme', pp. 221–5; Marguerat, *Le IIIe Reich et le pétrole*, pp. 65–6. 1931–2 governmental figures for nominal capital of loans placed in France ranked indebtedness of these states in descending order: Yugoslavia, Roumania, Czechoslovakia, and Poland. MAE, Papiers Tardieu, carton 693, 'Accords danubiens', undated, 'Rapports finan-ciers...'.

[14] Teichova, *An Economic Background*, pp. 25–6, 195–7; Soutou, 'L'impérialisme', pp. 235, 238–9.   [15] Soutou, 'L'impérialisme', pp. 225–35.

such a way as to induce commercial benefits'. The government also tried to link to its political treaties and treasury advances commercial accords advantageous to France. For example, in 1921 Paris insisted on protecting its investments in Poland by commercial accords onerous for Warsaw, and to which ratification of the bilateral political alliance of the same year was for a time subordinated.[16] The strategy of concentration by sector broke down in part because banks and other investors often preferred to diversify their participation, which, while more profitable, did not ensure the majorities deemed to be in the national interest.[17]

The inadequacies of French commerce in Central Europe were greatly increased by the world economic crisis, which in France took the form of a protracted stagnation, due in part to a refusal to devalue the franc, coupled with a domestic agricultural crisis. The predominantly agrarian French economy had traditionally lacked complementarity with the Danubian and East Central European economies. The protectionism which France adopted in the face of the world crisis strangled its scant trade with the allies. In 1931, in an attempt artificially to maintain domestic prices and so attract peasant votes in the 1932 elections, André Tardieu, as Minister of Agriculture, reinforced the Méline tariff system (1892), particularly where it affected grains and animal products, key Central European exports. A highly restrictive quota system, it was based on percentages rather than quantities. Because the colonies were exempt, colonial trade almost doubled by the mid 1930s. As a direct corollary, foreign agricultural purchases fell by more than one half.[18] The reinforcement of the French quota system in the wake of the world crisis created a rare unanimity of opinion within the allied camp. States such as Yugoslavia and Czechoslovakia sought to maintain French imports during the crisis, not only in order to facilitate debt repayment, but also in the hope of stimulating French purchases. To their embitterment, these hopes were in vain. Figures of Yugoslav exports to France demonstrate the virtual collapse of the

---

[16] Soutou, 'L'impérialisme', pp. 221–2 and note 7; 231–5.

[17] Soutou ascribes original adoption of this strategy based on the multiplying effect of investments to a desire to replicate Germany's highly successful pre-1914 strategy of penetrating foreign banking systems, which Paris supposed to be sufficient to lead in time to growing commercial imbrication with the host country. The French adaptation neglected important realities of Germany's pre-1914 commercial position, notably the richness of the German market for Danubian exporters and the superiority of German industrial potential, as well as the relatively high level of French prices.

[18] A. Sauvy and A. Hirsch, *Histoire économique de la France entre les deux guerres*, 4 vols. (Paris, 1965–75), II, pp. 385–6, 448–57; IV, pp. 9–34; Kaiser, *Economic Diplomacy*, pp. 41–2.

French market: purchases of 156,927,000 francs in 1930 dwindled to 19,655,000 francs in the first nine months of 1935, before the application of sanctions against Italy further disrupted the Yugoslav economy.[19]

From the onset of the world economic crisis, the Central European states were also buffeted by the withdrawal of foreign short-term loans, the inherently erratic form assumed by much post-war investment. French money did not return as the crisis levelled off. Throughout Central Europe, but perhaps especially in Poland, French investment came to be resented as much for its stagnation, which made the allied balance of payments negative, as for its proportions. Because the economic crisis ended French capital flow abroad, the Poles attached great importance to the transfer back to Poland of the savings of the sizeable population of Polish immigrant labourers swelling the French labour force since 1918. A 1934 letter from Polish war veterans to their French counterparts referred to these savings as 'the only heading in the Franco-Polish balance of trade which is favourable to Poland'. Treatment of these workers – made redundant by the crisis, out of proportion to their numbers among foreign workers, and subject to the misery and expense of sudden expulsion from France – rankled with the Poles.[20]

Charges of exploitation against the French investments position were also sharpened by the crisis, quite independently of German propagandising. The most notorious example was, again, a Polish one. The Zyrardów textile factory, one of the most important enterprises in Poland, came into the possession of the French industrialist Marcel Boussac immediately after the First World War, under the favourable conditions attached to ex-enemy possessions. What the Poles considered Boussac's grasping administration of Zyrardów gave rise to charges of fraud designed to evict Boussac's interests. Interminable negotiations and legal proceedings of unusual bitterness degenerated into almost open warfare, when the Swiss-born director of the factory was shot dead in the street, and a Polish administrator of Zyrardów driven to suicide by the virulence of the governmental press.[21] The Zyrardów affair, like the situation of the Polish workers in France, blighted bilateral relations for years.

[19] SHA, 'Roumanie', Delmas dispatch, 12 January 1936.
[20] Assemblée Nationale, 21 November 1934, annex: 'Lettre ouverte des anciens combattants polonais', pp. 21–2.
[21] Laroche, *La Pologne*, pp. 174–7; Wandycz, *Twilight*, pp. 124–5, 233, 345; A. Polonsky, *Politics in Independent Poland* (Oxford, 1972), pp. 365–8; L. Noël, *La Pologne entre deux mondes* (Paris, 1984), pp. 163–75.

A seasoned observer has characterised French external economic policy in the 1930s by comparing it to the Maginot line: 'This protectionist orientation held in all areas and is particularly well illustrated by the conception and construction of the Maginot line. The same psychology also existed in the economic realm...'[22] But as with the Maginot line, France's external economic policies were meant to have a multilateral component. Confronted with the devastation of Central Europe by the world crisis, Paris vetoed the 1931 plan for an Austro-German customs union, and attempted to act through leadership of international economic conferences. This sterile period encouraged, as has been seen, a reliance on Italy to supplant German commercial influence in Central Europe, and so further inhibited France's already small Danubian commerce.[23]

After the 17 April 1934 note, Barthou and the Quai d'Orsay began overtly political negotiations with Rome which eventually took the form of bilateral entente, intended by Paris to serve as a lure for a Danubian economic and political stabilisation. The economic element in these interlocking negotiations was to be a Franco-Italian sponsored merger of the two rival economic blocs in the region, the Petite Entente and the Rome Protocols groups. The merger was to be along the lines advocated by the economic conference held at Stresa in 1932: the extension by Germany and Italy of unilateral preferences to facilitate the absorption of Danubian agricultural surpluses without themselves being given equivalent customs preferences in Danubian markets. (At the 1932 conference, France and Britain had been asked to make financial contributions to the beleaguered Danubian states.) International efforts from 1932 to 1935 to promote a Danubian economic organisation were fruitless. During this period, France alone observed the principle of unilateral preference in its commercial treaties. It struck a virtuous pose in response to Central European complaints of the smallness of its purchases by pointing to the fact that France did not ask reciprocal privileges. The Reich in contrast rejected a Danubian preferential system as profiting Czechoslovakia, the most industrialised of the Danubian states, while it flooded Central European markets with its barter trade based on frozen marks.

The perils of this attachment to unilateral preference and the accompanying reliance on Italy to take up the commercial cudgels

[22] Pierre Mendès France, letter to the author, 24 October 1977.
[23] See above, pp. 19–20.

in Central Europe *vis-à-vis* the Reich were recognised in Paris.[24] The Quai d'Orsay's Political Directorate, aware of the damage being done by France's external commercial policies, struggled to maintain a commercial presence in Central Europe by even the slightest level of agricultural imports. In a letter to the recalcitrant Ministry of Finance after the Reich's conclusion of important commercial agreements with Hungary and Yugoslavia, Robert Coulondre, charged with the Quai d'Orsay's commercial policy, deplored 'our increasingly delicate situation in Danubian and Balkan Europe'. Alluding to strenuous German and Italian efforts in Danubia, he warned against leaving the impression of a French attitude 'very close to complete neglect'.[25] By and large, however, the Quai d'Orsay worked within the domestic, political, and economic constraints imposed upon it. Throughout 1936, its hopes were pinned on negotiations with Italy, which economically as well as militarily came to be seen as something of a panacea for France's ailing Central European ties. Berlin's exploitation of the rivalry of the Danubian economic blocs and of Franco-Italian discord during the Ethiopian crisis, rather than the inadequacies of French commercial policy, provided the Political Directorate's standard explanation for the Reich's growing centrality to Danubian economic life.[26]

TWO CASE STUDIES: YUGOSLAVIA AND ROUMANIA[27]

Of particular concern after the Rhineland reoccupation, the French situation of a stagnant external investment position coupled with negligible commerce cruelly redounded on its ability to supply its Central European allies with arms. At the time of Schacht's voyage, the clearest data on Paris's mishandling of the linkages between

---

[24] René Massigli murmured a protest in early 1933 when he transmitted to a departmental colleague the Czechoslovaks' fear that Paris's orientation, in favouring German and Italian commercial activities in Central Europe, would precipitate an Anschluss. If France, by espousing unilateral preference agreements and the establishment of quotas, abandoned the most favoured nation clause, a guarantee of multilateral trade, other states would do the same. International trade would collapse and the resulting proliferation of bilateral, rather than unilateral, preferential accords would bring an Anschluss closer. MAE, Papiers Massigli, 'Affaires de l'Europe centrale', Massigli-Coulondre letter, 16 February 1933.
[25] Finances, F30:2081, 7 June 1934.
[26] MAE, Papiers Massigli, 'Affaires de l'Europe centrale', 20 July 1936.
[27] The related case of Poland will be considered in chapter 4 under the heading of the Franco-Polish arms negotiations of 1936.

indebtedness, commerce, and arms sales came from Yugoslavia, the ally with the greatest distrust of Italy and 'the most sensitive spot' of the German commercial onslaught.[28]

Yugoslavia

The Yugoslav experience of the world crisis followed a standard Danubian pattern: proliferation of protectionist barriers, increased indebtedness, and difficulties in maintaining requisite levels of imported manufactured goods, all caused by a fall in world agricultural prices, the flight of short-term foreign loans, and participation in international conferences which brought little relief. An international conference indeed suppressed the reparations payments due to Yugoslavia from Germany.[29] The remedies suggested by French financial experts were classic: a balanced budget and the restoration of confidence by obtaining currency for payments abroad.[30] After a Treasury advance in 1931 and the concession of enlarged import quotas to Yugoslavia in 1932, the principal French succour was provided by debt adjustment – a moratorium on payments, debt reduction, and currency arrangements – inexpensive measures when France was still relatively unscathed by the crisis.[31] As a corollary, Yugoslavia signed accords with French investors in 1933 establishing technical financial collaboration between the two governments. A recovery fund in the Yugoslav central bank was instituted, of which a portion was reserved for foreign debt servicing in the national currency, and the rest for budgetary and monetary redress. As several of Yugoslavia's neighbours had suspended debt payments without the funds liberated being consecrated to national recovery, Paris regarded the technical agreements as a victory, but the Yugoslavs found the collaboration oppressive.[32]

The establishment of technical collaboration by Paris was related to its 1933 decision to institute clearing in trade with Yugoslavia. Franco-Yugoslav trade was much smaller than French trade with

[28] MAE, Papiers Massigli, 'Affaires de l'Europe centrale', 20 July 1936.
[29] Finances, F30:2080, Press summary, 9 May 1933; Naggiar dispatch, 29 January 1934; H. Raupach, 'The Impact of the Great Depression on Eastern Europe', *Journal of Contemporary History*, vol. 4, no. 4, October 1969, pp. 75–86.
[30] Finances, F30:2079, Note, 23 March 1932.
[31] Ibid., dispatch, 1 August; Note, 16 July 1932.
[32] Ibid., Notes, 4 August 1934; 8 November; letters from Banque de France inspectors, Gaudibert and Bolgert, 9 February, 14 June 1935.

Poland, Czechoslovakia, or Roumania, and the French application of clearing, conceived in terms of the balance of payments, further sacrificed commerce to a financially orthodox programme of retrenchment and debt repayment.[33] Diminished commerce in its turn limited the capability to repay debts and this deterred new French capital activities, with disastrous effect. By 1934, as German economic expansion began, the Quai d'Orsay actively discouraged investments and work by French enterprises in Yugoslavia, given the country's payments difficulties.[34]

The constraints imposed by French external economic policies were blatant: 'If there is no dispute of a financial character between France and Yugoslavia, the political and military collaboration of these two states raises on the other hand a financial problem whose solution appears extremely difficult.'[35] When the Yugoslavs requested financial aid in 1933 to buy arms in France, their indebtedness made the favoured means – the grant of a loan guaranteed by the French Government (*l'assurance-crédit*) – problematic. The recent debts moratorium disinclined the Quai d'Orsay to consent to further financial sacrifices, such as a less stringent payments schedule. The Quai d'Orsay's reticence was also the result of its reliance on Italy to dispute the Yugoslav commercial field with Germany. It dreaded arousing Italian resentment by arming the Yugoslavs. By June 1934, however, Barthou's diplomacy for an Italo-Yugoslav entente induced it to favour putting French arms stocks at the Yugoslavs' disposal, provided they proved amenable to a rapprochement with Italy to prevent an Anschluss. Barthou's visit to Belgrade led to an August 1934 decision by the *Conseil des ministres* to cede temporarily artillery and munitions from outmoded French reserves to their lamentably armed ally. The flaws in this compromise solution were such, however, that the problem of Yugoslav rearmament remained in effect to be posed.[36] While recognising the

---

[33] Finances, *Tableau général du Commerce et de la Navigation 1935–1937*; Finances, F30:2081, Press Summary, 4 November 1936. Oblivious to the effect on bilateral commerce, the Ministry of Finance originally opposed clearing as likely to diminish resources for servicing the external debt, and favoured urging the Yugoslavs to reduce their imports to a strict minimum. Finances, 2079, Flandin-Tardieu letter, 15 April 1932; 'Programme financier...', March 1933.

[34] Finances, F30:2080, Bargeton letter to Ministry of Finance, 6 February 1934.

[35] Finances, F30:2079, Note by Maxime Robert, 8 October 1934.

[36] For Weygand's parting protest of French policy in supplying arms to its allies as 'niggardly behavior which prejudices our highest interests', Dutailly, *Les problèmes de l'armée*, p. 296.

sizeable financial obstacles, the EMA advised Belgrade to purchase the rest of the war materials they required.[37]

Yugoslav negotiations with the private French arms firms, Brandt and Hotchkiss, were immediately embroiled in difficulty. A Ministry of Finance survey concluded that existing bilateral commerce could not support massive military orders. Commercial clearing, which was maintained by 80 per cent of Yugoslavia's export proceeds, already entailed a backlog of payments, while the remaining 20 per cent was ear-marked for the central bank fund. A settlement outside clearing was rejected as diminishing Yugoslav currency stocks and worsening the country's indebtedness. The sole recommendation made in a note of 8 October was to create a supplementary current of imports from Yugoslavia to allow eventual recourse to an *assurance-crédit*, although the Ministries of Commerce and Agriculture, the guardians of domestic production, would raise every objection.[38]

When Alexander was murdered the following day at Marseilles, the Yugoslavs let it be known that he had come to France to plead for arms. They were embittered by the subsequent French readiness to make debts concessions rather than lend effective arms aid.[39] Given Laval's determination to defuse the Marseilles affair and reach a trilateral entente with Yugoslavia and Italy, French Italophilia was almost certainly a factor. After Laval's visit to Rome in January, he was prepared to mediate in the arms negotiations, but the Yugoslavs considered their terms grasping. Brandt and Hotchkiss refused a proposal for arms payments from the Yugoslav state monopoly on tobacco, a means which would not have substantially altered the French quota system.

Laval sought to break the deadlock by suggesting a supplementary guarantee useful to France's incipient rearmament, Yugoslav copper from the Bor mines. Milan Stoyadinovitch, subsequently Premier of Yugoslavia, began his turbulent relations with Paris when, as Minister of Finance, he declined these supplementary copper sales. He remarked ironically that he could not oblige the Société française des Mines de Bor to sell copper in France. Rather than

[37] DDF I, 7, nos. 297, 318 note, 381; Finances, F30:2097, Note, 8 October 1934.
[38] Finances, F30:2097, 8 October 1934.
[39] Ibid., Note, 22 November; Bargeton letter to the Ministry of Finance, 31 December 1934. The tone of a request for aid to the strained Yugoslav Treasury from the Banque de France's inspector was typical: 'Yugoslavia ... to whom *more than ever* since 9 October we ought to give all our aid – especially when it is so easy!' Ibid., letter, 31 October 1934.

give supplementary copper guarantees, Stoyadinovitch renounced the Hotchkiss order. Paris, however, remained set on copper sales. The Quai d'Orsay asked the military attaché in Belgrade for a discreet study of Yugoslav mineral resources exportable to France in return for future arms purchases.[40] The study revealed that Yugoslavia's ordinary trade with France was so slight that clearing between the two countries had for some time been unable to sustain Yugoslav mineral exports. The drop-off in copper exportation, from which the Reich had directly benefited, had been critical: France, which in 1930 imported 6,400 tons of copper from Yugoslavia, imported none by 1934.

The crux of the French dilemma was clear. Béthouart wrote that, while Yugoslav mineral resources were suitable pledges for future arms transactions, 'it is very evident that one of the primary conditions of maintenance of the Franco-Yugoslav alliance is the reestablishment, and then the development of commercial equilibrium between the two nations. This is not the business of the military, but their action is none the less conditioned by it.'[41]

With some justification, the Yugoslav military reproached Paris that it was more concerned to make Yugoslavia privileged terrain for its industry than to aid an ally. The Brandt negotiations, limited to munitions and patents, lumbered on until May 1935, some twenty months after the original Yugoslav appeal. A tentative tobacco agreement, entailing interest and transport charges amounting to well over 40 per cent of the order, finally broke down over the definition of world tobacco prices, an index only acceptable to the Yugoslavs when computed in relation to the higher prices paid by Germany.[42]

The Reich's commercial offensive had started with bulk purchasing in Yugoslavia. That it burned to supply arms in France's stead was plain even before the imposition of sanctions against Italy threw the Yugoslav market wide open to German commerce. In March 1935, on the pretext of balancing clearing, the Yugoslavs agreed to buy German planes, a decision repeated French démarches did not reverse.[43] Six months later, Béthouart reported a grandiose

[40] DDF I, 7, no. 306; 9, nos. 95 and note 2, 105, 163.

[41] SHA, 'Yougoslavie', Béthouart dispatches, 15 April, 21 May 1935.

[42] Finances, F30:2079, Gaudibert letter, 9 February; SHA, 'Yougoslavie', Béthouart dispatch, 16 March 1935; DDF I, 10, no. 382.

[43] Dispatches in this period contain repeated references to French sales being vitiated by the internecine competition within its arms industry; in contrast, the Germans presented a well

German proposal to furnish Yugoslavia with all the war materials it needed, to be paid for by exportation of agricultural products and cattle.[44] The first significant German breakthrough in the strategic sector, however, came mid-way through the Ethiopian conflict in February 1936, when Krupp was given a construction contract for the armaments-related ironworks at Zenitsa, over French and Czech competition. The Reich had allegedly threatened to suspend its purchases in Yugoslavia if Krupp lost the Zenitsa contract.

Béthouart's remarks on the losing proposal from the French firm Delattre & Frouard are instructive. Struck by the illogicality of the Yugoslav plans for Zenitsa, which called for production much in excess of the country's current possibilities, the French firm completely transformed them, proposing a network of factories adapted to domestic production and situated close to sources of coke and to electrical installations. In contrast, Krupp conformed to the Yugoslav plans, with the calculation of progressively attracting contracts for the additional installations necessary to Zenitsa's inflated production.[45] When construction on the Zenitsa complex was begun soon after Schacht's visit, Stoyadinovitch extolled the creation of mineral processing plants in Yugoslavia: 'What we are doing today at Zenitsa for the iron industry, we will do tomorrow for the Bor copper industry and in the future for other minerals.' It would be inaccurate to present the French Government, least of all the General Staff, as opposed to allied domestic industrialisation, but the Reich was quicker than France to cater to the overweening scale of these plans.[46]

The Reich poured the proceeds from its commerce in Yugoslavia not only into construction of local industry but also into propaganda. Some months after Schacht's visit, scandal broke in the heavily censored Yugoslav press, usually at pains to downplay German penetration of the country, over subsidies being paid by the Reich to a domestic ultra-nationalist group called Zbor. German commercial agents negotiated directly with peasant cooperatives for agrarian goods, a shrewd practice which led the peasants themselves to press

coordinated front in their arms peddling abroad. SHA, 'Yougoslavie', 23 March, 24 September 1935; 4, 15, 26 June, 14 September 1936.
[44] SHA, 'Yougoslavie', 24 September 1935; Finances, F30:2081, press summary, 4 November 1936.
[45] SHA, 'Yougoslavie', Béthouart dispatches, 9 April 1935; 6 February, 30 March 1936.
[46] Finances, F30:2080, Dampierre dispatch, 23 June 1936; DDF II, 2, no. 418.

Belgrade for increased trade with Germany. In early 1937, working through a commercial society it had created to facilitate bilateral trade, the Reich purchased the entire plum output of the cooperatives for well over the ordinary market price and remitted the difference to the native Fascist movement, at which point scandal broke.[47]

Yugoslavia had been an early terrain for the recrudescence of German propaganda activities in the Balkans following Hitler's advent. Extensive use was made of propaganda films which, being the rage with the Yugoslav public, were also a commercial success. Even on a commercial basis, French film-makers were unable to compete because they lacked the banking facilities necessary to give several months' credit to Yugoslav purchasers.[48] In Yugoslavia, as elsewhere in the Balkans, the Reich heavily subsidised the press and engaged in wholesale 'cultural dumping' of finely printed books, and musical scores and programming.[49]

The German challenge to the French position in Yugoslavia provoked a series of alarmed dispatches from the Belgrade Legation. Rumours that Schacht had offered arms to the Yugoslavs reached Béthouart, who protested to the Chief of Staff that recent Yugoslav orders in Germany, more than double the amount frozen, could no longer be justified by a need to balance clearing. Schacht's visit also occasioned measures by the Yugoslav Government to promote commerce with Germany, including instructions to officials to place contracts with German industry. Béthouart was sceptical that the German commercial offensive would produce a 'healthy' Yugoslav revulsion from trade dependence on the Reich, as some in official French circles preferred to believe. Even before Schacht's visit, Béthouart had predicted that the bounty to be had with the frozen proceeds of German-Yugoslav clearing, a large and growing balance in Yugoslavia's favour, would quash any efforts of officers or bureaucrats wishing to prevent German industry from supplying weapons to the Yugoslav army. After Schacht's tour, he argued that the private interests of Yugoslav economic milieux were increasingly

[47] SHA, 'Yougoslavie', Béthouart dispatch, 2 March 1937; J. Hoptner, *Yugoslavia In Crisis, 1934–1941* (New York, 1962), p. 103.
[48] Finances, F30:2080, Chautemps letter to the Minister of National Education, 19 January 1934.
[49] Ibid., Commines dispatch, 26 June 1936; SHA, 'Yougoslavie', Béthouart dispatch, 5 January 1937.

Germanophile. The country's orientation *vis-à-vis* German arms
suppliers would depend on hard calculations of Franco-Yugoslav
commerce.

Ominously, a scattering of Yugoslav arms orders in France had
reached complete impasse. While anxious to buy French arms, the
Yugoslavs would pay only by clearing, but clearing payments,
months in arrears and constantly deteriorating, were refused by
French firms. It was necessary, Béthouart wrote, to prevent German
arms purveyance at any cost, while awaiting the time France could
resume its position on Yugoslavia's other markets. A restoration of
France's arms primacy could only bolster the desired Yugoslav
reaction against trade dependence on Germany. He urged that, if no
ordinary commercial solution could be found, Yugoslav raw
materials should be purchased by French arsenals, as a means to
establish a special clearing for arms. Indirect French imports of
Yugoslav minerals via Greece and Belgium (where they underwent
various treatments) had to be abandoned.[50]

In fifteen months, the French had ineffectually come full circle, to
return to the minerals expedient. They found the Yugoslavs no more
willing than in 1935 to mortgage their mineral production in return
for French arms. In late June 1936, when General Schweisguth met
the Director of the Bor mines, he was informed that the Yugoslav
Government had requisitioned 12,000 tons of copper to repay the
Škoda Works for Czech arms. No further copper could be made
available for arms clearing.[51] The air was fraught with recrimination: over past French failures to provide sanctions compensations
or arms, and over the exertions of the Banque de France inspectors
to maintain payment transfers in the face of Stoyadinovitch's
systematic sabotage of the programme for technical collaboration.
Lost prestige after the Rhineland reoccupation further impaired the
French position. A letter from a Banque de France inspector
lamented not the strangulation of bilateral commerce, but the
disintegrating situation of French investors:

They mock us: this is the conclusion at which I have arrived...the
diminution in our prestige is such that they are ready to treat French
investors as a negligible quantity...All the influence that we lose, moreover,

[50] SHA, 'Yougoslavie', Béthouart dispatches, 3 March, 4, 15, 26 June; Muzet dispatch, 10
March; Finances, F30:2080, Commines dispatch, 26 June 1936; DDF II, 2, no. 418;
DGFP, C, V, no. 376; Hoptner, *Yugoslavia*, pp. 46–7, 101.
[51] Schw., 1SC2 Dr9, 26 June 1936.

is gained by Germany... the commercial current between the two countries is increasingly apparent, but it is a current which does not produce currency to pay our loans.[52]

Roumania

In the summer of 1936, Franco-Roumanian economic relations afforded an important object lesson: even in the cases of effective governmental intervention to purchase a 'miracle export', an arms arrangement might be soured by insufficient ordinary commerce.

Throughout 1935, André d'Ormesson, Minister in Bucharest, and his military attaché, Colonel Delmas, had been anxious for the stability of the Francophile Government led by the liberal Tataresco. It was the first post-war Roumanian Government to make a serious rearmament effort. Meagre French purchases in Roumania meant that the Tataresco Government was chronically short of currency, able neither to meet its obligations to France nor to obtain French aid for its rearmament.[53] Like his military colleagues elsewhere in the Petite Entente and Poland, Delmas was an outspoken exponent of larger commercial exchange with his host-country:

The most effective support that a great power can now lend a smaller state whose friendship it wishes to assure is economic aid by means of commercial exchange. Roumanian opinion hardly dares to remonstrate openly with France... But it is very evident at this point that Roumania considers itself abandoned by France in the commercial domain and is disturbed and bitter.[54]

In straitened circumstances, the Tataresco Government pressed Paris in the summer of 1935 to accept an arrangement involving French arms in return for petrol. By tapping the national 'miracle export', it hoped to salvage an external trade swamped by foreign indebtedness. The Roumanian Government collected annual taxes in kind ('redevances') from petrol companies exploiting the country's oil fields. It then sold its quota on the national and international markets. The taxes amounted to just over 10 per cent of national production, worth in French terms 80 million francs a year. Despite protest in certain Roumanian industrial circles against mortgaging the country's principal source of revenues, Tataresco

---

[52] Finances, F30:2498, letters from Gaudibert to Ministry of Finance, 4, 25 June 1936; Hoptner, *Yugoslavia*, p. 102.
[53] SHA, 'Roumanie AE', Delmas dispatches, 30 July, 14 November 1935.
[54] Ibid., d'Ormesson dispatch, 30 July 1935.

proposed to cede the royalties to the French Government for a
period of twelve years. A fund of French currency would be
constituted for the repayment of Roumanian debts and military
purchases in France.[55]

Initially, Paris was reluctant to consider the Roumanian offer. Its
policy was to import largely unrefined petrol, whereas the
Roumanians were intent on exporting refined products. It was also
unwilling to alter its existing import structure which rested on the
USSR, Venezuela, and the US.[56] Once negotiations began, however,
agreement on the cession of the *redevances*, to be handled through a
Franco-Belgian consortium with interests in Roumania, was reached
relatively quickly. Inter-governmental financial talks proved more
laborious. The French desire to allocate part of the petrol proceeds
to Roumanian railway electrification caused difficulties as did the
payment schedules of the French firms Schneider and Hotchkiss,
which, by obliging the Roumanian Government to request an
important advance, would further eat into its resources for arms
purchases.[57] Moreover, alarmed by right-wing effervescence in
Roumania, which they saw as an Hitlerian menace to the country,
influential French political milieux pressured the Quai d'Orsay to
exercise close surveillance over Roumanian arms purchases made
with the petrol proceeds. It was known that the domestic
Germanophiles were pushing the commercial advantages available
to Roumania in Germany. It was thus feared in Paris that direct
cash transfers would be used by the Roumanians to place orders,
already prepared, for German arms.[58]

The German commercial-arms offensive in Roumania was fresher
than that in Yugoslavia, and no less vigorous. While the Reich
intended to lay hands on Roumanian petrol from the start,
commercial petrol negotiations in 1935 had offered German services
free of charge in organising the Roumanian war industry. This offer
and other advantageous arms proposals were refused at the insistence
of the French Minister, who also persuaded Titulesco to nullify

[55] Ibid., d'Ormesson dispatch, 3 August; 'Roumanie', Delmas dispatches, 20 July, 29
September 1935; Marguerat, *Le IIIe Reich et le pétrole*, p. 57.
[56] SHA, 'Roumanie', Delmas dispatches, 30 July, 29 September 1935; 'Roumanie AE',
Sarret dispatch, 21 May 1936.   [57] SHA, 'Roumanie', 14 November 1935.
[58] SHA, 'Roumanie AE', d'Ormesson dispatch, 3 August 1935; 'Roumanie: 1924–1939',
unsigned, undated note, marked 'même note remise à M. Laval/Discrétion'; MAE,
Papiers Léger, letter from Edouard Pfeiffer, Vice President of the Radical Party, to Léger,
6 January 1936.

secret German-Roumanian provisions enabling Roumanians to study in Germany.[59]

There were indications, however, of chinks in the armour that the Legation sought to fit over the Roumanian economy. Quasi-strategic orders had been placed in Germany, and a commercial accord of March 1935 was accompanied by transactions involving German petrol purchases and investments in the petrol and mining sectors. The Reich soon penetrated the Roumanian metallurgical sector. In 1935, it sold machines with a large cash loan to a state mining enterprise, and a German group obtained an important state contract for an installation treating gold, iron, zinc, chrome, and manganese, repayable in these products. The Legation was particularly watchful of the machinations of the industrialist Malaxa, who had influence with King Carol, and who was known abroad primarily for his strong interest in Resita, the largest metallurgical concern in Roumania. Malaxa, whose enterprises were among the few of any scale not under Franco-British-Czech control, maintained close relations with the German metallurgical industry, which he fostered against his Czech competition.[60] In the midst of the Franco-Roumanian negotiations, the Germans evidenced their desperation by proposing to trade the petrol *redevances* for cash, allowing Roumania to purchase arms in France.[61] The Reich's prime interest was not in bulk agrarian trade, nor even in the sale of arms, but in amassing raw materials for its war effort.

After considerable to-ing and fro-ing, the French reached an unworkable agreement with Bucharest in February 1936. The 7 February accords, ratified with *éclat* some weeks after the Rhineland reoccupation, were intended to be part of a complex system devised to reanimate bilateral commerce. The financing of Roumanian rearmament through orders to French industry was only one, if the most important, aspect of the system. During the negotiations, the Roumanian Government had implemented a series of measures to discourage exports to Germany, while encouraging them towards

[59] SHA, 'Roumanie', Delmas dispatches, 12 July, 14 September 1935; d'Ormesson dispatch, 9 April 1936.
[60] Ibid., Delmas dispatches, 22 August, 14 November 1935; 12 January 1936; d'Ormesson dispatch, 9 April 1936; 'Roumanie AE', Delbos-Daladier letter, 31 August 1937; Weinberg, *Foreign Policy*, pp. 118–19, 323–35; Marguerat, *Le IIIe Reich et le pétrole*, pp. 15–21, 45–9, 74–86.
[61] SHA, 'Roumanie AE', 21 May 1936; Marguerat, *Le IIIe Reich et le pétrole*, pp. 49–50, 85 note.

countries like France with strong currencies. The Reich mounted a determined counter-attack. It offered to take on export bonuses suppressed by the Roumanian Government, and succeeded in cutting short a flourishing recovery of Franco-Roumanian trade in the first part of 1936. In notifying Paris of the resulting regression in bilateral trade, the Bucharest Legation warned that, even if the Roumanians succeeded in their efforts to check German commercial expansion, only a proportional increase in French importation of Roumanian products, one considerably more substantial than that projected in the 7 February accords, could assure the desired scale of Franco-Roumanian commercial relations.[62]

Anaemic regular commerce with France sapped the strength of the February 1936 system and ultimately made it unworkable. The Roumanians explained to the British Minister that the petrol-arms agreement with France looked 'very pretty on paper', but had little actual value as France could not open its doors to Roumanian produce.[63] The French commercial predicament was everywhere the same: the problem of absorbing Central European products in adequate quantities. And, as elsewhere, the success of German commerce underwrote the Reich's propaganda: 'cultural dumping' of musical scores, fine editions, and films, subsidies to the Roumanian press and the funding of hundreds of ephemeral, small, pro-Hitlerian papers. The Bucharest Legation was struck by the insidiousness of German propaganda on the 1936 electoral campaign in France. It did not begin by speaking of Franco-Germany rivalry, but insisted on anti-Bolshevik and anti-Semitic themes, popular even with Roumanian Francophile opinion: 'Having prepared the ground, they attempt to demonstrate that France unfortunately has become the prey of Bolshevism and the Jews, another argument which carries weight in this country. And they finish by concluding that only Germany and its tribune can lead a people to grandeur.' Financed from the proceeds of German imports frozen by Roumanian currency restrictions, this propaganda had palpably altered the atmosphere of Roumanian life: 'Many facts remain, it is true, conjectural or too vague to ascertain with certainty...it is undeniable that Roumania is plunged into an atmosphere of occult intrigue,

---

[62] SHA, 'Roumanie', 9 April; 'Roumanie AE', 21 May 1936.
[63] Dissatisfied with the scope of the accords with France, the Roumanians offered almost immediately on their signature in February 1936 to sell oil to Britain in exchange for arms. PRO, FO 371, 20431 passim.

tension and disturbance, due to the underhanded, persistent and resourceful action of Germany.'[64]

In terms of indebtedness and arms, the situation of Czechoslovakia *vis-à-vis* France represented an anomaly. Ironically, had Czechoslovakia, the most financially sound of the Central European states, required an *assurance-crédit* to purchase arms in France, it would have been forthcoming without difficulty. Ranking among the seven largest weapon suppliers in the world, Czechoslovakia had no need to supplicate for arms as did Roumania, Yugoslavia, and Poland. However, it too demanded larger export quotas from France, partly in order to finance arms sales to its improvident Petite Entente allies.

Czechoslovakia, to which roughly 70 per cent of the industrial capacity of the Austro-Hungarian Empire had fallen, was the most industrialised of France's allies in Central Europe. After 1918, the industries Czechoslovakia inherited from Habsburg domination were faced with the problem of a shrunken home market, unable to absorb their production. Czechoslovakia had to export at least 30 per cent of its industrial output in order to survive.[65]

A large proportion of Czech trade had traditionally been with Germany. Autarchic tendencies reinforced by the world crisis, however, had transformed these trade relations. As Hans Raupach has analysed the change, 'bilateral relationships with long-term trade and clearing agreements hampered the multilateral mobility of each partner and enforced mutual dependence'.[66] For political as well as economic reasons, the Czechs attempted in 1935–6 to decrease their purchases in Germany, which only a few years before had been almost three times as large as those from any other Czech supplier. The Reich responded by relentlessly increasing its purchases in Czechoslovakia, and freezing the proceeds under a 1933

---

[64] SHA, 'Roumanie: SAE', 'SR' (Service de Renseignements), 6 March; 'Roumanie AE', d'Ormesson dispatch, 9 April 1936; Lungu, *Romania*, pp. 77–9, 110.

[65] Teichova, *An Economic Background*, pp. 24–5, and her essay, 'Industry', in Kaser and Radice, *Economic History of Eastern Europe*, I, which contains a valuable passage (pp. 234–5) on the effects of the Depression on Czechoslovak industry; Radice, 'General Characteristics', in ibid., p. 36; Z. Pryor, 'Czechoslovak Economic Development in the Interwar Period', in S. Mamatey and R. Luza (eds.), *A History of the Czechoslovak Republic* (Princeton, 1973), pp. 188–215.

[66] Raupach, 'The Impact of the Great Depression', p. 83.

clearing accord. In these circumstances, Prague resolved to resist the stranglehold of German trade by obtaining access to French and British markets.[67]

France had never given the new state the level of commercial satisfaction it demanded, and the complications of the world crisis in Czechoslovakia had done little to lessen French commercial astringency. In the mid 1930s, of French trade with its Central European allies, only Franco-Czech trade showed a chronic deficit for the smaller state.[68] Given the scale of French investment in Czechoslovakia, grave currency difficulties ensued from the recurrent deficit in bilateral trade, to which the German and Balkan habit of freezing credits due under clearing also contributed. The Prague Legation reported wild fluctuations in the national bank's currency holdings, which fell from 262 to 21 million crowns in the period July 1935–July 1936, rising again to 450 million by January 1937.[69]

Appealing to the French for increased quotas, the Czechs laid particular stress on their economic and military efforts for Danubian stabilisation.[70] For virtually the whole of its independent existence, Czechoslovakia had been a capital-exporting state. Its banks and industries, 'either themselves subsidiaries of foreign concerns or closely linked with them', exported capital to its neighbours, notably Roumania and Yugoslavia. The indebtedness of these states, however, disinclined them to close economic collaboration with Czechoslovakia, lest their common creditor be given means to exercise control over their finances.[71] The establishment of an Economic Council of the Petite Entente in 1933–4 had not met the expectations of the Czechs, who profited by only a moderate increase in trade, largely due to arms sales to Roumania on credit and to Yugoslavia, against tobacco and mineral (copper, zinc, and lead) deliveries. Even these essentially barter agreements were subsidised by the Czech Ministry of Defence.[72] In 1935–6, Hodža, as Prime

[67] PRO, FO 371, 20385, R1895/1167/67.
[68] Finances, *Tableau général du Commerce, 1935–7.*
[69] Finances, F30:1146, Monicault dispatch, 6 January 1937.
[70] Ibid., Czechoslovak Aide-Mémoire, 18 September 1936.
[71] Teichova, *An Economic Background*, p. 25; Finances, F30:2079, annex to note, 15 November 1934.
[72] Radice, 'General Characteristics', p. 59; Hauner, 'Military Budgets and the Armaments Industry', in M. C. Kaser and E. A. Radice, *Economic History of Eastern Europe* II (Oxford, 1986), pp. 59–60, 66. The chief obstacle to increasing Czechoslovakia's bilateral trade with its Petite Entente allies was the agricultural protectionism instituted by Hodža's party, the Agrarians, which hampered its trade of manufactured goods for Roumanian and Yugoslav produce.

Minister, advanced various programmes for the development of Czech economic expansion in the face of German commercial dynamism.[73] In the autumn of 1936, at Hodža's instigation, the most important Czech banks and industries banded together to form a Petite Entente economic centre. It aspired to draw on German methods to mobilise Central European economies against German commercial penetration.[74]

The Director of Živnostanská, the largest Czech bank, expatiated to the French Minister on the benefits for the industrialised countries in collaborating *à l'allemande* on the industrialisation of the less developed Petite Entente states by furnishing them with technicians, machinery, and capital. Živnostanská and the other enterprises of Hodža's Petite Entente economic centre whose production was largely dependent on raw material imports were particularly interested in the development of the Roumanian and Yugoslav metallurgical industries.[75] Czechoslovakia's recovery from the world economic crisis being brought about largely by rearmament, these projects had less publicised military underpinnings. The Petite Entente Chiefs of Staff had advocated since the early thirties standardisation of arms based on models in service with the Czech Army, and from 1935, the Petite Entente discussed the creation of metallurgical factories in Yugoslavia and Roumania, as a means of parrying the vulnerability of the Škoda Works to enemy attack.[76] The Czech Government also envisioned the transfer of a section of its war industry to a Roumanian Transylvanian citadel, a proposal officially adopted by the Petite Entente Chiefs of Staff.[77]

---

[73] Wandycz analyses the ambiguities in this planning, writing of Hodža's failed Plan of early 1936 for a Danubian federation: 'his hope was to reach eventually an accord with Germany. But he wanted the Central European bloc to act as a unit and to deal with the powers on an equal footing.' *Twilight*, pp. 420–1.

[74] Finances, F30:1146, Delbos-Auriol letter, 2 October 1936; Pryor, 'Czechoslovak Economic Development', pp. 198–200.

[75] Finances, F30:1146, Lacroix dispatch, 9 July; Delbos-Auriol letter, 2 October 1936.

[76] SHA, 'Yougoslavie', Béthouart dispatch, 9 April, 24 September 1935; 'Roumanie', Delmas dispatches, 1 December 1935, 19 May 1936.

[77] SHA, 'Roumanie', 19 May 1936, 22 January 1937. Cf. Hauner's important discussion of Czech arms sales abroad in depleting the country's military potential in 1938, 'Military Budgets', pp. 60–1, 78–80. While this was an issue of contemporary and post-war dispute, Hauner's discussion minimises the fact that the Czechoslovak military never intended to resist alone, outside of regional and international defence networks. He remarks only that the hopes of the Czechoslovak General Staff that Škoda's and Zbrojovka's arms supplies and technical assistance might in the long run secure control over Roumanian and Yugoslav armed forces went unfulfilled.

The Czechs and Roumanians developed a working industrial entente for defence work by the mid 1930s.[78] In July 1936, Zbrojovka, the state arms works at Brno, bought out Vickers' shares in Resita and the arms factory of Copsa Mica Si Cugir, and began to manufacture light machine guns and munitions using Czech prototypes, the best in the world for this weaponry. The Roumanians proved receptive to collaboration with Czech industry: their chauvinism was flattered by Prague's projects, and the country's possibilities of rearmament and wartime supplies were enlarged.[79]

Czech efforts in Yugoslavia were less successful. As Hauner comments, 'Most of the Balkan politicians, nevertheless, did not feel any particular loyalty to Škoda, and, once paid by the Czechs, they remained prepared to listen to the Germans next time.'[80] The Czechs were particularly embittered by Škoda's losing the Zenitsa iron works contract to Krupp in February 1936.[81] The Yugoslavs managed ingratitude even when the Czechs offered free arms. Shortly after Schacht visited Belgrade, the Yugoslav Government, forced to go back on an order for British tommy guns by a gift of Czech-manufactured guns, pronounced itself 'rather annoyed to find itself placed in a situation of obligation with regard to Czechoslovakia, whose pressure to develop its sales in Yugoslavia often lacked discretion and provoked impatience'.[82]

Czech arms diplomacy led to rivalry with France, a rivalry complicated by the fact that private French capital, particularly through the support given by Schneider's bank to Škoda, had long been involved in Czechoslovakia's arms production. The 1922 accords delimiting production between Schneider and its subsidiary

---

[78] Earlier defence entente had been held back by a 1933 scandal occasioned by a Škoda salesman who had joined in circulating rumours that Soviet troops were concentrating along the Bessarabian border, in order to receive a larger order from the Roumanians. Partly to restore its reputation, Škoda granted rights for Czech arms to be manufactured in Roumania and reduced its prices by almost half for guns manufactured in Czechoslovakia. Hauner, 'Military Budgets', pp. 62–3. These concessions conformed to the Czechoslovaks' interest, as they relied upon Roumania in a conflict to make available a portion of its petrol supplies. Czech T-120, 1041/1809/414113.

[79] By early 1937, eight contracts were concluded or under negotiation, including the construction of several factories in Roumania. SHA, 'Roumanie', Delmas dispatches, 19 May 1936, 22 January 1937; Marguerat, *Le IIIe Reich et le pétrole*, pp. 47–50.

[80] Hauner, 'Military Budgets', p. 61.   [81] Ibid., p. 67.

[82] SHA, 'Yougoslavie', 15 July 1936; and for a similar episode involving Czechoslovak attempts to save the Yugoslav market from Belgian competition, Hauner, 'Military Budgets', p. 66. On the other side, the Czechoslovaks complained that every Petite Entente conference occasioned Roumanian and Yugoslav demands for free war materials. Schw., 1SC2 Dr7, 7 January 1936.

Škoda allocated the East European market to Škoda.[83] Partition of arms sales was also touched upon in the 1933 Gamelin–Syrový meetings when Syrový requested that France not compete with Czechoslovakia for Central European and Balkan markets.[84] In practice, however, the involvement of the Czech Government sometimes compromised the accords from the French point of view.

This was illustrated by a Yugoslav arms contract being placed with the Czech Defence Ministry, which dashed Schneider's hopes of receiving a retrocession on part of an order given to Škoda. The contract being placed between governments, the Czech Defence Ministry became the sole arbiter of the distribution of orders and favoured Škoda. A portion of the contracts won by the Czechs went to the arms works at Brno, in which the Czech Government had a much stronger interest than in Škoda, and which was thus subject to fewer external pressures.[85] Czech arms purveyance also gave rise to financial acrobatics which directly clashed with French interests. By a 1936 tripartite payments schedule, Roumanian petrol sales to Yugoslavia were to be paid for in copper delivered to Czech industries executing Roumanian arms orders. The transaction prevented France from obtaining Yugoslav arms contracts on terms desired by the French General Staff.[86]

The Franco-Czech rivalry occasioned unfavourable contrasts in Bucharest and Belgrade between French and Czech arms purveyance. Singled out for praise were the rapidity of Czech arms deliveries and the important financial support and favourable payment terms given allied arms transactions by the Czech Government. Backed by the Czech Defence Ministry, Škoda, for example, sold anti-tank guns to Roumania at 50 per cent less than Schneider's asking price.[87] For their part, the Yugoslavs were not averse to playing on the competition between Škoda and Schneider,

---

[83] Teichova, *An Economic Background*, pp. 211–15. A concise history of the two principal Czech arms factories and their connections with French industry is given in Hauner, 'Military Budgets', pp. 72–83.

[84] SHAA, 2B98, 'Conversations franco-tchécoslovaques janvier 1933'.

[85] SHA, 'Yougoslavie', 24 September 1935; Teichova, *An Economic Background*, p. 199.

[86] SHA, 'Roumanie', Delmas dispatch, 24 September; for a similar clash of Franco-Czech-Yugoslav interests involving bauxite, see Finances, F30:1146, 'Bordereau à MG des F.', 28 August 1936; undated study; enclosure to Delbos-Auriol letter, 20 January 1937. These complicated barter arrangements were the province of Omnipol, the export-import division of Škoda, which on occasion marketed Roumanian and Yugoslav agricultural produce abroad in order to pay itself for arms sales.

[87] SHA, 'Yougoslavie', Béthouart dispatch, 1 April 1935; 'Roumanie', Delmas dispatch, 4 November 1936.

while steadily increasing their purchases in Germany. Prague's response was to press from the spring of 1936 for a combined, French-financed Schneider-Škoda effort, along with intensified Franco-Yugoslav commerce, to wrest Yugoslavia from the German embrace.[88]

French military attachés in the rest of Central Europe were given to harsh judgements of the Czech projects. Delmas especially reported delays and technical and financial difficulties in the implementation of plans for unification of Petite Entente war industrial efforts and systematisation of its arms. And he strove to alert the Roumanian Government to the collaboration possible with French industry: 'This country should be able to count upon its own national production and that of France.'[89]

The sharpness of Delmas's reaction revealed a concern to advance French industrial interests during the economic crisis (which in both France and Czechoslovakia took the form of protracted industrial stagnation). Foreign contracts also benefited incipient French rearmament. When *assurances-crédits* were granted in 1936 to Roumania and Poland, they included guarantees favouring French industry. This was unsurprising. After the Rhineland crisis, which, besides opening the sluice gates of allied arms requests, threatened to discredit the French pretension to lead an allied coalition in wartime, the EMA sought full credit for any help it could give.

Material and psychological contexts aside, the Quai d'Orsay was not unsympathetic to the Czech demand for increased quotas. Sentiment in official circles, however, was that Czechoslovakia was the Central European ally least in need of France's help. Despite its recurrent passive balance, Czechoslovakia maintained the greatest volume of trade with France, and in the 1920s and early 1930s apparently enjoyed far more favourable terms on loans placed on the Paris market than its neighbours.[90] The Czechs even acquired a patina of prosperity from their reputation as the arms salesmen of the Petite Entente.[91]

Persistence of the Quai d'Orsay's longstanding hopes for amalgamation of the rival economic blocs – the Petite Entente and that

---

[88] SHA, 'Yougoslavie', 24 September 1935; DDF II, 2, no. 143.

[89] SHA, 'Roumanie', Delmas dispatches, 1 December 1935, 19 May 1936.

[90] Finances, *Tableau général du Commerce 1935–37*; MAE, Papiers Tardieu, carton 693, 'Accords danubiens', undated 'Rapports financiers'. The low figure given for the servicing of loans to Czechoslovakia was queried, presumably by Tardieu or his *cabinet*, but it seems to have been correct, as it appears in successive memoranda.

[91] See, e.g., Schweisguth's remarks in Schw., SC4 Dr2, sdr b.

under Italian auspices – also fostered diplomatic ambivalence regarding the prospect of a Petite Entente arms buildup. The summer of 1936 represented a transitional phase in the Quai d'Orsay's approach to the ongoing Danubian economic and political crisis. Schacht's tour, while it goaded the French to counsel resistance to German commercial inroads, also made the Political Directorate fully aware of the importance of 'third party markets' to the Danubian states. A note of 20 July pointed out that pre-war commercial movements had completely changed, Austria carrying on only 35 per cent of its commerce with other Danubian states, Yugoslavia 30 per cent, Roumania 21 per cent, and Czechoslovakia merely 16 per cent. Indicating the privileged economic situation of Germany, able to thwart any system elaborated without it, these figures engendered defensive attitudes which made the Political Directorate even less willing to dispense with Italian commercial cooperation. Italy's cooperation was still deemed indispensable as a means to compensate for the French and Czech inability to absorb Danubian agrarian surpluses on an adequate scale. By taking up the commercial gauntlet *vis-à-vis* Germany at France's behest, Italy would become a force for Danubian pacification. The Political Directorate's 20 July note thus spoke nebulously of a French impetus to Danubian commercial recovery: 'To the extent that we are able, our action should complement [that of Czechoslovakia], while giving ourselves a wider field of action, that of an animating power.'[92]

ELEMENTS OF THE FRONT POPULAIRE'S RESPONSE:
MASSIGLI'S RECOMMENDATIONS AND THE
INTERNATIONALIST DEVALUATION OF THE FRANC

Such considerations on meeting the Danubian crisis and remedying the accompanying diminution of confidence in France also informed René Massigli's 9 July note, to which the Quai d'Orsay solicited the accord of the Blum Government. Massigli's recommendations were diverse and wide-ranging, without constituting a fundamental break with past policy. After alluding to the possibility of exploiting the putative natural resistance of the countries directly enmeshed with Germany, he placed an emphatically worded passage on the desirability of renewed Italian economic activity to regain markets

[92] MAE, Papiers Massigli, 'Affaires de l'Europe centrale', Note, 20 July 1936.

lost to Germany during the Ethiopian war: 'The immediate task of our diplomacy will be to make Italy assess the danger to itself that German penetration represents.' At the same time, the Quai d'Orsay rejected a negative policy with regard to Germany, and evoked the necessity for international monetary and commercial policies to permit Germany to reorientate itself towards normal commercial expansion.[93]

Massigli's international recommendations largely accounted for the cautious optimism, with regard to the German commercial onslaught, which reigned in French official circles through the autumn of 1936. For the Political Directorate, an essential element in this relative optimism was its continuing belief in the possibility of assigning a role to Italy. Massigli's remarks on the subject were reinforced by the note of 20 July, which reflected on the problem of increasing commerce with Central Europe, rather than on that of arms. On 11 July a critical event in the making of the Anschluss had intervened, the Austro-German accord, by which Austria, recognising itself as a German state, reached accommodation with Germany without Italy's protesting. Alluding to the unforeseeable consequences of the Austro-German accord, the author of the 20 July memorandum opined only that there would henceforth be considerable obstacles to too systematic a Danubian reorganisation. Instead, the note advocated bilateral accords in order to avoid any strengthening of the area's rival economic groups, from which Germany only profited: 'Each state should work individually for the improvement of its trade without subservience to the directives of a grouping whose very existence betrays its origin and political aims.' Overt bilateralism was in fact the only thesis acceptable both to Italy and the Reich. The Political Directorate's revised commercial blueprint – to which a unilateral preference stricture and traditional calculations on Italy were still important – thus depended on an 'invisible hand' operating amidst the economic mêlée to allay the threat of a German Mitteleuropa:

The increase in bilateral accords will lead to – and this is a good thing – the gradual interpenetration of the rival blocs that have been formed, and whose zone will always be insufficient to provide the relief demanded by the region of Europe under consideration. Germany will be among the

[93] DDF II, 2, no. 418.

beneficiaries, but not the only one. Italy will never give up the fight and if third countries, such as France and Britain – who absolutely must take more interest in the problem – make the necessary efforts, it will be possible to a certain extent, to thwart the German advance, without giving [the Reich] a reason to complain and revolt.[94]

The Italian theme was taken up by Delbos when he discussed the German accord before the Chambre's Foreign Policy Commission: 'On the economic plane, we can catch up with Germany. I envision a policy of bilateral accords concluded by the countries of Central Europe, to achieve an interpenetration of the Petite Entente bloc and the Austro-Hungarian-Italian bloc.'[95]

This belief that France could overtake Germany economically was shared by Blum himself, who was disinclined to derive comfort from the speculations on the impermanence of the Italo-German rapprochement entertained at the Quai d'Orsay after the Austro-German accord. Blum's receptivity to the proposals of the Massigli memorandum was inseparable from hopes connected with his conversations with Hjalmar Schacht, the President of the Reichsbank, who visited Paris in August 1936.

A late June visit from the departing French financial attaché had occasioned an invitation from Schacht for a disarmament overture. Freshly returned from his travelling salesmanship in Danubia and declaring himself favourably impressed by the Front populaire's ministerial declaration, Schacht opined that a French initiative for a disarmament accord would find support in Germany, provided the USSR participated.[96] Schacht was a known opponent of unlimited German rearmament, so that François-Poncet's dispatches soon joined Massigli's July memorandum in appealing for commercial and currency negotiations to include the Reich.

The German announcement of two year military service in early August provoked the Front populaire's major rearmament plan of September 1936. The first serious French rearmament programme, the government's defence expenditure in September 1936 exceeded the General Staff's estimates, amounting to 14 billion francs over a four year period. The very deterioration in the international climate, however, made an arms race more likely than ever. Fear of forever

[94] MAE, Papiers Massigli, 'Affaires de l'Europe centrale', 'Note pour le Ministre', 20 July 1936.   [95] Assemblée Nationale, Commission, 30 July 1936, pp. 19–20.
[96] DDF II, 2, no. 352.

losing the chance of a direct attempt to restore the German economy to a peacetime footing led Blum to arrange a meeting with Schacht soon after the German conscription announcement.[97] They discussed the satisfaction of German colonial demands in return for a disarmament agreement, envisioned by Blum as part of a general European settlement, including the USSR.[98] Schacht proved evasive in comparison with his French interlocutor. The European Left, however, had always seen Hitler as a product of the world economic crisis, and Blum's subsequent optimism about the talks came more from his reading of Germany's economic straits than from Schacht's actual negotiating counters.[99]

An unsigned memorandum written for Blum in this period began: 'Germany is on the eve of economic and financial catastrophe... This is what is behind the political gestures, which we must examine coolly to assess our present and future chances...' The writer maintained that dire economic difficulties had already led to the Rhineland reoccupation in an effort to distract the public from its discontents. The difficulties included the rise in world raw material prices, which obliged Germany to produce more to obtain less, the dwindling of stocks, and a slow-down in industrial production. The conclusion relevant to German commercial inroads in Central Europe was heartening: 'Germany has in effect exhausted all the advantages of bilateral accords.' Given the ceiling on its bilateral commerce, Germany could only recognise the errors of its ways and the necessity of pursuing a policy of international economic solidarity: 'Even as a stopgap, a war would not be logically desirable nor even possible for Germany at present. We thus hold the key to the situation, *to the extent at least that fear of compromising his prestige is not likely to provoke in Hitler a desperate determination.*' The memorandum's end argument was for an international economic conference: 'So it is up to us to finalize an international programme of economic

---

[97] Ibid., 3, nos. 196, 198, 210. The standard work on French rearmament in this period is Robert Frankenstein's *Le prix du réarmement français (1935–1939)* (Paris, 1982). The Front populaire's financial commitment to rearmament surpassed its expenditures on public works.

[98] While he was more prepared than Delbos and the Quai d'Orsay to negotiate with Germany without prior evidence of German goodwill, Blum insisted that bilateral Franco-German conversations would not suffice. As he had told the British the preceding month, a Franco-German arrangement, even guaranteed by Great Britain and Italy (a new Locarno), would not suffice to remove the danger of war. 'The perils which exist... do not directly oppose one of these powers to the other. It seems impossible to confine or to divide the peace.' DDF II, 3, no. 19.   [99] Ibid., nos. 213, 349.

recovery, in which there must be something for Germany, but which will allow us to demand of it substantial guarantees for the future.'[100]

The key point here is that the Blum Government linked these hopes for an international monetary and economic conference with the monetary operations under way in the autumn of 1936 – a Franco-British-American currency declaration and the devaluation of the franc. Official French circles looked to the devaluation and the accompanying tripartite currency declaration to compel a German devaluation, to be followed by the desired international monetary and economic conference in which the Reich would renounce its autarchic policies and frenzied rearmament, and provide security guarantees in the east. Blum was not self-deluded in believing that the Germans might devalue: Schacht had declared in Belgrade that, if France devalued, Germany would follow suit, and Blum had spoken afterwards to Beck in Geneva of a possible devaluation of the franc.[101] Immediately after the announcement of the tripartite currency declaration, René Massigli, in a closely argued letter to Léger, reflected on the monetary operations in progress. He found it difficult to imagine that Germany would not devalue. Without gold reserves, the Germans would require important foreign credits. A European settlement would thus be at hand provided that France, Britain, and the US agreed to link financial aid to preliminary German acceptance of its essential clauses. Massigli urged that France and Britain should immediately define their conditions rather than awaiting new Locarno negotiations.[102]

Historical analysis has highlighted the way in which Blum in his conversations with Schacht sought to induce the Reich to restore its economy to a peacetime footing by abandoning its break-neck rearmament through participation in an ill-defined colonial consortium underwritten by the British. Less remarked has been the strong correlation which existed between Blum's hopes for a European settlement including disarmament provisions to encompass both Germany and the Soviet Union, and France's

---

[100] Finances, F30: 1149, 'Dossier monétaire: Dévaluation du franc', unsigned, undated, 'Note au président du Conseil'. Italics in the original.
[101] Szembek, *Journal*, pp. 185–6; Czech T-120, 1041/1809/414106.
[102] MAE, Papiers Massigli, 'Violation de la Rhénanie', 26 September 1936. Seminal work has been done on the tripartite negotiations by R. Girault, 'Léon Blum, la dévaluation de 1936 et la conduite de la politique extérieure de la France', Colloque de Nanterre, 1977; for the reservations of J.-B. Duroselle, *La décadence*, pp. 311–14. Neither scholar deals with the documentation owed to René Massigli.

obligations to its eastern allies. The Front populaire's strategy was to obtain German security guarantees in the east and its return to a liberal economy which would lift the Reich's commercial mortgage on Central Europe.[103]

For Léon Blum, this strategy represented a solution to the problem of finding a specifically socialist contribution to a foreign policy otherwise marked by continuity and the threat of stagnation. The strategy did not appear chimerical at the time. For the officials at the Quai d'Orsay, as for Blum, Schacht's visit to Paris created the possibility of a *percée*, calling for diplomatic audacity, for the taking of well-calculated risks. Lengthy correspondence from François-Poncet in the summer of 1936 listed the negative inducements to negotiate: the possibility, acknowledged by high officials of the Nazi party, that its domestic economic crisis might force the Reich to turn eastwards in search of raw materials; and German misrepresentations of the French internal situation as chaotic and conducive to a Bolshevik take-over, which would entitle Germany to intervene in French internal affairs. The Ambassador took the view that the moment had come to reverse diplomatic roles and remove the initiative from Germany by forcing it to respond 'oui ou non' to a summons to negotiate.[104]

Implementation of the government's strategy was far from straightforward, however. Unsuccessful commercial negotiations in 1937 involved the Blum Government in a provisional agreement to sell iron ore to Germany in exchange for German coke.[105] While the maintenance of German coke imports had been indispensable to the

---

[103] DDF II, 3, no. 349; Finances, B12:619, Mönick dispatch, 17 October 1936. Foreign Office thinking on German economic expansion also proceeded from a view of Nazi adventurism as an economic phenomenon to reach diametrically opposite conclusions: the natural direction of German economic expansionism was towards Central and South-Eastern Europe, and such expansionism could be in the general interest of Europe. PRO, FO 371, 20385, C807/4/18, filed with R3731/1167/67; R3919/1167/67.

[104] Such German propaganda had a sharply defensive edge: rapid French economic progress but at the cost of social tumult was the Nazi press line to discontented German workers. It portrayed Blum himself as well-meaning, but as having lost control to his Communist electoral allies who were about to bring the country to unspeakable revolutionary catastrophe. François-Poncet saw this malignant sympathy for Blum as an indication of Nazi willingness to negotiate. MAE, Série Z, 717, François-Poncet dispatches, 2 July, 24, 27 August, 10, 25 September; Finances, B31.501, 15 August 1936.

[105] The Franco-German commercial negotiations of 1936–7 are treated in detail in Monique Constant, 'L'accord commercial franco-allemand du 10 juillet 1937', *Revue d'histoire diplomatique*, nos. 1–2, 1984. I am indebted to Monique Constant for her help in tracing documents on the Front populaire's involvement in these negotiations. As her article

French arms industry in Lorraine since the return of the Saar to Germany in 1935, the Blum Government was painfully aware that the iron ore supplied to the Reich at Schacht's insistence was being used for rearmament.[106] Its intention was to oblige Schacht on a temporary basis, in order to persuade the Reich to accept an agreement (French currency in exchange for more German coal) which would enable German tourists to visit the 1937 Exhibition, the Blum Government's answer to German propaganda excesses about the social climate in France.[107] At the same time, the Blum Government sought from allied Czechoslovakia an alternative source of the indispensable coke. Czech industrialists proved uncooperative and plans for importation of Czech coke across Poland financially unfeasible.[108]

The two-month agreement on iron ore and coke which the Blum Government reached with Schacht was clearly linked to its hopes of broader economic and political détente.[109] These hopes were disappointed when Schacht's visit to open the German pavilion at the 1937 Exhibition did not lead to substantive conversations. Surly and increasingly powerless at home, Schacht had been reluctant to return to Paris, letting it be known that he considered his August

points out, the Germans were able to buy more French raw materials with no accord at all than with the temporary accord of 1937 or the full-fledged commercial accord subsequently concluded. The breakdown in Franco-German clearing from 1935 meant that German raw material imports from France reached high points in the course of 1936, and, again, after the expiration of the 1937 temporary accord and before the conclusion of a regular commercial accord in July. Ibid., p. 115; Finances, B31.502, 12 July 1936.

[106] MAE, Série C, 'Tchécoslovaquie, 1 déc. 1936–31 mars 1937', 8, 26 February, 19, 22 March 1937; Finances, B31.483, 16 September 1936; B31.520, 5 July 1935, 'Note sur les règlements financiers franco-allemands'; Constant, 'L'accord commercial', p. 124. The turbulent history of France's dependence on German-controlled coke production after 1919 is summarised in Philippe Bernard, *La fin d'un monde 1914–1929* (Paris, 1975), pp. 154, 195.

[107] Constant, 'L'accord commercial', pp. 125–6, 132. The priority which the Front populaire gave to attracting German tourists to the 1937 Exhibition was thwarted by a revival of the Hitler Government's virulent press campaign alleging French internal disruption and by its special visas for travel to Paris only for visiting Nazis in groups. Both these tactics were the subject of French diplomatic protest. MAE, Série B (Relations commerciales), 302, 307, passim.

[108] MAE, Série C, 'Tchécoslovaquie, 1936–7', passim. By late March 1937, Lacroix, the French Minister in Prague, bitterly protested that Czechoslovak industrialists were concerned only with their own interests, while French industrialists preferred to purchase cheaper German coke. He raised the possibility of government subsidies to French industrialists for purchase of Czechoslovak coke, but the proposal was not retained by the Chautemps Government, in power from June 1937.

[109] MAE, Série Z: Allemagne, Delbos-Welczek conversation, 11 March 1937.

1936 visit a failure.[110] Blum's successor, Chautemps, and Georges Bonnet, his obliging Minister of Finance, did reach agreement in July 1937 with the Germans on a bilateral commercial treaty which not only regularised the iron ore-coal clause but entitled Germany to obtain other raw materials through the French colonies; this last proviso was intended as a means to lessen German colonial appetites. In fact, under Blum's successors, the negotiating terrain slowly shifted from talks on colonial issues to talks on ill-defined German penetration of Central Europe, in return for consideration of arms limitation/disarmament.[111]

Over the long run, then, hopes of abandoning the moribund Locarno negotiations for an offshoot of monetary operations which would bring a wide European settlement were disappointed. The Reich withstood all pressure to devalue. However, the atmosphere created by the reckoning that Germany might devalue took some time to settle. Significantly, it affected the timing of the Blum Government's own decision to devalue, which was delayed for some weeks in the summer of 1936, in order to allow the formation of a trilateral front to underwrite negotiations with Germany for a general settlement.

Had Blum succeeded with the wager implicit in the linkage between the hopes which arose from his talks with Schacht and the French devaluation of September 1936, Hitler would in effect have been stopped from being Hitler. As it was, Blum's conversations with Schacht, a known opponent of accelerated German rearmament, involved him in economic appeasement, the belief that the so-called German 'moderates' could be used to purchase a general settlement and the promise of European stability. Nazi brigandage *vis-à-vis* German Jewish citizens in the mid 1930s was thought at the time to be economically rooted.[112] It was thus widely believed in Western Europe that the return of the German economy to a more secure, peacetime basis would end Nazi domestic excesses, the régime's political and racial persecution in a bellicose search for 'internal enemies'. Blum's personal fault was to underestimate the supreme importance of ideology amongst his adversaries, while overesti-

---

[110] MAE, Série B, 302, 9 January; 307, 26, 27 May 1937; Constant, 'L'accord commercial', p. 110, n. 1.

[111] That this was in fact Schacht's design had been anticipated by French financial reports on the German press. Finances, B31.501, 21 December 1936.

[112] Schacht personally was known as an opponent of Nazi confiscatory measures against German Jewish enterprises, Finances, B31.483, 2 January 1936.

mating the power of rationality. In the fruitlessness of Blum's August 1936 conversations, there was the additional factor of Schacht's internal loss of standing.

An earnest of the new government's resolve to shore up allied faith in France after the reoccupation was that it did not intend to content itself with internationalism. In this vein, Massigli's note affirmed that France had a special effort to make, and owed its allies tangible proof that it intended to harmonise its economic and political relations and practise its alliances. Massigli advanced four 'national' proposals to brake the German advance through Danubia. The first proposal was for France to confine its efforts to those states – the Petite Entente, Poland, and Austria – with which it was most involved. The Petite Entente was meant to be the prime beneficiary of any supply of commercial oxygen. Austria was mentioned only in relation to a proposal that France grant export facilities, a proposal on which the Blum Government was already acting by granting special quotas to Yugoslavia. The Quai d'Orsay also sought the government's approval for the course long advocated by the Belgrade Legation, that France procure what raw materials it could from the Petite Entente rather than from non-allied suppliers.[113]

Shifting from commerce to arms, the Quai d'Orsay asked the government to facilitate the financing of credits and to grant *assurance-crédits* for allied, particularly Yugoslav and Polish, purchases of war materials. The award of *assurance-crédits* had in the past been governed by the credit of the buyer state, without distinction between the sale of arms and anything else. To overcome the problem of heavy allied indebtedness, Massigli, after pressing for adoption of commercial proposals to increase allied payments capacity, argued that future allied arms requests deemed indispensable by Daladier should be welcomed as of overriding national interest.[114]

The 9 July note bore the hallmarks of its author: lucidity, cogency,

---

[113] A commission for the revision of the customs system was also instituted to study a revision of the tariff system and the suppression of quotas, particularly in relation to allies, in anticipation of a return to free trade. Girault, 'Léon Blum', p. 16; Sauvy and Hirsch, *Histoire économique*, IV, pp. 37–8. Finances, B31.484, 4 February 1937 refers to a September 1936 declaration by Schacht that, under certain conditions, Germany was prepared to participate in negotiations for 'the return to economic and financial free trade'.

[114] DDF II, 2, no. 418.

and unequivocalness. It afforded a measure of the distance French governing circles had come in their appreciation of France's duties as an ally. Before June 1936, dismayed by the failure of the politico-economic strategies for continental predominance pursued in the immediate post-war period, and disconcerted by the xenophobic assertiveness of Central European domestic capital, French Ministers of Commerce had pursued 'a business strategy entailing advantages that compensate France for the services or benefits asked of her'. Approached by Beck in June 1934 for commercial concessions to finance naval purchases in France, Barthou's colleague at the Ministry of Commerce, Lucien Lamoureux, had vehemently protested Beck's 'blackmail' of the alliance: 'Naturally I refused to commit myself to that direction, which would have created a fearsome precedent, mixing foreign policy and military consider-ations with purely commercial objectives.'[115] Barthou and his successors acquiesced in this niggardly bilateral commercial policy, despite and on occasion because of the April 1934 note by which France signalled its resolution to assure its security through a search for great power allies. Lamoureux's 1934 response contrasts with candid conversations in the autumn of 1936 between officials from the Ministries of Commerce and Foreign Affairs. The representative of the Ministry of Commerce remarked bitterly that it was impossible to conclude allied commercial accords 'healthy' to France's interests given the Front populaire's political pressures to benefit the allies. The government, he protested, systematically subordinated France's economic interests to political necessities. The representative of the Quai d'Orsay defended the government's position: 'it is our entire policy in Central Europe which is at stake, a policy which is essentially based on economic and financial concessions and in which the choice open to France is essentially the following: make concessions or see these countries immediately turn to Germany'.[116]

The Massigli note also makes untenable the view that the French Government's preoccupation with the German campaign to realise,

[115] BDIC, Papiers Lucien Lamoureux, 'Souvenirs politiques 1919–1940', Chapter VII, 'Le Cabinet Doumergue 1934', sections 'L'accord franco-polonais', 'Autres accords', Microfilm 31. Lamoureux boasted to a legislative committee in May 1934 that he pursued 'a purely commercial and egotist policy'. Cited in Wandycz, *Twilight*, p. 353. For the allegation that his recalcitrant attitude towards Poland was prompted in part by his ardent defence of the industrialist Boussac, L. Noël, *La Pologne*, p. 168.

[116] The immediate context of La Baume's response was the recent arms negotiations with Poland. MAE, Série B (Relations commerciales), carton 88: 'Importation en France, 1936–7: Commission de revision douanière', 'PV de la séance du 12 nov. 1936'.

in Coulondre's phrase, 'a complete hegemony over Danubian and Balkan Europe' dated essentially from 1938, a view which has been suggested by J.-B. Duroselle.[117] The event on which Professor Duroselle focusses, the Alphand mission of November–December 1938 after a Central European tour by Funk, Schacht's successor, was played out in circumstances already familiar from the appraisals of 1936. By the time of Funk's voyage, not only had Czechoslovakia lost its autonomy, but the economic dependence of the Balkan countries on Germany had reached nightmarish levels. Contrastingly, the summer of 1936 represented a moment of initial clarity and resolve. The first important action taken by the Front populaire was a highly controversial grant of arms aid to Poland.

[117] Duroselle, *La décadence*, pp. 375–80.

CHAPTER 4

Blum and the military: the Franco-Polish arms negotiations of 1936

THE RAMBOUILLET ACCORDS AND AMBASSADOR NOËL'S
TESTIMONY

In September 1936, the Blum Government signed the so-called Rambouillet accords, by which it granted Poland two billion francs of arms aid. The Rambouillet accords represented a major step by the Front populaire towards its Central European allies, in conformity with René Massigli's emphasis on immediate, direct French action to counter that of Germany in Central Europe.

Massigli, in the 9 July note, observed that Poland's political rapprochement with Germany since 1934 had hastened economic cooperation in the form of such projects as the Pomeranian railway. These threatened to lead to military cooperation. The Reich, under the pretext of reducing credits, massively swollen by its refusal to pay its share of the joint railway venture in Pomerania, offered to apply the frozen credits to arms purchases.[1] Massigli argued that Poland would accept the German offers if the Blum Government did not respond favourably to Polish requests for financial and arms help, already several months old. Thus, while Schacht had not visited Poland in June, the Front populaire felt itself confronted by the same menace there as throughout Danubia. The Blum Government became actively involved in arms negotiations with Poland from July 1936, when it decided to send General Gamelin to Warsaw. In mid August, Gamelin visited Poland, meeting with Piłsudski's successor, Rydz-Śmigły, and touring Polish defence installations. Less than two weeks later, Rydz-Śmigły paid a long-awaited visit to France and concluded the financial accords signed at Rambouillet.

The standard source on the Front populaire's negotiation of the Rambouillet accords has been Léon Noël, the French Ambassador in

[1] SHA, 'Pologne: AM', 'Rapport...mai 1934 à mai 1936', 27 May 1936.

Warsaw from 1935 until the German invasion in 1939. In his memoirs, *L'agression allemande contre la Pologne*, M. Noël tells us that in June 1936 he met with the leaders of the new government and pressed Yvon Delbos to subordinate French assent to the Polish demands to two preconditions:

1 Technical guarantees that the Poles would not spend the greater part of the French credits on the construction of a national war industry.
2 The dismissal of the Polish Minister of Foreign Affairs, on the grounds that French opinion and the legislature would not accept a loan to Poland if Beck remained.

Noël considered the precondition regarding Beck absolutely necessary, given 'all the disappointments that his disreputable behavior had meant for us and the anxieties to which his subservience to Germany gave rise'. He claimed that Delbos readily acceded to his view: 'The Minister of Foreign Affairs approved my proposals concerning these two preliminary conditions. It was agreed, in particular, in the most explicit way, that he would undertake to make General Rydz-Śmigły understand that the government could not agree to what was being asked of it if Colonel Beck was not removed.'

Noël's 1946 narrative, which makes no mention of the German arms threat and treats Gamelin's visit to Warsaw as little more than a passing review of the Polish Army, next fastens on Rydz-Śmigły's voyage to France in September. At the Rambouillet talks, from which the Ambassador was excluded, Delbos defaulted on his alleged promise, refusing to demand Beck's dismissal 'contrary to what had been planned in the most categorical fashion...'. Rydz-Śmigły is said to have gone so far as to raise the subject himself, out of sympathy with Noël's campaign for Beck's dismissal, but Noël reports that Delbos replied with a remark almost discourteous in its insignificance. Noël's insistence that the question be taken up was disregarded, and the Rambouillet accords were negotiated and signed without any discussion of Beck or of his policy.

In a passage devoted to the motives of certain members of the government in treating Beck with kid gloves, Noël's speculations include: 'Did support which Col. Beck had been clever enough to arrange in certain clans operate in his favour? It is rather likely.'[2]

[2] L. Noël, *L'agression allemande contre la Pologne* (Paris, 1946), pp. 138–50.

Noël has since been more forthright, arguing that Beck was supported by Delbos and Alexis Léger because, he claims, all three were Freemasons.[3]

Nor did Delbos and Gamelin insist on the insertion in the September financial agreements of guarantees against Polish misuse of the French monies for the construction of a national war industry. Delbos's disregard of his second alleged promise of June 1936 had baleful consequences in 1939, when the Germans bombed the new Polish factories in the first hours of the war.

The version of events provided by *L'agression allemande contre la Pologne* is familiar from virtually all historical treatment of the subject.[4] Less common knowledge is the existence of an earlier version of M. Noël's recollections, in the form of a deposition which the Ambassador made for the Riom trials, organised by the Pétain Government to incriminate the Front populaire for the French defeat in 1940.[5] Noël's Riom deposition placed the disadvantages of Beck's staying in power in a somewhat different context, that of Beck's inability as a patent Germanophile to risk unpopularity *vis-à-vis* his own opinion by making necessary concessions to Germany in 1938–9. In his 1941 account of his June 1936 meeting with Delbos, Noël describes how he first offered himself to break the French preconditions to Rydz-Śmigły, in order to save the new government embarrassment. In this earlier variant, which puts even greater blame on the Blum Government, Noël recalls that his offer was brushed aside by Léger. While he approved of Noël's preconditions, Léger allegedly said that such a démarche exceeded Noël's diplomatic role and should be carried out by Delbos ('it is up to the Government to say plainly to the Polish General what is to be said'.) The three thus agreed that Delbos would demand Beck's dismissal. Noël's 1941 account of the war industries question is essentially the

---

[3] Conversation with Léon Noël, 11 May 1977; L. Noël, *La Pologne entre deux mondes* (Paris, 1984), pp. 132–3.
Etienne de Crouy-Chanel, Léger's private secretary, recalls Léger's dismay at sporadic rumours that he was a Freemason. He instructed Crouy-Chanel to track down the 'A. Léger' figuring on a list of Parisian masons. Crouy-Chanel's investigation revealed that the A. Léger in question was a hairdresser. Conversation with Etienne de Crouy-Chanel, 7 February 1979.

[4] Only David Kaiser's *Economic Diplomacy and the Origins of the Second World War* has called into question the Ambassador's account by comparing it with the printed French documentation, Kaiser, pp. 209–11.

[5] FNSP, Papiers Daladier, 4DA14, Dr3 sdrb, 'Procès-verbal, Cour Suprême de Riom, Déposition Léon Noël, 23 mai 1941'. According to a manuscript note by Daladier, Noël's testimony and that of his colleague, Robert Coulondre, were 'suppressed' by a special decision of the court when the trials began in February 1942.

same as those he later published, although his charge of shameful neglect on the part of the Front populaire was given sharper prominence by the Riom trials indictment, which included the fall of Poland in 1939. All of M. Noël's accounts, for the Riom trial and for post-war publication, focus exclusively on the negotiations following a fateful conversation with Delbos in June 1936. The negotiations, however, had an important history before the arrival of the Blum Government in power, one which calls into question the Ambassador's testimony.[6]

CRITICAL FIRST MOVES: THE EMA AND THE WARSAW
EMBASSY, OCTOBER 1935–MAY 1936

Polish arms demands were originally presented in October 1935 by the Polish Chief of Staff to d'Arbonneau, the French military attaché. Since the death of Piłsudski in May 1935, the French military had been attentive to the Poles' growing preoccupation with German rearmament and to a certain loss of nerve, attributable to the dwindling financial resources available to repair Piłsudski's failure in his last years to modernise the army. The final instalments of a French arms credit from 1924 were exhausted by 1935. When the Poles began to formulate new arms demands in the second half of the year, d'Arbonneau encouraged them to include all categories of material lacked by their army, and he urged Paris to grant an important *assurance-crédit*.[7] He also promoted talk in Franco-Polish military circles of a meeting between Gamelin and Rydz-Śmigły, the Polish Commander in Chief. Gamelin did not share his predecessor's strongly negative feelings about Poland, dating from Weygand's participation in the 1920 Polish-Soviet war. Weygand's retirement

---

[6] Noël's fourth and last account of the Rambouillet negotiations, *La Pologne entre deux mondes*, published three years before his death, in many respects takes up his Riom deposition. For example, absent from *L'agression allemande*, Léger figures in Noël's 1941 testimony and reappears in *La Pologne*. It also contains novel points redolent of Vichy: various principal actors in the negotiations are explicitly labelled as Freemasons, and Blum appears in the September 1936 negotiations, allegedly protesting that, as a Jew, he dare not risk offending anti-Semitic Polish opinion by demanding Beck's dismissal. This dubious recollection is unctuously glossed in *La Pologne*: 'I vainly insisted, vainly pointed out that he greatly exaggerated the disadvantage that his being an Israelite [polite French usage] carried in the minds of the Poles.' (p. 130) In fact, Noël had devoted several dispatches earlier in the year to his view that bloody clashes between Polish police and workers had involved Jewish Communists and intensified nationalist anti-Semitism, a subject to which he would return immediately after the Rambouillet negotiations. (MAE, Papiers Noël, 18, 19, 20 April, 29 September 1936).
[7] MAE, 'Pologne', Note, 26 October 1935; SHA, 'Pologne AM', 11 December 1935; for earlier Polish arms démarches, Rollet, *La Pologne*, pp. 250, 285, 292.

in January 1935 had improved Polish standing in French military circles. The Polish Army was increasingly seen as a counterweight to the Germanophilia of Beck and his circle in a contest for the allegiance of post-Piłsudskite Poland, but, impoverished and wavering, it was a counter-weight in need of strengthening.[8]

The Polish desiderata were conveyed without the Embassy's mediation when General Sosnkowski stopped in Paris after the funeral of George V. In the correspondence which ensued between the Ministries of War and Foreign Affairs, the War Minister expressed the view that practical discussion of material aid between staffs should be preceded by a political '*accord de principe*' reached through the Quai d'Orsay.[9] Apprised of Sosnkowski's overtures for an arms credit and loan for the development of a Polish war industry, Léger replied that such an operation should be envisaged in terms of French financial possibilities and appropriate assurances of Polish political intentions: 'The decision of the French Government must take into account, in this matter, not only the state of Franco-Polish relations, but also Polish attitudes towards its neighbours, and particularly towards Czechoslovakia.'[10] Without singling out Czechoslovakia, Maurin agreed that an important effort could only be made for an army 'whose aid in the event of a European conflict is assured us with the maximum certainty'.[11]

In fact, the General Staff's reading of Polish strategic usefulness had as much to do with Moscow as with Prague. The 2e Bureau's analysis of the Polish demands centred on the relationship between the Polish alliance and the still unratified Franco-Soviet pact. The 2e Bureau accepted d'Arbonneau's principal argument that the evolution of Franco-Polish relations since Piłsudski's death had lessened the danger of the Polish Army passing into the German camp. It assumed that, while Polish diplomacy since 1934 had weakened their alliance, Poland would honour its signature in the event of a German aggression on France. But for some months, it had been less certain of the Polish attitude in the event of a German-Soviet conflict, into which it feared France itself might be dragged

[8] Cf. the remark of a Polish officer at Piłsudski's funeral: 'Our colours are red and white, henceforth, it is a matter of knowing whether one adds – in a moral sense – a black band or a blue band. I can say that the great majority of the Polish Army hopes with all its heart that the band will be blue.' SHA, 7N3032, Note, 22 May 1935.

[9] SHA, 'Pologne: Accord de Rambouillet', Note, 29 January 1936.

[10] Ibid., Léger-Maurin letter, 28 February 1936.

[11] Ibid., Maurin-Léger letter, 18 March 1936.

by the operation of the Franco-Soviet pact.[12] In this case, the 2e Bureau feared a Polish intervention on the German side, against France. The military proved particularly susceptible to fear of a bloc in which Germany directly supplied an allied Poland with munitions and arms. The 2e Bureau advocated giving the Poles aid on condition that Poland would not intervene against France or any of its allies in the event of a conflict, or again, if it was certain that Polish military aid would be given to France in any European conflict in which it was involved. Since its consideration in spring 1935 of a Franco-Soviet accord concluded outside the framework of an Eastern pact, the EMA had taken the position that France would not be involved in a German-Soviet conflict provided Poland gave the necessary assurances that it would not take up arms against the USSR. Poland then was to supply the means by which the Franco-Soviet mutual aid pact would be emptied of potential French military obligation to the Soviet Union.[13]

This perspective, rather than that of arranging Soviet troop passage through Poland, guided the EMA's efforts to make the Soviet treaty compatible with the Polish alliance. Gamelin had responded to Laval's decision to ratify the Soviet pact by inviting Rydz-Śmigły to France, and he gave assurances about the scope of the Franco-Soviet pact to Rydz-Śmigły's colleague, Sosnkowski, when he visited Paris in February. Great care was also taken of Polish susceptibilities during the parliamentary debates on the pact's ratification, the bill's *rapporteur* declaring that Poland did not wish to envisage the passage of German or Soviet troops.[14] Noël successfully advocated a special Banque de France credit to support Poland's currency during the ratification debates, and the Ambassador joined d'Arbonneau in campaigning for arms and financial aid to Poland as an incomparable opportunity to efface the impression left by the Soviet ratification.[15] The Polish Counsellor in Paris, who had reported in May 1935 that France could be made to pay for the Franco-Soviet pact, was being proven correct.[16]

When Hitler seized on the Soviet ratification to reoccupy the

---

[12] SHA, 7N2520, Note, 24 April 1935, discussed above, pp. 70–2.
[13] SHA, 'Pologne...Rambouillet', Note, 29 January; 7N3000, 3 February 1936; DDF II, 1, no. 106; 2, no. 419.
[14] Schw., 1SC2 Dr7, 10 February 1936; SHA, 'Pologne AM', 13 February, 4 March 1936; J. Łukasiewicz, *Diplomat in Paris 1936–9, Papers and Memoirs of Juliusz Łukasiewicz*, ed. Wacław Jędrzejewicz (New York, 1970), p. 12 n.
[15] MAE, Papiers Noël, 8 February; SHA, 7N3000, 13 February 1936.
[16] Szembek, *Journal*, pp. 68–9.

Rhineland, the Polish Foreign Ministry manipulated the crisis to advance the Polish arms demands. As has been seen, Beck threw out ballast on the German side, while strengthening his assurances of loyal bilateralism as French inaction became more and more certain, culminating in an assurance that Poland would mobilise if France did so.[17] He then cannily exploited Paris's nonchalant response to his 'spontaneous' assurances to win Rydz-Śmigły's acceptance of his less than loyal diplomacy. Beck succeeded in presenting Paris as an ungrateful as well as an inept ally. A whispering campaign carried on by Adam Koc, the President of the Bank of Poland, served Beck's designs by charging that France was neglecting Polish rearmament. The Polish General Staff's vulnerability to Beck's machinations was demonstrated when the Polish Commander in Chief, having received a post-reoccupation promise from Gamelin of increased French offensive capacity, expressed fear that French factories would no longer be able to produce war materials destined for Poland.

Beck's manoeuvrings much exercised the Embassy, which presented them as a pernicious continuation of the struggle for army loyalties waged since Piłsudski's funeral. D'Arbonneau warned General Gérodias that intrigues were already forming around Rydz-Śmigły's negotiations with France, that Beck must not be allowed to consolidate his position and further diminish Rydz-Śmigły's favourable attitude to France.[18]

These developments were the more frustrating as the reoccupation had enhanced the value of Poland for the French military. As the General Staff's post-reoccupation planning centred on the defence of Czechoslovakia, Poland's role, geographically and demographically, was pivotal.[19] Accordingly, Gamelin after 7 March commissioned the study of strategic demands to be made of Poland, based on the liquidation of Eastern Prussia and aid to Czechoslovakia through Silesia; and anxious to impress the Poles by some military manifestation such as manoeuvres and a tour of the Maginot line, he arranged to have Rydz-Śmigły invited to France by his Minister, General Maurin. Saying that he would rather come to France at the end of the summer, well into the mandate of a new government, Rydz-Śmigły declined an immediate visit. The Poles explicitly

[17] See above, pp. 86–7.
[18] DDF II, 1, nos. 455, 506; 2, nos. 10, 11, 31, 45, 238; SHA, 'Pologne AM', d'Arbonneau-Gérodias letter, 15 April; dispatch, 29 April 1936.
[19] FNSP, Papiers Daladier, 4D1 Dr4 sdrb, Note III accompanying a Gamelin-Daladier letter, 10 July 1936.

indicated that they preferred not to deal with Sarraut's caretaker government.[20]

In late April, after Rydz-Śmigły's demurral, and between the two polling days of the French election, Léon Noël returned to Paris on leave. Since the London Conference, the Embassy had learned details of Polish governmental discussions at the reoccupation which confirmed its intuition that Rydz-Śmigły had been the force behind Beck's declarations of fidelity to the alliance, notably Beck's belated assurance that Poland would mobilise if France did. The Embassy's military attaché felt keenly that the Poles would have responded more surely to a French display of 'a strong manner' on 7 March. For Poland, d'Arbonneau wrote, Germany was 'the dangerous neighbour whom one is willing to knock out cold but not to annoy, lest one be bitten'. He and Noël went on to argue that the initial maladdress of inaction had been followed by diplomatic errors – the marked nonchalance with which Flandin had received Beck's Rhineland assurances – which served Beck's designs.[21]

Eager to recover this lost ground with Rydz-Śmigły, in Paris Noël personally alerted Gamelin to Beck's March mobilisation assurance. The French military had been told that Rydz-Śmigły had wished to march with France, and risk removing Beck should he be intransigently opposed to preventive war, but it had not been informed, much to its indignation, of an actual mobilisation offer.[22] Gamelin's recent experience of civilian-military tension resolved him to move quickly *vis-à-vis* Poland and Italy. (It was in this period that Gamelin authorised the organisation of a French expeditionary force.) His resolution in the Polish case was strengthened by Rydz-Śmigły's frustrating refusal to visit France before late summer, and accompanying apprehension that the Front populaire (promised by the first round of elections) would not comprehend the stakes involved in aiding Polish rearmament.

Since the Soviet ratification debate, Gamelin had looked on Poland as a foil to pressures for a Franco-Soviet military agreement, whereas it was clear that a left-wing French Government would include advocates of stronger ties with the USSR. There had been a foretaste of these internal pressures during the London Conference

[20] SHA, 7N3000, 18 March, 1 April; 7N3032, Gamelin-Ministry of Foreign Affairs letter, 27 March, d'Arbonneau dispatch, 9 April 1936; DDF II, 2, no. 238.
[21] DDF II, 1, no. 461; 2, nos. 71, 214; MAE, Papiers Noël, 13 March; SHA, 'Pologne', d'Arbonneau-Gérodias letter, 15 April 1936.
[22] Schw., 1SC2 Dr8, 4, 30 April 1936.

when one of the Radical ministers, Paul-Boncour, had instructed Léon Noël to ask the Poles to allow Soviet passage across their territory. A diplomat whose personal dynamism and independence were commonly acknowledged at the Quai d'Orsay, Noël had refused.[23] These factors, which Noël brought to Gamelin's attention, induced the General and a member of the government whose position was unaffected by the elections – President Lebrun – to authorise Noël to deliver an important assurance to Rydz-Śmigły during the interregnum, before Léon Blum took power.

Noël met with Rydz-Śmigły on 6 May, after the second round of the French elections. The printed French diplomatic documents contain a substantive discussion on the 6 May meeting between Noël and Rydz-Śmigły, but the printed documentation omits the critical point, assurances concerning the Polish arms demands which Noël transmitted on Gamelin's behalf and around which the discussion was organised.[24] A confidential letter from d'Arbonneau to General Gérodias of the 2e Bureau recounts this missing segment of the 6 May conversation.[25] The sum of the Polish arms demands had been known to the French since 9 March: a one-billion-franc credit to purchase arms in France, and a one-billion-franc loan for the development of a Polish national war industry, to include the constitution of stocks. The sums remained constant until after Gamelin's visit to Warsaw in August.[26] According to d'Arbonneau, Noël told Rydz-Śmigły that, while he had found French governing circles generally favourable to the Polish demands for a war industrial loan, he could give no assurance until the formation of the new government, and more reliable indications as to the evolution of the French financial situation. This was only prudent as, battered by

[23] Schw., 1SC2 Dr8, 30 April 1936. Like André François-Poncet, Noël entered the diplomatic service not by the traditional *concours* (competitive examination), but as an established *fonctionnaire* (bureaucrat) whose previous postings included the *Conseil d'Etat*, a prefecture, the Ministries of the Interior and War, and the Premier's office. He had also been director of the *Sûreté générale*, the investigative side of the French police. His first, highly successful diplomatic assignment was to Prague (1932–5). He had returned to Paris in early 1935, when his position as Secretary-General of Premier Flandin's office and mission to Stresa with Flandin and Laval brought him into direct rivalry with Alexis Léger. He took up the Warsaw Embassy in May 1935.

[24] According to the DDF (II, 2, nos. 170, 214–15), the 6 May conversation consisted of Noël's protest of Beck's March diplomacy and his denial of German and Polish press allegations that there were Soviet air bases in Czechoslovakia, an allegation which threatened to destroy all prospect of Polish-Czech rapprochement.

[25] SHA, 7N3032, d'Arbonneau-Gérodias letter, 13 May 1936. No trace remains of a personal letter to which d'Arbonneau refers, from Noël to Gamelin concerning his démarche.

[26] SHA, 7N3000, 3, 13 February; 7N3012, Maurin-Flandin letter, 18 March 1936.

capital flight even before its formation, the Front populaire government would have more difficulty than its predecessors in envisioning the transfer of important sums of liquid capital outside the country.

On the other heading of the Polish demands, however, Noël was far more positive, transmitting a firm assent in principle to an *assurance-crédit* for the purchase of arms in France.[27] He added an invitation from Lebrun and Gamelin to Rydz-Śmigły to attend the French manoeuvres of September, while d'Arbonneau was to request from Stachiewicz a precise rearmament programme, detailing the categories and quantities of material desired, firms to undertake work in Poland, and suppliers in France.[28] Noël's 6 May démarche then was to reassure and secure the allegiance of the Polish army, after the diplomatic convulsion of the Rhineland affair and before the formation of the new French Government, by a firm promise of arms aid.

The contemporary documentation thus appears to contradict M. Noël's account. His firm promise of an *assurance-crédit* in May 1936 modifies the problem of preconditions in the negotiations. By transmitting clear French acceptance of a large part of the Polish arms demands in early May, Noël in effect made it impossible for the Blum Government to postulate preconditions, notably that of Beck's dismissal, once it took power in June.[29]

On 6 May, Noël did broach the subject of Beck, complaining to Rydz-Śmigły of the malaise in bilateral relations engendered by Beck's double game. Although Noël recorded Rydz-Śmigły's defence of Beck's loyalty to France, he believed Rydz-Śmigły to be fundamentally sympathetic to his remarks. In return for the assent in principle to the *assurance-crédit*, Noël, having spoken frankly about Beck, received Rydz-Śmigły's assurances on the subject, 'that in any event, we could be assured that Rydz-Śmigły would follow Polish

---

[27] Gamelin explained to his subordinates that the government could not actually grant the *assurance-crédit* in the interregnum, before the meeting of the new legislature. Schw., 1SC2 Dr8, 30 April 1936.   [28] DDF II, 2, no. 170.

[29] While the Ambassador did not commit Paris to financing a Polish war industry in May 1936, M. Noël has stated in a letter to the present author that he wishes historians to interpret the promise which he claims to have extracted from Delbos in June 1936 as pertaining to French assent to both headings of the Polish demands – an *assurance-crédit* as well as a war industrial loan. Letter from Léon Noël, 10 August 1981; cf. Noël, *L'agression*, pp. 140–1. None of M. Noël's accounts of the negotiations reveal that he promised an *assurance-crédit* to the Poles before the arrival of the Blum Government in power.

foreign policy closely, and we could have every confidence in him'.[30]
To understand the spirit in which Noël received these assurances
regarding Beck, they should be placed in the context of the hopes
with which the Embassy surrounded Rydz-Śmigły.

His experiences after arriving in Warsaw in 1935, as well as the
influence of his previous posting in Prague, convinced Léon Noël of
Beck's blatant bad faith, and of the undesirable lengths to which
Beck carried Piłsudski's policy of understanding with Germany. On
the topic of Beck's ministerial staying power, Noël was to show
himself an optimist; the key to his optimism was Rydz-Śmigły. The
Embassy had detected the dawn of a new epoch in Polish
governmental changes in October 1935, which coincided with the
first Polish military approaches for French aid. The Embassy
received confidential reports that, under repeated attacks from
Rydz-Śmigły, Beck's situation had almost been compromised on the
eve of the formation of the new ministry.

Rydz-Śmigły allegedly had only abandoned his pressure for an
immediate change in foreign policy after lengthy conferences with
the new Premier and an intervention by the President of Poland,
Mościcki. Mościcki's protectiveness, according to Warsaw gossip,
was in response to Beck's solicitude for Mościcki's two sons, who
were talented at placing themselves in delicate situations. Of the
strengths of Beck's clique – its combativeness, its control of the
government press and secret funds – Mościcki's patronage was
believed to be the most important factor in Beck's tenacious hold on
the Ministry of Foreign Affairs.

Intimates of Rydz-Śmigły assured the Embassy that he had not
renounced his struggle against Beck, that the present governmental
changes were only a stage in the evolution of a government led by
Rydz-Śmigły, with General Sosnkowski as Foreign Minister. The
Embassy was already aware of Rydz-Śmigły's effort to neutralise the
connections Beck had established in the Polish Army by appropriate
transfers. It predicted that Rydz-Śmigły would not only shield the
army from traditional political pressures, including involvement in
Czechophobe manifestations, but intended personally to exercise an
effective influence on the government. Henceforth, Beck's influence
would be sensibly diminished and his actions controlled. A month
later, Noël reported increasingly open attacks on Beck and rumours
that he would step down in January 1936. These optimistic

conclusions were treated by the Embassy as cause to assent to the Polish arms demands. Noël was certain of Rydz-Śmigły's opposition to Beck.[31]

Beck of course made no exit in the months that followed. After the reoccupation, Rydz-Śmigły excused Beck's diplomacy on the grounds of Polish unpreparedness, which he pointedly blamed on French neglect, while the Embassy played down Warsaw's careful fostering of a link between the inadequacies of its diplomacy and its arms demands. It depicted Rydz-Śmigły as prudently awaiting the moment when he could impose a governmental change on Mościcki.

The Rhineland affair appears to have altered the Ambassador's counsel with regard to Beck's future. In early 1936, Noël shared the conviction of Polish opposition circles that French arms credits to Poland could only be considered if Beck were replaced by someone more acceptable to Paris.[32] After his démarche to Rydz-Śmigły in May, however, Rydz-Śmigły's position was consolidated by the French promise of aid, without any explicit undertaking on the General's part to dismiss Beck. The tactic underpinning the démarche was evidently to reassure Rydz-Śmigły after Flandin's mismanagement of Polish affairs at the reoccupation, in the belief that Rydz-Śmigły could be relied upon to get rid of Beck.[33]

When Noël spoke with Rydz-Śmigły in May, a Polish governmental shuffle was in the offing, and Noël debated whether Rydz-Śmigły would content himself for the time being with asserting his authority over Beck, or whether he was ready to adopt 'a more radical attitude'.[34] Although Beck retained his place in the May reshuffle, Noël and his colleagues lived in hope. A close collaborator of Rydz-Śmigły, Colonel Koc, was at work on a governmental programme to serve as a point of departure for the 'regrouping of national forces within the keynote of national defence', which Rydz-Śmigły announced in a May 1936 speech. The Embassy was given to understand that Koc's programme would be published on the eve of the formation of Rydz-Śmigły's long-awaited Government. In June, d'Arbonneau reported that Rydz-Śmigły's authority daily

---

[31] MAE, 'Pologne', Noël dispatches, 2, 14 October; Political Directorate Note, 26 October; Papiers Noël, 27 November 1935.

[32] DGFP, C, V, no. 106. Having previously warned against any French governmental commentary which could be construed as intervention in Polish internal affairs, the Ambassador in early 1936 may have been prompted unofficially to align himself with opposition to Beck by the journalists Pertinax and Mme. Tabouis, who spread the rumour that Noël had recently made a démarche to the Polish Government which had had the effect of keeping Beck in power. MAE, Papiers Noël, 13 October 1935, 24 January 1936.

[33] DDF II, 2, no. 71.   [34] Ibid., no. 170.

increased and that the General was taking an ever greater part in the country's political direction. D'Arbonneau speculated whether Mościcki would not resign in the face of Rydz-Śmigły's rapid ascent, a development which would open the way for the implementation of Koc's plan and Beck's dismissal.[35]

THE FRONT POPULAIRE AND THE ARMS NEGOTIATIONS

It was at this juncture that the Front populaire arrived in power. Its opening deliberations on aiding Polish rearmament were dominated by Polish blackmail. In late May, Berlin began to repudiate a plan for German currency payments of the railway debt awarded Beck after his useful attitude at the reoccupation.[36] Offers by Schacht to pay in weaponry the Reich's share of a joint railway venture in Pomerania had been bruited for months. The Polish General Staff told the Embassy that it had received new offers, this time for arms, and pressingly appealed for French support. In early July, it informed the Embassy that a study of the German arms proposals was underway.[37] Rydz-Śmigły personally exploited the climate created by Schacht's recent activities, in an attempt to extract from the new government acceptance of both Polish financial demands before he left Poland to attend the French manoeuvres.[38]

Neither the Embassy's official correspondence with Paris nor interministerial correspondence during the first weeks of the new government's existence contains any reference to the substance of Noël's May démarche to Rydz-Śmigły. The Blum Government authorised a Polish study commission to examine war materials purchasable in France, as a result of d'Arbonneau's follow-up to the 6 May conversation, but perhaps unsurprisingly, there is no indication that the Blum Government was ever told of Noël's firm promise of an *assurance-crédit*.[39]

Noël's closeness to military channels was still very much in evidence, however. D'Arbonneau and Noël asked the EMA to

---

[35] Ibid., no. 240; MAE, Papiers Noël, 28 August, 29, 30 September 1936; 20 February 1937; SHA, 7N3000, 10 June 1936.
[36] SHA, 'Pologne AM', 27 May 1936; DDF II, 1, no. 238; Kaiser, *Economic Diplomacy*, pp. 147–9.
[37] SHA, 7N3012, Daladier-Delbos letter, 1 July; DDF II, 2, nos. 349, 364; MAE, Papiers Noël, 7 July 1936.   [38] SHA, 7N3000, 2 July 1936.
[39] A 2e Bureau letter of 1 July to the Quai d'Orsay implied that discussion of the Polish demands had been in abeyance since the reoccupation. SHA, 7N3012, Daladier-Delbos letter.

pressure the government for approval of the Polish demands, presumably to be communicated through ordinary diplomatic channels, before Rydz-Śmigły's voyage to France. D'Arbonneau informed Gérodias that he and the Ambassador were pressing for a rapid governmental decision, not only for an *assurance-crédit* for arms purchases in France, but also for some measure of aid for the development of a Polish war industry and stocks, regarded by the Embassy as an indispensable, if lesser, part of the Polish demands.[40]

The Embassy's benevolent reading of Rydz-Śmigły's behaviour afforded another example of the very effective way in which the Polish army since Piłsudski's funeral had engendered an atmosphere of Franco-German rivalry for its loyalty. In a dispatch of early July, d'Arbonneau conveyed Rydz-Śmigły's pious assurances that Polish arms purchases in Germany would not betoken any change in the alliance with France:

Sincere assurances on the part of their author. What force have they, however, against the ineluctable consequences of such an event and against the currents of opinion to which it would give rise. What would be thought here, even in the milieux favourable to us, on seeing that France's abstention obliges Poland to arm itself in Germany. And for those who do not like us, such as Colonel Beck, will they not find in this an occasion for triumph by proving that France cannot be counted on...[41]

This was the anti-neutralist constant in the Embassy's pressures for meeting the Polish arms demands. French assent was to prevent Rydz-Śmigły from allegiance to Beck's baleful policies. In the first instance, it was to strengthen the friends of France rather than toppling its enemies.

With regard both to his own May initiative and to the Polish arms blackmail, Noël was not in a position in June 1936 to ask the new government to pose conditions to its assent to the Polish demands. In the controversial matter of Beck's future, while it is impossible to exclude that, when on leave in Paris in early June, Noël advocated to his superiors a French 'nudging' of Rydz-Śmigły in September, the contemporary documentation shows that Noël's priority in these weeks, as before the advent of the Front populaire, was to encourage

[40] Ibid., d'Arbonneau-Gérodias letter, 6 July 1937. In a 28 June telegram imploring the Blum Government to offer immediate satisfaction to the Poles in order to parry the German offers, Noël indicated that aspects of the negotiations less amenable to rapid solution, e.g., the war industrial demands and the exact figures of French aid, could be reserved. DDF II, 2, no. 364.   [41] SHA, 7N3000, 2 July 1936.

Paris to satisfy Rydz-Śmigły's demands. Would it not have been logically inconsistent for M. Noël, having obtained an indisputably firm promise from Delbos to level major preconditions on a Polish loan when Rydz-Śmigły visited Paris in September, to insist that his government agree to a loan on the spot in late June? Again, the contemporary material does not support Ambassador Noël's claim to have pressed the Blum Government for a hard line in the negotiations, but suggests that the Ambassador worked in May and June 1936 to obtain as much satisfaction for Rydz-Śmigły as possible. Beck's situation would change as a result of the French aid, rather than as a condition of it.

In early July, the Embassy's pressures for giving Warsaw immediate satisfaction were taken up by Daladier, as well as by Massigli and the Political Directorate, as a matter of overriding national interest.[42] The government responded by announcing on 18 July its decision to send Gamelin to Warsaw. The Gamelin mission was prompted by the need to maintain some room for negotiation despite the German arms threat, in the face of which the Embassy was prepared virtually to abandon high level discussion, e.g., on Czechoslovakia, in order to strengthen Rydz-Śmigły against neutralist currents. Daladier furnished a staccato explanation to d'Arbonneau:

> The Government sees an interest in preliminary questions for the grant of a credit to be discussed between soldiers. Given their importance, this can only be between Generals Rydz-Śmigły and Gamelin. No firm engagement on our part can be taken before this conversation. If we are proposing that General Gamelin go to Poland, it is in order not to adjourn the conversation until Rydz-Śmigły's voyage.[43]

Léon Noël, who was not consulted on the government's decision, protested in a telegram of 18 July. D'Arbonneau reported the Ambassador's anxiety that the Poles might actually refuse to receive Gamelin.[44] Noël had already crossed swords with the new government over the volatility of the Poles' moods. Soon after its arrival in power, anxious over the German arms threat, it had instructed him to sound Rydz-Śmigły about visiting France sooner than the autumn. The Ambassador had sent back a stiff message that insistence on an earlier visit would give Rydz-Śmigły an

---

[42] SHA, 7N3012, Daladier-Delbos letter, 1 July 1936; DDF II, 2, no. 418.
[43] SHA, 'Pologne...Rambouillet', 2e Bureau note, 25 August; ibid., 7N3032, 20 July 1936.
[44] MAE, Papiers Noël, 18 July; SHA, 7N3032, 18 July 1936.

impression of French distrust and would facilitate domestic manoeuvres to persuade him to renounce his trip. To the news of Gamelin's mission, Noël again replied that Paris should stand by the date and conditions of the visit accepted by Rydz-Śmigły in May. Noël's position suggests that he was solicitous of Rydz-Śmigły's Francophilia after his May remarks on Beck to Rydz-Śmigły had caused the Poles to close ranks.[45] He feared lest a brusque opening move by the new government disrupt favourable internal developments under Rydz-Śmigły's leadership, and risk the situation against which the Embassy repeatedly warned, in which Beck and his neutralist clique turned the negotiations to their own advantage.

Delbos responded with a justification of his and Blum's decision to send Gamelin.[46] Delbos's instructions for Noël on the occasion of Gamelin's visit provide the key to the expectations with which the Blum Government made its 1936 arms agreement with Poland. The government felt obliged to assent only after receiving assurances about the military hypotheses in which the arms would be used, and more generally, about Polish foreign policy. For Blum in particular, a determination to clarify Franco-Polish relations was inextricable from the decision to aid Poland.[47] Delbos wrote to Noël that normally such questions would be negotiated between the Embassy and the Wierzbowa, but, given the governmental situation in Warsaw, it would be wise to inform Rydz-Śmigły directly of Paris's views and preoccupations. Lest the Polish Government and Beck in particular take umbrage at this, Gamelin, speaking to him as one general to another, would conduct the conversations on the French side.[48]

On the issue of Beck, so important for Noël, there was to be plain speaking, but no talk conducive to his dismissal. For Delbos, the equivocalness of Franco-Polish relations was the result of ambiguities in Polish action, not of textual obscurity in the treaties. The perennial issue of formal revision of the 1921 treaties, outmoded by their references to a possible Soviet aggression against Poland, could be bypassed for the time being, given post-7 March exchanges.

---

[45] MAE, Papiers Noël, 22 June 1936; Łukasiewicz, *Diplomat in Paris*, pp. 12–15.
[46] FNSP, Papiers Daladier, 1DA7/Dr2/sdr e, 30 July 1936, with emendations by Alexis Léger.
[47] Blum vividly described after the war his reaction to the reigning atmosphere of distrust between the allies, *CE Témoignages* I, pp. 129–30.
[48] Blum told the British that Gamelin was sent because he could 'short-circuit' Beck by directly confronting Rydz-Śmigły. PRO, FO 371, 20764, C6041/981/55.

There was no question of asking the Poles to denounce the showpiece of Beck's diplomacy, the 1934 accord, which diminished tension on the Poles' western frontier. Delbos disclaimed any intention of recruiting Poland to a policy systematically hostile to Germany, but in his view the practice of the Franco-Polish alliance should entail concordant diplomatic action. Rydz-Śmigły was to be told, in phrases which could have come straight from Noël's plaints of 6 May, that since the 1934 accord Beck's diplomacy and press had too often given the impression that the Polish Government was more concerned to affirm the total independence of its policy than to stress its common interests with France.

This particularly pertained to Czechoslovakia. The Blum Government made a condition of its aid to Poland the loyal search for rapprochement with Prague. Delbos largely discounted the notion that Beck had committed Poland to participate in a German attack on the Czechs, but he argued that Warsaw's systematic hostility to Prague could be interpreted as a disturbing symptom of German-Polish collusion. He wanted assurances that Germany was not entitled to include Polish neutrality in its calculations. He argued that well-known Polish complaints against Czechoslovakia – minority grievances and the recurrent, false allegations of Czech-Soviet aviation links – could be overcome by mutual goodwill.

The government did not expect Polish-Czech agreement, indispensable to the effective operation of the French alliance, from Gamelin's visit alone. Their quarrel plainly could not be liquidated overnight. Gamelin's mission would be a double one. He was given discretion as to the discussion necessary for the military problems posed by the Polish aid request and eventual Franco-Polish collaboration. Politically, his role was to enable Rydz-Śmigły to understand the reasons obliging the French to link political to technical problems, or, in Delbos's phrase, to admit the need for a negotiation. Gamelin would demonstrate the nefariousness of existing Polish-Czech relations, make clear the French Government's firm desire to end such a situation, offer its mediation, and obtain Rydz-Śmigły's assent in principle to redressment. Rydz-Śmigły's verbal assurances, which might one day be 'lost from view', would not suffice. Delbos's instructions were that Rydz-Śmigły explicitly approve in writing a detailed summary by Gamelin of the political conclusions of their conversations. Noël would then examine with Beck the consequences of Rydz-Śmigły's acceptance of the various political principles outlined by Delbos, notably the necessity for a Polish-Czech entente.

Gamelin's visit was to give Rydz-Śmigły every interest in supervising the second tier of the negotiations preceding his voyage to France, the conversations between Noël and Beck. Rydz-Śmigły was to exercise a certain supervision over these conversations. He was being cultivated as a make-weight against Beck in the formulation of Polish foreign policy. It was not to be excluded that he might eventually replace Beck, but this was not the principal thrust of the Blum Government's efforts. Delbos was emphatic that the diplomatic conversations should not estrange Beck: 'you will have every possibility of pursuing the conversation on the diplomatic terrain without excluding the mediation of M. Beck, towards whom it would be maladroit on our part to manifest a systematic hostility'. After these instructions of July, Noël could have had few illusions as to the Blum Government's priorities: a clarification of Franco-Polish policy, particularly on Czechoslovakia, rather than the removal of Beck. These passages deprive of their drama Noël's claims of pained surprise that Delbos did not press for Beck's dismissal in the September negotiations in Paris.

Gamelin arrived in Warsaw on 12 August.[49] After a cordial first conversation with Rydz-Śmigły, Gamelin drafted a note in which, as he put it, he attempted to transpose to the military plane the essence of Delbos's instructions to Noël. In the note's composition, Gamelin had the cooperation of the Ambassador. From the plain-spoken passage in Delbos's instructions on the independence of Beck's policy, Gamelin and Noël extracted for Gamelin's presentation to Rydz-Śmigły only the expression, 'tout en sauvegardant la pleine autonomie de nos politiques': 'We simply consider that the practice of our alliance, while safeguarding the full autonomy of our policies, entails a normal concordance of view on military problems which might be posed to our armed forces.'

Delbos's instructions regarding Beck were a casualty of this almost exclusively military tenor, as, more seriously from the government's point of view, was its insistence on recognising Czechoslovakia as an integral part of the day-to-day working of the Franco-Polish

---

[49] The following account is based on three documents, long thought lost: Gamelin's report to Daladier with annexes, 'Exposé...par le général Gamelin au général Rydz-Śmigły', and 'Exposé...par le général Rydz-Śmigły au général Gamelin', 13, 14 August 1936, FNSP, Papiers Daladier, 1DA7/Dr2/sdr e.

alliance. The almost exclusively military bias adopted by Gamelin and Noël represented a continuation of their collaboration of the previous spring, when, having transmitted to Rydz-Śmigły Gamelin's denials of Czech-Soviet military ties, Noël sent word to Beneš to orient the Czech General Staff towards resuming collaboration with Warsaw. Believing a Polish-Czech political détente unlikely to manifest itself for some time, Noël and the EMA decided instead to promote a resumption of contacts between the Czech and Polish staffs, both concerned at German rearmament.[50] In Warsaw, Gamelin lent scant authority to recruiting Rydz-Śmigły to a political rapprochement ending all appearance of Polish-German complicity. Gamelin's unassertiveness on the topic of Czechoslovakia was compounded by the absence of the substantive conversations between Noël and Beck desired by Delbos.[51] This absence was unsurprising, once Noël and Gamelin chose to discuss the Polish arms requests on the basis of military collaboration between Poland and Czechoslovakia, without obtaining Rydz-Śmigły's assent to the principle of a Polish-Czech political entente. Gamelin's mission evolved into a kind of boycott of Beck, who was neither brought into the negotiations, nor into the topics discussed. The government's desire directly to negotiate a change in Polish-Czech relations was thus forfeited.

Gamelin read aloud his note and added comments during his second conversation with Rydz-Śmigły. The note began with the announcement of the Blum Government's acceptance in principle of both sets of Polish demands, the acceptance for which the Embassy and EMA had solicited the government for weeks. As the basis of conversation, Gamelin proposed the mutual obligation not to contract third-party engagements likely to block execution of the Franco-Polish treaties. His largely strategic discussion proceeded logically from the tenets of his planning for a war of coalition: the Reich's fortification of its western border, a German attack in the east, and Poland as the salvation of Czechoslovakia. His prime concern was to ensure a two-front war. Whichever country bore the brunt of attack – here, Gamelin echoed the public doctrine of the EMA on the unpredictability of the direction of the initial German attack – its task would be to contain and then to resist the German offensive, while its ally would pin down a maximum of German forces: 'In the development of our operations, it is evident that we

[50] DDF II, 3, no. 275.   [51] Conversation with Léon Noël, 11 May 1977.

cannot coordinate them closely, as if we operated in the same theatre; but it is important to combine them in such a way that the adversary cannot by a series of shuttles, confront us in turn.' Gamelin sought Rydz-Śmigły's undertaking that, from a period of political tension, France and Poland would take parallel measures. In an actual conflict, he proposed an exchange of liaison missions.

Gamelin took an oblique approach to the problem of reconciling disparate French treaty commitments in Central Europe.[52] His note for Rydz-Śmigły was discreet about what it termed the delicate points of France's obligations to Czechoslovakia and the USSR. On the topic of a Polish-Czech rapprochement, Gamelin diffidently linked staff talks to French arms aid: if Poland was obliged to concert operations with Czechoslovakia, especially over Silesia, France would be prepared to help, as it would be in the case of armaments. He reiterated Noël's earlier denial of staff talks between Czechoslovakia and the USSR, adding that there was nothing in Czech-Soviet relations harmful to Poland. After his offer of unstinting French mediation efforts in Prague, whose vulnerability he did not seek to conceal, Gamelin consigned the principle of a Polish-Czech entente to the province of the diplomats.

On the subject of the USSR, Gamelin's tone verged on the apologetic. In concluding its pact with the Soviets, France had been motivated only by desire to prevent an attack on the Polish rear when Poland sided with France against Germany. France had not had staff talks with the USSR and would have none without informing the Poles of their occurrence and aims. Gamelin's note contained only the slightest suggestion of eventual direct Soviet aid to Poland: the remark that, as with Czechoslovakia, there was nothing that would not be useful when the time came.

In his memoirs, Gamelin claimed to have proposed a combined Polish-Soviet land operation in Eastern Prussia. The contemporary evidence suggests a much less concrete approach on the subject of the USSR. Gamelin's talk of a war of coalition stressed Italy, not the Soviet Union. He extolled Italian action through Austria as permitting France to aid Czechoslovakia, and an Italian presence with the French army as assuring land and sea communications with Poland: 'The more we present the Germans with an extended front,

---

[52] In the margins of a proposal for revision of the problematic 1921 accords, including specific references to Soviet air and material support, Gamelin had minuted: 'Is there interest and possibility concerning the articles referring to the Soviets?' SHA, 7N3032, 'Projet d'une nouvelle convention militaire secrète franco-polonaise', n.d.

the more we will pose them a difficult problem.'[53] Gamelin concluded by assuring Rydz-Śmigły that Poland was not being asked to commit itself to an anti-German policy. Here, Delbos's instructions acknowledging the benefits of the 1934 declaration were adopted almost line for line. Delbos's language presumably appealed to Gamelin's prudence.

Rydz-Śmigły pronounced himself in general agreement with Gamelin's exposition. Singling out the USSR and Czechoslovakia, Rydz-Śmigły alluded to the griefs his country nursed against each. On the question of Soviet aid to Poland, Rydz-Śmigły echoed Gamelin's temporisation, saying that it should be discussed 'when the time came, as the situation took shape'. On Czechoslovakia, Rydz-Śmigły gave his personal word on a contingency already discounted by the Quai d'Orsay, that Poland would not join Germany in a war against Czechoslovakia. But there was at least the semblance of more substance. Poland would envisage a Silesian operation 'when the time came', supple phrasing in which Rydz-Śmigły took his cue from Gamelin's note. On Polish strategy, Gamelin's report to Daladier recorded little discussion, save Rydz-Śmigły's reflection that German fortifications in the Rhineland indicated a German intention to direct their opening offensive against Poland.

Rydz-Śmigły's written response was more restrained. Rydz-Śmigły and Beck had reached agreement shortly before Gamelin's arrival on an iron-clad bilateralism as their negotiating principle, and this was conspicuous in his note, despite assurances on the unconditional execution of mutual obligations. He formally assented to Gamelin's plan for Franco-Polish cooperation: common action from a period of political tension and an exchange of liaison missions in a conflict. As for Czechoslovakia and the Soviet Union, he merely returned Gamelin's assurances, saying that Poland had no engagements against either state. Had Gamelin on either occasion pressed for a formal guarantee to Czechoslovakia, Beck and Rydz-Śmigły had agreed that Noël would be summoned, and indignantly told

---

[53] Cf. Gamelin, *Servir* II, pp. 228–30. Gamelin afterwards claimed that Rydz-Śmigły divulged his war plan; that it involved Polish concentrations in the desired areas (East Prussia from a period of political alert, and Silesia), but that, at Rydz-Śmigły's request, he informed only Daladier and his immediate collaborators. However, according to a confidential EMA note of February 1937, with extensive citations from the August 1936 conversations, the modalities of Polish response to a German aggression were not precisely defined, a situation the note explained by the Poles' uncertain security with regard to the USSR. SHA, 'Pologne EMA/2', Note, 17 February 1937.

that Poland would agree to political conversations only in the framework of a 1934 Polish note expressing reservations about strengthening ties with Czechoslovakia.[54] As it was, any such Polish tactic was obviated by Gamelin and Noël's handling of Delbos's instructions. Rydz-Śmigły's note concluded with the promise that the Polish rearmament proposals would soon be sent to Paris, and it welcomed the successful alignment of their military perspectives.

Having consulted with Noël, Gamelin reported, 'I told Rydz-Śmigły that we were in agreement.' While he transmitted the Blum Government's assent in principle to both categories of Polish demand – arms and industry – Gamelin spoke in firm figures only of the *assurance-crédit*. Aid relating to the war industry remained subject to sundry technical difficulties and a review of the entire Polish rearmament programme, and was to be negotiated in Paris when Rydz-Śmigły attended the September manoeuvres. Gamelin and Noël were both at pains to impress upon the government, as the Embassy had been earlier, that the Poles attached great importance to realisation of their war industrial plans. While the immediate crisis had been ended by the promise of one billion francs for arms, the government's task was not over.

In separate dispatches, Gamelin and Noël justified their favourable verdict on the Polish note. Symptomatic of the military insecurities engendered by the 1934 pact and the Polish exploitation of Schacht's arms offers was the pleasure with which Gamelin recounted General Stachiewicz's enthusiasm over his visit as a demonstration that there was 'absolutely nothing between Germany and Poland, save the 1934 declaration of which everyone knew'. Such exuberance over the Franco-Polish alliance had considerable weight in the atmosphere prevailing among the General Staff after 7 March: 'at a time when, faced with the dangers of the international situation, it was more than ever necessary to draw up a balance-sheet of one's friendships'.[55] Gamelin was particularly pleased by the Polish assurance that there were no Polish-German engagements against the USSR, an assurance vital to his campaign against a French military accord with the Soviet Union. He consistently relied for his policy calculations on the personal relationships he forged with foreign generals; his relationship with Badoglio had until 1936

---

[54] Szembek, *Journal*, p. 189. According to Łukasiewicz, the Poles had been virtually certain of a French demand for new Polish obligations to Czechoslovakia since a maladroit intervention by the Soviet Ambassador in Paris. Łukasiewicz wrongly attributed to Potemkine's intervention the French decision to send Gamelin to Warsaw. Łukasiewicz, *Diplomat in Paris*, p. 15.   [55] SHA, 'Pologne EMA/2', 17 February 1937.

been the most striking example. Gamelin reported to Daladier that Rydz-Śmigły's personal attributes made his undertakings all the more valuable, an assessment which Noël shared.

The Ambassador lent his full support to Gamelin's mission, 'a mission which he accomplished, moreover, in complete agreement with me'. Noël was aware that the purpose of the Gamelin visit was to ensure discussion of the important preliminary questions between the two governments before Rydz-Śmigły's visit to Paris. He also knew that Gamelin had transmitted the government's assent in principle to the Polish demands. Like Gamelin, he was satisfied with the Polish counterparts, and he knew that with transmission of the Blum Government's assent to both sets of the Polish demands, the bulk of the negotiations had taken place in Warsaw. 'Overall, I do not think that in the present circumstances, and in any case as long as M. Beck remains in charge, it would be possible for us to obtain from Poland more complete guarantees and more extensive engagements.'[56] Léger afterwards told the British that it was Gamelin who had confronted the Poles over their attitude to Germany; very little had been done with Rydz-Śmigły in Paris.[57] In the September negotiations, in holding the ring against the Blum Government, the Polish delegation in Paris – Rydz-Śmigły and Beck's vigilant new Ambassador, Łukasiewicz – enjoyed substantial advantages: Gamelin and Noël's past promises, the intervening German conscription extension, and an aggressive Polish negotiating offensive on behalf of a national war industry.[58]

Blum recalled after the war his personal dissatisfaction with Gamelin's negotiations in Warsaw. 'I do not know if he posed [the question of whether the Poles were our allies or not] with the firmness and categorical strictness which I would have hoped.'[59] When Rydz-Śmigły paid his long-awaited visit to Paris, the government attempted to patch over the sketchiness of the Warsaw conversations. As Rydz-Śmigły's host, Gamelin first presented him

---

[56] DDF II, 3, no. 153. Cf. Noël's account of Gamelin's mission in *La guerre de '39 a commencé quatre ans plus tôt* (Paris, 1979), pp. 115–16. Noël attempts to use his exclusion from the discussions during the accord's discussion in September to argue that he had no real part in the Franco-Polish arms negotiations, but, given the importance of the Gamelin mission, this is misleading. Gamelin's mission is discussed more in *La Pologne entre deux mondes*, but Noël still gives little idea of the substance of Gamelin's mission or of his own part in it.

[57] PRO, FO 371, 20764, C6144/981/55.

[58] Beck had appointed Łukasiewicz to Paris in June 1936, after purging the Embassy of Łukasiewicz's predecessor, Chłapowski, and his colleagues, whom Beck held responsible for attacks in the French press on himself and his policy. MAE, Papiers Noël, 20 June 1936.

[59] *CE Témoignages*, I, p. 130.

with a memorandum from Beneš, and then at Delbos's behest, posed a series of pointed questions from the Czech Embassy in Paris, concerning Poland's attitude in the event of a German attack on Czechoslovakia.

Beneš had seized on the occasion of General Schweisguth's attendance at the Czech manoeuvres in mid August to propose sending Gamelin a note on Czechoslovakia's quarrels with Poland.[60] He wanted Gamelin to insist in the Paris talks that France would not tolerate continuing Polish animus against Czechoslovakia. After a shrill opening, reviewing former, spurned diplomatic approaches to Poland and offers of minority negotiations, Beneš renewed offers of a wide-ranging friendship treaty and stated Czechoslovakia's willingness to resume military collaboration, once certain that Poland had no malevolent intentions.[61] Political subjects studiously avoided by Gamelin in Warsaw were thus reinstated in the Franco-Polish negotiations. According to Colson, Gamelin was reluctant to show Beneš's note to Rydz-Śmigły. When he did so, he took pains to distance himself, describing it as Beneš's personal gesture. Gamelin's only contribution was to read aloud the juridical and minority assurances for which he said he could vouch personally. Rydz-Śmigły promised to read it, but could make no response. Gamelin accepted this in good grace 'repeating to him that, personally, I insisted on not going beyond my role'.

The following day, Delbos gave Gamelin precise questions from Osuský, the Czech Ambassador, concerning the Polish attitude to an attack on Czechoslovakia. Gamelin was to put them to Rydz-Śmigły when he returned Beneš's note. To the direct question, what would Poland do at a German attack on Czechoslovakia, Rydz-Śmigły smoothly replied that Poland would be faithful to its League commitments to Czechoslovakia, and to the alliance with France, a reply embittering the Czechs who saw in it no more than a promise of Polish neutrality.[62] He then asked whether the Czechs so distrusted Poland. Aware that Osuský was threatening an extension of Czechoslovakia's fortifications along the Polish frontier, Gamelin mentioned this. Rydz-Śmigły laughed, saying it would be 'a waste of money', banter on which Gamelin seized, asking if it could be relayed to Prague.[63] D'Arbonneau, who was also present, held out

---

[60] Schw., 2SC2 Dr5, 'Mission en Tchécoslovaquie', Conversation with Beneš, 21 August 1936.   [61] DDF II, 3, no. 215.   [62] Ibid., no. 326.
[63] Gamelin transmitted Rydz-Śmigły's assurances to the Czechs the same day, *Servir* II, pp. 237–8.

the lure of the 1921 treaty, remarking that, at a German menace to Czechoslovakia, France and Poland would be bound by the treaty to hold staff talks. Rydz-Śmigły agreed in passing that this was so, but handed back Beneš's memo, about which he repeated he could make no personal response. His behaviour conformed to the entente he had reached with Beck in early August. To the question of what Poland would do in the event of a Czech-German war, he effectively refused any response extending Poland's obligations.

The financial negotiations in Paris were turbulent. Rydz-Śmigły's arrival had been preceded by Polish financial proposals which considerably exceeded the framework of previous Polish demands. The Poles exploited the German conscription extension of 24 August to raise the total amount under discussion from two billion to two billion, five hundred million francs. The one billion francs originally demanded for arms was whittled down to 800 million francs, thus increasing the money to be spent in Poland on a national war industry to 1,700,000,000 francs.[64]

While Rydz-Śmigły was being squired round French military installations, the Polish delegation rejected the first French financial proposals, for 800 million francs for French arms, an additional 200 million for purchases in France for the Polish war industry, and the abandonment of French claims on the last, overdue instalments of a 1921 arms credit. In effect, Paris's solution offered the one billion francs to be spent in France already promised by Gamelin, plus an attempt at financial sleight of hand. No liquid funds were to be transferred. The opening French gambit owed everything to the civilian ministries, the Quai d'Orsay, and particularly Finance. The Finance representatives were motivated in the main by the technical difficulties of loan transactions on the Paris market with a devaluation imminent. They also shied away from parliamentary debate. The Chambre des Députés and Senate had in the past been truculent about lending money to Central European countries less than assiduous in repaying their debts. While more nuanced, the Quai d'Orsay's position was similar. Besides wishing to avoid a parliamentary vote, it sought to retain some lever should the negotiations not produce the desired effect of binding the two

---

[64] SHA, 'EMA/2 Pologne', 'Accord de Rambouillet', 2e Bureau note, 25 August 1936. The Poles also demanded that revised commercial accords meet their financial obligations to France. This demand was left to Paul Bastid, the French Minister of Commerce, when he visited Warsaw later that month.

countries together, and the Poles later exploited their independence in war manufacturing to distance themselves from France.[65]

The Poles intransigently held to their demand for a war industries loan. Poland, they insisted, needed to develop its own arms industry; it would be useless merely to increase existing stocks of arms. When the French countered by again asking for a rough outline of the Polish rearmament programme on which to base a decision, the Poles turned abrasive. What was at stake was a question of international military collaboration, not 'an ordinary financial transaction'. It was up to France to respond to the Polish proposals; the Polish military would not draw up a rearmament programme until the size of the French credit was known.[66] Łukasiewicz, in particular, adopted an 'abrasive tone', giving the Polish financial demands the character of an ultimatum. He intended the demands for arms and war industries to be indivisible.[67]

Sympathetic to the latter demands, the EMA pressed for a settlement on the issue before Rydz-Śmigły returned to Poland. Schacht's voyage made the military's traditional policy of encouraging allied war industries appear more timely than ever. German commercial-arms penetration in the Balkans was accompanied by strenuous efforts to gain contracts in local defence-related industries, such as that won by Krupp for the Zenitsa installation in Yugoslavia. German ambitions to infiltrate Yugoslav and Roumanian factories provoked fears that, by controlling the progress of allied rearmament, the Reich could determine the most favourable time for aggression.[68] Anxious to thwart such influences in Poland, the French military pressed to combine industrial and arms support. In interministerial meetings, only the military were liberal with regard to the monies to be spent in Poland, proposing that the Poles be granted the first annuity (200–300 million francs) of a loan, and that study be made of subsequent aid to develop war manufacturing. This proposal resembled a compromise solution advocated by d'Arbonneau and the Embassy in June and July. Since the beginning of the arms negotiations, the Embassy and the EMA

---

[65] Ibid., undated 2e Bureau note, 'Armaments polonais: aide financière demandée à la France'; Note, 2 September 1936.   [66] Ibid., 2e Bureau note, 31 August 1936.
[67] Ibid.; Łukasiewicz, *Diplomat in Paris*, p. 17; Szembek, *Journal*, p. 210. Polish attachment to the transfer of large liquid sums reflected also the long-standing economic bitterness between the two countries, and Warsaw's expectation that the Blum Government would collapse amid civil disorder in the fall. Szembek, *Journal*, p. 183.
[68] DDF II, 2, no. 157; Schw., 1SC2 Dr10, 10 December; SHA, 'Yugoslavie', 11 December 1936.

had agreed on the wisdom of regarding the Polish war industrial demands as an integral, if lesser, part of the Polish desiderata.[69]

Indignant at Łukasiewicz's negotiating style, the military was adamant that the pro-German lobby which they believed had manoeuvred for months to win over Rydz-Śmigły should not at the last hour deprive him of an impressive settlement. Schweisguth confided to his journal: 'The Ambassador plays Beck's game and is intransigent, so that Rydz-Śmigły will return empty-handed.'[70] A 2e Bureau note advocated a substantial effort to meet the Polish demands, reserving till last a 'psychological reason of the greatest importance':

Vis-à-vis his country and certain members of his government, it is indispensable that General Rydz-Śmigły should take back to Poland precise assurances of French financial aid, if not, the adversaries of Franco-Polish rapprochement would have too easy a game in demonstrating the futility of this policy and would definitively distance Poland from France, whom they see as incapable of translating into concrete facts a policy only manifested in the realm of sentiment.[71]

The Reich's conscription extension was key to the effectiveness of this argument in September. The accelerated reconstitution of German military force made more pertinent than ever Gamelin's early summer advocacy of rapprochement with Poland with its large population and border on Germany, in order to re-establish the Franco-German balance imperilled by French demographic weakness. Eager to put Rydz-Śmigły's visit to diplomatic and propaganda purposes, the EMA called for redressment of the Franco-Polish alliance as a retort to Hitler's announcement.[72]

Fissures duly appeared in the Ministry of Finance's opposition to a loan to be spent in Poland. A note by a leading official in the Ministry of Finance, Jacques Rueff, destined exclusively for the EMA, pronounced the question essentially a political one, at least as long as the Polish Government's refusal to furnish a rearmament

---

[69] Under the heading of a national war industry, the Embassy and EMA grouped both the development of war manufacturing and the amassing of stocks. The Poles were known to be critically short of ammunition. (Their abandonment after the Rambouillet negotiations of plans to use the French funds to amass stocks would alarm the Ambassador and d'Arbonneau's successor as military attaché, General Musse.) SHA, 7N3000, d'Arbonneau, 3 February, 2 July; Noël, 5 February; 7N3012, Maurin-Flandin letter, 18 March 1936.

[70] Schw., 1SC2 Dr10, 2 September 1936.

[71] SHA, 'EMA/2 Pologne', 'Accord de Rambouillet', Note, 2 September 1936.

[72] Łukasiewicz complained that one of Daladier's speeches during the visit put an 'unpleasant stress on French strength'. Łukasiewicz, *Diplomat in Paris*, p. 17; DDF II, 3, no. 247.

programme prevented realistic assessment of the utility of its proposals. Rueff's argument was cold-blooded, but it broadly conformed to those of the EMA: 'It is a question of knowing whether we judge it indispensable for the purposes of national defence to buy at the price set by the government of Warsaw or at a price approaching it the political or military guarantees which it seems to have offered.'[73]

Successful compromise proposals were hammered out shortly before Rydz-Śmigły's departure, when it was agreed to loan the Poles a total of two billion francs – the sum discussed between Rydz-Śmigły and Gamelin in Warsaw – over a period of four years. The sum was to be divided between a credit of 800 million francs for purchases in France, and the remainder, 'moyens financiers' from several different operations worth 1,200 million, to be consecrated to the development of the Polish war industry. The figures were somewhat deceptive: the provisions' net effect was to ensure that at least half the total funds ended up in French pockets. These arrangements would necessitate a parliamentary vote, but Auriol saw no difficulty in this, given the Reich's extension of military service. To smooth the way for ratification, the proposal included stipulations clearing French debts in Poland as part of the loan for a Polish war industry, and giving French industries a share in its construction. Auriol was insistent that the EMA be given the right to supervise the Polish use of the funds. The 2e Bureau had previously recommended verification of the military uses of the funds at Poland's disposal, with provision for their suspension, a recommendation prompted by the Quai d'Orsay's fears of a more independent Polish policy.[74]

Although the Poles accepted the French compromise proposals, financial negotiations went down to the wire. Experts at the Ministry of Finance worked through the night of 5–6 September to elaborate a financial agreement to be initialled at Rambouillet on the 6th, Rydz-Śmigły's last day in France. By the time of President Lebrun's luncheon that day, the experts were still deadlocked over interest rates and the French insistence on a military control clause

[73] SHA, 'EMA/2, Pologne', 'Accord de Rambouillet', Note, 2 September 1936. A minute on the note – 'Has not been submitted to the Minister of Finance – do not refer to this' – suggests the distrust of the *Direction du Mouvement général des Fonds* for Auriol and the government.
[74] Ibid., and 2e Bureau note, 5 September 1936; G. Sakwa, 'The "Renewal" of the Franco-Polish Alliance in 1936 and the Rambouillet Agreement', *Polish Review*, XVI (1971), p. 59.

(*droit de regard*) for the use of funds to be spent in Poland. In
desperation, the experts motored to Rambouillet, where a meeting
over after-lunch coffee turned, in Łukasiewicz's phrase, into 'a lively
discussion' of the contentious points. The French insistence on a
control clause affronted Rydz-Śmigły, who at one point appealed to
Gamelin: 'Why do you want to spoil, by a clause which entails
suspicion of us, the value of the generous gesture which France is
making?' Blum then intervened, explaining to the General that
France wanted to be certain that the money would not be used
against Czechoslovakia or the USSR, and that it would not be spent
elsewhere than in Poland. To make his thought perfectly clear, Blum
added, 'In Germany, for example.'

Various assurances were forthcoming from the Poles, although
they were not novel. When Delbos directly posed Osuský's questions
to Rydz-Śmigły, the French were again told that it would be a waste
of Czech money to fortify the frontier with Poland. Łukasiewicz's
account of Rambouillet, in which he denies that Rydz-Śmigły
answered Blum and presents himself as intransigent on the subject of
guarantees, is tendentious. According to one of the Polish financial
officials present, Łukasiewicz actually offered to insert into the
agreement Rydz-Śmigły's phrase that the Czechs need not fortify
their border with Poland. Although the phrase was not inserted, the
offer doubtless misled Paris as to Polish goodwill.[75] Gamelin tersely
reported to Daladier that Rydz-Śmigły agreed to what Blum asked,
and so the problem of the control clause was settled. In fact, the
clause was dropped. The finished agreement stipulated only the use
of financial aid in France and Poland, without an explicit *droit de
regard*.[76] The government's acquiescence is attributable to the
pressure to reach a settlement before Rydz-Śmigły's departure.

Friendly references to Germany served to soothe Polish sensibilities
after Delbos's pointed questions on behalf of Osuský, and Blum's
strictures on the French money to be spent in Poland. Delbos and
Blum spoke reassuringly to Łukasiewicz of French desires for
rapprochement with Germany. (It is important to remember that
Rydz-Śmigły's visit followed not only on the German announcement
of two year service, but also on Schacht's conversations with Blum,
which had briefly opened the vista of an international economic/

[75] DDF II, 3, nos. 301, 308; *CE Témoignages*, I, p. 130; Szembek, *Journal*, pp. 205–8;
Łukasiewicz, *Diplomat in Paris*, pp. 18–19; Wieslaw Domaniewski, 'Umowa w Rambouillet', *Zeszytg historyczne*, no. 47 (1979), pp. 226–7. I am indebted to Henry Rollet for
calling my attention to this information.   [76] DDF II, 3, no. 308.

disarmament conference.) They did not intend to sanction Beck's attitude. However, even if the Blum Government had been in a position to exert pressures for Beck's departure – which, as has been shown, it was not in September 1936 – there is reason to doubt that it would have done so. Jules Moch, chief of Blum's secretariat at the Matignon, recalls Blum's sentiment that it was not for his government to depose its opposite numbers.[77] Vulnerable to the hostility of foreign governments with its Socialist premier and Communist backing, the Front populaire reckoned it the better part of wisdom not to intervene flagrantly in the internal affairs of other states. Its tactic remained fostering an evolution in Polish policy that would sweep Beck along, rather than estranging Warsaw by attacking Beck frontally.[78]

The lack of coordination between French and Polish foreign policies, a subject avoided by Gamelin in Warsaw, was discussed during Rydz-Śmigły's week in France. Łukasiewicz recalled that Daladier complained of it, and Blum at Rambouillet elicited from Rydz-Śmigły a statement of his resolve to exercise over Polish foreign policy 'an absolutely decisive control and sovereignty', a statement more forcefully put than the General's promise of May to Noël, and consistent with the government's desire to involve Rydz-Śmigły in foreign policy formulation.[79] Admittedly, the original governmental impulse had been to elicit written recognition of political aspects in the negotiations, along with Beck's participation in conversations on Czechoslovakia. Acceptance of Rydz-Śmigły's various undertakings entailed risk. Evidence of his control over Polish foreign policy, notably as regarded Czechoslovakia, was to follow rather than precede the completed arms deal.

STORMY SEQUEL: BECK, CZECHOSLOVAKIA, AND THE
POLISH WAR INDUSTRIES QUESTION

The affair of the control clause or more exactly, the Polish assurances given in exchange for the clause's disappearance, occasioned immediate controversy. Soon after Rydz-Śmigły's departure, an article in the semi-official *Le Temps* predicted a Polish-Czech rapprochement and alluded to the statements dismissing the need for

[77] Letter from Jules Moch, 11 August 1977.
[78] This characterisation belongs to Robert Coulondre, Assistant Political Director in September 1936. DDF II, 4, no. 218.
[79] Łukasiewicz, *Diplomat in Paris*, p. 19; *CE Témoignages*, I, p. 130.

Czech fortifications on the Polish border which the Poles had offered to put into the Rambouillet accords. Beck and the Paris Embassy gave no quarter in denying *Le Temps'* information. The governmental press agency declared that there could have been no mention of Czech fortifications during the Paris conversations, concerned as they were exclusively with Franco-Polish relations. A virulent campaign opened in the Polish press denouncing the recent action of the Czech Government in trying a group of Poles accused of sedition in Teschen. It gave Beck occasion to exploit one of his favourite themes, that Franco-Czech relations were entirely independent of France's relations with Poland.[80]

After the maladroitness of *Le Temps* gave him an opportunity to show his hand, Beck, whom Noël believed had done everything possible to prevent Rydz-Śmigły from going to Paris, pursued his campaign to entrench himself and his policies by appropriating Rydz-Śmigły's French triumph. Photographs of the two showed a smiling Beck welcoming Rydz-Śmigły back to Poland. Beck borrowed glory on the French side by claiming Rambouillet as the product of his assurances at the reoccupation. To the Germans and Roumanians, he presented Rambouillet as a confirmation of the bilateralism of his French policy, accepted by Germany in 1934. But if Noël was justly indignant at Beck's behaviour, he was certain that Rydz-Śmigły had returned to Poland devoted to the French alliance.[81]

In the weeks after Rydz-Śmigły's return, the Ambassador anxiously awaited a government reshuffle. Noël saw in the French devaluation of late September a possible catalyst, via a Polish devaluation, for the removal of Beck. The chief Polish proponent of devaluation was Adam Koc, the collaborator of Rydz-Śmigły who had quit the presidency of the Bank of Poland several months earlier over a government decision to implement exchange controls rather than devalue. For Noël, the Rambouillet accords' invalidation of Koc's whispering campaign of spring 1936 was an accomplishment on a par with their enhancement of Rydz-Śmigły's domestic position. He pinned his hopes on a Polish devaluation, which by setting President Mościcki, its prime opponent, against Koc would compel Mościcki's resignation, and clear the way for Rydz-Śmigły to act

---

[80] DDF II, 3, no. 275; MAE, Papiers Noël, 8, 11 September 1936.
[81] MAE, Papiers Noël, 11 September, 22 October 1936; DDF II, 3, no. 271; Łukasiewicz, *Diplomat in Paris*, p. 21.

against Beck.[82] Noël's hopes regarding Beck's dismissal continued unabated after the Rambouillet negotiations, when, as before, Beck's fate was linked to that of Mościcki.

Only in November did Noël acknowledge the disappointment of his hopes concerning Rydz-Śmigły. He rehearsed his past conviction that, after Rydz-Śmigły's voyage to France and the triumphant popular welcome on his return, the General would use his growing influence to neutralise, 'while waiting for better', Beck's personal tendencies, with the result that Polish policy would progressively undergo a profound transformation. It had been almost universally predicted in Warsaw, according to Noël, that Rydz-Śmigły would be rid of Beck as soon as Koc's programme appeared and a new government could be constituted. But neither Koc's programme nor the promised governmental reshuffle had materialised. After the government's decision not to devalue the zloty, Koc had decided to await an aggravation of economic difficulties in order to give maximum impact to the announcement of his programme. Polish opinion became restive, and Rydz-Śmigły's prestige had been affected. He had then unwisely accepted the baton of Marshal, a promotion vehemently criticised in Piłsudskite circles, and since early October, ill with appendicitis, he had not participated in visits of foreign dignitaries, such as the new Prime Minister of Roumania, Antonesco.[83] Beck, who, according to Noël, had believed that rapprochement with France would entail his fall, had been relieved by Rydz-Śmigły's inaction after his return and had jockeyed to improve his position, abetted by international developments such as Titulesco's disgrace, Belgium's deepening neutralism, several successes at Geneva, and a private visit to France, where he was received as a matter of courtesy by members of the Blum Government.[84]

Rumours of a governmental change still circulated, but, having so long awaited a reshuffle, Noël, like some character out of Beckett's *Godot*, concluded wearily: 'In any other country, such an imprecise situation...could not be prolonged beyond a short period. In Poland, it seems to me, to the contrary, that the incertitude and complexities that it entails are rather an element in its duration.' Noël's final word on the subject was the speculation that the ailing

[82] DDF II, 1, no. 540; 2, no. 45; 3, no. 433; MAE, Papiers Noël, 30 September 1936; FRUS 1936, I, p. 540.   [83] SHA, 'Pologne', 25 November, 8 December 1936.

[84] Blum and Delbos none the less took the opportunity to raise the issue of Czechoslovakia with Beck. Blum expressed himself negatively to the Czechs about the conversation: despite Blum's energetic approach, Beck was evasive. Czech T-120, 1041/1809/414109–10.

Rydz-Śmigły had set out to demonstrate to the country that he would use his influence only in exceptional cases, when major policy decisions were required.[85]

This view of Rydz-Śmigły acting as a *deus ex machina* at critical moments in the national destiny, while a marked retreat on Noël's part and a disappointment to French hopes, allowed the comforting belief that he would intervene to make the decision necessary to align Poland with Czechoslovakia in a conflict. In the meantime, Paris had to content itself with Beck's explanations for the conspicuous absence of a Polish-Czech détente. While Polish relations with Germany lost much of the intimacy formerly shocking to French opinion, Beck and his school directed it as before, if with more prudence. When Antonesco visited Paris in mid December shortly after a visit to Warsaw, he transmitted Beck's assurances that, while there was nothing grave between Poland and Czechoslovakia, it was necessary to be circumspect because Germany was watching closely for any Polish-Czech rapprochement.[86] Gamelin's immediate reaction was 'That's worth what it's worth', but in presenting the situation to his staff, he said more optimistically that, while Beck could not strengthen relations with Czechoslovakia without discontenting Germany, he desired their progressive amelioration. Gamelin took comfort from military intelligence: not only were the Poles constructing fortifications to protect the Silesian basin, as he had suggested, but the Polish General Staff was studying an offensive in Silesia with only a simple *couverture* against the USSR.[87]

To this extent, Gamelin's sense of injury at the Polish attitude during the Munich crisis was to be genuine. Rydz-Śmigły's involvement in the Polish operation in Teschen was as great an affront to him as Badoglio's leadership of Italy into the war in June 1940. When Rydz-Śmigły wrote to justify the Teschen seizure, denying that there had been any discussion of Czechoslovakia at Rambouillet and claiming to have given a negative response to Beneš's memorandum, Gamelin complained bitterly to Daladier of 'the policy of M. Beck to which the Marshal appears presently

[85] DDF II, 3, no. 433; MAE, Papiers Noël, 22 October, 18 November 1936; 20 February 1937. Noël's very retrospective comments on Rydz-Śmigły's inadequacies in *L'agression allemande*, pp. 149–50 can be compared with his admission of having relied on Rydz-Śmigły to topple Beck in *La Pologne entre deux mondes*, pp. 118, 144; these passages in *La Pologne* on their own considerably soften the Ambassador's otherwise reiterated claim (ibid., p. 122) to have urged that Beck's departure be a strict precondition of the French loan.
[86] Schw., 1SC2 Dr10, 22 December 1936; 1SC2 Dr11, 13 January 1937.
[87] Ibid., 8, 13 January 1937.

pledged'.[88] Czechoslovakia was the victim of the policy advanced by
the Embassy and EMA, according to which reinforcement of Rydz-
Śmigły's domestic position represented the most effective way to
transform the Franco-Polish alliance.

If the months after the Rambouillet negotiations were critical for
Léon Noël's calculations on Rydz-Śmigły and Beck, they were, if
anything, more critical for his concern over Polish allocation of the
French monies. As will be recalled, according to the Ambassador, in
June 1936 he put to Delbos and Léger two conditions, of which the
first pertained to his fear that the Poles would squander the greater
part of the French monies of the construction on a national war
industry. He claimed to have persuaded the Quai d'Orsay to draft
a text, in effect the control clause, for the financial accords, but it was
abandoned in September by Gamelin, Blum, and Delbos, with
disastrous consequences. This is a plausible account. The Poles
suddenly raised their demands in late August, although they did not
obtain all that they had asked in September. There was indeed an
affair of a control clause, omitted at the last minute from the
September agreement. For the veracity of his claims, however, the
central question is: are there contemporary indications that Noël
acted several months in advance of the September negotiations to
prevent the Poles from using the greater part of the Rambouillet
proceeds for a national war industry, for the project which later
came to be known as the Polish security triangle?

In the period before the Blum Government, the Embassy and
EMA were agreed in urging on the Quai d'Orsay assent to both
headings of the Polish demands. With the advent of the recalcitrant
Front populaire, the Embassy's documented pressures were for some,
for any measure of governmental support for the war industries
section of the Polish demands. Noël was prepared to work through
military channels to extract the government's decision. His channels
of communication with the EMA and Gamelin personally were
excellent. It is thus striking that, given the EMA's direct involvement
in the question, no echo of Noël's allegedly profound concern in June
1936 with the threat posed by the Polish designs reached Daladier,
Gamelin, or through d'Arbonneau's correspondence, Gérodias of
Army intelligence.

In contrast, it is possible to follow minutely the alarm caused the

[88] SHA, 5N579, 'Cabinet du ministre', Gamelin-Daladier letter, 12 October 1938.

Embassy by Polish plans for an industrial security triangle at the end of 1936. In correspondence between Léger and the Ministry of War concerning the Embassy's justified fears, there is no reference to such plans having been bruited since the early summer.[89] It might be argued that, having disregarded the Ambassador's prescient counsels of June, Léger and Daladier had no interest in including such a damning reference in official correspondence, were it not for two dispatches in Noël's own papers. On 31 October, Noël reported that the Polish General Staff had not yet fixed its projects for the French credits to be spent in Poland, but that a struggle between industrialists for their partition appeared to be going on:

It is to be feared, in these conditions, that the financial effort to which France has agreed will not be used according to the degree of real importance and order of urgency of outlay to be made. What matters most of all is the build-up of stocks – *at present insignificant* – in munitions and raw materials, beginning with coal.[90]

Alluding to the failure at Rambouillet to establish a military control clause, Noël suggested that the negotiations for a revalorisation of the credits after the French devaluation could furnish an indirect means of supervising their allocation. The clause did not result from the revaluation negotiations, and several weeks later, on 25 November, Noël sent word of the grandiose investment plan for a security triangle. He strongly deplored the project as hampering the build-up of the indispensable munitions stocks: 'The information reaching me in this regard, *reinforces the fears which I expressed to Your Excellence on 31 October*, indicating that it was to be feared that the credits opened by France would not be used according to the degree of urgency of outlay to be made.'[91] If, in June 1936, Noël had feared a disaster with the French credits to be spent in Poland and had spoken out forcefully on the subject, why did he date his very generally phrased concern from autumn 1936? Noël's new military attaché, Colonel Musse, also dated the Embassy's fears of Polish misuse of the French funds from the same period, and, in two letters, took credit for prodding the Ambassador on the subject.[92]

The precise corroboration provided by the contemporary docu-

[89] SHA, 7N3000, Léger-Daladier exchange of letters, 28 November, 10 December 1936.
[90] MAE, Papiers Noël, 31 October 1936; italics in the original.
[91] Ibid., 25 November 1936; my italics.
[92] SHA, 7N3000, 8 December; 7N3012, Musse-Gérodias letters, 11 November, 8 December 1936.

mentation for Noël's alarm over the Polish financial projects in October–December 1936, and the absence of any documentary corroboration in the quarters in which one would expect reference to it in June and July 1936, strongly suggest the inaccuracy of this part of Noël's account of his June conversation with Delbos. Noël doubtless supported a proviso stipulating that the Poles should communicate their arms programme, but there was nothing exceptional in that. The Embassy and EMA had attempted to obtain the Polish programme since before the advent of the Front populaire. Throughout the period of Gamelin's visit, Noël had no reason to believe that the Poles would not communicate their arms programme. Rydz-Śmigły promised to do so in Warsaw, and Noël and Gamelin gave every sign of believing him. The essential point, however, is that, in supporting the proviso, the war industrial developments to which the Ambassador later linked it had not yet arisen in his own mind. Nothing indicates that June 1936 marked a turning point in Noël's appreciation of the Polish demands. While doubtless a matter of regret to the Embassy as to the EMA, abandonment of the control clause in September in the face of Rydz-Śmigły's consternation was a logical consequence of the policy they had advocated for months.

In the controversy over the Polish war industry in late 1936, the EMA stood firm, finding itself for the first time at cross-purposes with the Embassy. To an indignant letter from Musse, Gérodias minuted:

the General [Gamelin?] has just read your letter; he thinks that while keeping watch over the affair, we cannot act as guardians or rather as a judicial council. You know moreover that he feels that after having built up the indispensable stocks, it is important for a country to have factories ready to function from mobilisation.[93]

The Embassy's plaints found more of a hearing among the civilians. Meeting Beck at Geneva in early 1937, Delbos, acting in the main on suggestions from Daladier, pointed out that the Polish industrial programme cost some six times the promised credits. He advised Beck to combine plans for construction with the build-up of stocks and increased production in existing factories. He also queried the location of new roads to be built with French credits, suggesting that roads in southern and eastern Poland could alarm the Czechs

[93] SHA, 7N3012, 8 December 1936.

and Soviets.[94] Delbos had no success in extracting Polish under-takings to streamline the proposals. Warsaw proceeded with construction. Rather than censuring the Polish attitude, Gamelin was annoyed by Delbos's démarche, minuting on a letter from the Quai d'Orsay: 'I continue to think that all of this is very delicate – that we risk, without any very clear advantage, offending the Poles – why not let the soldiers settle the greater part of this among themselves.'[95]

In the months before the war's outbreak, the disproportion in the accord's application between monies spent in France and monies spent in Poland grew, as industrial difficulties and military–political factors caused the French to honour less than 20 per cent of the Polish arms credit in France.[96] It is true that, as Noël points out, the new Polish arms factories only opened their doors in time to be bombarded by the Luftwaffe. For this policy, the General Staff bears the principal responsibility on the French side.

RAMBOUILLET: A REASSESSMENT

The Blum Government has been much criticised for the flaccidity of its diplomacy towards Poland, for its failure to secure the removal of Beck or to alter Polish policy towards Czechoslovakia. The consequences have seemed momentous in retrospect: Rambouillet was the last Franco-Polish negotiation before Munich. The most outspoken critic of the Front populaire's conduct of the negotiations has been Léon Noël. The force of Noël's criticism rests in his claim that it was practical politics for the Blum Government to rid itself of Beck as the most efficient means of reversing Poland's policy to Czechoslovakia. Noël's account, based on the claim that in June 1936 he presented to the new government cogent and prescient policies concerning Beck's future and a possible Polish misuse of the French funds, has played an important part in the historiography of Franco-Polish relations before the war.

The contemporary documentation, however, suggests another reading, in which the Franco-Polish negotiations emerge as long and complex. The project for French financial aid inherited by the Blum Government already bore the two features which would most

[94] SHA, 7N3000, Daladier-Delbos letter, 10 December 1936; Léger-Daladier letter, 20 February 1937; DDF II, 3, no. 308.
[95] SHA, 7N3012, Gamelin minute to Léger-Daladier letter, 20 February 1937.
[96] Łukasiewicz, *Diplomat in Paris*, p. 21.

influence its elaboration: first, the Warsaw Embassy's great faith, shared by the EMA, in Rydz-Śmigły; second, the EMA's consideration of the Polish demands in terms of the consequences of the Franco-Soviet ratification debate, the related Rhineland reoccupation, and the Front populaire's supposed Russophilia.

News of Rydz-Śmigły's opposition to Beck during the Polish governmental changes of October 1935 reached the Embassy with the first Polish solicitations for aid. From October 1935 until November 1936, Noël cherished the hope that Rydz-Śmigły would oust Beck. The Embassy's faith in Rydz-Śmigły, not just as a privileged spokesman on the problems of Franco-Polish relations, the role in which the Blum Government sought to cast him by sending Gamelin to Warsaw, but as the ideal agent for Beck's suppression led the Ambassador to downplay such episodes as Rydz-Śmigły's defence of Beck in May and his attempt to blackmail Paris over the German arms offers in June. Noël's sense of drama was an illusion. Whatever tensions had existed between Rydz-Śmigły and Beck, by August, when Gamelin went to Warsaw, they had reached a working agreement on the line to take with the French. Rydz-Śmigły's view of the negotiations had strong affinities with Beck's, namely the belief that the most important consequence of a rapprochement with France would be to raise Poland's stock in Berlin.[97] Rydz-Śmigły's entente with Beck was reflected in the fundamental ambiguity of his assurances to the French. He never pledged to alter Polish foreign policy, only, in a promise on which he did not make good, to involve himself in its direction. For the rest, in his eagerness to obtain French arms, he countenanced the discussion of topics antipathetic to Beck. These could always be downplayed afterwards, as Beck and Łukasiewicz ensured that they were. The prime casualty of these miscalculations concerning Rydz-Śmigły was Czechoslovakia.

The effect on the Rambouillet negotiations of the military's ruminations on the Soviet pact was equally marked. The EMA from the start regarded the Polish arms démarches from the vantage of its own relations with the USSR. Polish assurances of continuing equilibrium between Germany and the USSR far outweighed in value for the EMA any attempt to reconcile the Polish and Soviet

---

[97] Szembek, *Journal*, p. 207; for Beck's assurances to Berlin after Gamelin's visit that he and Rydz-Śmigły were agreed that nothing had changed in Polish foreign policy, DDF II, 3, no. 169.

alliances. These assurances were deemed vital both to an eventual second front against Germany, and to safeguarding France's distance from the Soviet embrace. The Rhineland reoccupation and the Left's electoral victory in the spring of 1936 led Gamelin to authorise important initiatives towards the two allies, Italy and Poland, whose importance had been enhanced by the disappearance of the Rhineland statutes. In the case of Poland, Gamelin's initiative coupled assent to a substantial part of the Polish arms demands with assurances of the falsity of rumours concerning Soviet air bases in Czechoslovakia, in a move to foster the EMA's long-standing goal of Polish-Czech rapprochement.

When the Front populaire took power, its negotiating position in Warsaw – circumvention of the issue of revision of the 1921 treaties, acceptance of German-Polish détente, and the demand for a loyal search for a political and military rapprochement with Czechoslovakia, rather than its immediate realisation – was not inflexible, but it was subverted by Noël and Gamelin, who agreed that Paris's priority should be a revival of Polish-Czech staff contacts, rather than a Polish-Czech political entente. They turned the government's military bias into an almost exclusively military démarche. Their preference for a loose-jointed Polish-Czech military connection represented more than Noël's repugnance at involving Beck in the negotiations or Gamelin's penchant for relying on foreign generals. It had strategic underpinnings in the EMA's extreme caution in the matter of provoking Germany. The EMA considered it certain that, even an accord comprising France, Czechoslovakia, and Poland, without the USSR, would be regarded by Hitler as an attempt at encirclement and broken before it could be realised.[98] Its approach then was deliberately low key, the creation of an infrastructure for Polish-Czech entente rather than a conspicuous flurry of finished agreements. French liaison at a conflict as a kind of hinge between Poland, Czechoslovakia, and the USSR was crucial to this scheme of things. Indirection was characteristic of Gamelin, especially as regarded the USSR, and Rydz-Śmigły's acceptance of a liaison mission in a conflict seemed to promise him leverage to influence Polish military reaction in a Czech-German crisis. Gamelin saw little interest in pushing the Poles and Czechs into an inseparable peace-time entente when the Soviet mortgage still hung over Czech policy,

[98] Schw., 1SC2 Dr9, 25 June 1936.

and especially when the Blum Government's attitude to a military pact with the USSR was still fluid.[99]

The real significance of June 1936 for the fledgling negotiations was twofold. For the EMA, the Front populaire's assumption of power led to Cot's destabilising pressures for a Franco-Soviet military entente in aid of Czechoslovakia. For the Embassy, there were dangerous delays in the new government's acceptance of the Polish demands, and the harrowing prospect of its insensitivity to the delicate Polish internal game, on which it thought so much depended. Léon Noël's accounts consign the negotiations to an historical vacuum. Virtually all the factors shaping them are omitted or misrepresented, as are many of his own most pertinent actions. By focussing on June 1936, Noël invites the reader to compare his own perspicacity with the weakness and indeed the foolishness of the Front populaire and of General Gamelin, as much a pariah in 1941 as in 1946.

It is not incidental that the thrust of M. Noël's narrative corresponds closely with the Riom indictment. The influence of the politicised proceedings at Riom on this period's historiography is for the most part a saddening aspect of its study. Riom afforded a stage for the festering of personal and ideological convictions relating to responsibility for the calamities of 1939–40; to these powerful emotions was sometimes added the desire for self-exculpation.[100]

Far from displaying unusual prescience in June 1936, Noël had already embarked on a collaboration with Gamelin which effectively deprived the French Government of the option of pre-conditions in the negotiations. For the Ambassador's preoccupations – Beck and Polish allocation of the French funds – the pulse points in the negotiations were to be found in his May démarche to Rydz-Śmigły; in his continuing collaboration with Gamelin in Warsaw in August; and, lastly, in the period after the Rambouillet negotiations, when Noël was forced to admit the futility of his hopes that Rydz-Śmigły

---

[99] Rydz-Śmigły's presence in France in September was to be opportune, abetting the military in deflecting pressures from within the government to retort to the German conscription by consolidating French ties with the USSR. Cf. P. Cot, *Le procès de la République*, II (New York, 1944), p. 340.

[100] It should be said that already in the spring of 1937, on the defensive *vis-à-vis* the Czechs and the Polish opposition who had counted on Beck's fall as a condition of French aid, Noël sought to shift blame for Beck's retention of power to the Blum Government. Slávik dispatch, 8 April 1937, no. 75 in *Europäische Politik 1933–1939 im Spiegel der Prager Akten* (Essen, 1941), pp. 70–1.

would dismiss Beck, and when Warsaw made known its plans for a national war industry.

The tendentiousness of Noël's various accounts has obscured the turbulent negotiating climate in which the Blum Government found itself. Franco-German competition for the loyalties of the Polish Army and the post-Rhineland miasma of Franco-Polish relations would have constrained any French Government. So would the unspoken assumption of both sides in the negotiations that arms and financial aid were being used to supplant extensive French obligations. The structure of the negotiations, in which the bulk of hard political discussion took place in Warsaw, meant that the margin of diplomatic manoeuvre left the Blum Government in September was small. Remaining negotiating slack was virtually taken up by the Reich's conscription extension. At Rambouillet, in order that there should be an arms accord, the government succumbed to a form of the exclusive reliance on Rydz-Śmigły's personal uprightness and loyalty to the alliance, which had previously been the preserve of the Embassy and the military. In the last resort, the issue for the government, as Blum implied in 1947 testimony, was that elusive diplomatic entity, the restoration of trust. Describing the malaise in the alliance before Gamelin initiated his government's negotiations with the Poles, Blum compared international to personal relations: 'Really, this kind of existence was no more bearable on the plane of international politics than it is on that of personal relations.'[101]

The question left by the contemporary documentation is not so much why the Blum Government signed an arms accord in return for inadequate counterparts, as why Blum entrusted the negotiations, including those on the essential matter of Czechoslovakia, to the EMA. The answers are partly in immediate circumstances – the need, as Blum described it, to short-circuit Beck; partly in the new government's commitment to national defence and its readiness to utilise the newly reorganised military bureaucracy; and partly in a traditional dilemma of radical governments, whether to rely on experts of uncertain loyalty.[102] Blum's response to this dilemma was related to the nature of his exercise of power. He was concerned

---

[101] *CE Témoignages*, I, p. 130.
[102] Blum's dependence on Gamelin appears relatively unforced, given the semblance of loyalty Gamelin bestowed on the new government in its first months, see above, p. 105, n. 38. The passages in *Servir* on the Franco-Polish negotiations as such are consistently untrustworthy.

throughout his mandate to maintain bridges to conservative bastions, such as the Senate and the Army. This concern often impinged on external relations: it was again visible during the 1937 Franco-Soviet military conversations. For the French ruling classes, the burden of proving legitimacy rested entirely with the Front populaire. Blum felt keenly the burden of proving himself a Prime Minister responsive to all aspects of the national interest. (Among the ironies surrounding his government was that slogans such as 'Mieux Hitler que Blum' sought to deny him precisely this political legitimacy.) It should also be said that the stakes of military loyalty were particularly high for Blum. In the crackling tensions of 1936–7, the threat of civil war and external intervention was rarely to be disregarded.

CHAPTER 5

Blum and the diplomats: the Franco-Petite Entente negotiations, I

As well as conducting major negotiations with Poland, the Front populaire became the only French Government to negotiate with the Petite Entente as such. Largely thrust on the Blum Government by the Petite Entente's discontents, the Franco-Petite Entente interlude demonstrated the full extent of Central European centrifugal forces. The negotiations were vitiated by the collapse of the pivots of France's involvement in Central Europe, its reliance on Italy and Russia.

LE PROJET TITULESCO

There were ominous signs of the Petite Entente's disarray when its heads of state assembled in Bucharest in early June 1936. Titulesco had sent Paris an SOS in May for energetic action to restore French prestige in Central Europe, prestige which, he warned, had been seriously damaged by the Rhineland reoccupation. In Bucharest, this was amplified. Titulesco and Beneš predicted that Hitler would shortly bring about an Anschluss and then fall on Czechoslovakia and Roumania. They made it plain that the Petite Entente's lack of any advance position with regard to an Anschluss and a German attack on Czechoslovakia was intended to provoke Paris and London into manifesting their attachment to the Central European status quo. Continuing great power inadequacy, they warned, would compel Czechoslovakia and Roumania to reach accommodation with Germany.[1] The Petite Entente Chiefs of Staff, meeting in mid June, reached a similar conclusion: commitment against German expansionism only if assured of French military support. The Roumanian generals said that, if France isolated itself, and the Central European states were forced to choose between

[1] DDF II, 2, no. 291; PRO, FO 371, 20385, R3572/1644/67; R3723/1644/67.

188

Germany and the USSR, they would choose the Reich. They voiced ardent hopes for a military alliance between France and the Petite Entente.[2]

Titulesco, France and Russia

From the Petite Entente meeting in Bucharest, Titulesco journeyed in mid June to an international conference in Montreux, summoned to resolve Turkish claims to reestablish sovereignty over the Straits. France was represented by Joseph Paul-Boncour, the former Foreign Minister and long-time political ally of Pierre Cot. Soon after the Montreux conference began, Paul-Boncour and Litvinov came to grips with a problem which had recently preoccupied Paul-Boncour, Soviet passage through Poland and Roumania to Czechoslovakia.[3] Both before and after his attendance at the June session of the League in Geneva, Paul-Boncour patronised conversations at the ongoing conference in Montreux on a mutual aid pact between Titulesco and Litvinov. These conversations, according to Paul-Boncour, envisaged precise formulae for Soviet troop passage across Roumania. In his 1932–4 negotiations with the Soviets, Paul-Boncour had made overtures for a mutual aid network to include the USSR, France, Poland, and the Petite Entente. His memoirs suggest that his mediation in the unofficial conversations at Montreux was a sequel to this earlier diplomacy. At Montreux, he provided sustenance for Titulesco's hopes for a French-sponsored accommodation with the USSR by fostering the elaboration of an effective French 'protectorate' over the Petite Entente, linked to an overall Franco-Soviet military understanding to which Litvinov might also adhere.[4]

For Titulesco, the logic of entente with the USSR had been irresistible since the French sought to manoeuvre the Petite Entente into an anti-Anschluss alignment pivoted on Italy. In January 1935 at the Petite Entente meeting at Ljubljana, Titulesco had appealed for accelerated French negotiations with the USSR, arguing that an

---

[2] DDF II, 2, no. 365.

[3] Paul-Boncour, *Entre deux guerres*, III, pp. 60–2; Schw., 1SC2 Dr8, 30 April 1936; DDF II, 2, no. 358.

[4] Paul-Boncour, *Entre deux guerres*, III, pp. 58–60; DDF I, 5, nos. 88, 139, 193; II, 2, no. 475. As to the previously insoluble problem of troop passage, no explicit mention was to be made of Bessarabia: the USSR was to undertake not to leave its troops on the Roumanian side of the Dneister river after hostilities ended.

eastern pact including Roumania was indispensable to the operation of the Rome Accords. The Petite Entente countries could not turn to Central European questions until assured of their eastern frontiers.[5] The Czech-Soviet pact of June 1935 forced him to conclude that, in a conflict, his country would be used with or without its permission as a conduit to Czechoslovakia. In the Roumanian-Soviet talks which followed, unfounded Roumanian claims to have obtained a formal French guarantee for a passage formula sparing Bessarabia suggest that Titulesco sought to underwrite his negotiations with Litvinov by a precise French commitment which would replace explicit Soviet recognition of the disputed Bessarabian frontier.[6] Once the Soviets had let pass what he regarded as the psychological moment for an accord, immediately after signing their pacts with France and Czechoslovakia, relations dramatically worsened between Titulesco and the Soviet Minister, whom he suspected of fostering a Popular Front formation in Roumania.[7] Titulesco sought to make use of the Soviet Union by opposing its force to Germany's, but he remained on guard, 'a warm partisan of the Franco-Soviet pact, but...not for all that, an admirer of the Front populaire formula'.[8]

At the Petite Entente's meeting in June 1936, King Carol had renewed Titulesco's year-old mandate to enter into conversations for a Roumanian-Soviet pact modelled on that between Czechoslovakia and the USSR. The Bucharest conference brought the problem of Soviet passage to the fore when it accepted Czech-inspired and financed plans for a strategic railway line to assure a Czech-Soviet linkage across Roumania.[9] Titulesco's ambivalence towards the USSR induced him from the time of the Bucharest meeting to contemplate a direct appeal to France.

During a break in the Montreux conference, Titulesco went to Geneva for the June League session. Virtually on arrival, he sought out René Massigli, to whom he proposed 'a single treaty of alliance with the Petite Entente' which he disingenuously described as the

[5] MAE, 'Tchécoslovaquie-Petite Entente', Remerand dispatch, 12 January; Naggiar dispatch, 26 January 1935; *International Affairs* (Moscow, 1963), 'The Struggle...for Collective Security', II, p. 123.   [6] PRO, FO 371, 19499, R4616/1/67.
[7] DDF II, 2, no. 303.   [8] SHA, 'Roumanie: SR', 25 December 1937.
[9] Czech T-120, 1041/1809/414097/414110–11. The Roumanians had refused an earlier Czech project involving a more conspicuous Soviet link. PRO, FO 371, 20385, R3723/1644/67; SHA, 'Roumanie', Delmas dispatch, 11 June 1936.

proposal of the Petite Entente heads of state.[10] Massigli dismissed Titulesco's initial approach, but the next day, when Titulesco returned to the subject 'with an extraordinary vehemence' at a luncheon given by Delbos, Massigli realised, as he wrote privately to Léger, that it was 'a manoeuvre...likely to produce serious consequences'. Titulesco insisted that France had everything to gain from Roumania and Yugoslavia's assuming towards it engagements similar to those France had to Czechoslovakia. In return, France should promise aid at any aggression against Roumania and Yugoslavia.[11]

Massigli inferred from Titulesco's excited exposition that, in practical terms, such a treaty would be directed against Italian aggression. Titulesco accompanied his remarks with a diatribe against Italy, blasting its equivocal policy and 'the double game' of Laval's diplomacy. When Massigli interrupted to argue that excluding Italy from a new Central European alignment would precipitate an Italo-German entente, Titulesco exploded with rage, accusing the Quai d'Orsay of systematic Italophilia. His attack on Italy was meant to rally the Yugoslavs, whose wavering had been conspicuous at the Bucharest meeting, held during an early June period of Italian military alert. The Bucharest meeting, like the Petite Entente's preceding meeting in Belgrade, had been dominated by Yugoslav fears that, having defeated Ethiopia, Italy would turn on Yugoslavia.[12] The Yugoslavs had approached the French for aid in case of Italian attack, but hopes by the Blum Government in June to revive collective designs, including a Mediterranean pact to protect Yugoslavia against all attack, led it to offer only a routine reiteration of its obligations under the 1927 treaty. The Yugoslavs regarded this as virtually useless.[13] Their fears reached alarming proportions. The Yugoslav General Staff took the view that the defeat of Germany would only play the game of Italian imperialism.[14] In Geneva, Massigli observed that the Yugoslav representative, Pouritch, seemed much keener for precise French assurances than for Titulesco's 'new pieces of paper'.

---

[10] Titulesco had agitated at the Bucharest meeting for a military mutual aid pact with France against German, Italian and Polish aggression, but his proposal had not been formally adopted. DDF II, 2, no. 475.

[11] MAE, Papiers Massigli, 'Affaires de l'Europe centrale', Massigli-Léger letter, 27 June 1936. [12] DDF II, 2, nos. 291, 304.

[13] PRO, FO 371, 20436, R4727/1627/92.

[14] DDF II, 2, no. 365; Czech T-120, 1041/1809/414097.

With the French delegation, Titulesco attempted to capitalise on the blackmail at the recent Petite Entente meetings, announcing that a Franco-Petite Entente treaty would abolish cause for fear of Yugoslav or Roumanian 'turns at the waltz' with Germany. Massigli did not doubt that Titulesco would attempt to sway Delbos by another outburst, or perhaps 'he already thought of invoking [Delbos's] refusal to hasten an evolution towards the other side', i.e., towards Germany. He suggested that it would be desirable to ascertain if Beneš was aware of Titulesco's latest manoeuvre: 'Beneš would understand immediately that, by wanting to ask us too much, the Petite Entente would obtain nothing and he would know how to bring his partner round to more reasonable views.'[15]

Perhaps motivated by Pouritch's presence at Delbos's luncheon, Titulesco made no mention of the Soviet Union, but, before the Geneva session ended, he brought into talks with the French delegation his Soviet *arrière-pensées*. His remarks indicate that he regarded a new round of Soviet conversations as part of a wider framework in which France would undertake additional obligations to Roumania, in return for Roumania's extension of its obligations to Czechoslovakia and involvement with the USSR. He argued that a reinforcement of the Petite Entente, its acceptance of engagements to intervene against Germany, the improvement of Roumanian-Soviet relations in the interest of Czechoslovakia and so of France – all of these things would be easier to realise if France intervened to assume an assistance obligation *vis-à-vis* the Petite Entente as a whole.[16] Massigli remembers: '[the Quai d'Orsay] was hardly favourable to these grand schemes. The reason for our reserve was simple: Titulesco was fundamentally anti-Soviet; it was as a protection against the USSR that he conceived the western alliance...' Massigli was sceptical of *le projet Titulesco* for another reason: he rightly judged that Titulesco's vehemence owed something to a fragile domestic situation.[17]

After Delbos was coolly non-committal in response to his proposals in Geneva, Titulesco returned to Montreux. When their con-

---

[15] MAE, Papiers Massigli, 'Affaires de l'Europe centrale', 27 June 1936.
[16] Ibid., Note, 6 October 1936.
[17] Massigli letter to Nicholas Rostow, the historian of Anglo-French relations, 7 February 1978. In the view of French diplomats, Titulesco linked these calculations, seeking to disarm intense internal opposition to his policy of entente with the USSR by the impression that he had adopted it at France's demand.

versations resumed there, Litvinov turned on Titulesco, questioning the representativeness of his policy and expressing doubt that a pact could be signed at all.[18] For Litvinov, the main obstacle in bilateral relations was Roumanian internal politics. Recrimination in Bucharest against Soviet attempts to foster a Popular Front was matched by resentment in Moscow of the Tataresco Government's tolerance of domestic Fascist organisations and its less than clear-cut allegiances to entente with France and collective security.[19]

Moreover, Litvinov was angered by Delbos's reaction to Titulesco's proposal for a Franco-Petite Entente pact. Since 1933, the Soviet attitude to Roumania had been cavalier, the Soviets calculating that Petite Entente policy would be determined by that of France. As Léon Blum had seen in 1934:

The Soviet Government wishes to guarantee the 'security' of its European front by a system of international conventions if possible, by the support of resolute powers if necessary. Nothing is more logical or more legitimate. Only, whether it is a question of general conventions or of particular supports, France becomes the key piece on the board. It is in France that are situated the essential conditions of 'security' for Soviet Russia.[20]

After the signature of the USSR's pact with Czechoslovakia whose operation was formally subordinated to its mutual aid pact with France, Litvinov had refused overtures from Titulesco for a mutual aid pact with Roumania until ratification of the French pact. Ostensibly prompted by a reluctance to embroil the USSR in Central European complications arising from the Ethiopian war, this refusal had been accompanied by threats. If France made a Soviet policy of eastern collaboration impossible, the USSR would disinterest itself in the west and abandon Eastern Europe to Hitler.[21] In the summer of 1936, the Soviets were avid for a military pact with France and were to subordinate even their relations with Czechoslovakia to this end. Litvinov's diplomacy calibrated direct involvement with the states separating the USSR from Germany with ever greater levels of French involvement.

After clashing with Litvinov in Montreux, Titulesco, despite Paul-Boncour's attempts at dissuasion, telephoned his resignation to

---

[18] I. M. Oprea, *Nicolae Titulesco's diplomatic activity* (Bucharest, 1968), pp. 102–4; DDF II, 2, no. 304.   [19] Lungu, *Romania*, pp. 77–9.

[20] L. Blum, *Populaire*, 13 July 1934.

[21] MAE, Papiers Massigli, 'Pacte franco-soviétique', Note, 20 September 1935.

Bucharest. He apparently wanted to provoke a show of force with his own government which would enable him to renew negotiations with Litvinov.[22] He also faced a showdown with the Soviet Minister in Bucharest. Titulesco explained his resignation to Ostrovski as caused by Litvinov's 'step backwards' and by France's unfavourable reception to what Ostrovski called 'his project for a single pact encompassing all of the political ties of France in Central and Eastern Europe' – an ambitious formula which is a remainder that the resurrection at Montreux of proposals for a revised Eastern pact coincided with setbacks in the Soviets' attempts to influence the Franco-Polish negotiations.[23] On the topic of Roumanian internal politics, Ostrovski was if anything more virulent than Litvinov. Rather than an entente with a Roumanian Government as dubious as Tataresco's, he told Titulesco, Moscow would prefer an open hostility: 'authorising it to envisage from the present plans for a campaign destined to make of Roumania the battleground in the eventual war between Germany and the USSR'. He also threatened to unleash the Soviet press on the themes of Bessarabia and of the 'Hitlerization' of Roumanian policy.[24]

Given Ostrovski's language, it is not surprising that, once the King had refused Titulesco's resignation, a group of Cabinet ministers accepted his condition for remaining as Minister of Foreign Affairs: the drawing up of a document setting down the broad lines of Roumanian foreign policy, particularly towards the Soviet Union. To d'Ormesson, Titulesco exulted that he had received a real gentlemen's agreement signed by his government in support of his Soviet policy. The document stipulated that the first objective of Roumanian diplomacy was the conclusion of a Franco-Petite Entente alliance against aggression. It then renewed the full powers previously granted Titulesco to conclude a mutual aid pact with the Soviet Union. Auxiliary clauses reaffirmed the government's opposition to domestic Communism and provided for surveillance of foreign legations in order to curb external interference in Roumanian politics, in a proviso directed against Ostrovski.[25]

In a final shuttle between Montreux and Geneva, Titulesco resumed his attempts at cross-pollination of the Russian and French

[22] Paul-Boncour, *Entre deux guerres*, III, p. 63.
[23] Łukasiewicz, *Diplomat in Paris*, pp. 15–16.
[24] MAE, Papiers A. d'Ormesson, 14 July 1936.
[25] Ibid., 15 July 1936; Paul-Boncour, *Entre deux guerres*, III, pp. 63–4; Hoover Institution, N. Titulesco Collection, 13/040.

negotiations. In Montreux, Litvinov, chastened by the affair of Titulesco's resignation, agreed on 21 July to initial draft clauses drawn up by Titulesco, although, for both sides, the draft had little independent existence outside the larger project involving France.[26] Litvinov allowed that a final version of a bilateral pact might be signed at the September League session, but was anxious that word of it not be bruited. At his request, Titulesco agreed not to send a copy of the draft back to Bucharest, but personally to deliver it to the King in the autumn.[27]

From Montreux, Titulesco paid his inevitable call on Delbos, in Geneva for the League session ending sanctions. Armed with his government's confirmation and bolstered by the conversations with Litvinov, he officially presented his proposal for a Franco-Petite Entente pact.

The Quai d'Orsay's response

From late June, Delbos was subjected to strong negative argumentation from the Quai d'Orsay's administration. Massigli had immediately alerted Léger to his impression that, while aware of the difficulties in meeting Titulesco's demands, Delbos hoped to be able to do something for him. Once Massigli's letter reached Paris, Paul Bargeton, the Political Director, undertook to undermine the general principles of Titulesco's project.

Bargeton's memoranda revealed a pervasive vulnerability. In a note of late June outlining France's juridically and politically disparate treaty obligations in Central and Eastern Europe, the Political Director hailed planned reforms in the League of Nations as the only suitable means to unify the French system, by placing all accords in a common framework which would create obligations between France's allies. His distaste for the existing arrangements

---

[26] Paul-Boncour, *Entre deux guerres*, III, pp. 58–60. The Hoover Institution's Titulesco collection (14/557) contains Titulesco's working draft modelled on the Czech-Soviet pact, with marginalia initialled by Titulesco and Litvinov and dated 21 July. The draft made no mention of a Franco-Petite Entente pact. However, by refusing to initial the clause which subordinated the pact's effectiveness to French action on the grounds that 'there was no proper alliance between Roumania and France' (Lungu, *Romania*, p. 81) Litvinov forced Titulesco to turn back to France for supplementary assurances. Professor Lungu summarises the draft, but mistakenly writes that the USSR's pacts of 1935 explicitly named Germany as future adversary. He also interprets Litvinov's veto of the clause as genuine, rather than as a manoeuvre.

[27] Paul-Boncour, *Entre deux guerres*, III, p. 64; Oprea, *Nicolae Titulesco's Diplomatic Activity*, pp. 105–6.

was blatant: 'The result of the present situation is not only weakness. It is also to concentrate against France any effort made on peace, France constituting – and how inadequately – the only link between the countries which would be willing to oppose such an attempt.'[28]

Bargeton's lengthier appreciation of 8 July attacked Titulesco's proposals in terms which again manifested the Quai d'Orsay's critical distance from the Petite Entente. He gave short shrift to the notion of a French alliance with the Petite Entente, which he presented as neither juridically nor politically coherent enough to conclude an all-embracing treaty with France. Bargeton's essential critique of a policy of alliances was that no serious result could be obtained from states which did not owe each other mutual aid: 'It is essential that these states should be engaged to lend each other aid, especially as, for the most part, they are not in a position to aid France directly.' Pointing to Poland's opposition to Soviet passage through Roumania, he expressed scepticism that these states acting only in their own security interests could reach an understanding: 'This is only one aspect of the actual situation which, as long as it lasts, makes any attempt at constructing a system of alliances illusory.' The Political Directorate thus dismissed the potential advantages of Titulesco's project: aid to Czechoslovakia via a Roumanian-Soviet entente, and an operational anti-German orientation for the Petite Entente. It also rejected immediate aid engagements explicitly directed against Germany:

we would appear, contrary to everything that French governments have affirmed until then, no longer as opposed to the aggressor whoever it might be...but as *a priori* adversaries of Germany...We could not defend ourselves from [the charge of] having organised an encirclement, not of the aggressor, whoever it might be, but expressly of Germany with the reactions which would then seem justified.

Its panacea was to cleave to a reformed League covenant by which the Franco-British entente could be maintained, regional military pacts organised, and Italy rallied to the defence of the Danubian status quo.[29]

By the time this 8 July note was circulated, Central European security dilemmas had been intensified by the Austro-German Accord of 11 July. Struck by Czech pessimism in the accord's

[28] DDF II, 2, no. 372.
[29] MAE, Papiers Massigli, 'Affaires de l'Europe centrale', Note, 8 July 1936.

aftermath, the Prague Legation began to champion Titulesco's project. Lacroix expressed alarm that renewed German overtures in Prague would provoke no more response from France than that Czechoslovakia should await a new Locarno conference to review their relations with Germany. He feared that the country would fall into the Reich's orbit. The Czechs would survive this, he warned, but France could not remain a great power once separated from Central Europe.[30]

Lacroix's warning could not have been clearer, but he enjoyed slight status at the Quai d'Orsay, having been posted to Prague in 1935 to tone down France's presence after the tenure of the dynamic Léon Noël. In the end, despite the Prague Legation's impassioned advocacy, the Political Directorate's view prevailed. Fearful that Italy would be provoked into joining the German camp, Léger, with Gamelin in tow, acted to dissuade Blum and Delbos from reinforcing Roumania and Yugoslavia's treaties with France. Delbos accordingly told Titulesco in Geneva that France was not yet prepared to assume new obligations.[31] Delbos's response, however, was tentative. In a Foreign Policy Commission meeting in which he championed a revived Danubian pact as a rejoinder to the Austro-German agreement, Delbos spoke solicitously of the Petite Entente's post-Rhineland insecurity, in terms allowing for an eventual French adherence to a Franco-Petite Entente pact.[32]

Cot and Titulesco: a study in lost connections

So much is reasonably clear. In contrast, a narrative of the last weeks of this first phase of the Franco-Petite Entente negotiations, before Titulesco's fall from power on 29 August, is a study in lost connections. The bare outlines of Titulesco's movements are plain. After his conversation with Delbos placed him in a diplomatic cul-de-sac, he journeyed to the south of France. There, according to Paul-Boncour, he telephoned Blum, imploring him to send one of his ministers. Pierre Cot was sent; he arrived in Cap Martin on 14 August.

The choice of Cot was not incidental. After the indifferent reception at a June CPDN meeting of his plan for an inter-allied

---

[30] DDF II, 2, no. 475.
[31] SHA, 1N43, 17 July 1936; Paul-Boncour, *Entre deux guerres*, III, p. 64.
[32] Assemblée Nationale, Commission, 30 July 1936.

aviation front, Cot had returned to the charge at a second CPDN meeting in late July. Uncompromising as to the Soviet nucleus of his plan, Cot locked horns with the General Staff over its Italian strategy ('the use of its land forces in Central Europe being subordinated to the hypothesis of simultaneous alliance with Italy and Yugoslavia, which seems an unlikely hypothesis'). Partly in response to an intra-governmental polemic generated by Blum's recent declaration at Geneva that France would remain faithful to its mutual aid obligations, he insisted that only the Air Force was capable of an offensive strategy outside French territory. Roumania was an early focus of Cot's air diplomacy. Roughly simultaneously with the July CPDN meeting, Cot began negotiations with the Roumanians for the fitting out of airfields for inter-allied use; there was some discussion of French financing of the fields.[33] Cot's mission in the south of France then was part of this wider strategy with its Soviet tincture.

Another layer of interpretation can be extracted from a 1937 military intelligence report. According to a former collaborator, Titulesco at one time envisaged Soviet troop passage through Roumania, but a delegate of the Red Army suggested that it was unnecessary as they could enter Czechoslovakia through Poland. Titulesco then envisaged a pact limited to permission for Soviet planes to fly over Roumania, reinforcing Roumanian squadrons or flying directly to Czechoslovakia. A Soviet general was said to have visited Roumania to examine means of this aid.[34] No dates were given, but all that is known about his Soviet diplomacy indicates that the shift from land to air passage took place in the final weeks of Titulesco's ministry. Despite the difficulty of fitting the report closely to the documentation on his meeting with Cot in Cap Martin, it is intriguing for two reasons. Its emphasis on Poland corresponds to Soviet readiness in 1936–7 to negotiate troop passage through Poland, and it suggests that, after the second French refusal of his Petite Entente project, Titulesco may have busied himself with an alternative air diplomacy.

Whatever the connection between his talks with Cot and his Soviet diplomacy, the ground was cut away from Titulesco when, still in the south of France, he was ousted from the Tataresco

---

[33] Paul-Boncour, *Entre deux guerres*, III, pp. 64–5; SHAA, 2B93, Léger-Cot letter, 27 November 1936.   [34] SHA, 'Roumanie: SR', 25 December 1937.

Government. Professor Oprea's monograph maintains that a precipitating factor in Titulesco's dismissal was his decision in August, once German and Italian aid to Franco was known, to sign over to the Spanish republicans cannons and fifty planes ordered by the Roumanian Government in France, a decision about which the King was not consulted. The French archives offer no confirmation, although it is quite conceivable. Blum testified in 1947 that, once Italy had supplied planes to Franco, the Air Ministry under Cot dispatched planes to the Republic by repurchasing planes manufactured in France for unspecified foreign states, rather than sending materials from French arsenals.[35] Plainly Carol wanted a pliable minister who wold lend himself to the royal desire for less dangerous diplomacy. Carol's other motives were dislike of Titulesco's opposition to the domestic right-wing, which enjoyed court sympathy, and dismay at the way in which his foreign policy had estranged the Italians over sanctions, and the Poles and the Germans over the tattered issue of Soviet passage. Paul-Boncour is probably correct in implying that the slight results of Titulesco's diplomatic exertions in July were detrimental to him in Bucharest, where German and Polish pressures were being deployed to frustrate any Soviet passage arrangements. The Roumanian archives contain advice to dispense with Titulesco's services sent by Hitler to Carol through the Roumanian Fascist, Christian Goga, in July 1936.[36] The Soviet response to Titulesco's departure was particularly virulent.

THE NEUTRALIST DILEMMA: THE PETITE ENTENTE BETWEEN GERMANY AND THE USSR

The Czech security plight

With Titulesco's departure, the cause of a Franco-Petite Entente pact was largely taken over by the unflamboyant Czechs. Shortly before Titulesco's fall, Osuský, the Czech Minister in Paris, had discussed the project with Delbos. Adapting Bargeton's argument that France could do nothing until stronger ties bound the other states, Delbos replied that a Petite Entente mutual aid pact should

---

[35] Oprea, *Nicolae Titulesco's Diplomatic Activity*, p. 40; *CE Témoignages*, I, p. 219; Schw., 1SC2 Dr9, 27 July 1936.
[36] Oprea, *Nicolae Titulesco's Diplomatic Activity*, pp. 165–7; Paul-Boncour, *Entre deux guerres*, III, p. 66.

be concluded before France would consider a pact with the Petite Entente.[37]

Osuský's advocacy was related to the renewal of German offers in Prague, dreaded by Lacroix since the Austro-German accord. German proposals for direct negotiations on the Sudetendeutsch in July were followed in mid August by a renewal of Hitler's post-reoccupation offer of a non-aggression pact. The official Czech response was to delay until the prospects for international negotiations became clear, but a situation in which Prague felt able neither to accept nor reject the German offers was materialising.[38]

The Quai d'Orsay does not appear to have been as distraught as Lacroix over the Czech dilemma. Before the Chambre Commission in late July, Delbos had alluded with equanimity to the German overtures, saying that Beneš was attempting to stretch German proposals on the Sudetendeutsch to fit League requirements. The British, who had long favoured a Czech-German non-aggression pact, approached Bargeton in late August with inflated rumours that an agreement had actually been reached. Bargeton responded that, while the Quai d'Orsay had never been enthusiastic about bilateral accords, it would not object to the conclusion of such an accord.[39] It is much less certain that Blum, who began his conversations with Schacht on the same day, was prepared to abandon a collective framework for a Czech-German agreement. Schacht later claimed that, in a September sequel to their colonial/disarmament talks, he sent Blum an offer from Hitler of non-aggression assurances *vis-à-vis* the USSR and Czechoslovakia, and that Blum only modified the document on one point concerning the USSR.[40]

The Czech security predicament appeared more stark after an abortive approach in August to the Soviets. Word of the Austro-German accord had prompted Krofta, the Czech Foreign Minister, to wonder aloud whether Czechoslovakia should not proceed to military talks with the Soviets and say so.[41] When the Soviet Marshal Segorov took the waters at Karlsbad in August, he was invited to Prague for talks. According to one version of the conversations, the Soviets pressed for the overall security arrange-

[37] DDF II, 3, no. 207.
[38] Assemblée Nationale, Commission, 30 July 1936; DDF II, 3, nos. 57, 320, 326.
[39] Assemblée Nationale, Commission, 30 July 1936; PRO, FO 371, 20377, R4978/1162/12; Weinberg, *Foreign Policy*, pp. 316–17.   [40] DDF II, 3, nos. 8, 213; 4, no. 311.
[41] DDF II, 2, no. 446.

ments outlined by Ostrovski in July. Struck by the Czech military's fear of Germany and elusiveness on the topic of French intentions, Moscow reasoned that, if France intended to aid Czechoslovakia, it should make this clear by concerting measures with the USSR, Poland, and the Petite Entente; if not, the Petite Entente should be left to make what terms it could with Hitler. The Czechs were told that Segorov and his government considered a staff accord of little interest before staff talks with the French. Some weeks later, the Soviet Ambassador flatly told Schweisguth that a Soviet-Czech military accord was subordinated to one with France. To Schweisguth's cavalier response that the two 1935 pacts had been signed independently, Potemkine countered that the existing Czech-Soviet pact subordinated common intervention to French collaboration.[42]

When the Petite Entente met at Bratislava in mid September, the Czech position was anguished. Beneš fell back on a campaign to win approval for the Petite Entente mutual aid pact counselled by Delbos. Here, he had to contend with the incipient Italo-Yugoslav commercial negotiations which arose out of the pacification démarches that Italy, at Britain's urging, had made in the Balkans, and which resulted in late September in a bilateral trade agreement.[43] Beneš attempted to use financial means, increased Czech investments in Yugoslavia, to offset the advantageous Italian offers.[44] But inured against Prague's largesse, the Yugoslavs kept a low profile at Bratislava. Beneš's campaign for a Petite Entente mutual aid pact was reduced to a dialogue with Titulesco's canny successor, Antonesco.[45]

Beneš's draft for a Petite Entente pact contained a clause whereby the Petite Entente would conclude agreements with neighbouring great powers only as a corporate whole, rather than as individual states at a disadvantage *vis-à-vis* Germany, Italy, and the USSR. This applied the so-called external action theory adopted at the

---

[42] DDF II, 3, no. 274; PRO, FO 371, 19880, C6630/92/62, C7262/92/62; Schw., 1SC2 Dr10, 23 October 1936. Schweisguth obtained Beneš's assent on 24 August to the principle of an informal entente before either country entered into Soviet military conversations. The Czechoslovak overture probably having predated this, Beneš heartily concurred with Schweisguth's request in the knowledge that a French tandem was indispensable to the strengthening of Czech-Soviet ties. Ibid., 2SC2 Dr5, 24 August; Faucher-Schweisguth letters, 8, 21 October; 5 November 1936.   [43] DDF II, nos. 268, 299.

[44] Ibid., nos. 266, 274, 459 note.

[45] PRO, FO 371, 20375, R5827/32/12; 20385, R5984/1644/67. The Petite Entente project mooted by Beneš and Antonesco, in conformity with Paris's priorities, was directed against no state in particular and it did not clearly differentiate itself from the Danubian pact.

Petite Entente's June meeting. To Lacroix, Beneš aired grandiose plans for the Petite Entente, declaring his ideal to be a transformation of the group into a single great power, but he made it plain that this diplomatic parturition could only be accomplished with French forceps.[46]

Projects for Petite Entente pacts – of mutual aid with the USSR and of non-aggression with Germany – were mooted under the heading of 'virtual fusion' of the Petite Entente states. The elevated sentiments of unity with which they were put forward at the Petite Entente's meetings in Bratislava and later in Prague, only half-concealed the group's drift into neutralism. Beneš assured Lacroix that the proposed German-Petite Entente non-aggression pact would be negotiated in close liaison with a new Locarno. He came close to putting his cards on the table, however, when he admitted to doubting that Germany would be prepared to conclude a non-aggression agreement with the Petite Entente, adding that the Reich might well accept such a pact with Czechoslovakia.[47] The use of a Soviet-Petite Entente pact as a means for Prague to draw closer to the recalcitrant Soviets did not escape Antonesco, who, while at first lavish with assurances that he would continue Titulesco's policy towards the USSR, had strong reservations abut the Czech draft. Antonesco subsequently complained to Eden of the collective clause, arguing that, just as Czechoslovakia might wish especially close relations with the USSR, Roumania might desire improved relations with Poland. Antonesco claimed to have told Beneš that a looser Petite Entente diplomatic system, one based on complete confidence, would enable each state's allies to mediate between it and its antagonists.[48] By early October, Antonesco began to advocate a Soviet-Petite Entente pact in Geneva, as a means to facilitate Yugoslav participation in an agreement with the USSR without a separate Soviet-Yugoslav agreement. By the time he visited Prague at the end of the month, he spoke openly of a Soviet-Petite Entente agreement as a means to extricate himself from Roumanian-Soviet negotiations, while countering Czech pressures for entente with Moscow. Antonesco's advocacy of a Soviet-Petite Entente pact, like his practice of shielding behind the Yugoslavs, was a diplomatic way

[46] DDF II, 3, nos. 434, 448.
[47] Ibid., no. 448. Beneš's royal allies in the Petite Entente, Carol and Prince Paul of Yugoslavia, had long favoured a Czechoslovak-German entente.
[48] PRO, FO 371, 20436, R5724/1330/37.

of temporising with his French and Czech allies, closer to the Soviet Union than Roumania after Titulesco wished to be.[49]

The Comintern and the Soviet mortgage on the Front populaire

By autumn 1936, the situation with regard to direct Soviet involvement in Central Europe was far graver than the Czechs were prepared to admit. As Roumanian irritation with the Soviet Legation's zealous courtship of domestic parties suggested, it was widely believed in the region that the Comintern had set out to exploit Blum's electoral victory by installing a chain of mini-Popular Fronts. The Polish and Yugoslav Governments were extremely apprehensive of the sudden growth, fuelled by the misery of the Depression, of native Communist parties.[50] Even the Czechs, who had received promises of non-interference from Stalin on the signature of the Czech-Soviet pact, had to contend with Soviet nervousness at the unresponsiveness of Czech socialists to Comintern overtures.[51]

The attempts of the newly arrived Blum Government to dissociate itself from increased Soviet activity in Central Europe – such as a message to Warsaw in June that 'the French Government was not at all pleased by the Soviets' increasing interference in questions concerning Central Europe' – were ill-fated.[52] The state of the other West European Popular Front, that of Spain, inflamed the doubts of Central European observers concerning the French internal situation. Within two weeks of its outbreak, the Spanish convulsion, which many Yugoslavs believed would soon extend to France, had 'almost unhinged' Paul's mind on the subject of a Communist menace. The war palpably increased Yugoslavia's determination to refuse any association with the Soviet Union, lest it engender, as it was considered to have done in Spain and France, an unwieldy Soviet presence in domestic politics. The Regent also had nightmares of being dragged by the Franco-Soviet pact into a war provoked by

---

[49] PRO, FO 371, 20385, R5984/1644/67; Lungu, *Romania*, pp. 106–7.
[50] DDF II, 2, nos. 238, 295.
[51] DDF I, 11, no. 50; II, 2, no. 376; Schw., 2SC2 Dr5, Faucher-Schweisguth letter, 21 October 1936. In Beneš's view, opposing social conceptions were more likely to cause conflict than treaty violations; accordingly, he stressed the indispensability of maintaining order in France. Schw., 1SC2 Dr10, 12 August 1936.
[52] Szembek, *Journal*, p. 184.

204 *The Popular Front and Central Europe*

the Soviets, in which Yugoslavia would be compelled to fight Germany without effective French aid.[53]

The Spanish conflict and the continuing Russo-German military build-up, including extended conscription in the Reich's case accompanied by virulent anti-Bolshevik rhetoric created general anxiety in Central Europe that German-Soviet war was imminent.[54] In Roumania, Titulesco's dismissal was followed by intensive neutralist propaganda against involvement on behalf of France or any other state in a German-Soviet war, propaganda abetted by Ostrovski's declarations that the Red Army would turn the buffer states into a battlefield. Soon to be bolstered by Belgium's defection from the French camp, the Roumanian neutralist campaign was orchestrated by Titulesco's old adversary, Georges Bratiano, whose theses resembled those of Beck.[55]

These indigenous reactions were aggressively fostered by German propaganda. Its effect was an ideological polarisation, placing France, Czechoslovakia, and the USSR on the opposite side of the barricade from Poland, Yugoslavia, and Roumania. Despite France's sponsorship of a policy of non-intervention by the great powers in Spain, German exploitation of the Spanish theme gave its anti-Bolshevik/anti-Czech campaign new life. It also licensed the Reich to take a direct interest in French internal politics.[56] Using inflated allegations from *Je suis partout*, the German press was unleashed in early August on the subject of the secret dispatch of French planes to the Spanish Republic. In virulent attacks on the Soviet Union, France was depicted as an advanced base – a West European Czechoslovakia – for the Soviets in the Spanish war. Although Hitler did not mention France at Nuremberg in September, the rally was the scene of violent exhortations to real war against the Soviet Union.[57] Hitler had told a prominent foreign visitor to the Berlin Olympics that France would soon know the same fate as Spain, and the alert was maintained by German diplomats,

[53] PRO, FO 371, 20436, R4727/1627/92; DDF II, 3, nos. 428, 464.
[54] DDF II, 3, nos. 174, 198.
[55] Ibid., nos. 266, 372, 378; SHA, 'Roumanie', Delmas dispatch, 15 November 1936.
[56] The controversy over Blum's decision not to intervene in Spain, which led to the diplomatic farce of the Non-Intervention Committee, has been analysed by A. Adamthwaite, *France and the Coming of the Second World War* (London, 1977), pp. 42–5; Colton, *Léon Blum*, pp. 234–69; Dreifort, *Yvon Delbos*, pp. 31–54; J. Lacouture, *Léon Blum* (Paris, 1977), pp. 341–96; and most recently, by Glyn Stone, 'The European Great Powers and the Spanish Civil War, 1936–1939', in Robert Boyce and E. M. Robertson (eds.), *Paths to War* (London, 1989), pp. 212–24.   [57] DDF II, 3, nos. 88, 174, 250, 254, 469.

who conducted business throughout this period with frequent reference to the French internal situation.[58]

Disquiet at the besmirching of France by German propaganda lent edge to Blum's resolve in his talks with Schacht to negotiate a general disarmament settlement. In pleading the merits of a general settlement ('all the problems are connected'), Blum rejected ideological barriers to European entente and included an impassioned defence of the French internal situation: 'There is something that you must really understand. Popular movements like those which have occurred in our country increase the internal power of a people.'

To Schacht's interjection, 'Yes, communism has become national', Blum retorted:

It is not only that. It is that national sentiment has taken another form...Chancellor Hitler considers Communism a danger to civilisation. He fears that France will allow itself to be infected...But if Chancellor Hitler really wants to deliver France from the Soviet danger, I am going to tell you what would be the most sure method: it would be to deliver France from the fear of German danger [by a general settlement, including a disarmament accord].[59]

In an interview with François-Poncet soon after Schacht's return to Berlin, Hitler brushed aside Blum's claim that the recent social crisis in France had reinforced national resolve. Ignoring the Ambassador's assertion that French Socialists and Radicals would not tolerate attempts by Communists to foment civil or general war, he announced: '*If Communism triumphed in France, it would be impossible for him, Hitler, to consider this event as an internal French affair.*'[60] Schacht's visit and Hitler's alleged assent to non-aggression assurances for Czechoslovakia and the USSR heightened the prospects for a general settlement, but the brutal German concern with French internal affairs was disquieting, the more for being voiced at a time that rumours were being spread by the Soviets concerning an imminent German attack in the west.

---

[58] Ibid., nos. 100, 232, 294, 306, 328; SHA, 7N2522, 2e Bureau, 'Note au sujet de la possibilité d'un conflit en Europe', n.d.   [59] DDF II, 3, no. 213.

[60] Ibid., no. 334; italics in the original. In late October, Delbos formally protested Hitler's attitude to the German Ambassador. Welczek retreated, opining that Hitler's statements should be heard as authorising Germany to proceed to 'defensive measures', such as remilitarisation and fortification of the Rhineland and diplomacy to sever the ties between France and the USSR. MAE, Z:717, 31 October 1936.

In early September 1936, after Schacht's visit to Paris had violently alarmed the Soviets, the Soviet Ambassador in Paris tried to hasten Franco-Soviet military talks by informing the French that, according to Soviet intelligence, military circles in Berlin favoured attacking France in the autumn, when Poland and Czechoslovakia could not yet aid it and Britain would remain neutral. Potemkine added that, in the absence of a military pact with France, the USSR would abandon collective security. The Blum Government was reported to be shaken by the prospect of virtual isolation in the event of an early German attack.[61]

Potemkine's activities reinforced the apprehensions the Quai d'Orsay had nursed since the summer of 1936 regarding a full-scale German military build-up in the Rhineland.[62] Delbos gave Eden a 22 September memorandum which stated flatly that the new German military effort was directed towards the west.[63] When Schweisguth returned from the Red Army manoeuvres (19–23 September) bearing fresh Soviet warnings of a German attack in the west, Léger agreed with Soviet declarations that Hitler's vehemence against Russia at Nuremberg masked aggressive plans against France, while he refused the object of the Soviets' war-mongering, a Franco-Soviet military agreement.[64] The EMA joined in this period in combating Soviet attempts to manipulate Paris's anxiety over the German military build-up in the Rhineland to provoke the conclusion of staff accords. Their prime weapon was the report on Red Army manoeuvres by General Schweisguth, whose mission from the outset had been inseparable from Soviet overtures for staff conversations.[65]

The General Staff and the Schweisguth report

The Schweisguth report was a wilfully Manichaean response to a glowing report on the 1935 Soviet manoeuvres by General Loizeau, which was being politically exploited within the Blum Government. The 1936 mission was distrustful of the iconoclastic, theatrical character of Soviet manoeuvres, impressive to earlier observers such

[61] PRO, FO 371, 19880, C6630/92/62.
[62] Schw., 1SC2 Dr9, 'Rapport', 7, 9 July; 1SC2 Dr10, 'Rapport', 6 October 1936.
[63] DDF II, 3, nos. 14, 276.
[64] Ibid., no. 343; Schw., 1SC2 Dr10, 8 October 1936; FRUS, I (1936), pp. 357–8.
[65] Schw., 2SC2 Dr6, undated account of a 30 June 1936 Hirschfeld–Schweisguth conversation; DDF II, 3, no. 343.

as Loizeau and Cot. The Schweisguth mission judged the Soviet army strategically unprepared for war against a great power. Whereas the air factor had been acclaimed previously, now it was the war material supplies – but the mission doubted the continuing capacity of Soviet industrial mobilisation.

Drafted in fact by Paul de Villelume, the General Staff's liaison officer to the Quai d'Orsay, the final section of the Schweisguth report drew highly politicised conclusions from Soviet attempts to prod the French to intransigence *vis-à-vis* Germany.[66] The Soviets plainly wanted maximum support from France in the event of a German attack on the USSR, but, Villelume argued, much preferred that the German maelstrom break over France. The Soviet Union would then emerge as arbiter at the end of a conflict devastating Western Europe, as the United States had done in 1918. The existence of such a Soviet design had been a commonplace for some time in French political circles. Its plausibility derived from Soviet defensive concerns in the Far East, and was assiduously cultivated by the Germans. Göring in his 1935 Warsaw meeting with Laval insisted that the Soviets 'seek to utilise the system of pacts to unleash a war against Germany, in order better to be able ultimately to bolshevise the peoples exhausted by this struggle'.[67]

In a scenario of duplicity and drive for hegemony, Villelume depicted the Soviets as manipulating France and Germany, in order to realise their hopes for Franco-German war. The Spanish war would be exploited and France stampeded into provocative gestures towards Germany, on the false premisses that Germany was

---

[66] Schw., 2SC2 Dr7, sdr a; *CE Témoignages* IX, p. 2742. SHA, 7N2520 contains a much underscored 2e Bureau document of 9 November 1935 which reported in detail on a speech by the Italian Communist Togliatti on the danger of war at the August 1935 meeting of the Comintern. In the face of the Comintern's dismantling of its mission to foment proletarian revolution abroad, Togliatti reiterated the old Bolshevik line that, in the event of international war, civil war should be the Comintern's motto. Officially, proletarian revolution was to be postponed in favour of anti-Fascism in alliance with declared enemies of the revolution, but the EMA feared, as the Comintern's Dimitrov privately acknowledged, that the proletarian revolution might begin as a people's anti-Fascist struggle. Retrospectively, the August 1935 meeting of the Comintern, in fact its last, has appeared as the death rattle of the Comintern, which was stripped of its revolutionary *raison d'être*; cf. E. H. Carr, *Twilight of the Comintern 1930–1935* (New York, 1982), pp. 403–27, and P. Frank, *Histoire de l'Internationale communiste* (Paris, 1981), pp. 713–24.

[67] Schw., 2SC2 Dr7, sdr b; MAE, Papiers Rochat, 'Pologne', 18 May 1935. Sarcastic mimicry of these threats by the Soviet Ambassador in Paris figures in J. Fabry, *De la place de la Concorde au Cours de l'intendance* (Paris, 1942), pp. 75–6; Potemkine's more serious rehearsal of them in a report to Moscow appears in Haslam, *Soviet Union*, pp. 101–2.

insufficiently prepared, and that any softness would make France its first victim. Insinuating that Soviet overtures for a military entente only served these manoeuvres, Villelume pointed to Soviet unconcern at the prospect of exacerbating the German encirclement complex by Franco-Soviet military talks. With Germany, Soviet incitement would take the form of a demonstration that, badly defended by an undisciplined army, France was easy prey: 'this could be the reason for the demoralization that the Third International, according to very recent information, is attempting to continue at present among [our] troops'.[68]

The speculative exercise ending the Schweisguth report embodied some of the deepest fears of the General Staff. With the paralytic wave of strikes in the early summer, which he attributed to Soviet influence, Daladier had predicted unchecked Communist agitation in the army, a fear which had besieged the military since the Front populaire's formation.[69] The Spanish conflict redoubled the military's concern over France's volatile internal situation. Matters were not clarified by the Blum Government's evolving policy of relaxed non-intervention, which involved covert transport of Soviet arms bound for Spain across France.[70] The Spanish war induced in the military a sense of being in the direct line of fire, and the Germans exploited it. Haranguing François-Poncet in early September 1936, Hitler whipped up fears that the French Army would experience a trauma similar to that of their Spanish colleagues:

Will this country still have the clearsightedness and energy necessary to stand up to Communism? How would its army behave if it had to intervene? The officers would bravely and honestly do their duty, like the Spanish officers. But the troops, would they fire on revolutionary masses?[71]

In Paris, the German military attaché preached anti-Bolshevism to Gamelin's staff.[72]

For the General Staff, these were troubled waters in which German and Comintern sources were not always distinguishable. Gamelin's entourage believed that the French Communist paper,

---

[68] On again/off again Comintern subversion in the French Army between the signature of the Franco-Soviet pact and the advent of the Front populaire is analysed in Haslam, *Soviet Union*, pp. 84, 87, 102, 104.

[69] Schw., 1SC2 Dr9, 25 June 1936; SHA, Papiers Fabry, 'Journal de marche', passim.

[70] For the reminiscences of the French customs official charged with the contraband shipments, D. Grisoni and G. Hertzog, *Les brigades de la mer* (Paris, 1979), pp. 104–12.

[71] DDF II, 3, no. 334.   [72] Schw., 1SC2 Dr10, 6 October 1936.

L'Humanité, was receiving large German subsidies, while German penetration of Communist party cells preoccupied the government.[73] In the weeks after his report's circulation, Schweisguth alluded in his diary to intense fears amongst the EMA that the French Communists would foment war or civil war. Georges, one of its more conservative members, told Schweisguth in mid October that a general strike, which he considered entirely possible, would immediately be exploited by Hitler to stage a *coup de force*; the following month, General Gérodias informed him that army intelligence believed that a strike at the Renault works would be generalised and army leaders assassinated. The most reliable elements in the state from the General Staff's point of view – the security services, Pétain, Daladier, and President Lebrun – were said to take these reports seriously.[74]

Litvinov in Geneva

In so tense an atmosphere, Schweisguth's report was bound to cause a sensation, but its rapid circulation to the highest civilian authorities was ensured by the flurry of activity in which Litvinov engaged at the autumn Geneva session.

Litvinov was alarmed by the knowledge that Blum was in Geneva to press the British, in the event unsuccessfully, for a common démarche in the Schacht talks and for an international economic conference, as a sequel to the Tripartite Declaration and the devaluation of the franc. The French delegation also left to one side its projects for League reform, previously supported by Litvinov as sanctioning negotiations between France and its eastern allies. Remarks he made to Eden in Geneva suggest that, already fearful of the 'larger Manchurian conflict' which broke in July 1937, Litvinov dreaded the effects on France as British indifference to Czecho-slovakia deepened with heavier imperial concerns in the Far East.[75] Litvinov thus confronted Blum on 2 October 1936, extracting two promises. After negotiations for a new Locarno, or once it was clear

---

[73] PRO, FO 371, 19857, C4248/1/17; DDF II, 3, no. 472.
[74] Schw., 1SC2 Dr10, 22, 30 October, 30 November 1936. These charged passages from Schweisguth jar with the picture of placid relations between officers serving in France and the Blum Government in Martin Alexander's 'Soldiers and Socialists: the French officer corps and leftist government 1935–7'.
[75] PRO, FO 954/24, SU/36/16; 954/8, Fr/36/22–5; Fr/36/30; Fr/36/32; DDF II, 3, no. 276.

that such negotiations would not be held and Blum was said to be pessimistic, his government would be prepared: to unify its obligations to the USSR, Poland, and the Petite Entente in some kind of pact of mutual guarantee; and to embark on military conversations with Russia, provided these conversations had no official character and entailed no written obligation. Blum allegedly felt obliged to agree to Litvinov's demands, subject to the Locarno proviso, because Litvinov threatened to countenance a Petite Entente accommodation with Germany unless France put its Central European interests in order.[76]

A proposed systematisation of France's eastern ties and unofficial military talks leaving unaltered the 1935 Franco-Soviet pact would not literally contravene the terms of the Blum-Schacht conversations, in which Blum had specifically reserved the maintenance of France's treaty obligations. He of course hoped that the Reich could be persuaded to give non-aggression assurances concerning the USSR and Czechoslovakia. In the existing ideological climate, however, there could be little doubt that Blum's promises to Litvinov for the post-Locarno period represented a deviation from the Quai d'Orsay's policies. Villelume and Massigli promptly telephoned from Geneva to instruct that the Schweisguth report be handed to Léger.[77]

The promises which Litvinov sought from Blum revealed aims much like those which had led the Soviets to lend themselves to Titulesco's Franco-Petite Entente proposals. In Geneva, Litvinov also renewed his approaches to the Roumanians. His conversations with Antonesco were turbulent, Litvinov repeating the complaints about the Roumanian internal situation with which he had confronted Titulesco. Antonesco, who disclaimed first-hand knowledge of Titulesco's conversations with Litvinov, retaliated by reviving the Bessarabian question. He found liable to misinterpretation the provision for evacuation of Roumanian territory at the end of a conflict, which Litvinov told him Titulesco had accepted at Montreux. The practical consequence of the two conversations with Litvinov was Antonesco's recommendation to Massigli that France immediately sign a mutual assistance pact with the Petite Entente.

[76] PRO, FO 371, 19880, C7057/92/62, C7102/92/62, C7262/92/62.
[77] Schw., 1SC2 Dr10, 7, 8 October 1936. The Quai d'Orsay's nervousness was increased by the fact that the Soviets in late September 'moved perilously close to breaking with the non-intervention committee'. Haslam, *Soviet Union*, p. 119.

Antonesco's phrasing was almost identical with Titulesco's in June.[78] Massigli's response was that no project should be put forward which made a Locarno conference more difficult.[79] In Geneva, then, the Locarno stipulation was brought to bear on interlocking Franco-Petite Entente and Franco-Soviet conversations.

Within two weeks, the Belgian monarch proclaimed his country's aim of an 'independent' foreign policy, binding it to neither power bloc. The deliberate leakage of Leopold's 14 October statement to the Belgian cabinet was a giant step taken by Brussels to extricate itself from its Locarno obligations, including its remaining military arrangements with France. The Blum Government acquiesced not only because the Belgians ably exploited fears that they would accept pressing German offers for a non-aggression pact, but because the British supported Brussels.[80] While Paris was at pains to present Leopold's speech as motivated mainly by internal political considerations, the Belgian descent into neutralism had strong affinities with Central European neutralism. In both regions, France's ties to the USSR and problems of passage had been passionately debated since the Rhineland remilitarisation increased the importance for the French military of a war on the peripheries.[81] Leopold's speech sent shock waves through the French camp. In Roumania, the press was so extreme on the neutrality theme that even Belgium's Minister in Bucharest protested.[82]

The Quai d'Orsay was immediately reassuring, in order to curtail the damage caused by the Belgian decampment, without substantially altering France's position in the languishing Petite Entente

---

[78] In a related manoeuvre, Litvinov declared to Kamil Krofta that as the USSR could no longer count on France in the event of war with Germany, the 1935 Czech-Soviet pact should be severed from the Franco-Soviet pact. Such a gesture did not accord with the Soviet position on a Czech-Soviet pact, but, by threatening to increase the chances of unguaranteed Soviet passage, it also compelled the Roumanians again to turn to France for guarantees. SHA, 7N3107, 'Roumanie SR', 5 October 1936. Soviet diplomacy in 1935–6 consistently used the Petite Entente to pressure Paris.

[79] MAE, Papiers Massigli, 'Affaires de l'Europe centrale', Note, 6 October 1936.

[80] Belgium's repudiation of its reciprocal ties to France was facilitated by a 20 November declaration in the Commons by Anthony Eden on the British commitment to defend Belgium and France. The War Office regarded Belgium's disastrous drift away from France as enhancing Britain's chances to stay clear of a war beginning in Central Europe. Eden's declaration and Delbos's 4 December reply are sometimes mistaken for a high-water mark in Anglo-French relations in this period. Kieft, *Belgium's Return to Neutrality* (Oxford, 1972), p. 140 and note.

[81] DDF II, 3, nos. 14, 67, 128, 172, 287, 296, 300, 346, 358, 386, 388, 397, 411, 421, 438, 454, 477, 508; Kieft, *Belgium's Return*, pp. 135–45.   [82] DDF II, 3, no. 370.

negotiations. The circular dispatched by Delbos warned against attempts by German propagandists to exploit the Belgian initiative, particularly in Roumania. Delbos also alluded to the vociferously neutralist leanings of the Czech Agrarians after Leopold's speech. As Delbos well knew, Krofta and Beneš were themselves in need of steadying with regard to the temptation of a bilateral agreement with Germany.[83] A section of the French press, in the wake of Leopold's speech, having seized on revived international discussion over France's offensive capacity against Germany, Delbos dispensed platonic assurances that France would not abandon the principles inspiring its relations with Czechoslovakia in order to assure its own security. After reiterating that France could not agree to a solution allowing Germany to blame it for a failure in the Locarno negotiations, he took a prudent half-step towards assent to Franco-Petite Entente talks: either in the event that the Locarno conference led to a general settlement, or that its failure obliged the parrying of new German initiatives, the French Government was prepared to examine in what forms and under what limitations the solidarity of France and the Petite Entente could be reaffirmed.[84] Subsequent dispatches made clear that the Quai d'Orsay maintained its insistence that an internal Petite Entente pact precede a pact involving France.[85]

Wedged between the necessity of warding off German attempts to isolate Czechoslovakia and France on account of their involvement with the Soviets, and the threat of Soviet abandonment of Czechoslovakia to Germany, Delbos fought shy of commitment to the Soviet-shadowed Franco-Petite Entente scheme. His unspoken stress was on the limitations of solidarity. Blum's undertakings to Litvinov were not, however, to go unhonoured. The government deliberated on them by early November 1936, amid violent inter-ministerial conflict over Cot's projects for collaboration with the Petite Entente and the USSR. The full-scale disarray of the Petite

[83] Lacroix had recently made strenuous attempts to dissuade Beneš and Krofta from their view that, in the absence of a Locarno conference, a *tête-à-tête* with Berlin, hedged with safeguards, represented the new diplomatic wisdom for Prague. To Paris, he had harked back to his arguments of July in support of a Franco-Petite Entente pact: 'If, as one might suppose, we have come to a turning point in European history, France should ask itself if the relationships instituted since the war with the resuscitated or enlarged states of Central and Eastern Europe do not constitute the essential condition of its necessary position as a great power?' Ibid., nos. 320, 352.   [84] Ibid., no. 391.
[85] Ibid., nos. 448 note, 467 note.

Entente and further deterioration in the international climate placed Paris in a situation in which prudence came to seem more of a risk than commitment.

France and Italy

A state visit by Carol and Antonesco to Prague in late October 1936 signalled the defeat of Delbos's priorities in the negotiations. The French had known since the Belgian affair broke that Roumania was reluctant to accept a tightening of its Petite Entente ties without prior certainty of increased French support. Antonesco reiterated this in Prague.[86] Mounting evidence of the failure of the Petite Entente's negotiations for a mutual aid pact coincided with indications of growing Italo-German entente.

From his 1 November 1936 Axis speech, Mussolini noisily extolled a diplomatic partnership with the Reich dedicated to dividing Europe into warring ideological camps. This prospect repelled Blum, who since June 1936 had made it known to Rome that he did not intend to behave as a doctrinaire anti-Fascist.[87] The Blum Government then acted to meet all of the demands formulated by Mussolini in conversations with French journalists and visitors in June 1936. These were: a conciliatory ministerial declaration, a sign to which Mussolini attached real importance; action in London to oppose sanctions and obtain the lifting of British assurances of protection in the event of Italian aggression, which had been provided to small Mediterranean states in autumn 1935; and diplomacy at the League to spare Italy problems over the recognition of its conquest.[88]

The wisdom of such conciliatory behaviour towards Italy was called into question, when on 11 July 1936, a week before the outbreak of the Spanish conflict, Mussolini stepped aside as the Austrians signed a pact with the Reich – a move seriously con-

---

[86] Carol's aide-de-camp more candidly told the British military attaché that Roumania would retain its liberty of action in the Belgian fashion and watch Britain. Ibid., nos. 362, 448; PRO, FO 371, 20384, R6508/578/67.   [87] See above, pp. 99–100.
[88] DDF II, 2, nos. 275, 289, 311, 324, 328, 329, 332, 339, 359.

templated in Vienna since the onset of the Ethiopian war. Franz von Papen, Hitler's special emissary to Vienna, began his exertions for a bilateral accord in late summer 1935, when European chancelleries buzzed with talk of Italy's African designs. The Austrian tack in the negotiations was to reduce a bilateral treaty to a gentlemen's agreement, with abundant, vague declarations of goodwill.[89] The Reich did not prove amenable to this, and Austrian resolve weakened when Italy invaded Ethiopia in October. Describing himself as 'with his back to the wall', the Austrian Foreign Minister told Gabriel Puaux, the French Minister, that he could no longer decline governmental conversations with Papen, but would remain faithful to the idea of the Danubian pact. Berger left Puaux in no doubt that Ethiopia lay behind his decision:

to speak frankly, he did not want to run the risk, by refusing a German offer, of exposing his country to a bid for power, as in July 1934, when Austria was no longer so sure of being able to count on immediate and effective aid.[90]

Austrian acquiescence was temporarily forestalled by Italian military assurances, and by a ministerial reshuffle increasing the influence of Mussolini's Austrian admirer, Prince von Starhemberg.[91] Papen was not crushingly discouraged by what the French documents reveal to have been his near-miss of October 1935. He could afford to bide his time. By early 1936, hard-pressed by his Ethiopian venture, Mussolini peddled his Austrian wares in Berlin. He informed the Germans that: 'If Austria, as a formerly quite independent state, were thus in practice to become a German satellite, he would have no objection.' When Mussolini's protégé Starhemberg was dismissed from the government in May 1936, the way was wide open for an Austro-German agreement, a proposition whose attractions for Vienna had been increased by the Rhineland reoccupation.[92]

An essay by Professor Bariéty on the Austro-German negotiations takes as its point of departure the Austrians' post-Rhineland despair that Hitler intended to execute his pan-German programme. Such

---

[89] DDF I, 12, nos. 17, 23, 81, 302; Czech T-120, 1041/1809/414161, 414163; J. Gehl, *Austria, Germany and the Anschluss* (Oxford, 1963), p. 109.   [90] DDF I, 12, nos. 366, 390.
[91] MAE, 'Autriche', Puaux dispatch, 4 December 1935; Gehl, *Austria*, p. 110.
[92] DDF I, 2, no. 85; 3, no. 41; DGFP C, IV, no. 485; Gehl, *Austria*, pp. 110–11.

depression in Vienna did not date from the Rhineland affair. Identical fears in late 1935 had prompted Austria's fervent support of Franco-British attempts to placate Mussolini. Reporting abnormal German troop concentrations on the Austrian border in December 1935, Berger told Puaux that he believed that, in the case of Anglo-Italian conflict, the Reich would carry out an Anschluss: '"This would be the end of Austria", concluded the Minister, who added "and immediately afterwards, the end of Czechoslovakia."'[93] By closely following the memoirs of Gabriel Puaux in not referring to the Austro-German negotiations in the later half of 1935, Bariéty's account strongly suggests that the absence of an Austrian policy was the prerogative of left-wing French governments.[94] In fact, Austria had little to hope from France, which had no Austrian policy without Italy, and this was true regardless of the political colouring of the government in Paris. The Austrians were well aware that only Italy had ever been inclined to protect Austria against a camouflaged Nazi aggression. As Berger delicately put it, 'the principal safeguard for Austria...is Germany's fear of a direct Italian intervention in accord with France'.[95] In January 1936, Puaux, who strenuously opposed the negotiations, could offer only words: a reaffirmation of the Stresa declaration on Austrian independence. When the intensification of Italian military involvement in Africa threatened to leave Austria bereft of any guarantees, Pierre Laval beseeched the Petite Entente to prevent Austria from drifting into the German orbit.[96]

In May and June 1936, Chancellor Schuschnigg reopened the conversations with Papen, while the Quai d'Orsay vainly tried to coordinate the raising of sanctions with London. Paris was no closer than in the past to resolving the central dilemma of its Central European policy and the question to which Franco-Austrian relations had been reduced since 1934: the problem of Italian intentions. The *Front populaire's* apparent unresponsiveness in

[93] MAE, 'Autriche', Puaux dispatch, 4 December 1935.
[94] J. Bariéty, 'La France et le problème de l'Anschluss mars 1936 – mars 1938' (15. Deutsch-französisches Historikerkolloquium, Bonn, 1978). MM. Puaux and Bariéty place the burden of the Austrian decision to come to terms with Germany not on Mussolini's African diversion, but on French silence after an Austrian overture in the spring of 1936 for a collective negotiation guaranteeing Austrian independence. Puaux, *Mort et transfiguration de l'Autriche* (Paris, 1966), pp. 81–3; Bariéty, 'La France', p. 6. As the Austrian overture was also an attempt to mediate between France and Italy, Flandin's conversations with the Italians in April and May 1936, to which neither writer refers, may be taken as a response.
[95] DDF I, 13, no. 294.   [96] DDF II, 1, no. 34.

dealing with Vienna can be explained, if not justified, by the paralysis in its relations with Italy. After the Austro-German accord, Puaux complained of the absence of directives from Paris in the final phase of negotiations. He had felt unable to evoke continuing French allegiance to a projected Danubian pact in his last conversations with Schuschnigg, who was left with the impression – understandably painful to Puaux – that France was no longer interested in the fate of Austria. Delbos subsequently refuted the charge of abandonment with a sharpness only increased by his own powerlessness with regard to Italy.[97]

The finished accord left intact only the façade of Mussolini's defence of Austrian independence. The Schuschnigg Government agreed to bring Austrian Nazis into the Cabinet, in return for a formal promise from Hitler not to interfere in its internal affairs, and to coordinate its foreign policy with that of the Reich. Henceforth, the Austrians refused obligations involving military action, presumably including passage rights, against Germany, a position which effectively nullified the Franco-Italian military planning of 1935. As a corollary, they spoke of refusing the Reich the right to utilise Austrian territory in an aggressive enterprise, although Austrian military fidelity to this proviso was called into question by subsequent reports that Austria might grant passage to German troops against Czechoslovakia.[98] Vienna's sympathy for Prague as threatened with a common fate had withstood the first phases of the Reich's diplomatic exertions.[99] With the great powers' inaction over the Rhineland, references to solidarity with Prague ceased, while the Austrians were plainly susceptible to the German propaganda concerning the Franco-Soviet pact which accompanied the reoccupation.[100] François-Poncet treated the accord as heralding the fulfilment of Chambrun's June prophecies of a neutralist, anti-Czech group of powers, drawn by Germany's triumphant bilateral diplomacy. His interpretation seemed to be substantiated by Goebbels' remarks on the accord's significance, including talk of

---

[97] DDF II, 2, nos. 444, 465. It is often supposed that the Blum Government was ideologically averse to that of Schuschnigg on account of the Austrian Government's suppression of Viennese workers in February 1934; cf. Blum's declaration to Eden in late June 1936 that Schuschnigg should be given all possible financial and diplomatic support, PRO, FO 954/8, Fr/36/13.

[98] DDF II, 2, no. 254; 3, no. 12; Schw., 1SC2 Dr10, 15 October 1936.

[99] DDF I, 12, no. 81; 13, no. 396.   [100] DDF II, 1, no. 332.

compelling the Czechs to abandon the USSR for an agreement with Germany.[101]

These were disconcerting indications for the government, pre-occupied by the exposed situation of Czechoslovakia. Blum later described the accord as a turning point which convinced him that 'a real rapprochement between Italy and France was no longer possible'. He doubted that a Danubian pact, to include the Italian guarantee for Prague desired by the EMA, could be concluded after the Austro-German accord, precisely on the grounds that the accord signified Italy's abandonment of its Central European interests and the shift in its ambitions to the Mediterranean littoral.[102]

Against a pessimistic reading of the Austro-German accord were the views of Delbos and Gabriel Puaux. Puaux's estimate of the accord was that its dangers were diffuse and would not fall due for some time. He appealed for an international negotiation to stabilise Central Europe in its entirety, and to this end, urged that Paris take the initiative for 'a candid and friendly explanation with Italy'. Since the Italo-German bloc was essentially improvised, it remained possible to procure Italian collaboration, but Puaux's message was *tempo alla breve*.[103] A resolutely unalarmed Delbos addressed the Chambre's Commission des Affaires étrangères along these lines at the end of the month. Describing the accord as guaranteeing Austrian independence, and rejecting the idea of interference, Delbos concluded: 'Its characteristics can justify the attitude of the Austrian government... We should not then consider this accord as essentially bad.'

Delbos's concern rather was with the Italo-German rapprochement which, as he and Puaux saw it, presaged Europe's division into Fascist and democratic arms of a cross: 'This new formulation leads us to fear an imminent war, a war of religion which would not fail to embroil all of Europe in an appalling conflagration.' Doubtless, the Spanish events intensified his fear. Delbos – like Puaux and Chambrun, if more guardedly – did not view the Italo-German entente as definitive: 'I would be surprised if Italy was so tied to Germany – a seesaw policy is an Italian tradition.'[104]

Another indication of growing Italo-German entente appeared on 12 July, when Italy refused an invitation to meet with the Locarno

---

[101] DDF II, 2, nos. 272, 432, 452; 3, no. 43.   [102] *CE Témoignages* I, pp. 125, 220.
[103] DDF II, 2, nos. 444, 482; 3, nos. 6, 41.
[104] Assemblée Nationale, Commission, 30 July 1936.

powers in London on the grounds that Britain's Mediterranean assurances were still in force, and that Germany was to be excluded from the first sessions. Having insisted on Italian inclusion in the London meeting, Delbos's reaction to the refusal was a circumspect sounding in Rome rather than the candid, friendly talk urged by Puaux. In reply, Ciano offered only a bilateral meeting in preparation for a conference to include Germany.[105] In remarks which showed his debt to the Political Directorate's advice of June to seek a tactical middle way in dealing with the Fascist régime, Delbos commented on the failed démarche in Rome:

We wanted to avoid running after [Italy], as well as manifesting our bad humour, which would have been equally maladroit. We are keeping to our stand, with the hope that Italy will return of its own accord.

The result of this manifestation of French dignity was Italy's absence from the London Conference on 23 July. Before the Commission des Affaires étrangères on 30 July, Delbos's evenhandedness warred with disappointment:

We have done the most that we could for rapprochement with Italy. We have not obtained the awaited results and we have no official indication that our attitude has influenced Italy. She remains very reserved, too reserved in our eyes.[106]

The London Conference did allow the Front populaire to claim a small diplomatic triumph, in the form of the British decision to rescind their Mediterranean assurances of late 1935. Some weeks previously, immediately after Britain and then France had called for an end to sanctions, Mussolini and Ciano had granted audiences to two Frenchmen, J.-L. Malvy, a former minister, and Hubert Lagardelle, the corporatist socialist. To Lagardelle, Mussolini declared that he would be prepared to examine a Mediterranean pact once the British assurances were withdrawn. With Malvy, the Italians played on the day's discrepancy between French and British sanctions announcements to demand that France forestall any decision at Geneva refusing Italy recognition of its Ethiopian conquest. Malvy reported that Mussolini would not demand explicit recognition at that time of his *fait accompli*: '*No decision* one way or another, gaining time, would be the procedure which suits him.'

[105] Increasingly impatient with British attempts to keep Italy at arm's length, Delbos had warned London that the continental situation was too serious for Italian susceptibilities not to be spared as much as possible. DDF II, 2, nos. 408, 431, 479; 3, no. 6.
[106] Assemblée Nationale, Commission, 30 July 1936.

There was the usual edge of menace – French failure to accomplish the next series of tasks would be considered far graver than sanctions – along with the customary talk of close collaboration on all fronts once France undertook the newest labour assigned by Rome.[107] As a result of retouched accounts of these interviews, a distorted view of the Front populaire's diplomacy towards Italy circulated at Vichy and has since enjoyed a somewhat uncritical reception.[108]

At the time, with the success of French pressures for London's withdrawal of the Mediterranean assurances, the Quai d'Orsay still contemplated Italian reintegration into such collective schemes as the Mediterranean and Danubian pacts. Delbos thus resumed in London his campaign for a Mediterranean pact, an advocacy rooted in preoccupation with Italo-German entente. London remained dilatory, in part because of the growing turmoil in the western Mediterranean, and in part because it had no interest in renewed naval bargaining.[109]

Over these Mediterranean proposals, as over sanctions, the French felt themselves penalised by their fruitless attempts to coordinate policy with London. Why then, given Rome's apparent amiability, did the Quai d'Orsay not encourage the Blum Government to leave to one side the policy it had advocated since

[107] DDF II, 2, no. 275, Blondel's italics; PRO, FO 954/8, Fr/36/13.
[108] Italian entry into the war in 1940 was a matter of particular sentimental regret for those in Vichy circles. A case in point is Lucien Lamoureux's account of the Mussolini-Malvy interview included in E. Bonnefous's *Histoire politique de la Troisième République*, vol. 6 (Paris, 1965), pp. 410–11. Lamoureux's account of the interview, supposedly recounted to him by Malvy in spring 1937, is chronologically confused and differs on important points from Malvy's summary to the Rome Embassy (DDF II, 2, no. 339). In Lamoureux's version, the Quai d'Orsay was said to be hostile to the visit and Malvy to have gone to Rome as an ordinary tourist, whereas Blondel's dispatch alludes to Léger's briefing of Malvy and arrangement of the meeting with Mussolini through the embassy. Lamoureux has Mussolini bitingly critical of the Front populaire, whereas Malvy described the interview to Blondel as very friendly. Most importantly, Lamoureux's version contains statements of which there is no hint in Blondel's dispatch. Mussolini is made to say that Italy would become Germany's ally for better or worse, and that it could not then be said that, in the case of war, Italy would not be in the camp of its allies. Blum is thus personally made to incur responsibility for the 1940 defeat by refusing Mussolini's 'overture'.
When another of Mussolini's visitors in June 1936, Bertrand de Jouvenal, claimed to a congress of the Parti populaire français after the Anschluss in 1938 that Mussolini had charged him with a similar message for Blum, the diplomat Massigli indignantly protested to Léger that Mussolini's actual remarks were of a completely different colour and in much less precise form. Nothing in Jouvenal's account to him at the time, he wrote, entitled the interpretation that Jouvenal had been charged with any 'message' whatever for Blum. MAE, Papiers Massigli, 'Correspondance personnelle 1932–1938', 13 March 1938. Massigli's original note on Jouvenal's conversation with Mussolini is in DDF II, 2, no. 275.
[109] DDF II, 3, no. 121.

the failure of attempts for a compromise peace in April 1936 – a policy coordinated with London to bring Italy back to Geneva – and instead press the Italians to participate in regional negotiations? The answer was that France was bound to Britain in the summer of 1936, as in the past, less by common policies than by fears. Among these was the recurrent fear of Anglo-German rapprochement. The French had been alarmed by the lack of visceral British reaction to the denunciation of Locarno, and by British susceptibility to Hitler's proposals for bilateral accords in Central Europe and to a revised role, closer to mediation than enforcement, for the Locarno guarantors. British behaviour during the last phase of the Ethiopian war, and the reluctance with which the British agreed to meet the new French leaders in July amplified the fears, which had come to the fore in Paris after the reoccupation, of finding themselves alone against Germany. Had the Quai d'Orsay attempted to confront London with a diplomatic *fait accompli* providing Italian guarantees in Central Europe, there was a large risk that it would lose on both sides. Italy, after all, no longer needed to carry out 'diplomatic preparations' for its Ethiopian venture, which, along with the half-concealed desire to dismantle the Petite Entente, had provided the original impetus for its willingness to discuss a broader Danubian settlement.

As for the Danubian pact which had figured in the government's June ministerial declaration, Delbos again proposed it after the Austro-German pact, as a means of averting the war of religion that he feared from an Italo-German entente. Danubian negotiations figured prominently in the Political Directorate's plan for a League of Nations reformed according to the lessons of the Ethiopian war, a League in which endless deliberation would be replaced by smoothly functioning regional military accords. A League arrangement would also contain any Italian revisionist impulses, such as a desire to revive the Four Power pact at the expense of Czech, Polish, or Roumanian territorial integrity.

Despite the abrasions caused by the Spanish conflict, the Quai d'Orsay hoped to bring Italy back to Geneva by negotiating gradual recognition of its Ethiopian conquest. In September 1936, Avenol, the League's Secretary-General, went to Rome to sound Mussolini and Ciano on the acceptability of a procedural expedient which would unseat the Ethiopian delegation at the September Geneva session, and so allow Italian representation at the League without engaging the Assembly on the issue of the Italian conquest. Avenol's trip to Rome took the guise of a personal initiative, but it was preceded by a favourable campaign in the semi-official French press, and Avenol took advice beforehand from the Quai d'Orsay's influential legal advisor, Basdevant.[110] Ciano was receptive, but Avenol's confidence in his ability to stage-manage the League session with French help was badly misplaced. A small power revolt, abetted by Litvinov, ensured that the League Assembly ratified a decision by the credentials committee to accept the Ethiopian credentials for that session. It was all the French could do to keep the rebellious states from freezing the League indefinitely into an anti-Italian posture. Having vainly tried to soothe the Italian delegation, Massigli lamented to Léger: 'It is strange that it is the countries which most fear war which, by their attitude, work to cement the Italo-German bloc.'[111] The disastrous effect of the affair was increased by the fact that 'with bags virtually packed and tickets in hand', Ciano and his aides had awaited in Rome the news that the Ethiopian delegation had been unseated.[112]

Brushing aside Paris's pleas for moderation, Ciano described the Italian position with regard to the League as 'A *de facto* rupture without a legal rupture', and he reserved for Paris the first concrete sign of his fury at the September fiasco.[113] It took the form of another affair of accreditation, that of René de Saint-Quentin, who was named to replace Chambrun as Ambassador in Rome two days after the adverse League vote. The Palazzo Chigi demanded that Saint-Quentin be accredited to the 'Emperor of Ethiopia', that is, a unilateral French recognition of the Italian conquest, terms that exceeded the procedural accommodation Rome had been prepared to accept in early September.[114] The decision to replace Chambrun was made before the Geneva fiasco, and so dated from the halcyon period in which an Italian return to Geneva was deemed imminent. According to Blum, difficulties were not anticipated from the

---

[110] Barros, *Betrayal*, pp. 126–36.
[111] DDF II, 3, nos. 239 and note, 277. The era of aggressive anti-Bolshevik rhetoric in Italian foreign policy dated from these months.
[112] Barros, *Betrayal*, p. 140; for Ciano's amiability in September 1936, Shorrock, *From Ally to Enemy*, p. 191. French involvement behind the scenes in Avenol's failed manoeuvre, involvement which in effect complied with Mussolini's requests of June 1936, demonstrates that the Blum Government was not so unresponsive to Italy as Professor Shorrock believes. Delbos ruefully acknowledged to the Chambre's Foreign Policy Committee that the blame in the collapse of Franco-Italian relations in 1936 had to be shared.
[113] DDF II, 3, nos. 281, 286.   [114] Ibid., nos. 318, 329.

nomination of Saint-Quentin, an African specialist who had worked in late 1935 on the cession proposals, highly favourable to Italy, which had formed the basis for the Hoare-Laval plan.[115]

Before the Chambre's foreign policy committee, Delbos addressed the argument that France could have Italian friendship at the price of a gesture and that the present quarrel was absurd. He observed that this might be so, but Rome had recently absolved the USA of any obligations to accredit their Ambassador to the Emperor of Ethiopia: 'This unequal attitude is offensive to us. Italy has the right to defy the League of Nations and to deal it another blow, but it will not be France which gives the signal for this new blow... We claim to play a leading role in Europe, in harmony with other states. We will continue our policy to that end.'[116] The dénouement was hardly satisfactory for the Quai d'Orsay: for two crucial years, from November 1936 until François-Poncet's arrival after Munich, French diplomacy in Rome was executed by Blondel, the Embassy's Counsellor. Nor was the Blum Government, as is sometimes implied, oblivious to the harm being done by the situation.[117]

The French responded immediately to the collapse of bilateral relations by expressing renewed interest to the British in a multilateral Mediterranean pact. Massigli implored Eden for a joint response to disarm Italian suspicions of Franco-British intentions, but his démarche was to little avail. The British desired a bilateral détente with Italy. To Delbos's protests at France's exclusion from the burgeoning Anglo-Italian entente, Vansittart replied smoothly that if a policy of bilateral pacts was reprehensible in Central Europe, where it played into German hands, it was not the same in the Mediterranean, where it would prevent Italo-German rapprochement.[118]

Easily the most dramatic result of the September League fiasco was a visit by Ciano to Berlin in mid October for the launching of the

---

[115] Colton, *Léon Blum*, p. 222; see also Fouques-Duparc's comments in *Léon Blum chef du gouvernement* (Paris, 1967), pp. 363–4, and the firm views of Sir George Clerk, PRO, FO 371, 20685, C2499/18/17. Chambrun and Léon Noël have insisted that Chambrun's removal had an intensely Italophobe motivation, Chambrun, *Traditions et souvenirs* (Paris, 1952), pp. 220–8; Noël, *Les illusions*, pp. 108–9.

[116] Assemblée Nationale, Commission, 27 November 1936; DDF II, 3, no. 340.

[117] Cf. Shorrock, *From Ally to Enemy*, pp. 192–4, 197–9. In May 1937, when, despite misgivings as to Italian policy, Paris sought British support for Geneva's *de facto* recognition of the Italian conquest, Delbos asserted that Franco-Italian relations were gravely handicapped by French inability to accredit an ambassador to Rome. MAE, Papiers Massigli, 'Italo-Ethiopie...', Delbos dispatch to Corbin, 1 May 1937.

[118] DDF II, 3, nos. 276, 314, 456, 485, 489–90, 499.

Italo-German diplomatic partnership.[119] The Reich agreed to recognise the Italian conquest in Ethiopia, as well as to harmonise its economic interests in Danubia with those of Italy by dividing possible outlets, an ominous prospect for Paris given the Italo-Yugoslav economic accords of September. The anti-collective security bent of the visit was reinforced by overt coordination of German and Italian positions in the Locarno negotiations. The Quirinal's position from October 1936 was that any reference to particular French pacts or to League intervention would abort negotiations for a new Locarno. Rome also maintained for the first time that the Franco-Soviet pact was incompatible with Locarno, and depicted France – against the backdrop of the Spanish war – as an unfit ally, mined by Comintern intrigue. The Berlin Embassy after Ciano's departure warned that, if the German and Italian Locarno conception did not prevail, the two revisionist powers would confront the democracies with a continental bloc.[120]

Mussolini's Milan speech of 1 November consecrated Ciano's labours. Denouncing collective security, Mussolini proclaimed the creation of an Italo-German axis, grouping 'all the peaceful states of Europe'. As for France, after deploring its attitude of 'reserved expectancy', Mussolini left it to one side and went on to make overtures for bilateral entente to Britain and Yugoslavia. Isolation again threatened Paris and Prague.[121]

The General Staff and Italy, 1936–7

The General Staff's appraisal of Italy's value appeared entirely unaffected by the hindrances to Franco-Italian diplomatic relations. Lecturing in November to the newly formed 'Collège des hautes études de la Défense nationale', Schweisguth acknowledged that Italian policy was fluid, but declined to predict Italy's ultimate alignment: 'what I want to impress upon you is the capital importance for our national defence of the decision [Italy] will reach'. Schweisguth did this by setting out hypothetical Italian alignments. Italian hostility would separate France from Central Europe, and so alter naval, air, land, and allied strategies as to completely alter the conduct of a war of coalition. Italian neutrality, the case Schweisguth had been asked to consider, would make

---

[119] Ibid., no. 410.   [120] Ibid., and nos. 381, 412, 469.
[121] Ibid., nos. 432, 473; Czech T-120, 1041/1809/414113–14.

French sea links with Central Europe uncertain, land links impossible, and, by requiring *couverture* of the Alpine frontier, it would diminish the possibility of inter-allied aid. Echoing Gamelin's tenets on the defence of Czechoslovakia, Schweisguth compared Italy with Poland as indispensable but capricious elements of victory: 'Italy, which can separate Central Europe from the west; Poland, which can separate it from the east; both almost as precious to Germany for their neutrality as for their cooperation, both seeming bound to fly to the aid of victory.' Alluding specifically to Czechoslovakia, Schweisguth told his select military listeners that the reoccupation and the recent revision of Belgian policy made the dispatch of a French expeditionary force to Central Europe more important than ever. A few weeks before his lecture, Schweisguth had shown Czech and Yugoslav military over the French fortifications. Their doubts as to France's offensive capabilities had been visible beneath their professed admiration. Schweisguth's argument was that French influence in Central Europe was in direct proportion to the offensive capabilities attributed to France, and that these depended in the first instance on Italy.[122]

The study of an expeditionary force, which Gamelin had instituted after the reoccupation, was not complete until Schweisguth's second set of lectures at the CHEDN in April 1937. Schweisguth gave his April lectures in the grim atmosphere engendered by the Italo-Yugoslav political pact of March. With the General Staff study in hand, he was, if anything, more adamant on the topic of Italy. The EMA's study, which postulated a rather friendly benevolent Italian neutrality, was precise 'right down to verification on the ships themselves of load capacity'. It envisaged a force of some 230,000 men transported along three possible naval routes – the Adriatic ports, Salonika, and the Black Sea – and able to intervene in a Danubian conflict within four months of embarkation, according to optimal calculations. Naval transport being cumbersome, the General Staff suggested shrinking the expeditionary force by reducing the infantry, as the allied armies were rich in men. It also recommended preceding the dispatch of the expeditionary force with materials such as heavy artillery and tanks that could not be obtained elsewhere, e.g., from the Soviet Union, and a French command capable of coordinating allied operations. This relatively

---

[122] Schw., SC4 Dr2 sdr b, 'Les données militaires actuelles d'une guerre de coalition européenne...', 5 November 1936, 20 April 1937.

rapid aid could be supplemented by the action 'limited but almost instantaneous' of the French Air Force, provided an adequate infrastructure had been organised in advance. The initiative for these various recommendations was Gamelin's. In a preparatory meeting for Schweisguth's second round of lectures, Gamelin had insisted on the narrowness of the Franco-German frontier and the necessity of enlarging it in Belgium or in Central Europe 'if only by a rapid, symbolic detachment, while awaiting the possibility of a large-scale operation'.[123]

Having impressed upon his listeners the complexity of the proposed operation, Schweisguth permitted himself a professional observation. An autonomous French policy in Central Europe, independent of such geographical realities as entente with Italy, was an illusion: 'From all the preceding, the impression emerges that the formulae so abundantly employed by statesmen and journalists, of "collective security" and "mutual aid" are in reality difficult, slow and limited in implementation.' In the EMA's view, projects such as a Franco-Petite Entente mutual aid pact amounted to little more than a pious wish without Italian friendship, the essential condition of France's remaining a continental power. By releasing Alpine troops for the expeditionary force and by permitting the use of its excellent railroads to the Yugoslav frontier, Italian support would ensure that the first French troops arrived on the Danube within three days and the entire expeditionary force within three weeks.[124] The moral of Schweisguth's cautionary tale was that, with Italian amity, all would be well. The Soviet role in Schweisguth's Central European *Kriegspiel* was limited to supplies, a particularly important function, he had told Léger, should Italy be hostile.[125] Schweisguth dismissed out of hand Soviet land intervention. Of the overall efficacy of Soviet air aid, he was sceptical, referring to 'a part of the [Russian] air force effectively out of breath...'.[126]

The EMA's attachment to Italy ostensibly rested on the orthodoxy that, as General Debeney said of the Belgian volte-face, nothing could modify geography.[127] From the Salonika discussions of the early 1930s, the EMA had been encouraged to pursue technical studies, in which diplomatic appreciations of alignments in a conflict

[123] Schw., SC4 Dr2 sdr b, 'Les données militaires...' and 1SC2 Dr11, 24 February 1937.
[124] Schw., SC4 Dr2 sdr b, 20 April 1937.
[125] Schw., 1SC2 Dr10, 8 October 1936.
[126] Schw., SC4 Dr2 sdr b, 5 November 1936.
[127] Schw., 1SC2 Dr10, 4 December 1936.

were absent, and in which its own fixation on a war of extended
fronts sometimes pushed into the background important military
elements, such as the complexities of Italo-Austrian relations and the
inadequacies of the Italian army in a European war.

The military's reliance on Italy in 1936–7 was also fostered by
French domestic factors. As its domestic disaffection with the Blum
Government grew, the EMA's wounded infatuation with Italy
deepened, a state of affairs which seemed to feed on the new Italo-
German entente. Rather than adapt its strategy, the military
preferred to fault the Blum Government for Mussolini's decampment, thus sowing several acres of the bitter sentimental harvest
gathered at Riom.[128] Italian diplomatic obstreperousness, for which
the military blamed the Blum Government, paled beside the dark
designs which the Schweisguth report attributed to the USSR: the
weakening of France and its army through Comintern activity, in
order to bring about a European war. The General Staff thus
dug in its heels over the position that an Italo-Polish front for the
defence of Czechoslovakia was incompatible with the Soviet
rapprochement aggressively pursued by Litvinov outside the
government and by Pierre Cot within it.

The decision to negotiate with the eastern allies

In this climate, Schweisguth's seemingly objective remarks on Italy
were intimately related to Pierre Cot's agitation for an inter-allied
coalition predicated on a Soviet military pact. In early September,
Cot had insisted to Delbos that the *Conseil des ministres* be informed
of his plan. Delbos's assent in principle was emptied of substance by
his stipulation that any collaboration entail minimum disadvantage
from a political point of view, and by a detailed critique of Cot's
ideas for inter-allied air cooperation. He said that air collaboration
with the Soviets should be renounced in favour of French utilisation
of Soviet war factories, that is, a policy of apolitical technical/
industrial accords with due regard for secrecy, rather than Cot's
plan, which Delbos and the EMA were convinced would look like an
attempt to encircle Germany.[129] Delbos's services then appealed to
Schweisguth for yet another note on the disadvantages of Soviet

---

[128] As attested by the memorandum which Gamelin circulated at Riom: 'The so-called
Popular Front policy would completely distort our positions abroad, by introducing its
dangerous ideology.' FNSP, Papiers Blum, 3BL3 Dr1, p. 12.

[129] DDF II, 3, no. 279.

conversations. Cot turned to Blum, obtaining the Premier's authorisation for an interministerial committee to examine his project of immediate allied air conversations, excluding Italy. Cot's only concession to Delbos was a delay in accepting an invitation to visit Bucharest.[130]

Called at Cot's request, the 6 November interministerial meeting represented an internal struggle for control of French policy. It deliberated on proposals for Soviet military talks and a reshaping of France's ties with the Petite Entente, a variant of the double agenda in abeyance since Blum's October conversation with Litvinov. As far as Blum was concerned, the Belgian decampment and Mussolini's Axis speech threatened to remove altogether a Locarno framework, into which a Czech-German accord could be placed. Blum saw a pressing need for negotiations to shore up Czechoslovakia and prevent a breakdown of the Petite Entente. Schweisguth's journal tersely records the meeting's conclusions: 'Everyone agreed to instigate a strengthening of the Petite Entente's internal military ties and ours with them... As to staff conversations, after a lively discussion between the Daladier-Chautemps and Cot-Rucart groups, it was decided that Cot would postpone his trip to the Petite Entente, and that we would ask the Soviets via the military attachés for their concept of mutual aid...'[131] Gamelin fixed on this form of Franco-Soviet staff contacts in order to thwart Cot's design to embark on a Soviet entente by way of aviation.[132]

Schweisguth, who would actually carry on the Soviet conversations, met with Bargeton the day after the interministerial meeting. They agreed to delay the talks until the arrival of the new Soviet military attaché at the end of the year, 'so that only a single Russian [military attaché] was in on the secret'.[133] In late December 1936, as preparations for the Soviet conversations began, Gamelin and Daladier could still agree in the candour of a closed-door meeting that an Italian rapprochement was 'the crux of maintaining peace'.[134]

Traces of the design to refurbish France's eastern ties with Soviet aid, the original connection between the two proposals adopted on 6 November, subsisted in Lacroix's short-lived success several days

[130] DDF II, 3, no. 394; Schw., 1SC2 Dr10, 10 October 1936.
[131] Schw., 1SC2 Dr10, 7 November 1936; 2SC2 Dr7 sdr b, undated manuscript note on the Soviet conversations; CE *Témoignages*, I, p. 127.
[132] Schw., 1SC2 Dr10, 20 October, 'Rapport'; 26, 27 October, 7 November 1936.
[133] Ibid., 7 November 1936.   [134] Ibid., 22 December 1936.

later in canvassing members of the government on Prague's plan for
a Franco-Soviet-Petite Entente pact; in a 3e Bureau memorandum
of early 1937 which advocated as a distant priority a unification of
France's eastern obligations into a single multilateral pact; and in
Cot's subsequent negotiations with Bucharest.[135] In practice, the two
negotiations were conducted independently. This decision reflected
the consensus between the military and diplomats that Russian
collaboration should be largely confined to industrial aid, gradually
phased to disarm Central European suspicions and to minimise the
semblance of preparations for a preventive war which Berlin might
exploit. In the Quai d'Orsay's view, extensive reliance on the Soviets
could only lead to uncontrollable ideological contagion and conflict
with Germany. Léger's response to the Schweisguth report had been
to discourse on the 'psychological disadvantages' of a Soviet
rapprochement, deploring the web that Communism was extending
over all countries.[136] Blum himself was hardly insensitive to the
danger of neutralism fed by Comintern action. The new French
Ambassador in Moscow, Robert Coulondre, was thus instructed to
tell Litvinov on 10 November: 'A psychosis is being created
according to which the Soviet entente leads to Communism; this fear
tends to neutralise that which is inspired by the German threat and
to paralyse cooperation among the pacific powers at the very time
when this current ought to intensify.'[137]

The Petite Entente negotiations were, relatively speaking, expe-
dited. On the day Coulondre met with Litvinov, 10 November,
Delbos notified the Petite Entente that the French Government was
prepared to negotiate 'without pointless haste, but also without
waste of time', a Franco-Petite Entente pact. The negotiations were
to be carried on simultaneously with negotiations for a Petite
Entente mutual aid pact; the two pacts would then come into force
at the same time.[138] The issue remained whether the agreements
would be placed under the strategic auspices of a Franco-Soviet or
a revived Franco-Italian entente, and more immediately, whether

[135] Ibid., 17 November 1936; SHA, undated EMA note, 'Tchécoslovaquie', communicated
by M. Jean Nicot.   [136] Schw., 1SC2 Dr10, 8 October 1936.
[137] DDF II, 3, nos. 472, 497, 506; R. Coulondre, *De Staline à Hitler* (Paris, 1950), pp. 30–46.
To similar Czech complaints, the Russians retorted: 'Bolshevistic propaganda in these
countries, if it exists, is an absolute dwarf compared to the systematic and brilliant
propaganda of Germany. It would be good if...[Roumania and Yugoslavia] concerned
themselves with the German danger before it is too late.' Czech T-120, 1143/2028/444464.
[138] DDF II, 3, no. 457.

Petite Entente negotiations could avert bilateral Czech-German accommodation.

To summarise, the proposal for a Franco-Petite Entente pact originated with the Roumanian Foreign Minister, Titulesco, in June 1936. Titulesco had Soviet ulterior motives in proposing the pact to Paris. After he fell from power, the project was taken up by the Czechs, anxious at the conclusion of the Austro-German accord. While sympathetic to the plight of the Czechs in the aftermath of the Rhineland reoccupation, the Quai d'Orsay for some months did not lend its approval to negotiations with the Petite Entente. Instead, it encouraged the Petite Entente first to conclude a mutual aid pact. Its position was gradually eroded by growing neutralism in the allied camp, and by burgeoning Italo-German rapprochement which blocked European-wide security negotiations. For its part, the French General Staff was dismissive of the Franco-Petite Entente negotiations. It remained attached to the moribund entente with Italy, for the state of which it blamed the Blum Government. In November 1936, restive at continuing military/diplomatic reliance on Italy, the Air Minister, Pierre Cot, pressed, as Titulesco had done, for unified French obligations in Central Europe; Cot's project included Franco-Soviet military conversations. He persuaded Léon Blum, increasingly anxious to reassure the Czechs and sceptical of Mussolini's goodwill, to call a cabinet meeting on the subject in early November 1936. The 6 November meeting was a direct sequel to the June CPDN. Divergent conceptions of French security – the refurbishment of France's eastern ties with Soviet aid as opposed to the military preference for a Petite Entente reliant on Italy and Poland – again clashed. The outcome was a provisional separation of the Petite Entente negotiations from the question of Soviet military talks.

CHAPTER 6

Blum and the diplomats: the Franco-Petite Entente negotiations, II

ECONOMICS, MINORITIES AND PROPAGANDA

The Czechoslovak draft

The Czechs responded to Delbos's assent at once, sending separate drafts for Petite Entente and Franco-Petite Entente pacts. They proposed that agreement be reached on a text, which would then be presented in Belgrade and Bucharest as French-inspired. In deference to Delbos's views, the Franco-Petite Entente draft had the veneer of a Danubian pact, open to other states which could choose between mutual aid, consultation, and non-assistance to an aggressor. (Not incidentally, these provisions encompassed Beneš's aspirations for a Czech-German agreement.) The substance of the draft, however, was based on the Franco-Soviet pact's regional application of article 16.[1]

René Massigli scuttled the Czech draft in his commentary. By virtually reproducing the text of the Soviet pact, Massigli argued, the Czech draft would occasion further German encirclement propaganda and offend international opinion, traumatised by the Spanish war. He opposed any arrangement which might appear 'an indirect means of creating a vast political group of the USSR, France and the Petite Entente'. Massigli advocated engagements patterned on the British accords of late 1935 with the Balkan states, a diplomatic formula in line with Paris's hopes for British mediation in rallying the Yugoslavs to a Petite Entente mutual aid pact. At the same time, able neither to rely on Italy nor to renounce its support, and anxious that the pact not be seen as a rigid counter-move to the

---

[1] DDF II, 3, nos. 467–8, 483. The Soviet bias of the Czech draft was supplemented shortly afterwards by Lacroix's representations in Paris to unnamed, allegedly favourable members of the government concerning Prague's plan for a Franco-Soviet-Petite Entente pact. Schw., 1SC2 Dr10, 17 November 1936.

formation of an Italo-German bloc, he presented the Franco-Petite Entente pact as 'in some way the residue' of France's 1935 Danubian pact diplomacy. As for the French role, he strenuously objected to the Czechs' failure to subordinate the operation of a Franco-Petite Entente pact to that between the Petite Entente states. Massigli concluded that the Franco-Petite Entente pact should give France a more modest role.[2]

Robert Blum's mission

The Quai d'Orsay delayed the elaboration of its own Franco-Petite Entente draft while extensive soundings of the Petite Entente were carried out for much of December. For the Blum Government's attempts to invigorate the ailing Petite Entente negotiations, the most obvious source of difficulty was the growing estrangement of the Yugoslav Prime Minister. Stoyadinovitch's coolness provoked even Beneš to a blast of irritation: 'Now that he sees himself as the object of the attentions of Rome and Berlin, he is happy, he is conceited, he imagines himself presiding over a great power like Poland. When I speak to him of reciprocal military aid, as though he believes that I am more menaced than he, he responds evasively.'[3]

The German economic threat had of course been blatant since Schacht's tour. Paris's response to increased Italian activity in Belgrade was more ambivalent. Italy, seeking to recover its pre-sanctions position in the Balkans, had signed a commercial agreement with Yugoslavia in September 1936. The initial French reaction had not been vehemently negative. When Ciano visited Berlin in October, and there was talk of respective economic spheres in Central Europe, it became harder for French diplomats to hold on to their traditional position that the Reich's commercial dynamism could be counterbalanced by an Italian economic presence in Danubia. Yet Delbos continued to react with *sang-froid* when the Yugoslavs after Mussolini's Axis speech spoke to him of their desire for improved relations with Italy.[4]

The Blum Government first counted on commercial negotiations with Belgrade to remedy past French negligence and to save Stoyadinovitch from Italian and German blandishments. A politically motivated decision by the Front populaire to accord substantial commercial concessions to the Yugoslavs in the form of

[2] DDF II, 3, no. 503; 4, nos. 9, 81.   [3] DDF II, 4, no. 81.
[4] DDF II, 3, no. 464; 4, nos. 11, 148; Hoptner, *Yugoslavia*, p. 85; Schw., 1SC2 Dr10, 7, 12 November; SHA, 'Yougoslavie AM', 11 December 1936.

customs rebates on grain purchases predated French involvement in negotiations with the Petite Entente. The commercial negotiations, however, had been postponed until the size of the French harvest was known. Beginning at roughly the moment the government entered the Petite Entente negotiations, they were subject to Blum's strong pressures on the chronically reticent Ministry of Agriculture, pressures inseparable from his desire for a consolidated Petite Entente. Envisaging a strategy which timidly replicated Schacht's, the government offered to purchase 200,000 tons of Yugoslav grain, with the proceeds to be used for Yugoslav arms purchases in France.[5]

The Yugoslavs flatly refused to sell the quantities of grain necessary to finance arms purchases. Instead, they combined grain with other agricultural products less in demand in Germany and Czechoslovakia, which offered more attractive arms packages. To bulk grain sales, that would have financed arms purchases in France on far less advantageous payments schedules, Belgrade preferred a piecemeal dismantling of the hated French quota system. The untimely arrival of a German delegation in quest of further wheat purchases rushed Paris into an agreement which provided neither the desired arms settlement nor political capital in the Franco-Petite Entente negotiations. Paris's only slight consolation was Yugoslav assent to resume direct exports of copper, useful for French rearmament.[6] Hardened by his dealings with Laval, Stoyadinovitch had dispensed with any hope of French military support. He was embarking on a policy of doing business with Italy and Germany in order to reconcile Yugoslavia's minorities, while attempting an external equilibrium between these states on the one hand, and Britain and France on the other.[7]

At this delicate stage, Blum sent his son, Robert, on an unorthodox diplomatic mission to Central Europe. Robert Blum and his wife had lived in Belgrade for a year in 1931 on an assignment from the firm Hispaño-Suiza, for which Blum was an engineer. They counted from their stay many close Yugoslav friends, including Milan Stoyadino-vitch – in 1931 an opposition politician who had seemed progressive and democratic to the younger Blums. Scheduled to return to Belgrade on business in December 1936, Robert Blum, at his father's

---

[5] The Ministry of Finance regarded the concessions being offered, notably a renunciation of discussion of Yugoslav debts to French investors, as so abnormal that they should be kept rigorously secret. Finances, F30: 2081, Baumgartner Note, 21 November; 2498, Rueff-Delbos letter, 28 December 1936.

[6] Finances, F30:2079–81, 2097, 2498, passim.   [7] DDF II, 4, no. 165.

request, secretly requested interviews with Stoyadinovitch. Renée Blum, who accompanied her husband, remembers the great importance her father-in-law attached to the conclusion of the Petite Entente pacts. Preoccupied by the recent unsatisfactory soundings on the subject, Léon Blum wanted to try again on a more intimate plane, in the hope that Stoyadinovitch would feel more free to confide his reservations, and that his son could eventually obtain a favourable response. The initiative was timely: both the British and German ministers in Belgrade were encouraging Stoyadinovitch to have nothing to do with the Franco-Petite Entente project.[8]

The younger Blum spent six days in Belgrade, meeting with Stoyadinovitch three times and the Regent once. In Stoyadinovitch's complex arguments against a Franco-Petite Entente pact, economics were dominant. Pointedly dismissive of the recent economic accord with the Front populaire, he dwelt on French niggardliness during sanctions, which he contrasted with the Reich's voracious appetite for Yugoslav trade. Obsessed with Ciano's reported division of spoils in Berlin, Stoyadinovitch feared that a Franco-Petite Entente alliance would produce a consolidation of the Italo-German entente, possibly even an Axis partition of Central Europe for eventual colonisation. He mentioned in this connection the internal minority troubles fanned by Germany and Italy, which economic distress might ignite. His intense preoccupation with his country's internal troubles led him to extol an ambitious Greater Balkan entente, requiring a Yugoslav rapprochement with Bulgaria, a policy which would pacify Yugoslavia's Macedonian minority. Stoyadinovitch accompanied his dissociation from the Petite Entente or more precisely, Czechoslovakia, the only Petite Entente state not in the Balkan Entente by an hostility to bloc politics, which he likened to the British stance. He sweetened his refusal of the Franco-Petite Entente pact by assurances that, in a crisis, Yugoslavia would be at France's side, but remarked that to proclaim this in advance would only subject Yugoslavia to economic reprisals from Italy and Germany. Stoyadinovitch spoke less ingratiatingly when he called for direct Franco-German agreement.

Robert Blum reluctantly concluded from his visit that the Yugoslav response was negative. The blatant opportunism of the Premier's policy towards Germany and Italy, however, and the

[8] Hoptner, *Yugoslavia*, p. 56.

strength of popular affection for France persuaded him that British mediation and French economic guarantees might yet force Stoyadinovitch's assent. Such hopes, he warned, were only practical if immediate action were taken in the way of cultural exchanges and propaganda to regain lost ground in Yugoslav political and intellectual circles. In this, he joined the French military attaché in Belgrade who had insisted shortly before the Blums' arrival that only vigorous cultural, industrial, and political propaganda could ensure the effectiveness of French commercial concessions.[9] Robert Blum attached particular importance to the propaganda proviso ending his report, and he took pride after his visit to Belgrade in the parliamentary vote of credits to increase numbers of scholarships to France and professorships in *Instituts français* in Central Europe, and to renovate French libraries abroad. Privately, he and his wife were shocked by the change in Franco-Yugoslav relations from the early 1930s, when Yugoslavs of all classes had been intensely Francophile. For the Blums, 'All of Central Europe had been cast off', and they asked themselves why the Quai d'Orsay had abandoned these countries culturally to the German onslaught.[10]

By 1936, the inadequacies of French propaganda abroad were egregious. The efforts of the existing propaganda organisations, under the authority of four different ministries as well as of private groups, were disorganised and lopsided. In the words of an indignant deputy: 'one is appalled by the number of groups which draw on propaganda funds. Each is working in a particularist spirit incompatible with an overall plan.' Moreover, the central propaganda service headed by Pierre Comert at the Quai d'Orsay was run on a shoestring, while large sums were lavished on the semi-official Havas agency and on propaganda/information services in Alsace-Lorraine.[11] Among the Alsatian organisations heavily subsidised by the French Government after the First World War was the *Comité alsacien d'études et d'informations*. The Comité's field of action included Central Europe, especially Czechoslovakia, which was believed to

---

[9] SHA, 'Yougoslavie AM', 11 December 1936.
[10] DDF II, 4, no. 180; conversation with Renée Robert Blum, 2 June 1977. Robert Blum's authorship can be identified by comparing the report's second section on his visit to Prague and Léon Blum's 1947 testimony, *CE Témoignages* I, p. 129. The Regent confidentially informed the British Legation of Blum's visit (PRO, FO 371, 20436, R7570/83/6), but, within the Quai d'Orsay, Blum's mission was not widely known. He had not signed his report, at his father's request.
[11] Ernest Pezet, cited in Assemblée Nationale, Commission, 20 March 1936; ibid., 17 March 1937; P. Amaury, *Les deux premières expériences d'un 'Ministère de l'information' en France* (Paris, 1969), pp. 12–25.

share with Alsace a frontier mentality *vis-à-vis* Germany. Its correspondents, including Hubert Beuve-Méry in Prague, filed confidential intelligence reports sent directly to the seven highest members of the French Government. While the Comité's archives in Strasburg are closed, official contemporary evidence suggests that governmental subsidies cultivated intelligence gathering in allied states at the expense of propaganda. The meagreness of French propaganda in Central Europe was such that one Petite Entente Foreign Minister boasted that his country spent more on press subsidies in France in one month than the French did in a year in his country.[12]

This aversion to intensive propaganda reflected *mentalités*, some of them profound and relinquished with difficulty. Parliamentary transcripts from this period show a complacency also apparent with British information services abroad. Propaganda as carried on by Germany and Italy was regarded as unsuitable to the aims of a democracy – not world conquest, but the prevention of a kind of moral conquest of its allies: 'We need to combat mendacious propaganda more than we need to establish our influence abroad by official means. It is enough for us not to hide France's true face from the world.'

Propagandising was thought unbecoming, both to the French as a people and to France's democratic régime, whose freedoms it would menace. This argument only half concealed fears, generated by the divisiveness of domestic politics, that a governmental campaign of slogans representing official truth would immediately provoke a counter-campaign of slogans from the domestic opposition 'which would demolish those of the government'.[13]

Pierre Laval had provocatively dismissed strong pressures from the Foreign Policy Commission in 1935 for a fundamental reorganisation of the propaganda services: 'I do not believe in propaganda. When a country has a good army, a good foreign policy, when it is strong, its propaganda makes itself. Hungary has the best propaganda. It spends considerable sums. Do you believe that it profits from that?'[14] Laval's resistance also sprang from wariness of parliamentary infringement on his ministerial prerogatives, which included allocation of the sizeable part of the budget of the *présidence du Conseil* earmarked for propaganda. The Quai

[12] M. Vaïsse, 'La mission de Jouvenal à Rome', p. 93.
[13] Assemblée Nationale, Commission, 17 March 1937.
[14] Assemblée Nationale, Commission, 13 March 1935.

d'Orsay was similarly opposed to parliamentary pressures for reform.[15]

Two months before his son's mission, Blum had appointed an interministerial committee, composed of Camille Chautemps, his Minister of State, and two Under Secretaries of State from the Quai d'Orsay and the Matignon, to study reform of the propaganda apparatus.[16] Chautemps appeared before the Chambre's Foreign Policy Commission in March 1937 to report his committee's decision not to create a Ministry of Propaganda. He justified his decision as being less disruptive of existing ministerial demarcations and as requiring fewer credits, a pertinent criterion after Blum's recent declaration of a financial 'pause'. Before the Chambre commission, Chautemps advocated continuing with his committee, which he whimsically described as 'without means, without resources, and without legal authority to impose itself on the services which are already in place', in order to coordinate the existing propaganda organisms and press subsidies rather than undertaking the vigorous reforms desired by observers such as Robert Blum and Colonel Béthouart.[17]

Chautemps's more promising conceptions in March 1937 relied on the generosity of private or semi-private business rather than the coordination of impecunious ministries. Personal representations by the Minister had already persuaded various publishers to give the government substantial discounts, and Chautemps spoke of using French commercial agencies abroad as purveyors of national propaganda. As to cinema, a prime medium for German propaganda, Chautemps, who disposed of not a *sou* for French propaganda films, could only point to his committee's stimulation of an incipient awareness of its national duty within the film industry. In radio, a medium particularly attractive to Central European listeners and one in which the Germans excelled with their technical mastery, polyglot programming and high-quality artistic broadcasts, Chautemps's inquiry revealed rebarbative French attitudes. His Commission changed the name of the station broadcasting abroad from 'Radio-colonial' to 'Radio-France'. For the rest, Chautemps and the government looked to the 1937 Paris Exhibition to restore

[15] Assemblée Nationale, Commission, 20 March 1936; Amaury, *Les deux premières expériences d'un 'Ministère de l'information'*, pp. 12–15.

[16] Amaury, *Les deux premières expériences d'un 'Ministère de l'information'*, pp. 17–19.

[17] Ibid., p. 52. Blum's brief second government in 1938 included a ministerial portfolio for propaganda.

France's prestige by rivalling the Berlin Olympics.[18] The Exhibition's failure was badly demoralising for many in French official circles. Their despairing, unspoken assumption, increasingly powerful, was that it would be naive to believe that money spent on propaganda would be sufficient to refurbish the image of France in the world. The task could only be accomplished by a dramatic internal transformation.[19]

After his disturbing days in Belgrade, Robert Blum proceeded to Prague. He had only received instructions from Hispaño-Suiza to go there once he reached Belgrade. Thus there were no directives from his father for this part of his trip. In Prague, Robert Blum dined with a journalist much in Beneš's confidence, Hubert Ripka, and several members of the Czech Government. As the younger Blum's report on his mission made clear, whatever the differences between Czechs and Yugoslavs, both were caught by minority issues which gave economics a primacy that crippled political will. Stoyadinovitch had described his country's dilemma: 'Such a renewal of domestic agitation [on minority issues] would find a terrain all the more favourable as commercial reprisals [by Germany and Italy] would plunge the country back into economic difficulties, and these would maintain discontents susceptible to exploitation...'[20]

The Czechs emphasised to Robert Blum that the Sudetendeutsch were more the victims of economic hardship, willed by the Reich, than of Czech oppression. In 1935–6, Czechoslovakia had cut back on its German purchases, only a few years before almost three times as large as those from any other supplier, in order to avoid trade dependency on Germany. The Reich responded by relentlessly increasing its purchases in Czechoslovakia and then freezing the proceeds under a 1933 clearing accord. It manipulated these currency difficulties to discourage German tourists from summering in Marienbad or Karlsbad, areas whose tourist, glass, and textile industries had been devastated by the Depression. This exacerbated Sudetendeutsch grievances against Prague, while worsening low Czech currency reserves, which in turn strained the servicing of debts to France.[21]

---

[18] Assemblée Nationale, Commission, 17 March 1937; Amaury, *Les deux premières expériences d'un 'Ministère de l'information'*, pp. 53–61.
[19] MAE, Papiers Massigli, 'Correspondance personnelle', Massigli-J. Paul-Boncour letter, 7 January 1938, misdated 1928.   [20] DDF II, 4, no. 180.
[21] Finances, F30:1146, Lacroix dispatch, 17 June; Aide-Mémoire, 18 September (appended to Delbos-Bastid letter, 3 October) 1936.

Not only was much of the attractiveness of Henlein's *Sudetendeutsch Partei* rooted in economic hardship, but the Foreign Office's encouragement of Henlein's plaints caused concern to the Czech ministers who dined with Blum. The Foreign Office's sympathies, shaped by the Prague Legation and its Permanent Under Secretary's contacts with the 'moderate' Henlein during his periodic visits to London, were grimly anti-Czech. Vansittart minuted in August 1936: 'I too of course think – as every perspicacious man must – that the Czechs have ruined [them]se.[lves] by their follies and corruptions...' Vansittart for some months had urged Henlein to devote his efforts to economic rather than political grievances. An appeal by Henlein to the League Council, of which Eden was president, provided the Foreign Office with opportunity to raise the Sudetendeutsch question in Paris. Delbos staunchly maintained that the Czechs were gradually introducing reforms.[22]

Nevertheless, the Quai d'Orsay and the Ministries of Finance and Commerce were not responsive when the Czechs pleaded for French concessions – enlarged quotas and advantageous loan terms – to benefit the Sudetendeutsch.[23] When Prague drew attention to its sacrifices for its Petite Entente and Soviet allies, in an attempt to influence the revision of the quota system after French devaluation in September, that too was of no avail. To the Ministry of Commerce, Delbos wrote:

Responding to arguments of the same kind, the French Government has always been opposed to the idea of financing by special concession the political or economic concessions which Czechoslovakia, in a just appreciation of its own interests, may be led to make in Central Europe, parallel moreover to the efforts of French policy.[24]

The British Legation in Prague observed without regret that the Czechs were being pushed into negotiations with Germany by the

[22] PRO, FO 371, 20374, R2126/32/12, R2128/32/12, R3290/32/12; 20375, R2526/32/12, R6726/32/12, R6894/32/12; 20385, R7651/1644/67; DDF II, 4, nos. 180, 295, 329; Czech T-120, 1041/1809/414118; S. Grant Duff, *The Parting of the Ways* (London, 1981), p. 171.

[23] Finances, F30: 1146–7, passim; MAE, C: 'Tchécoslovaquie: Relations commerciales 1936–7', passim. Delbos was also aware of Czechoslovak jealousy of the Poles' good fortune at Rambouillet.

[24] Finances, F30:1146, 3 October 1936; DDF II, 2, nos. 48, 209. The Ministry of Commerce questioned Prague's figures for trade imbalance between the two countries. It maintained that the deficit in Czechoslovakia's trade with France could be accounted for by Czechoslovak purchases of finished wool products from France, which were re-exported to the Balkans, with payment dates months after those to French exporters. Finances, F30:1146, 28 August, 15 October 1936.

lack of French response.[25] The anger at Paris in some circles in Prague underscored the possibility of a split within the governmental majority, which would pit Beneš's forces against Hodža's Agrarian Party. Aghast at Comintern activities under the aegis of Soviet military aid to Spain, the Agrarians contemplated accommodation with Germany through the Sudetendeutsch, with whom they allegedly wanted to form a domestic anti-Communist coalition.[26]

The Czech-German negotiations of the autumn and winter of 1936–7 have been admirably recounted by Gerhard Weinberg.[27] The prospect of increased trade figured from the first in the Czech response to approaches from the *Dienststelle Ribbentrop's* Albrecht Haushofer, the driving force on the German side for reaching an agreement to neutralise Czechoslovakia. At Beneš's invitation, Haushofer and an official from Seldte's veterans' organisation, Trauttmannsdorff, twice visited Prague in November and December 1936, Trauttmannsdorff returning a third time in early 1937. In November, the Germans offered an unconditional, ten-year non-aggression pact. Beneš's refusal to renounce Czechoslovakia's obligations to France and the USSR at a German attack, or to eschew League terminology, shifted discussion to reaffirmation of the 1925 arbitration treaty, coupled with a large increase in trade to benefit the Sudetendeutsch. For some weeks into 1937, Beneš and his colleagues believed in an imminent accommodation. But, unlike his emissaries, Hitler was unconcerned by the well-being of the Sudetendeutsch, and untempted by an agreement which would have stabilised the Beneš Government by leaving its treaties intact. The negotiations were eventually dropped, by the German side.

Robert Blum's impromptu arrival in Prague on 18 December actually coincided with the second round of the German talks, of which rumours appear to have reached Paris only in January 1937.[28] A mid December interview between Delbos and Osuský suggests that Prague was already preparing the transition from Franco-Petite Entente to German negotiations. Osuský declared to Delbos that were the Franco-Petite Entente negotiations to fail, his government would be prepared to negotiate with Germany: 'we would be

---

[25] PRO, FO 371, 20375, R7445/32/12.
[26] Ibid., R7445/32/12; Finances, F30:1147, Lacroix dispatch, 10 March 1937.
[27] Weinberg, *Foreign Policy*, I, pp. 316–21, and 'Secret Hitler-Beneš Negotiations in 1936–37', *Journal of Central European Affairs*, 19, no. 4, January 1960, pp. 366–74.
[28] DDF II, 4, nos. 383 and note, 393, 439 note, 442; Schw., 1SC2 Dr11, 15 February; 1SC2 Dr12, 2 April 1937.

prepared to make all necessary concessions, even on matters in which we were clearly in the legal right, to avoid the risks of war in conditions in which we would be too heavily handicapped...'[29]

This did not mean that Beneš intended to jettison his loyalties to France. While Haushofer's transcripts suggest that they may have been cavalier about the extent of their treaty commitments, the Czechs intended to keep their defensive treaties.[30] The Agrarian Hodža, the chief proponent of a German agreement within the Czech Government, expected Czechoslovakia to be attacked in 1938; the Czech military, on the basis of the *Reichswehr*'s latest manoeuvres, continued to plan for a German-Hungarian attack. The emerging wisdom in Prague appears to have been that buying time and avoiding provocation should guide policy. A signed agreement with Hitler would make Poland and Yugoslavia better disposed to Prague, while the Reich's subsequent violation of its commitments would rally Britain and France.[31] It was typical of Beneš's diplomacy that his messages to Robert Blum should have included a countervailing query on the progress of Cot's air planning. Soviet air support had been for some months a matter of keen interest in Prague.[32]

Neutralisation of the Franco-Petite Entente negotiations by a brief flurry of counter-negotiations was as necessary to ultimate German success as was the tactic of preserving a grievance by perpetually raising Henlein's demands. At a critical point in the Franco-Petite Entente negotiations, when Blum himself espoused the project, the Czech-German conversations were taken as an indication of temporary German innocuousness by the Czechs and the Yugoslavs, who were kept informed by Hodža. Beneš sent a message to Robert Blum as the Blums boarded the train for Paris that there was no immediate German menace to Czechoslovakia.

In something of a post-scriptum to Robert Blum's mission, Beneš added that an anti-Stalin clique headed by Marshal Toukhatchevsky was engaged in secret negotiations with Berlin. Either during his December 1936 visit, or at an earlier stage in the conversations, a 'slip of the tongue' by the German envoy Trauttmannsdorff had informed Beneš of Toukhatchevsky's alleged treason. This was the

[29] DDF II, 4, no. 165.
[30] DDF II, 4, no. 209; Weinberg, 'Secret Hitler-Beneš Negotiations', pp. 368–9.
[31] DDF II, 4, nos. 116, 442; Schw., 1SC2 Dr10, 18 December 1936; 1SC2 Dr11, 'Rapport', 5 January 1937; PRO, FO 371, 20375, R7427/32/12.
[32] PRO, FO 371, 20374, R4430/32/12; R4734/32/12; 20378, R3673/1799/12; 20385, R3723/1644/67; Schw., 1SC2 Dr9, 4 June 1936.

opening ploy of the Toukhatchevsky affair, an intrigue to decapitate the Red Army fabricated by the Gestapo with the complicity of the NKVD.[33] The Czech-German conversations provided a perfect opportunity for a leakage by the SS, which, unlike the German Foreign Office, was kept informed of the talks.[34] Beneš duly transmitted the rumour of Toukhatchevsky's treason to Stalin, but not without first sending word to Léon Blum by the chain of messages which Ripka gave the younger Blum in the Prague railroad station.[35] The 'revelations' concerning Toukhatchevsky were in the long run used to justify to the hilt the French General Staff's stance against closer relations with the USSR.

Antonesco in Paris

Neither Yugoslav refusal of the Petite Entente pacts, confided by Blum to Ripka, nor their own hopes of accommodation with the Reich, encouraged the Czechs to maintain a leading role in the ongoing Franco-Petite Entente negotiations. This fell to the Roumanians. Antonesco spent a week in Paris in mid December, a visit which coincided with Robert Blum's to Belgrade. He set out to ingratiate himself with his hosts, wishing to obtain the upward revision of the commercial part of the petrol settlement of February 1936. Recently returned from Warsaw, he delivered a soothing apologia for Beck's policy, while his prognosis for the Franco-Petite Entente negotiations was more hopeful than anything the French were hearing from Belgrade or Prague. Antonesco told Delbos and Blum that Roumania and Czechoslovakia were agreed on Petite Entente and Franco-Petite Entente *resserrements*, as was Yugoslavia, on two conditions: that it not be required to draw close to Russia and that Britain be involved.[36]

Cooperation with the Soviets became even more suspect after

[33] R. Conquest, *The Great Terror* (New York, 1968), pp 217–20; J. Erickson, *The Soviet High Command* (London, 1962), pp. 403–73; N. Rutych, 'L'affaire du maréchal Toukhatchevsky', *Revue des deux Mondes*, 15 April 1961; FNSP, Papiers Daladier, 1DA7 Dr5 sdr c.
[34] Weinberg, *Foreign Policy*, p. 317; Erikson, *The Soviet High Command*, p. 220.
[35] DDF II, 4, no. 180; *CE Témoignages*, I, p. 129. Beneš's memoirs, which are selective on the Czech-German negotiations, date his knowledge of the Toukhatchevsky affair from a conversation between Trauttmannsdorff and the Czechoslovak Ambassador in Berlin in the second half of January 1937, E. Beneš, *The Memoirs of Dr. Beneš* (London, 1954), pp. 14–20 and note. Another more obscure account by Beneš is in W. Churchill, *The Second World War: The Gathering Storm* (Boston, 1948), pp. 288–9. The combination of Robert Blum's report and his father's 1947 testimony conclusively demonstrates Beneš's error.
[36] DDF II, 4, no. 213 and note; Schw., 1SC2 Dr10, 22 December 1936; PRO, FO 371, 20430, R7716/646/37.

Germany and Japan signed the Anti-Comintern pact in November 1936. The pact marked the Reich's success in squeezing the USSR in diplomatic pincers by a doctrine which drew no clear line between Bolshevik and Popular Front governments. Accompanied by declarations that it had been necessitated by the establishment of Popular Fronts which allowed Comintern participation in power, it provoked a rapid response from the Quai d'Orsay: assurances to Tokyo of the limitations of the Franco-Soviet pact, and a repetition of warnings to Moscow against ideological agitation. In Central Europe, the result of the Anti-Comintern pact was heightened fear of great power ideological rivalry. This was apparent not only in Polish, Austrian, and Yugoslav refusals of German invitations to join an anti-Comintern front, but also in Yugoslav, and less conspicuously, Roumanian hesitation to accept the French project for Petite Entente pacts. However readily Antonesco broached the subject of Franco-Petite Entente negotiations in Paris, the Bucharest Legation had reported several weeks earlier that the Roumanians feared being drawn by the Czech-Soviet entente into a general conflagration arising from the Spanish war. In such an eventuality, Carol and Antonesco had implied, they would at all costs avoid taking sides. This neutralism meant a deepening of the isolation of Czechoslovakia, which, if it did not come to terms with Germany, would certainly be one of the first German objectives in a German-Soviet war.[37]

Antonesco and Delbos also tried to unravel the tangle caused by Stoyadinovitch's diplomacy *vis-à-vis* Bulgaria. Eager for a friendship treaty with Sofia, the Balkan Entente's traditional enemy, the Yugoslavs had sounded Delbos before Antonesco's visit. Delbos assented in principle, but delegated the task of setting conditions in the negotiations to the Roumanians, who feared that such a treaty would nullify the Balkan Entente. He cautioned the Yugoslavs that an accord would open the way to influences beyond the Balkans, and that too exclusive a diversion of Yugoslav energies to Balkan problems would weaken the Petite Entente's cohesion. With Antonesco in Paris, Delbos actively mediated, proposing a compromise clause maintaining prior Yugoslav treaty obligations. Prague,

[37] DDF II, 4, nos. 25, 36, 49, 86, 105, 116, 153. Cf. Antonesco's line with Eden, that he had pressed for London's involvement in the Franco-Petite Entente negotiations because he felt that he could count upon its disapproval. Given his preference for a Czech-German agreement, Antonesco implied, he naturally turned towards London. PRO, FO 954/23, Ro/32/2.

however, unconditionally approved the Yugoslav-Bulgarian pact, forcing Antonesco to abandon his conditions.[38]

The Yugoslav-Bulgarian pact was disruptive: the Roumanians were annoyed by the Czechs' lack of consultation before responding, and the French because their priorities in the negotiations were ignored. Daladier was incensed by the treaty after the French commercial sacrifices of December, and he threatened to withdraw the decrepit French war materials stored in Yugoslavia.[39] The Yugoslav-Bulgarian episode transposed Yugoslav allegiances from the Petite Entente to the Balkans, which Stoyadinovitch described as anchoring Yugoslavia in the British sphere. Troubling indications of German connivance in the negotiations soon emerged, however. François-Poncet's interpretation of the pact as representing the Reich's successful prospecting in the Balkans was corroborated by Hitler's 30 January speech, in which he extolled the 'new realities in Europe', Italy, Poland, and the Balkans, and by Yugoslav press coverage of the pact exclusively in Balkan terms, without reference to France or Czechoslovakia.[40] It thus provided a foretaste of the Italo-Yugoslav treaty of March 1937, the consummation of Stoyadinovitch's Balkan ambitions.

EARTHSLIDE: THE NEGOTIATIONS COLLAPSE

The French draft

In this unpromising atmosphere, the Quai d'Orsay finally circulated its draft for a Franco-Petite Entente pact.[41] It codified Massigli's objections to the Czech draft. The Political Directorate's guiding consideration remained the subordination of French obligations to the operation of a Petite Entente mutual aid pact. Ingenious drafting gave full scope to the Franco-Czech tie. Roumania and Yugoslavia would each assume new obligations to France and Czechoslovakia, while France's reciprocal obligation would be activated only by the Petite Entente mutual aid pact, except in the case of a German attack on Czechoslovakia. Paris was eloquently silent as to the

---

[38] Beneš justified his precipitant assent to the pact by arguing that Petite Entente flexibility in this instance might make Belgrade more receptive to a Petite Entente pact, but the Prague Legation presented Beneš's behaviour as carrying over his hopes for accommodation with Germany. DDF II, 4, nos. 165, 192, 359, 387.

[39] Schw., 1SC2 Dr11, 4 January 1937.   [40] DDF II, 4, nos. 253, 240, 355, 386.

[41] Ibid., no. 281.

The Popular Front and Central Europe

modalities of its aid once the Petite Entente pact was operative. The diplomatic advantage for Prague and Paris was plain, less so for Roumania and Yugoslavia. By a supple negotiating posture (it was willing to postpone signature of an initialled pact until the outcome of the Locarno negotiations was known, in deference to Yugoslav wishes, and to accept collective amendments from the Petite Entente), the Blum Government pressed for a rapid, face-saving agreement to shore up Czechoslovakia.

There was never a joint Petite Entente response. The delays in the draft's elaboration had completely altered the configuration within the Petite Entente from June 1936, when Titulesco had originally proposed a Franco-Petite Entente pact as a means of inducing a Roumanian-Soviet entente and of protecting Yugoslavia from Italy. By early 1937, neither Roumania nor Yugoslavia had any real interest in the project, only in letting the French down gently. Prague's response was governed by an impulse towards accommodation with Germany. The Czechs' first reaction to the French draft was clouded by an open reference to the Czechs' November draft, which Prague had repeatedly asked be kept secret.[42] Beneš made no objection to the French draft which held no surprises after Massigli's November criticisms, but he resisted French pressures to threaten the Yugoslavs with an end to Czech arms supplies and exclusion from the Petite Entente if Yugoslavia refused to initial the French draft.[43] The Czechs had no intention of jeopardising the offer from Berlin which they expected from Hitler's 30 January 1937 speech. Far from shepherding the Yugoslavs back into the French fold, they pursued a policy of imitating Belgrade, as they struggled to accommodate themselves with grace to Belgrade's various Balkan and Italian diplomatic enterprises.[44] Indeed, Beneš was said to be attempting to enlist Roumanian and Yugoslav support for pressure on Paris for a Franco-German agreement, without which Czechoslovakia would make its own deal with Germany rather than waiting to be crushed.[45]

It was Antonesco who approached the French in Geneva with alternative treaty proposals to free a Franco-Petite Entente *resserrement* from subordination to a Petite Entente pact. The same

---

[42] Ibid., no. 318. The Czechs may have come to believe that their negotiations with Berlin were short circuited by leaks in the Petite Entente negotiations.

[43] Ibid., nos. 338, 358, 387.   [44] Czech T-120, 1041/1809/414041.

[45] DDF II, 4, nos. 213, 442; Orville Bullitt (ed.), *For the President Personal and Secret* (Boston, 1972), p. 204.

bent was visible in the Czech draft, but for Antonesco it had quite another origin. Since November, Beck had advised Antonesco that entente with Czechoslovakia would be folly. The proposal favoured by Antonesco was for three French treaties, one with each Petite Entente state, modelled on the 1921 Franco-Polish treaty.[46] In a rare moment of candour with Delbos, Antonesco made it plain that Roumania saw no advantage to compromising itself for Czechoslovakia, but for the rest, and less credibly than in December, he shielded behind Belgrade.[47]

Behind Antonesco's amendments, the Quai d'Orsay scented a Roumanian desire for cheap assurances against Russia and Hungary. It was also apprehensive that the Yugoslavs would use a Franco-Yugoslav pact to increase their value to Germany, as it believed the Poles had done. Its position was unyielding: bilateral treaties were useless because they would not oblige Roumania and Yugoslavia to aid Czechoslovakia, and the German danger would only manifest itself via Czechoslovakia. Delbos rejected any project showing reticence towards Prague, a reticence which, he argued, in itself would justify changes in Czech policy.[48]

In rebutting Antonesco's proposals, Delbos made no mention of what the French Legation described as Bucharest's 'profound aversion for direct or indirect political ties with the USSR'. The silence suited both sides. In approaching the French in Geneva, Antonesco had been over-eager that his proposals not be seen in an anti-Soviet light, protesting that there were advantages in being able to maintain relations with the USSR by 'the Czech detour'. Pierre Cot, however, sought to force his hand.

Pierre Cot and Caranfil

After the decision of the November interministerial meeting that he should postpone a voyage to the Petite Entente, Cot carried on negotiations from Paris with the Roumanians for a mutual air aid pact, entailing the fitting out of their airfields for French or allied use. Cot explicitly postulated Soviet use of the refurbished fields.[49] Caranfil, his Roumanian counterpart, agreed to technical talks within the framework of the Franco-Petite Entente negotiations,

---

[46] DDF II, 4, nos. 334, 344, 379; MAE, Papiers Massigli, 'Affaires de l'Europe centrale', Massigli-Thierry letter, 25 January 1937. [47] DDF II, 4, no. 344.
[48] Ibid., nos. 334, 338 and notes, 401; MAE, Papiers Massigli, 'Affaires de l'Europe centrale', Note, 12 February 1937. [49] SHAA, 2B93.

but, while the two air ministries wrangled over the size of the French advance to finance the infrastructure, a behind-the-scenes stalemate developed. In early December, apprehensive that Roumanian air bases would come under Russian control, King Carol stepped in to refuse Cot's demands.[50] To break the deadlock, Cot sent an emissary, General Gérard, to conduct negotiations with Caranfil during Antonesco's visit to Paris. Gérard was to capitalise on the diplomatic goodwill emanating from Antonesco's visit to cajole the Roumanians to enter rapidly into construction. To Gérard's pressures for deployment of 'French or allied' air forces on Roumanian soil, Caranfil gave only verbal assent, subject to governmental ratification. Caranfil's timid complicity with Cot caused his eviction from the Roumanian Government in January, after hostile parliamentary questions. Schweisguth noted drily that Caranfil was being sacked, like Titulesco, for Russophilia.[51]

Cot's aims and brash tactics affronted Antonesco, who confided to Eden that his concern to avoid arrangements enabling the USSR to use Roumania as a base in aiding Czechoslovakia lay behind his objections to the Franco-Petite Entente pact. It was difficult, he said, to express his apprehensions directly to the French, given France's close relations with the USSR, with whom Roumania could not afford to quarrel.[52]

Having separated the Petite Entente and Soviet negotiations in November, the Quai d'Orsay was loath to see the Soviet issue return to the Franco-Petite Entente proceedings. The week Caranfil fell, a private letter from Jean Paul-Boncour, the Legation's Counsellor, drew Massigli's attention to the impossibility for Roumania of accepting the French draft which, based on article 16, indirectly implied an engagement to allow Soviet troop passage to Czechoslovakia. He continued: 'I do not mean to say that at the moment of danger Roumania will not even resign itself to the passage of air squadrons; but even within these limits, there can be no question of stipulating anything whatsoever on this topic at the moment.' Massigli accepted this and did not quarrel with the Legation's emphasis on discreet, non-Soviet, technical collaboration as a possible solution to Roumanian objections to the politicised

[50] Schw., 1SC2 Dr10, 10 December 1936.
[51] Schw., 1SC2 Dr11, 18 January 1937.
[52] PRO, FO 954/23, Ro/37/2–3. On increasing Roumanian attraction to Britain, unlikely to try to force the Roumanian hand in dealing with the USSR, and on the amicably vague British response, Lungu, *Romania*, pp. 113–14.

engagements of the French draft. Czechoslovakia remained the locus of his concern: 'But it remains true that Czechoslovakia is "up in the air", that it is troubled and that we must find some way of reassuring it, lest it follow the example of its Polish neighbour. But how?'[53]

Blum, Stoyadinovitch, and Mussolini

In January 1937 there were indications from Belgrade that the Petite Entente negotiations were being obviated by Yugoslav hopes of entente with Italy. Requests from Belgrade to postpone the conclusion of a Franco-Petite Entente pact until after negotiations for a new Locarno were a transparent pretext for substituting negotiations with Italy for those with France.[54] In a sequel to his son's mission, Léon Blum was directly informed of the unfolding Italo-Yugoslav negotiations. Stoyadinovitch instructed Pouritch, the Yugoslav Minister in Paris, to tell Blum confidentially that the Italians wanted to 'liquidate' all controversial questions between the two countries, and to obtain Blum's reaction. Only later would Blum be officially informed through the Quai d'Orsay. Besides repeating various arguments he had used with Robert Blum, Stoyadinovitch justified his receptivity to the Italian overtures by invoking the Anglo-Italian gentlemen's agreement of early January as a diplomatic paradigm. The agreement declared bilateral acceptance of the Mediterranean status quo, and Stoyadinovitch said that he interpreted it as a British guarantee for Yugoslavia. Pouritch was to take this line with Blum, to make him understand why Belgrade preferred a rapprochement with the Italians to one with the Petite Entente:

> After the signing of the Anglo-Italian declaration in Rome and the improvement of Franco-Italian relations, it is probable that the French Government will be less insistent about the [Franco-Petite Entente] pact. It must be clear to every Frenchman that the Czechoslovak guarantee was less interesting to us than Italy's, especially now that we have England's. And without any obligation on our part.[55]

No trace has remained of Blum's response to Stoyadinovitch's glib assertions about the Anglo-Italian agreement, but it can hardly have

---

[53] MAE, Papiers Massigli, 'Affaires de l'Europe centrale', Paul-Boncour-Massigli, Massigli-Thierry letters, 20, 25 January 1937.

[54] DDF II, 4, no. 326; Schw., 1SC2 Dr11, 18 January 1937.

[55] Hoptner, *Yugoslavia*, pp. 57–8; PRO, FO 371, 21200, R835/835/92, R1114/835/92; DDF II, 4, no. 460.

been enthusiastic. Mussolini had successfully persuaded London to exclude the French from the Anglo-Italian talks, despite the obvious importance Paris attached to association with any exchange of declarations between London and Rome.[56] Much as the French manifested *contre mauvaise fortune bon coeur* – an Anglo-Italian accord being preferable to another exercise in Anglo-German diplomacy – Paris considered the Anglo-Italian negotiations, which involved colonies and excluded discussion of massive Italian troop intervention in Spain, a painful end to the long and uneven process of liquidating the Ethiopian war.[57] After the negotiations, Mussolini poured even more troops into Spain. The discomfort of the Anglo-Italian accord was followed by a direct Italian approach to the French, which Blum regarded as little more than an insult. Exalting the invincibility of a Franco-Italian bloc of 80 million Latins and declaring 'a kind of insurmountable revulsion' for Hitler, Mussolini offered Blum a Franco-Italian entente. Italy would enlist Franco's sympathies for France, in return for France's dropping its interest in the Spanish Republic, and tolerating the installation of Franco's régime. Blum replied that the surest means to improved Franco-Italian relations would be mutual fidelity to the existing non-intervention engagements. Blum later described the Italian request for unilateral French disengagement as 'a little, rather childish war trick... to make easier... the aid that from his side, Mussolini was determined to continue to give Franco'.[58] In the succeeding weeks, Paris was to view even Italy's Balkan diplomacy from the Spanish perspective.

The British refusal to mediate

The Blum Government's last hope for the Petite Entente negotiations rested with British mediation in Belgrade. When Eden visited Paris in late January, Blum personally pressed him for a supportive

---

[56] DDF II, 4, nos. 30, 170, 188, 245.

[57] Ibid., nos. 325, 327. François-Poncet reported particular German interest in the 'realistic character' of British policy demonstrated by the Anglo-Italian colonial accord of late January, which broke the monopoly of Ethiopian traffic through French-controlled Djibouti by giving Italy access to ports in British Somalia. Ibid., no. 367.

[58] *CE Témoignages* I, pp. 220–1; DDF II, 4, no. 182; 5, nos. 13, 42. In this period, a Quai d'Orsay memorandum defined long-term French policy on Spain as the establishment of a *cordon-sanitaire* by non-intervention, followed by a compromise peace to be effected through great power mediation; it also postulated only short-lived Italo-German entente, DDF II, 4, no. 325. For the importance of Spain in Franco-German détente in these weeks, ibid., no. 211; Bullitt, *For the President*, p. 198.

démarche in Belgrade.[59] Notwithstanding Eden's equivocation (caused by well-grounded fears that, if he were forthright, Paris would be able to blame him for the negotiations' failure), the Foreign Office from the first had been indignant at the Blum Government's involvement without prior consultation in negotiations with the Petite Entente. The French draft elicited its stern opposition. Its principal arguments were a British right to limit severely French involvement in Central Europe, in return for British undertakings to defend continental France, and the view that the draft represented a provocation to Germany greater than its possible military effectiveness. The Foreign Office believed that its support for the draft would cement the Italo-German rapprochement; estrange moderate, supposedly Anglophile opinion in Berlin; and jeopardise the normalisation of Franco-Italian relations, although the British had not been particularly solicitous of these recently. Its clear preference was for a Czech-German agreement.[60]

Eden delivered a *coup de grâce* to the French scheme in early February. He claimed that, while he had not attempted any pressure on the Roumanians and Yugoslavs, all means of persuasion at the disposal of the British Government would have been unavailing. Unreceptive to the French Ambassador's protests that the Petite Entente states were gradually succumbing to Italo-German influence, Eden implied that the disintegration of the Petite Entente was natural, since Hungary had ceased to be an offensive threat, and acceptable, in that it entailed no diminution in the three countries' allegiances to France. Eden was complacent concerning future Yugoslav loyalties. As for Czechoslovakia, whose precarious position he could not deny, he observed that there were perhaps other means for its protection than a pact of such uncertain efficacity. Eden told Corbin that there was nothing to prevent France from periodically reaffirming its obligations to Czechoslovakia, a course the French followed until the last phase of the Munich crisis.[61]

[59] DDF II, 4, no. 325; Schw. 9 January 1937.
[60] A minute by Sir Orme Sargent put the matter squarely: a Franco-Petite Entente alliance should not even be attempted until Czechoslovakia had convincingly shown itself unable to reach 'an honourable and durable entente' with Germany. It was in keeping with the Foreign Office's animus against Czechoslovakia that Sargent should go on to express scepticism that such an accord could be reached. DDF II, 4, no. 474; PRO, FO 371, 20436, R7570/83/6; 21136, R501/26/67, R1234/26/67, R968/26/67.
[61] PRO, FO 371, 20436, R838/26/67; FRUS I (1937), p. 51; DDF II, 4, no. 104.

The Quai d'Orsay's 12 February note

The Political Directorate considered the import of the collapse of the negotiations with the Petite Entente and the significance of Eden's remarks in a lengthy memorandum of 12 February 1937. The 12 February note demonstrates that the importance of the negotiations for the Quai d'Orsay lay less in their chequered course than in the conclusions which, always sceptical of the wisdom of conducting such negotiations with the Petite Entente, it reached after their failure.

The memorandum began with clear-eyed characterisations of Yugoslav and Roumanian policy. Stoyadinovitch's policy was presented as sacred egoism. His marked solicitude for Germany was at least as much the result of intensified bilateral economic relations as of fear of the Reich, while his flirtation with Italy was compatible in his own mind with the maintenance of friendly relations with France. Roumanian policy was described as 'fear mixed with admiration for Germany, fear mixed with hatred of Russia'. The Roumanians and Yugoslavs were loath to take up obligations to Czechoslovakia, at once menaced by Germany and on good terms with Russia. Titulesco and Beneš's old dream of turning the Petite Entente into an instrument of European policy would have to be relinquished, and the Petite Entente allowed to revert to being an organisation principally directed against Hungarian revisionism.

The 12 February note directly addressed the problem of the terms on which a French presence in Central Europe could be maintained. As Massigli's correspondence with the Bucharest Legation had shown, the Political Directorate was not averse in principle to technical accords with the Petite Entente states as a means of permitting 'the remaining political sympathies to be manifested actively at a moment of danger'. However, such accords could only be prepared in view of specific hypotheses. Whereas the hypothesis was relatively clear in the case of Czechoslovakia, it was much less so for a Petite Entente state such as Roumania. The memorandum implied that the political disintegration of Franco-Petite Entente relations was perhaps too far advanced for technical accords to be practical. At the least, Paris would henceforth be justified in asking for assurances that its technical aid was being given to states that would defend it from an aggression. The theme of political unreliability led the Quai d'Orsay to urge the compilation of a balance sheet: 'What could we expect from our friends? To what extent can we count on them? This is both a military and a political problem.' If the results of such an examination were negative, the government itself would have to take responsibility: 'it remains for the French Government to decide how, reserving the future, the position that we have acquired can be preserved and how precautions can be taken to avoid the sympathies which we enjoy in the Danubian states being further diminished'.

The Political Directorate for the present wished to impose a more general conclusion on the Blum Government. 'As for pursuing an active policy in these regions, it would perhaps be better to renounce it. At the least, it is necessary to cease pursuing it alone...' It argued that a Danubian policy could only be validated by substantive British support. The memorandum speculated that British detachment from Central European problems rested on the assumption that Paris still exercised diplomatic control over the countries in question. A French threat to liquidate its policy of friendship with the Danubian states might galvanise Eden into giving the desired directives in Belgrade and Bucharest. If not, the Political Directorate was prepared to dispense with an active policy in Central Europe.[62] While the Quai d'Orsay had sought British good graces since the start of the Franco-Petite Entente negotiations, the 12 February memorandum marked the passage of British involvement from implicitly to explicitly conditioning any involvement by the Quai d'Orsay in a constructive French policy in Central Europe. In this respect, it commenced the phase of Franco-Czech relations which ended in Munich.

In a conversation several days later, Corbin, Ambassador in London, capitalised on the sangfroid with which the Foreign Office had greeted rumours of an imminent German attack on Czechoslovakia to ask whether British detachment would not encourage the Reich in such an attack. He implored Vansittart to consider a

---

[62] MAE, Papiers Massigli, 'Affaires de l'Europe centrale', unsigned memorandum, 'La France et la Petite Entente', 12 February 1937.

French Treasury difficulties in early 1937 reinforced the emergent Franco-British tandem in Central Europe. Appealing to London for support for implementing his plan for fiscal recovery, Auriol made use of Paris's difficulties in underwriting its alliances in the form of aid to Czechoslovakia, Poland, and Roumania, a sterile adoption of the ploy the Czechs had used with unsuccess *vis-à-vis* Paris. R. Girault, 'L'influence de la situation économique française sur la politique extérieure de la France 1936–9' (Anglo-German Historical Conference, 1980), pp. 16–19.

parliamentary declaration resembling that on Austrian independence made by Sir Austen Chamberlain in the Commons in March
1936, after which the Germans had come up with a League-
guaranteed agreement with Austria. The British Legation in Prague
had already detected some receptivity in French diplomatic circles
there to British promotion of a Czech-German agreement, which
would allow the French Government to 'bow to the inevitable'. Nor
were Czech governing circles slow to draw conclusions as to the new
importance of British influence and its uses in moving forward the
blocked Czech-German negotiations.[63]

The Italo-Yugoslav political pact, March 1937

The Italo-Yugoslav negotiations gained momentum in early
February, when the Quai d'Orsay was officially informed that a
Yugoslav diplomat was being sent to Rome to negotiate a
gentlemen's agreement on the Anglo-Italian model.[64] The Yugoslavs
combined procrastination in the Franco-Petite Entente negotiations
with profligate assurances of fidelity to France. They reminded the
French that the composite character of Yugoslavia required it to be
on good terms with all of its neighbours, an argument also coming
to the fore on the subject of Czechoslovakia. Then, in late March, the
Yugoslavs suddenly announced that Ciano would visit Belgrade.

Infuriated by this news, Delbos fixed on the Spanish imbroglio.
He argued that by freeing Italy of Balkan preoccupations, a political
accord would allow further Italian engagement in Spain. He
acknowledged that the Quai d'Orsay had long hoped for an Italo-
Yugoslav entente, but implored the Yugoslavs not to add to the
difficulties in the Western Mediterranean, and to take elementary
precautions, initialling rather than signing an accord until the
international atmosphere was more propitious.[65]

Ciano and Stoyadinovitch signed a political accord and an
accompanying economic accord the day of Ciano's arrival in
Belgrade, 25 March. There was truth in the observation of
Dampierre, the French Minister in Belgrade, that the terms of the
accord conformed to those which France had always wished to
govern Italo-Yugoslav relations. The provisions of the political pact

[63] PRO, FO 371, 21134, R968/26/67, R2210/26/67; 21136, R1068/26/67.
[64] DDF II, 4, no. 395; 5, nos. 43, 89, 100, 152–3; Schw., 1SC2 Dr11, 29 January, 2 February
1937.   [65] DDF II, 5, nos. 152–4, 190.

were relatively innocuous: Italian recognition of Yugoslavia's existing obligations cancelled out a provision whereby the two states agreed to remain neutral if either was the object of an unprovoked aggression. The extent of Italian concessions made it difficult to blame the Yugoslavs for signing the treaty. When Prince Paul visited Paris several months later, Delbos likened the reaction of a section of French opinion to the agreement to that of a jealous lover, but he conceded that for Belgrade the moment to negotiate had been well-chosen.

The pact placed France before a *fait accompli* and, like the Gentlemen's Agreement, it had been concluded outside a League framework.[66] In Stoyadinovitch's apologia for the pact, the old theme of Italo-German rivalry figured prominently. If Stoyadino-vitch could be believed, all was not lost. Although certain that there would be an Anschluss, he claimed to be convinced of the fragility of the Axis. A Franco-Italian rapprochement was sooner or later inevitable, at which time the Italo-Yugoslav entente would bear its fruit.[67]

Paris was not consoled. Heavily influenced by the immediate Mediterranean context, the Quai d'Orsay ascribed the extent of Mussolini's concessions in the negotiations to his search for an immediate success to compensate for his stinging defeat at Guadalajara, and it correctly assessed the pact as portending a renewed Italian onslaught in Spain.[68] Its reading, however, was muddied by British influences.

The Foreign Office had been kept minutely informed of the progress of the negotiations, and had counselled the Yugoslavs to resist Italian pressures for alliance. Most of the draft articles that troubled the Foreign Office had been successfully rejected. Taking the view that Italy's main preoccupation since January had been the coordination of its foreign policy with Germany's, Eden promoted instead 'a brief, anodyne text on the lines of the Anglo-Italian declaration'. He regarded the ensuing limited Italo-Yugoslav negotiations benevolently, minuting: 'It is perhaps pertinent to remember that this (of which I do not take an unduly pessimistic view so far) could not have happened had we not set the example

[66] C. Seton-Watson, 'The Anglo-Italian Gentlemen's Agreement' (Anglo-German Historical Conference, 1980), p. 7; Hoptner, *Yugoslavia*, pp. 70, 86; Ciano, *Diplomatic Papers*, p. 103.
[67] DDF II, 5, nos. 190, 201, 212, 240, 418.
[68] Schw., 1SC2 Dr12, 2 April; 'Rapport', 6 April 1937.

with the Anglo-Italian declaration.'[69] Once it was clear that the pact would not be accompanied by Yugoslav declarations placating France, London used its good offices to soften French resentments. The Foreign Office's orientation had been apparent in the semi-official press even before announcement of the pact's signature. The pact was described as solidly in the context of Franco-British hopes in 1934–5 for Italo-Yugoslav entente and of the Anglo-Italian Gentlemen's Agreement. The Foreign Office urged the Quai d'Orsay to keep a diplomatic stiff upper lip, advice potentially applicable to Czechoslovakia. The Paris Embassy pressed the line that 'Diplomatic successes and failures at the moment were largely questions of psychological effect. If the French press said that France had suffered a defeat... [the pact] would be considered a defeat.' The result, an Embassy official noted, was that the French Government's public line corresponded closely with that of *The Times*.[70]

As for Prague's reaction, a resentful Beneš followed Ciano to Belgrade, but returned proclaiming Yugoslav attachment to France and the Petite Entente. Stoyadinovitch rallied Beneš by giving the wholly inaccurate impression that German influence was weak in Yugoslavia, and by presenting Italy as without credit in Austria and motivated by desire for a front with Yugoslavia.[71] His Belgrade visit prompted Beneš to make an overture to the Italian Minister in Prague, a démarche which bore strong traces of the opportunism of his reaction to the Bulgarian-Yugoslav pact. Announcing that the pact might be made to harmonise with his own policy of supporting an Italo-Petite Entente rapprochement to prevent Anschluss, Beneš grasped at straws when he indicated openness to an overture from Rome. To Lacroix, disconcerted by his erratic behaviour, Beneš confined his objections to the absence of consultation and to the pact's timing.[72]

Had the French and Czechs been privy to the conversation

[69] PRO, FO 371, 21197, R889/224/92; Vansittart minute, R1169/224/92; 21198, R1450/224/92, R1623/224/92, R1688/224/92; Sargent minute, R2014/224/92. When the British reproached Stoyadinovitch for putting too much into the Italian pact, he replied cynically that Yugoslavia would not honour its obligations. Schw., 1SC2 Dr12, 28 April 1937. Within the Foreign Office, only Vansittart had viewed Yugoslav diplomacy with distrust, although Eden afterwards came to share the impression of having been duped by the Yugoslavs. PRO, FO 371, 21198, R1623/224/92; 21199, Eden minutes, R8283/224/92, R8392/224/92.

[70] PRO, FO 371, 21199, R2529/224/92; 21136, R2187/26/67.

[71] Ibid., 21198, R2190/224/92; DDF II, 5, no. 240.

[72] DDF II, 5, no. 241; PRO, FO 371, 21199, R2397/224/92; J. B. Hoptner, 'Yugoslavia as Neutralist: 1937', *Journal of Central European Affairs*, July 1956, p. 1.

between Stoyadinovitch and Ciano at the pact's signature, their worst fears would have been confirmed. Before Ciano's visit, Stoyadinovitch seems genuinely to have aspired to a policy of equilibrium in relations with all of the great powers. Subbotić, the chief Yugoslav negotiator, withstood Italian pressures for an alliance and successfully refused an Italian draft clause forbidding either state to enter into understandings with third powers which might be directed against the other. Once Stoyadinovitch and Ciano met, however, the outstanding fact in the negotiations became the pleasure each took in the pose struck by the other. Their congeniality led Stoyadinovitch to go further than he intended in providing oral assurances beyond the text of the pact. In particular, he heralded an eventual Italo-Yugoslav alliance as 'natural and inevitable'. He declared his aim to be the establishment of Yugoslavia as the principal power in the Balkans, an aim to which Italian support was indispensable. Like the overwhelming majority of European statesmen in 1937, Stoyadinovitch saw the Reich's expansionism in pan-Germanist terms. Regarding an Anschluss as inevitable, he sketched for Ciano a post-Anschluss period in which an Italo-Yugoslav Axis would deter the Reich from a move towards the Adriatic. Stoyadinovitch considered such a 'mad attempt' by Germany, however, unlikely, evidencing its alacrity in promoting good Italo-Yugoslav relations. He gloated over his own excellent relations with Berlin, telling Ciano: 'Belgrade's collaboration with the Rome-Berlin Axis may be considered ensured.'

Stoyadinovitch made it clear that his collaboration with the Axis should include arms purchases in Italy and Germany. The French, he told Ciano, had lent money at a usurious rate and had not given Yugoslavia a single bayonet. He deplored the 'truly deleterious and disruptive influence of the Jewish, Masonic and Communistic mentality of the France of Blum'. One of the official Yugoslav explanations for the pact abroad was to be as a means of obtaining military supplies. This excoriation of the Blum Government was deeply unjust, for, as has been seen, the Front populaire made a greater effort than its predecessors to supply the Yugoslavs with arms, an effort spurned by Stoyadinovitch.[73] Nor, of course, did Stoyadinovitch acknowledge the Czechs' generosity in arms purveyance.

[73] PRO, FO 371, 21199, R3375/224/92; DDF II, 6, no. 141.

On the subject of the Petite Entente, Stoyadinovitch, who attached great importance to Roumania's resources of grain and petrol, told Ciano that relations with Roumania would remain cordial, whereas those with Czechoslovakia would be emptied of substance. He spoke of renewing his advice to Prague to conclude a Czech-German agreement. His remarks on the future of the Petite Entente were shrewd: 'I consider that formally at least, it will not undergo any transformation. It is entirely in Czechoslovakia's interest to let matters lie, so as not to make it obvious where the rift in the lute is, how it came there and how big it is.'

Ciano's thrust throughout the negotiations was to wrest Yugo-slavia from the Franco-Czech orbit. He concluded his note on his conversations with Stoyadinovitch by announcing that Italy would shortly take France's place in Yugoslavia, and he boasted to foreign diplomats that he had broken apart the Petite Entente.[74] Ciano's remarks on Germany required more subtle interpretation. Through-out the negotiations, Belgrade was attentive to Ciano's suscepti-bilities *vis-à-vis* Germany. Ciano had described it to Subbotić as not only a dangerous adversary, but a difficult friend, adding that Italy and Yugoslavia should not turn against Germany but should organise their collaboration with it. Ciano's larger design emerged in a Belgrade conversation with Prince Paul: 'our pact should attract other countries into our orbit. An understanding with Hungary is desirable. When Vienna becomes the second German capital, Budapest should be ours.'[75]

The inescapability of Anschluss, and the necessity of creating a second line of defence against a German push to the Adriatic by falling back on Yugoslavia had become factors in Italian policy as early as 1933.[76] Italian acquiescence in the Austro-German accord and the imperatives of the Spanish conflict ensured Italian receptiveness to German pressures for an Italo-Yugoslav political pact in the autumn of 1936. A bilateral political pact with Yugoslavia in effect would restructure the Rome Protocols around the Axis.

The diplomatic impetus for the Italo-Yugoslav political pact originated largely in Berlin, as a reaction to the Petite Entente negotiations. After Petite Entente discussion of mutual aid pacts at Bratislava in September 1936, Stoyadinovitch sought German advice and was counselled by Hitler to refuse a Petite Entente pact

[74] Ciano, *Diplomatic Papers*, p. 105; Hoptner, *Yugoslavia*, p. 85; PRO, FO 371, 21136, R2231/26/67; DDF II, 5, no. 247.   [75] Hoptner, *Yugoslavia*, pp. 67, 83.
[76] Aloisi, cited in Robertson, *Mussolini*, pp. 42, 66.

and to distance himself from Czechoslovakia. German-Yugoslav talks, of which the French were apparently unaware, ensued. Their terms, extrapolated by Professor Macartney from subsequent German offers to Roumania, included German arms supplies and a guarantee of Yugoslav territorial integrity. The important point for Yugoslavia's future was that the Reich systematically set about removing 'any dangers with which renunciation of the French alliance might threaten Yugoslavia' by mediating with the states involved.[77] Hitler and Neurath then pressed Ciano to reach entente with Yugoslavia when he visited Berlin in October 1936. German action during the negotiations took several forms. The Reich, which had for some months stifled the protests of its minority in Yugoslavia, advised Rome to improve treatment of Slav minorities in Italy, a key negotiating point for Belgrade, and Hitler successfully urged that Italy channel Hungarian revisionism against Czechoslovakia rather than Yugoslavia. Berlin otherwise softened Ciano's abrasive diplomacy in Belgrade by transmitting assurances that Yugoslavia would not be required to renounce its other friendships, and that Italy would ultimately be content with something less than the alliance demanded by Ciano.[78]

Ciano's bravado in Belgrade aside, the power realities of this new arrangement were soon transparent. The case of Italian commerce was illustrative of the outcome of Yugoslavia's new course. In the first nine months of 1937, the Yugoslav economy boomed. Stoyadinovitch's foreign policy of conciliating Yugoslavia's great-power neighbours paid sizeable commercial profits; it was thus very important to the task of internal consolidation set by the Stoyadinovitch Government. By the March 1937 economic agreement accompanying the political pact, Rome promised to import more from Yugoslavia, paying in scarce hard currency, and to grant Yugoslavia most favoured nation status. With sanctions ending as the September 1936 and then the March 1937 economic accords entered into force, the volume of Italo-Yugoslav trade in 1937 increased elevenfold from 1936. The 1937 figures, however, represented a significant decrease in bilateral trade in comparison with 1935. Economically anaemic as a result of its foreign adventurism, Italy proved unable to resume its pre-sanctions place

[77] C. A. Macartney, A. W. Palmer, *Independent Eastern Europe* (London, 1962), p. 356; PRO, FO 371, 21191, R3587/2760/37; Lungu, *Romania*, pp. 104–6, 110.
[78] Ciano, *Diplomatic Papers*, pp. 58–60; Hoptner, *Yugoslavia*, pp. 56–7, 74–6; PRO, FO 371, 20436, R6814/2472/92, R7407/2472/92.

in the Yugoslav economy. Italian economic vitality was largely spent in competition with Czechoslovakia for Yugoslav outlets. In an exact correspondence between political and economic realities, given Italy's disruption of the Franco-Petite Entente negotiations, Italian re-entry into the Yugoslav market diminished the importance of Czechoslovakia without impeding the continued growth of German trade. Germany's share of Yugoslavia's external trade expanded from 26 per cent to 33 per cent from 1936 to 1937. Official Yugoslav analyses point to the importance of the formation of a creditor balance in Yugoslavia's favour as a psychological inducement to trade. The Reich's frozen mark system provided this psychological inducement, whereas the Czech-Yugoslav credit balance in 1937 was in Prague's favour – ironically, partly on account of Škoda's arms-ores transactions, made in a futile effort to maintain Yugoslav friendship.[79]

The Quai d'Orsay was not slow to discern the shifting concerns of Italian policy. In early May 1937, after Mussolini made plain to Schuschnigg in Venice that he would do nothing to prevent Austria from falling into German hands, Delbos sounded Eden as to a *de facto* recognition of Italy's Ethiopian conquest at the next Geneva session. Delbos had few illusions as to Italian gratitude: 'At the most they would remove a pretext for new complaints. The choice is between disadvantages.' The Quai d'Orsay's prognosis of a series of Italian diplomatic retreats before the Reich's dynamism showed the Political Directorate in the act of renouncing its reliance on Italy as a constructive force in European diplomacy:

It is important to know if the British Government regards the events of these last months in the same light as we do, and if so, renouncing the optimism with which it has tried to please Italy, and which the facts have so often contradicted, whether it also considers that, having committed itself above all to the Spanish affair and thus given up much of its freedom of action, Mussolini will find himself almost inevitably led to abandon Italy's own interests in Danubia, once the weakening of the Petite Entente is assured, in order to bring his effort to bear on the Mediterranean, presenting this evolution, imposed by Germanic pressure, as a normal consequence of the creation of the Empire.[80]

The evolution of this climate accounts for the world-weary tone in

[79] Finances, F30: 1147, 'Renseignements sur les finances publiques', 11 November 1937; Czech T-120, 1041/1809/414047–8.
[80] MAE, Papiers Massigli, 'Italo-Ethiopie', Delbos dispatch to Corbin, 1 May 1937; DDF II, 5, nos. 242–3, 290, 429; Schw., 1SC2 Dr12, 'Rapport', 27 April 1937.

Schweisguth's April CHEDN lecture, which propounded the impracticability of any French strategy in Central Europe without Italy.

The plight of Czechoslovakia and the tandem of Franco-British policies were the dual realities henceforth impelling French diplomacy. In glossing a conversation with Robert Vansittart, the French Ambassador in London reminded his Minister of a fundamental divergence in recent Franco-British security conceptions: 'While we think of the immediate peril, of the necessity of putting minds at rest and of discouraging troublemakers, the Foreign Office is above all preoccupied with the solidity of the foundations on which European peace reposes. To pacts whose practical value is debatable, it prefers nothingness [le néant].'[81] Of this British preference for a diplomatic void, Paris was given another painful example when it embarked on military exchanges with the Soviet Union.

LE NÉANT DIPLOMATIQUE: THE FRANCO-SOVIET NEGOTIATIONS

Under the aegis of aid to Czechoslovakia, Franco-Soviet military conversations had been on the government's agenda since its acceptance of Soviet and Petite Entente negotiations in November 1936. With the arrival in late 1936 of Semenov, the new Soviet military attaché in Paris, conversations began. With Colonel de Villelume acting as interpreter, General Schweisguth first met with Semenov on 8 January 1937, several weeks before the demise of the Franco-Petite Entente negotiations. Marked by many of the same concerns, notably the defence of Czechoslovakia, the Franco-Soviet negotiations soon took on a troubled existence of their own.

Both sides at the opening talks were pursuing a double policy of overtures in Berlin. At a meeting with de Gaulle in the course of the Second World War, Stalin acknowledged the vicious circle of mutual distrust which had prevented pre-war Franco-Soviet intimacy:

When we concluded the Franco-Soviet pact, we did not completely understand. Later, we understood that Laval and his colleagues did not really consider us as allies. In signing an accord with us, they wanted to pin us down and to prevent us from signing an accord with Germany. And we

[81] DDF II, 4, no. 474.

Russians, we did not have on our side complete confidence in the French. This reciprocal distrust ruined the pact.[82]

From late 1936, unknown to the French, an emissary from Stalin carried on abortive talks with Schacht for the opening of bilateral negotiations. Stalin's decision to approach Berlin in the wake of the Anti-Comintern pact was doubtless influenced by the continuing attraction for the Blum Government of talks with Schacht.[83] Blum's insistence during his August conversations with Schacht on the necessity of maintaining the Soviet tie and on the indivisibility of peace apparently did nothing to lessen the distrust of the Soviets, who made no secret of their preference for a government headed by the more Russophile Herriot.[84] For their part, the French considered that the beginning of Soviet conversations need not entail renunciation of hopes for a general settlement. In late January, the General Staff admonished Pierre Cot as to the necessity for absolute secrecy over the conversations, lest publicity jeopardise Blum's recent overture to Berlin in a speech in Lyons.[85] The General Staff's desire for secrecy was intensified by foreknowledge of the scale of Soviet ambitions for the talks. Advance reports from Warsaw, Semenov's previous posting, had indicated that Semenov intended to rent an entire residence in Paris to house his personnel of twenty. For the French military, Soviet swagger lent itself to Schweisguth's hypothesis that the Soviets were pressing France for talks in order to provoke Germany to war in the west.[86]

The Franco-Soviet conversations were also burdened from the start by Beneš's message of December about Toukhatchevsky's alleged dealings with the Germans. Blum recalled in 1947 that his enthusiasm for Franco-Soviet staff talks had been dampened by Beneš's message.[87] This was doubtless so, but it should not be taken as the last word on the subject. Having carried out his instructions to admonish Litvinov on Comintern zealousness, Robert Coulondre, the new Ambassador in Moscow, soon reported that the Soviets were

[82] 2 December 1944 de Gaulle-Stalin conversation, *Sovetsko-frantsuzskie otnocheniia, 1941–1945* (Moscow, 1959), pp. 346–7. I am indebted to General de Gaulle's translator, Jean Laloy, for calling my attention to this passage and transcribing it in a letter of 7 July 1981.

[83] Erickson, *Soviet High Command*, pp. 432, 453; Weinberg, *Foreign Policy*, I, pp. 220–2; Haslam, *Soviet Union*, pp. 123–8. As for some months in the past, Hitler firmly refused to proceed from economic to political negotiations with the Soviets. Haslam, *Soviet Union*, pp. 100, 106, 127.   [84] PRO, FO 954/8, FR 36/15.

[85] Schw., 1SC2 Dr11, 25 January 1937; DDF II, 4, no. 325.

[86] SHA, 'Pologne AM', 22 December 1936.

[87] *CE Témoignages* I, p. 129; Coulondre, *De Staline à Hitler*, p. 83.

losing interest in fomenting discord in Spain and were settling on a more moderate policy with regard to Comintern activities abroad. He believed that Soviet pursuit of a policy based on *raison d'état*, rather than ideology, depended on the guarantees given Moscow. These French internal arguments had obvious relevance to the government's willingness to hold talks – although on a low flame so as not to compromise French security – despite the uncertain Soviet internal situation.[88]

Alexis Léger informally and antiseptically told the Soviets of these priorities. At a Soviet Embassy luncheon soon after the talks began, Léger pointedly renewed the traditional French injunction that a direct relationship existed between French internal stability and the ease with which Paris could reach entente with Moscow. He also spoke to the Soviets of the need for Paris to reach a preliminary entente with Britain.

With his consummate skill at reconciling ministers to the Political Directorate's viewpoint, Léger had taken Blum aside in early February and assured him that the Ministries of War and Foreign Affairs would loyally follow the government's policy with regard to military accords, but he asked that matters not be precipitated, in view of London's aversion to Franco-Soviet military dealings. Schweisguth recorded: 'Blum understands this and resists the Communists and Herriot who are pressuring him.' Blum's natural caution was fostered by the Quai d'Orsay, partly out of dismay at recent British policy, which had facilitated the Belgian decampment and drawn closer to Italy without particular regard for France. As Léger impressed upon those around him in these weeks, Britain was less at the side of France than he liked to say.[89]

The operative governmental consensus determined the unofficial instructions repeatedly given Schweisguth to draw out the talks, without provoking a renewal of the USSR's Rapallo collaboration with Germany: 'It will be necessary then... not to rush but to avoid giving the Soviets the impression that we are playing with them, which could drive them into a political volte-face.'[90] Formally, Schweisguth's task was to probe the intentions of the Soviet military concerning aid to France and Czechoslovakia in a conflict.

[88] Schw., 1SC2 Dr11, 8 February 1937; DDF II, 4, no. 325; 5, no. 16; FRUS I (1937), p. 53.
[89] Schw., 1SC2 Dr11, 8, 9, 15 February 1937. For Blum's inclination through early 1937 more to rely on the British than on the Soviets, see the testimony of Victor de Lacroix in ibid., 1SC2 Dr10, 26 November 1936, and of Pierre Cot in *Le procès*, II, pp. 341–2.
[90] Schw., 1SC2 Dr11, 8 January 1937.

Schweisguth was to say that, for France, the existence of a common frontier with Germany made its contribution simple. The introduction of other services into the discussion and the decision to proceed to full-fledged staff talks would depend on the results of the conversations with Semenov.[91]

The first major Soviet positioning in the conversations was prompt and serious. On 17 February, the Soviet Ambassador Potemkine, with the approval of the entire Soviet Government, called on Blum, while Semenov met General Colson, the head of Army Headquarters. According to the Soviet General Staff, the USSR could aid France or Czechoslovakia at a German attack through Poland or Roumania with all of its forces, or should this prove impossible 'for incomprehensible reasons', Soviet troops could be sent to France by sea and the Soviet Air Force dispatched to France and Czechoslovakia. The Soviets could also furnish war materials for the French and Czech war efforts. But, in all cases, formal accords between the states involved were indispensable to the Soviet General Staff. General Gérodias, who had previously asked why the Soviets could not march through Lithuania, was told that they intended to rely on France entirely for passage arrangements. Alongside formal military accords, this 'political aid' constituted the Soviet priority in the talks. The Soviet staff also wished to know what aid France could lend the USSR and what armaments it could provide.[92] Potemkine read aloud to Blum, who was said to be shaken by it, a letter from Stalin which was very warm on the subject of a military alliance.[93]

In late February, Schweisguth, Gamelin, Georges, and Colson concerted a response to Potemkine's démarche, which they submitted to Daladier for presentation to Blum. Their plan was to declare the Soviet démarche technically unsatisfactory: while informative as to the nature of possible Soviet aid, it left its scope and execution obscure. The military pressed for continued conversations between Schweisguth and Semenov, postponing until their conclusion the governmental decision on more substantive conver-

---

[91] Franco-Soviet-Petite Entente relations were not broached in depth in the opening conversations. Gamelin informally mooted with his colleagues strategic arrangements involving the Petite Entente: a road with halting places up to the point of Czechoslovakia, an apparent revival of a 1935 plan for circumscribed Soviet passage across northern Roumania; supplies of Russian tanks; and Soviet aid against Hungary. Schw., 1SC2 Dr11, 'Note', 5 January; 9 February 1937; 1SC2 Dr10, 22 December 1936.

[92] DDF II, 4, no. 457.

[93] Schw., 1SC2 Dr11, 18 February; 1SC2 Dr12, 19 March 1937.

sations.[94] Daladier was more dilatory still, leaving the generals to cool their heels for several weeks before meeting with them in mid March, on the very morning of Schweisguth's next scheduled conversation with Semenov, who was scheduled to leave afterwards for Moscow. Daladier also aimed to postpone the evil day of a governmental decision. He spoke to Gamelin and Schweisguth of the restiveness of other government members: Blum, disconcerted by Stalin's letter, and Cot, more enthusiastic than ever at the prospect of collaboration with the Soviet Air Force.[95]

From late 1936, Cot had endured a series of defeats in his programme of severing the Air Force from the strategic apron strings of the Army and creating an inter-allied air coalition by negotiating Soviet air passage to Czechoslovakia with the Roumanians.[96] When Daladier refused his request of late January 1937 to carry on joint army–air force talks in Moscow, Cot stormed at his exclusion from the talks, threatening resignation at a Matignon meeting if air accords were not instituted. But, by early February 1937, Schweisguth and Léger believed that Cot, like Blum, was resigned to a prudent pace in the negotiations.[97]

With Cot, however, appearances had a way of being deceptive. After a mid February session of the CPDN refused his plan to expand the Air Force for the second time in as many months, Cot privately sought out Blum to argue that only an air accord with the Soviets would permit France to confront German forces. The two decided that Cot would discreetly build a bridge to the Soviets via the Czechs. Having indicated support for the overture during Robert Blum's visit, Beneš responded by sending Hubert Ripka to Paris. Ripka and Cot concluded that existing treaties could be adjusted to serve as a base for Franco-Czech-Soviet collaboration. Cot regarded his understanding with Blum and contact with Ripka as a prolongation of the technical collaboration with the Soviet Union imposed by the Blum Government as an interministerial policy in June 1936. He knew that the Soviets were dissatisfied with piecemeal technical exchanges and the uneven level of response among the

---

[94] Schw., 1SC2 Dr11, 18, 23 February; FNSP, Papiers Daladier, 1DA7 Dr5, sdr c, Note, 23 February 1937.　　　[95] Schw., 1SC2 Dr12, 16, 19 March 1937.

[96] When the Blum Government announced its important rearmament plan in autumn 1936, Gamelin had disputed Cot's stress on inter-allied collaboration as indispensable to the Air Force, contending that France should maintain parity with Germany for both aviation and tanks: 'which is only a question of matériel and money'. Schw., 1SC2 Dr10, 'Rapport', 20, 26 October 1936.　　　[97] Schw., 1SC2 Dr11, 25 January, 8 February 1937.

different French defence ministries: 'As might have been expected, our Russian friends wanted to see broached in its entirety the negotiation for a military alliance. They wanted the problem of Franco-Soviet collaboration to be treated as a block rather than piece by piece.'[98] Notwithstanding the absence of a Soviet representative at his conversations with Ripka, Cot was well enmeshed in what his adversaries on the General Staff dreaded as an *engrenage* producing a military alliance. It was only a matter of time until he attempted a more substantive manoeuvre.

While organisation of Soviet air aid to Czechoslovakia represented the most strategically accessible of the Soviet staff's hypotheses, French military appreciation of the subject was mixed. Schweisguth, in his November CHEDN lecture, had cast doubt on the effectiveness of the Soviet Air Force acting on Czechoslovakia's behalf, and, above all, there was the vexing problem for the EMA of separating conduct of the talks from Cot's overweening ambitions for Franco-Soviet relations. There was inconclusive talk of Soviet air assistance in Daladier's meeting with his generals in mid March. Daladier remarked on the difficulty of Soviet air action without intermediate bases and queried the real possibility of persuading the Roumanians to grant air passage. When Gamelin observed that the Soviets could give formal guarantees to Poland and Roumania, Daladier undercut further discussion by saying that, in a conflict, France could do without Soviet aid but not that of the British, who were profoundly averse to Franco-Soviet military ties. The introduction of the British factor had obvious connotations for active French involvement in the Czechs' defence. Daladier sought to paper over the chasm by rhetoric when he announced that he intended to go to London and rouse the British to the dangers of allowing Germany to reconstruct a Mitteleuropa on the Baghdad Axis.[99]

In their meeting on the same day, Semenov bluntly told Schweisguth that the Soviet staff would refuse to answer his most recent questions, which were the province of official conversations authorised by the two governments. Even the technical questions proposed for discussion were subordinated to a transformation of Roumanian and Polish diplomatic attitudes by French mediation.[100]

[98] Cot, *Le procès*, II, pp. 343–50; *CE Témoignages* I, pp. 272–3; Coulondre, *De Staline à Hitler*, pp. 33–4; Erickson, *The Soviet High Command*, p. 364; FNSP, Papiers Daladier, 1DA7 Dr5 sdr a; Schw., 1SC2 Dr9, 25 June 1936.
[99] Schw., 1SC2 Dr12, 16, 19 March 1937.   [100] Ibid.

During Semenov's three week absence, Paris assessed the strategic repercussions of the increased threat to Czechoslovakia from Belgian neutralism. The Quai d'Orsay had been involved since early March in trilateral negotiations with Brussels and London to release Belgium from its Locarno obligations, including participation in the defence of France. These negotiations were the materialisation of the policy announced by Leopold's October 1936 speech and secret, high-level Franco-Belgian meetings in late 1936–7.[101] Although Gamelin placed ill-starred hopes for a revival of Franco-Belgian cooperation in his personal contacts with the Belgian General Staff, the potential consequences of the Belgian estrangement in a war over Czechoslovakia were sobering. The closing of the Belgian *porte de sortie* meant that, in the West, France could freely act against Germany only along an as yet unfortified 150 km. line from Karlsruhe in the Rhineland to Luxemburg. Delbos predicted to William Bullitt, the American Ambassador, that, given the narrowness of the so-called Rhine-Moselle front, 'a small portion of the German Army could hold up the French Army, leaving the major portion of the German Army to operate against the Czechs and the Austrians'.[102] A 9 March note written by the head of the 2e Bureau, Gauché, argued that, while Germany was still incapable of waging total war, it was prepared to unleash 'a powerful and rapid war of aggression against a country of least resistance in Central or Eastern Europe', Czechoslovakia being the specific case adopted in the text.[103] The essential condition of German success against Czechoslovakia, he postulated, was the advance assurance of benevolent neutralities and complicities, such as those of Italy, Belgium, and Poland. As Gamelin had pointed out in a CPDN meeting before the start of the trilateral negotiations, the German war plan entailed full *couverture* against France, but only a weak *couverture* on the Polish border: 'which seems to indicate that this

---

[101] Kieft, *Belgium's Return*, pp. 166–72.   [102] FRUS, I (1937), pp. 91, 96.

[103] Dissenting from his colleagues on the EMA, Gauché took the stand that active defence of Czechoslovakia remained a French interest: 'The Czechoslovak defeat would have for us, as much from a foreign policy as from a moral point of view, such grave repercussions that the victorious issue [of a general war] would be compromised. In particular, there is no doubt that success of this scope would be of a nature to catapult into the German camp the hesitant powers of Central and Eastern Europe.' SHA, 7N1522–1, 'Réflexions sur un conflit éventuel en Europe', 9 March 1937. For steadfast opposition within the EMA to Gauché's advocacy of direct, unilateral French aid to Czechoslovakia across southern Germany, see SHA, 1N46, 10 April, and General Georges' impatient note of 5 August 1937 opposing a French crossing of the Rhine to aid Czechoslovakia.

operation, in present circumstances, can only be accomplished with a certain connivance on the part of [Poland] '.[104] These arguments had a distinctly anti-Soviet tinge. Belgium's defection made the General Staff more wary than ever of pushing countries from neutralism into complicity with the Reich by an insistence on their closer association with the USSR. (The EMA's own susceptibility to the politics of anti-Bolshevism obscured the fact that Italy, Belgium, and Poland had never shown the slightest pro-Czech inclination.)

Others in Paris counselled a Soviet antidote to the Belgian defection. In early April, Cot broke ranks to carry on negotiations with the Soviets, sending Pierre Keller of the Air Staff to Moscow. Although a French governmental decision on staff talks still awaited Semenov's return to Paris, Keller offered the aid of the French Air Force. Vorochilov refused his offer of technical conversations as an attempt to separate air from land questions. He informed Keller that, as the only French response had been more questions, the conversations were at a dead-end until the Blum Government approved regular, across-the-board staff talks. Keller returned to Paris stressing the seriousness with which talks were regarded in Moscow, which, he argued, necessitated greater seriousness on the French side: a prior inter-service accord, an understanding with the Czechs and consultation with the British.[105]

Word of Keller's failure coincided with the brief resumption of the Paris talks. Semenov brought the expected Soviet demurrer to an 8 April meeting. In an identical démarche, Potemkine called on Blum, and insisted that the USSR could most effectively maintain its obligations to its allies by amicable passage through Poland, or, failing that, intervention by sea. Potemkine pressed for a governmental decision before he left Paris at the end of the month to take up a new post, as Vice-Commissar of Foreign Affairs.[106] The Soviets used a negotiating tactic to become painfully familiar to the French and British in 1939. When their most attractive offer was accepted – in this case, air aid to Czechoslovakia – the Soviets partially retracted it, in order to secure a more difficult item on their negotiating agenda, in this case, passage through Poland. They believed that a German attack on the USSR would only be possible through Poland, while the most effective aid they could give

---

[104] SHA, 'CPDN Procès-verbaux', 15 February 1937.
[105] Schw., 1SC2 Dr12, 8, 9, 12, 23 April 1937.   [106] Ibid., 8, 9 April 1937.

Czechoslovakia was not to send troops into that 'narrow and partly encircled land', but directly to attack eastern Germany through Poland.[107] In terms of the critical question of railway gauges and efficiency, there was no question that the mass of the Red Army should pass through Poland rather than Roumania. Passage through Poland was a long-term Soviet aim, in which Soviet offensive and defensive postures were identical. By early April, the Franco-Soviet transactions were completely deadlocked.

While Semenov had been in Moscow, there had been indications of panic in Paris. Delbos spoke to Lacroix, on leave at the end of March, of hiding Franco-Soviet military accords from the British. Lacroix's confidant, Schweisguth, did not give reasons for Delbos's unwonted willingness to resort to secret accords, but surely the Soviet practice of what Schweisguth called 'double blackmail...the threat of rapprochement with the Reich, the threat of unloosing the French communists' had something to do with it.[108] In the volatile period after a clash at Clichy in March 1937 between the Parisian right-wing and supporters of the Front populaire, the powerful threat of internal disruption redoubled the Reich's attention to French internal events and gave the Blum Government's internal opponents the smell of its blood.[109] The Soviet threats carried all the more force as they coincided with a baffling lull in the Soviet internal convulsion: it seemed that, after being incriminated by Radek in the January purge trials, Toukhatchevsky had succeeded in dissipating Stalin's suspicions, an impression which lasted until the middle of May.[110]

Actuated by the Soviet threats and the stalemate in the conversations, Blum and Delbos approached Daladier, by far the most reluctant of the four French Ministers now directly involved in the talks. They stressed the effect on internal politics of driving the Soviets into the German camp. Blum was particularly anxious to maintain the loyalty of the working class to the cause of defence of the republic. In response, Daladier summoned Gamelin and asked him to meet secretly with a Russian military representative, perhaps at the coronation of George VI the next month. Gamelin did not

---

[107] FRUS, I (1936), p. 200; the phrase is Telford Taylor's in *Munich: the Price of Peace* (New York, 1980), p. 453.   [108] Schw., 1SC2 Dr12, 13 April 1937.

[109] For Laval's April and May soundings in the Francoist camp for aid in the event of a Communist coup in France, F. Kupferman, *Pierre Laval* (Paris, 1976), pp. 64, 97–9.

[110] Erickson, *Soviet High Command*, p. 455.

commit himself, except to insist that he would not act without informing the British and the Poles. Afterwards, he drew up what he called 'a written opinion' on the substance of the Soviet position. On the crucial issue of Soviet troop passage through Poland and Roumania, he argued that the two countries would require all of their rail resources for their own mobilisations. Past conversations with the Poles and Roumanians did not permit him to envisage a solution to the problem of passage. He concluded astringently: 'the only rapid aid which can be envisaged is that of aviation or motorised forces'. The EMA response to Soviet bluster in the talks was to limit its participation in the ceremonies surrounding Potemkine's departure to a polite letter.[111]

In April Daladier journeyed to London. He spoke privately of the trip as an occasion to acquaint the British with the pressures Paris was under, and so remove the untenable possibility of secret bilateral negotiations with the Soviets, or, given sufficient British opposition, of any substantive negotiations. As for the intention of rousing London's awareness of the German menace, which he had proclaimed to the General Staff, his personal policy during the trip had a somewhat different flavour: Franco-British collaboration, especially in the Mediterranean, and the cautious development of a Franco-German *entente cordiale* at the expense of the Soviet pact.[112] Daladier believed that closer ties with the USSR would lead to a Franco-Soviet preventive war against Germany, an eventuality which he was certain would be unacceptable to the French people. Another critical facet of Daladier's personal policy was his vigorous support over some months for extension of France's northern fortifications to cover the Belgian border, in opposition to the EMA's doctrine of 'forward defence' in Belgium. Schweisguth depicted this fortress mentality in his journal: 'he had just seen the mayors of Northern France who had asked him to protect them with "big" fortifications and then to let the Germans cry'.[113] The British obligingly told Daladier that, while France was naturally free to proceed to Soviet military conversations, the Germans were watching closely and Britain would not be surprised at the consequences. As for Soviet pressures in Paris, Corbin's preparatory soundings at the Foreign Office highlighted the dilemma of the Blum Government, caught between the devil and the deep blue sea.

[111] Gamelin, *Servir*, II, pp. 286–7; Schw., 1SC2 Dr12, 9, 13 April 1937.
[112] SHA, 7N2812, 29 April 1937.   [113] Schw., 1SC2 Dr10, 31 October 1936.

Vansittart had said that the Foreign Office would not dream of examining the justification for a military accord; it would simply see it as proof of the strength of the Communist party in France.[114]

The British were invited by Daladier to substantiate military objections to Soviet conversations, but, by the time he returned to Paris, increased Soviet pressures made it impossible for the government further to postpone a decision. Ministers began to discuss a démarche to be made by Coulondre, resembling that Potemkine had already made to Blum. Consistent with Blum's promises to Litvinov in October 1936, the French démarche would place a governmental decision in favour of staff talks under the aegis of the 1935 pact, without the signature of a full-fledged military pact extending its obligations.[115]

While Daladier was still in London, the EMA felt itself being outflanked by the government. On 27 April, Gamelin told his subordinates that, if compelled to meet with a Soviet representative, he would say that the French military were partisans of an accord, but could not admit any Russian interference intended to weaken the French army.[116] A Quai d'Orsay memorandum of the following day, on the basis of Gamelin's views of the most efficacious Soviet aid, neatly elaborated the démarche to be made by Coulondre. The Quai d'Orsay's premise was highly juridical: the Soviet desire for a military pact resulted from a confused conception of the purpose of treaties. The 1935 treaty having already created every possible obligation between France and the USSR, all further communication about military possibilities could be made under its aegis. The Soviets might be asked, in their own interest, for air support for Czechoslovakia and for local aid to the Petite Entente, but formal military discussions based on parallelism and reciprocity of forces had a political character which the Quai d'Orsay wished to avoid. The note did not define the French contribution, while it evidenced the military's obsessive fear that, distant from Germany's borders, the Soviets might well remain outside a conflict. The démarche itself carried two conditions: no publicity on technical talks, and Soviet acceptance of France's obligation to inform allied governments. Some weeks earlier, Bargeton had declared that Soviet staff talks would complete the dismemberment of the Petite Entente. This view

[114] Schw., 1SC2 Dr12, 19 March, 8, 25, 27 April 1937; DDF II, 5, no. 299.
[115] Schw., 1SC2 Dr12, 13 April 1937.
[116] Ibid., 27 April 1937; DDF II, 5, no. 285.

was implicit in the note's conclusion, which brushed disavowal: 'This would seem to be the character to give this communication – the question of its political opportunity in present circumstances does not fall within the scope of this note.'[117]

The evolution of a French démarche to break the stalemate in the Soviet conversations was paralleled by diplomatic shadowboxing between Paris and London over the issue of Czechoslovakia. The ongoing Belgian negotiations had caused acute disquiet in Central Europe. An early diplomatic manifestation of this disquiet was a query from Beneš as to whether France would object to Czechoslovakia's 'attempting to work out a more friendly relationship with Germany'.[118] Delbos gave his assent on 8 April, in the clear context of the importance of Britain to Czechoslovakia. Delbos adopted the dictum of the new British Minister in Prague, that the British attitude would be determined by the extent of genuine Czech conciliatoriness to Germany. He was plainly anxious that a negative Czech attitude not be attributed to France.[119] The assumptions underpinning Delbos's assent are clear from a 22 April conversation between Léger and the American Ambassador. Léger conceded that a Czech-German agreement on the model of the German-Polish declaration was possible; indeed, all the states of Central and Eastern Europe could henceforth be expected to attempt accommodation with the Reich. But Léger's base calculation lay elsewhere: 'neither Poland nor Czechoslovakia nor any other state of Central and Eastern Europe would have any confidence in any promises which Germany might make and while cultivating better relations with Germany would attempt to do everything possible to obtain additional support from France and England'.[120]

It soon became clear that Czech overtures for a non-aggression pact aroused no interest in Berlin. Pleading the damage done French security by Belgium's estrangement, Delbos broached the subject of a formal British commitment to Czechoslovakia in late April. It was, in effect, a standard French appeal after a West European diplomatic perturbation for British guarantees in Central Europe. Phipps, the British Ambassador retorted with equally standard equivocation.[121] Several days later, Delbos confided to Bullitt his despair at devising a policy to preserve peace. France was no longer strong enough to

---

[117] Schw., 1SC2 Dr11, 17 February; FNSP, Papiers Daladier, 1DA7 Dr5, Note, 28 April and Colson's response, ibid., 11 May 1937.   [118] FRUS, I (1937), pp. 77–8.
[119] DDF II, 5, nos. 217, 228.   [120] FRUS, I (1937), p. 79.
[121] Ibid., pp. 84, 88–9.

maintain the Central European status quo against Germany and Italy combined. It could take strong action only with Britain, but Britain was unlikely to give such an undertaking until its rearmament was complete.[122] The only stop-gap seemed to be recourse to the Soviets, thus parrying the worst eventualities while Britain rearmed.[123]

In the spring of 1937, the Czech problem as seen from Paris presented itself in three tiers. If repeated Soviet assertions were to be believed, the USSR would aid Czechoslovakia when, and only if, France did so. Since mid February, the Political Directorate had held that France should not undertake an active policy in Central Europe without Britain. The synthesis which suggested itself to Blum and Delbos was the formation of a Franco-Soviet-British front. Litvinov's appeals in this period for French mediation to bring about an Anglo-Soviet rapprochement implied that the Soviets would willingly lend themselves to this design.[124]

The British were directly informed of Paris's intentions during the coronation ceremonies. In a meeting with a disapproving Eden on 15 May, Delbos refused to postpone Soviet staff conversations although he whitewashed them, characterising them as an 'entirely harmless ... exchange of information' between military attachés. His apologia for firmness had two themes, the necessity of preventing a Soviet return to Rapallo and of defending Czechoslovakia. Delbos argued that talks would prevent Soviet 'preparatory measures with a view to a subsequent reorientation of Policy', a roundabout version of his and Blum's fear of the effects which a Germano-Soviet rapprochement would have on French internal politics. He also justified bilateral technical contacts as 'urgently needed from the purely aeronautical point of view, since Russian assistance would be indispensable if Czechoslovakia were to be attacked by Germany'. In a belated echo of Lacroix's dispatches during the Franco-Petite Entente negotiations, Delbos rested his case: 'We will not abandon Czechoslovakia. We cannot do it without disappearing from the

---

[122] Ibid., pp. 91–2.
[123] When, in May 1937, Daladier spoke of the desirability of reviving disarmament talks, Blum concurred, making clear, however, that he regarded them as linked to the progress of British rearmament. Labour opinion in Great Britain, like much of French opinion, would be more easily rallied to rearmament if it could be suggested that disarmament was near. SHA, 'CPDN Procès-verbaux', 19 May 1937.
[124] DDF II, 5, nos. 442, 470.

map of Europe as a great power.'[125] Delbos no doubt considered that
Czechoslovakia's exposed situation authorised such gravity. One of
the by-products of his late April conversation with Phipps had been
a consensus that Hitler could take Austria at any time without
serious international complications.[126]

After receiving Litvinov, who waxed strong on the subject of a
common Anglo-Franco-Soviet effort in defence of Czechoslovakia,
Blum spoke to the ubiquitous Bullitt of a tragic resemblance between
the international situation of 1937 and that of 1914. Blum's use of the
1914 analogy signified his despairing acceptance of the likelihood of
war. Hitler having seized the initiative in European politics, Blum
saw no other choice but to recreate the pre-1914 Anglo-Franco-
Russian alliance. The analogy was also politic. As a patriotic, supra-
ideological phrase, it called to mind Barthou, and in the turbulent
conditions of 1937, served to downplay the significance of the Soviet
purges. When Bullitt asked if Blum did not think 'the recent
wholesale exilings and shootings' would be an obstacle to Anglo-
Soviet rapprochement, Blum answered: 'he did not believe it would
be any more difficult for the British Government to work with the
present Russian Government than it had been before the war for the
French Left Governments to work with Czarist Governments. In
any case, he felt that there was no other alternative...'[127]

Two days later, on 22 May, a meeting of the three *Défense nationale*
ministers with Delbos, Blum, and Léger reached agreement on the
instructions for the démarche by Coulondre discussed within the
government since mid April. Schweisguth recorded their decision:
'In short, it is a matter of saying to the Soviets that the Franco-
Soviet pact maintains all of its value for us, that staff conversations
constitute its normal accompaniment, and that the French and
Soviet staffs can be authorised to engage in them.'[128] On the eve of
the ministerial discussion, Blum insisted to Bullitt on his determination to lead France to war should Germany attack
Czechoslovakia.[129]

The military reacted to the government's decision with profound
scepticism. Schweisguth wrote: 'The impression with which I am
left by this conversation is that the question of Franco-Soviet staff

[125] PRO, FO 371, 20702, C3620/532/62; C3685/532/62; DDF II, 5, no. 429.
[126] FRUS, I (1937), pp. 52, 79–80, 85.
[127] Ibid., p. 94. For the sea-change in Blum's personal views represented by the 1914 analogy,
    J. Bariéty, 'Léon Blum et l'Allemagne', *Les relations franco-allemandes*, pp. 38–9.
[128] Schw., 1SC2 Dr12, 26 May 1937.   [129] FRUS, I (1937), p. 97.

talks is still heavy with misunderstanding.' He criticised the government's decision on three points. The question of inter-service coordination remained unsettled, the phrasing in the démarche implying army leadership of the talks having occasioned a violent outburst from Cot in the 22 May meeting. Secondly, the Soviets, who had insisted in February and March on formal staff accords, expected staff talks to bring them something new, whereas the Quai d'Orsay believed that talks could be reduced to technical conversations without increasing treaty obligations. For the EMA, even technical talks under the aegis of the 1935 pact would heighten the chance of war by exacerbating the Reich's encirclement phobia. Lastly, the Political Directorate argued, that as the 1935 pact would be unchanged, Poland and Roumania would have no reason to be alarmed by staff talks. Schweisguth reckoned that the Quai d'Orsay underestimated the effect Soviet talks would produce on these countries, and the ways in which their alarm could be exploited by Germany.[130]

Crucial to Schweisguth's last point was an April trip to Bucharest by Beck, who had made headway in persuading the Roumanians of the folly of Soviet passage.[131] The aim of Beck's visit had been to strengthen Polish-Roumanian cooperation against the USSR by the revival and reinforcement of their 1922 military treaty.[132] Nor was Warsaw's campaign against the follies of association with the Soviets confined to Bucharest. In late May, Gauché of the 2e Bureau was visited by the Polish military attaché, more opposed than ever to Soviet passage. He informed Gauché that the Poles were prepared to appeal to the Germans, whose territorial ambitions they thought limited, against the Soviets, whose ideological ambitions they thought limitless.[133]

The effect of the talks on Poland and Roumania figured prominently in two EMA notes, which marked the most forceful

---

[130] Schw., 1SC2 Dr12, 26 May 1937.

[131] For corrosive Polish influence on Roumanian-Czechoslovak relations in the winter of 1936–37, DDF II, 4, no. 442, note; 5, no. 138.

[132] Schw., 1SC2 Dr12, 14 May 1937. The 1922 Polish-Roumanian treaty was originally directed against the Soviets, but, when Germany joined the League in 1926, it was extended to any unprovoked aggression. After the signature of the Franco-Soviet and Czech-Soviet pacts, Titulesco enlarged the 1922 treaty to imply a right for the Soviets to send troops through Roumania; his modification caused the treaty's non-renewal in early 1936. SHA, 'EMA/2 Pologne 19', Note, 1 July 1937.

[133] SHA, 'EMA/2 Pologne', Note, 29 May 1937.

opposition the military had yet mustered to Soviet talks.[134] Among the disadvantages of the government's decision, the military emphasised the risk of consolidating within the German camp a Polish-Roumanian bloc, capable of giving the Reich the foodstuffs it needed and of neutralising the USSR. Germany would then be liberated for a war against France: any intensification of relations with Moscow would thus imperil France's own security.

These military anxieties were striking in that, in important respects, it was as if the Rambouillet negotiations had never taken place. In February 1936, d'Arbonneau had evoked as a reason for French arms aid to Poland the possibility of Poland joining the German camp.[135] The EMA's language had come full circle by May and June 1937, when it sought to exploit the ambiguities it had deliberately fostered in the strategic discussions preceding the Rambouillet accords, again in the cause of warding off Soviet talks. It recommended a reexamination of French security, in which a choice would finally have to be made between Poland and the Soviet Union. They were well aware that the course they advocated, a Polish-Czech combination, carried the risk of a German-Soviet rapprochement, but they were perhaps less swayed than in the past by fear of a German-Soviet treaty. As Schweisguth told Bargeton, in 1933 the Soviets had been prepared to sign a treaty with France while maintaining a secret treaty, of which they none the less told the French, with Germany. The Soviets, he implied, were capable of anything. As for the hapless Czechs, for some time the French military had made no secret of the view that the Soviets would not march on their behalf.[136] In Gamelin's view, they would have to resign themselves to purchasing Polish support in a crisis with the cession of Teschen.[137]

The implication of these EMA notes was that the gains of the Rambouillet accords could only be safeguarded by retaining the goal of a Polish-Czech nucleus. The EMA contrived to ignore Poland's evolution since the autumn of 1936, which made a Polish-Czech front a pure illusion. The ink on the Rambouillet accords had hardly dried when Polish behaviour towards the Czechs filled the Political Directorate with renewed apprehension:

General Rydz-Śmigły told General Gamelin on his soldier's 'honour' that there existed no secret accord between Poland and Germany especially as

---

[134] DDF II, 5, no. 480; 6, no. 35.   [135] SHA, 7N3000, 3 February 1936.
[136] Schw., 1SC2 Dr12, 8 April 1937.   [137] DDF II, 5, no. 275.

concerns Czechoslovakia. We contented ourselves with this assurance, but it is very evident that the parallelism in the action of German and Polish diplomacy with regard to Prague constitutes a collusion in fact as dangerous as a written accord.[138]

For the General Staff in 1935–7, the hypothetical Polish-Czech front was inseparable from its use as a shield against Soviet negotiations. To an extent unrecognised by the EMA, the Belgian decampment had destroyed their expectations of August and September 1936 for a Franco-Polish-Czech strategic entente. In April 1937, Łukasiewicz confided to Bullitt, Beck's conclusion that, with the barring of Belgium to French troops, the French alliance was 'virtually useless'. The resultant weakening of Poland *vis-à-vis* Germany necessitated a major reconsideration of Beck's foreign policy.[139] The effect of his reappraisal was to intensify the Piłsudskite calculation that Poland's best chance of safety lay in the likelihood of a German move against Czechoslovakia and Austria, while Poland maintained its independence and acted as a buffer against the Soviet Union, recuperating Teschen in the process.[140] By summer 1937, what remained of the French alliance system had become a *noeud de vipères*, a nest of vipers. Virtually all of its strands were actuated by the calculation that the German attack might far better fall elsewhere, although Beck was singularly prepared to enter into complicity with Berlin.

The EMA was also categorical on the necessity of safeguarding what it rather euphemistically called the cordiality and candour of relations with London against jeopardy by Soviet talks. Capitalising on Eden's disapproval, it argued that French security rested on the British entente, which in 'power, certitude and constancy' was more valuable than any Soviet support.[141] This argument corresponded to a growing defensive mentality in French military and diplomatic circles under the impact of the Belgian negotiations. The diplomats' resignation to retrenchment was reinforced by the General Staff's reading of the defensive lessons of the Spanish conflict. Alongside the older calculation that the victors in the next war would be the belligerents with staying power, emerged a new willingness to concede to Germany 'large initial successes'. The British entente, with its discouragement of active French support of Czechoslovakia,

---

[138] MAE, Papiers Massigli, 'Affaires de l'Europe centrale', Note, 7 November 1936.
[139] FRUS, I (1937), pp. 77, 91.   [140] Rollet, *La Pologne*, pp. 264, 283–4.
[141] Schw., 1SC2 Dr12, 26 May 1937.

had an obvious part to play in these emergent calculations for a long war.[142]

With the circulation of these memoranda, Daladier and the EMA closed ranks. Daladier, as chief of the defence establishment, resolved in future to by-pass Cot entirely by preventing discussion of the Soviet conversations in CPDN meetings, and by himself assuring coordination of the *Défense nationale* departments, while Delbos supplied firm directives for Soviet questions jointly involving the Ministries of War and Foreign Affairs.[143] But Cot could not be contained by such procedural expedients. Once the Quai d'Orsay had drawn up its verbal note for Coulondre following the government's 22 May decision, Cot instructed Keller to seek out contacts with the Soviets. Cot's initiative was swiftly aborted on the Soviet side by the arrest of Vorochilov's deputy, Toukhatchevsky, and of many of his colleagues. His effort to obtain for the French Air Force the first fruits of the 22 May decision never received a response.[144]

Toukhatchevsky's disgrace began in mid May when he was demoted, and then on 26 May dismissed and arrested. As late as the May-day celebrations, however, Toukhatchevsky had not been ostracised, and the Blum Government's deliberations on the 22nd were not influenced by the opening steps in his disgrace. The first mention of Toukhatchevsky's downfall in the surviving French documentation is an EMA note of 9 June recommending postponement of military conversations until the wave of purges passed.[145]

The Moscow executions liberated the EMA from any pretence of accepting staff conversations. Gauché read aloud to the EMA a note on the executions which concluded: 'No moral guarantee exists *vis-à-vis* this army and its chiefs.' Gamelin vigorously seconded Gauché: 'This should make us more prudent than ever; do not break off [with the Soviets], in order not to risk throwing Stalin into Hitler's arms, but do not commit ourselves and do not show the Russians anything of interest. The USSR is increasingly outside the European game...' He advocated renewed appeals to the Poles and Roumanians against the German danger, appeals which could be made

---

[142] FRUS, I (1937), pp. 78, 96–7.   [143] Schw., 1SC2 Dr12, 27 May 1937.
[144] Ibid., 1SC2 Dr13, 14 June 1937. Pierre Cot's various accounts of his negotiations with the Soviets omit any reference to their curtailment by Stalin's military purges.
[145] Haslam, *Soviet Union*, p. 138; DDF II, 6, no. 35.

with a clear conscience since the purges effectively removed any possible discussion of Soviet passage:

this must be explained to Poland and Roumania by developing this argument: we wanted to suppress on your behalf the danger of a Russian threat to your rear lines; this country is annihilating itself; you see very well that Germany remains the only danger for you and here, our interests coincide with yours... Above all, we must not breathe a word of Russian passage across their countries; those people have placed themselves outside humanity.[146]

The announcement of Toukhatchevsky's execution was met with diplomatic silence in Paris. Scheduled to obtain authorisation from the interministerial committee for the delivery of the démarche by Coulondre, Delbos was in no hurry to do so. The Soviets did not desist from pressing for negotiations.[147] Nor were the most ardent advocates of a military understanding with Russia – Cot, Herriot, and Paul-Boncour – discouraged by the purges. They argued that the Moscow executions showed the danger of a Soviet rapprochement with Germany, and that it was all the more necessary to conclude staff accords since the treason had been unmasked.[148] The General Staff easily had the last word, however. As Schweisguth told Bargeton, 'If we had listened to them, we would have had an accord now, which would have been signed [by] Toukhatchevsky.'[149]

The French silence *vis-à-vis* the USSR deepened with the fall of the Blum Government on 21–2 June. It has been suggested that Blum chose to fall *à gauche* over financial matters on account of the collapse in France's external position.[150] In a speech of July 1937 at Bordeaux, Blum himself lent substance to this interpretation, referring to the *Leipzig* incident which opposed the Spanish Republicans and the German navy in the Mediterranean. But inextricably related internal factors also stressed by Blum at

---

[146] Cited in Le Goyet, *Le mystère*, pp. 205–6.

[147] For an assessment of growing Soviet insecurity in the context of the worsening situation in the Far East, F. C. Jones, *Japan's New Order in East Asia* (London, 1954), pp. 70–1, and note 4.

[148] Coulondre, *De Staline à Hitler*, p. 83; Schw., 1SC2 Dr13, 23 June 1937. The advocates of Franco-Soviet entente later used the argument that the purges had made of the Red Army a more Jacobin force, as dangerous to underrate as the French armies of 1792; for Herriot and Blum's talk to this effect after the Anschluss, Churchill College, Phipps Papers, 1/20, 26 March; 1/21, 18 November 1938. [149] Schw., 1SC2 Dr13, 23 June 1937.

[150] R. Girault, 'Les relations internationales et l'exercice du pouvoir pendant le Front populaire', *Cahiers Léon Blum*, no. 1, May 1977, p. 42; Professor Girault's argument is taken up by Jean Lacouture in *Léon Blum*, pp. 417–22.

Bordeaux should not be neglected.[151] Jules Moch, who was present at the *Conseil des ministres* after the Senate's refusal of *plein pouvoirs* to Blum, recalls that Blum decided to acquiesce in the Senate's veto only after receiving word that extremists within the SFIO wished to rally militants to demonstrate in front of the Senate. He emphasised how grave the situation could become if the Minister of the Interior was obliged to protect the Senate against pro-government demonstrators. A new Clichy would be possible: he refused to envisage such a hypothesis.[152] Several months earlier, referring to Hitler's attention to civil discord in France, Blum had insisted on his commitment to an orderly transfer of power, should his government fall: 'He considered the international situation too grave and the possibilities of action by Hitler too great for him to envisage for one moment any action which would diminish the strength of France in international affairs.'[153]

Blum remained as Vice-Président du Conseil in the succeeding Chautemps Government. Cot also remained under Chautemps, although he was never again in a position to exert the influence he had in 1936–7. His continuing presence, like that of Blum, was linked to a commitment by the new government to a trickle of covert aid to the Spanish Loyalists.

The incident of the Soviet military purges ensured that the critical debate concerning the defence of Czechoslovakia, begun in the CPDN in the first weeks of the new government and posed in its most extreme terms in the EMA notes of May and June 1937, was never formally resolved. The collapse of the Franco-Petite Entente negotiations has been explained in this chapter in terms of Italo-German-Yugoslav diplomacy, and of the prospect of French military conversations with the USSR, an episode which signified Blum's personal acceptance of the imminence of war. By June 1937 and the failure of the projected military conversations with the USSR, Barthou's diplomatic initiatives towards Italy and the USSR had been exhausted in such a way as to leave pulverising ideological divisions. This, and the isolation of Czechoslovakia in the ideological currents of the War of the Spanish Obsession constituted the necessary obverse of what Gerhard Weinberg has called Hitler's

[151] Colton, *Léon Blum*, p. 262; *L'oeuvre*, IV-2, pp. 34, 39–40.
[152] Moch, *Rencontres*, pp. 235–6.   [153] FRUS, I (1937), p. 56.

Diplomatic Revolution of 1936–7, the indispensable preparation for his triumphs in 1938–9.

The contours of Munich were already visible in the Germans' jubilation over the Toukhatchevsky affair, their successful intrigue to decapitate the Red Army. As always after one of their *coups*, they lost no time in lulling the French. After Toukhatchevsky's execution, the cordial German military attaché boasted to Schweisguth that the Red Army was no longer to be feared. The *Reichswehr* had maintained relations with it only to obtain a technical apprenticeship impossible under the Weimar régime, and wished for no further contact. Kuhlenthal threw in a soldierly reminiscence. He had attended a luncheon at the Kremlin in 1929 for thirty-six guests, of whom only two were still alive. In a deft allusion to Mussolini's 1933 proposals for extensive territorial revision in Central Europe and an arms limitation settlement, he added that the only solution to Bolshevik perfidy was a revival of Mussolini's conception by which the four great powers would reach an understanding to assume the direction of Europe.[154]

[154] Schw., 1SC2 Dr13, 17 June 1937.

CHAPTER 7

The great eastern crises, *1938–1939*, and the fall of France

THE CZECH CRISIS

Yvon Delbos, who retained the Foreign Affairs portfolio under Chautemps, discussed the future of French policy with the American Ambassador the month after Blum's fall. The picture Delbos drew for Bullitt was composed of the Quai d'Orsay's conclusions, after the breakdown of the Franco-Petite Entente negotiations, and the lessons extracted by the Chautemps Cabinet from the Spanish War:

Insofar as he [Delbos] could foresee the future, the position that France would take would depend entirely on the position of England. France would not undertake to fight Germany and Italy. The position of France would be the same as her position in the Spanish affair [i.e. formal non-intervention]. If England should wish to stand firmly by the side of France against Germany and Italy, France would act. If England should continue to hold aloof, France could not act. France would never be caught in the position of having the Soviet Union as her only ally.[1]

The conspicuously Spanish imprint of Delbos's language revealed fears such as that evoked by the Chairman of the *Chambre des députés* Foreign Policy Commission earlier in the year – that a Sudetendeutsch uprising, perhaps with the dispatch of German 'volunteers', would transform Czechoslovakia into a second Spain. These fears were inextricable from the Soviet factor. As the Roumanian Antonesco had remarked, the Spanish war had made the Soviet Union into an object of fear throughout Europe, and this redounded against its ally, Czechoslovakia. In the words of another allied diplomat, 'who knows if around Brno [a centre for German emigré propaganda], a new Catalonia will not spring up?' Many in influential French circles shared the Central Europeans' dread of Comintern activity in Spain and Czechoslovakia. As with almost all

[1] Bullitt, *For the President*, p. 222.

other aspects of French diplomacy, official French perception of Czechoslovakia was heavily coloured by the Spanish war. One no longer heard Czechoslovakia compared to Alsace (as it had been in the relatively halcyon days of Franco-Czech amity) in its antipathy to German hegemony and its devotion to France. Instead, the formulation 'if not Spain, then not Czechoslovakia', or 'la non-intervention généralisée', in Simone Weil's phrase, had become current in French politics by mid 1937.[2]

Delbos's observations also encapsulated the conclusion which the Quai d'Orsay had drawn from the failure of the Franco-Petite Entente negotiations.[3] The Franco-British diplomatic tandem in Central Europe, which dated from the failure of these negotiations (and not, as is usually argued, from the immediate aftermath of the Rhineland reoccupation), launched the phase of Franco-Czech relations which ended in Munich, a phase marked by a renewed search for that elusive entity, an honourable Czech-German accord. For some months this policy commanded considerable consensus in Anglo-French circles, including pro-Czech opposition circles led by Winston Churchill and Léon Blum. Nevertheless, unofficial diplomacy, such as the visit of the British Foreign Secretary Halifax to Hitler and private conversations between Premier Chautemps, his Minister of Finance, Georges Bonnet, and Franz von Papen, all in autumn 1937, frankly betokened the sell-out that occurred at Munich. The international tide turned against Czechoslovakia from November 1937.[4]

A strategy with important implications for this diplomatic disengagement was elaborated in November and December 1937 by another carry-over from the Blum Government, Chautemps' Minister of Defence, Edouard Daladier. The cultivation of Franco-British collaboration in the Mediterranean, the arterial line of Britain's colonial interests, and the cautious development of a Franco-German *entente cordiale* at the expense of the Franco-Soviet pact had been Daladier's personal policy for some months. His talk to the military, before his spring 1937 visit to London, of rousing

[2] Jean Mistler in Assemblée Nationale, Commission, 3 March 1937; Szembek, *Journal*, pp. 214–15; DDF II, 4, no. 446; SHA, EMA/2, 'Tchécoslovaquie', Mittelhauser memorandum, 1 February 1926; L. Nöel, cited in *Le Petit Parisien*, 21 January 1935; S. Pétrement, *La vie de Simone Weil* (Paris, 1973), II, p. 113.
[3] See above, pp. 251.
[4] Czech T-120, 1143/2028/444495–7; DGFP, D, 1, nos. 22, 63; Earl of Birkenhead, *Halifax* (London, 1965), pp. 368–70.

Britain to the dangers of the German design to create a 'Mitteleuropa on the Baghdad Axis', however, showed that he took a less piecemeal view of German designs than Delbos and Bonnet. Daladier saw a great threat to French colonial interests in the Italo-German diplomatic partnership. By autumn 1937, he breathed fire on the subject of Italy, influenced by suspected Italian submarine warfare off Spanish waters and by a tightening Italo-German partnership which shifted Italian interests from Austria to the Balkan and Mediterranean littoral, a shift perceptible not only in the Italo-Yugoslav political accord but in Italian territorial claims against France itself. In a CPDN meeting of November 1937, he informed the military that, whereas previous planning had postulated a French conflict with Germany, events made timely the study of a Mediterranean conflict: 'What has been merely a variation until now risks becoming the essential.'[5]

When the military chiefs actually deliberated on his proposal the following month, Daladier was milder on the preponderance of the Mediterranean theatre, whose value he now presented as a means to enlist the support of London: 'The principal preoccupation of the English at this point [is] the Mediterranean area…It is only there that one can try to tie them down…It is on this terrain that we must act.' Gamelin was lukewarm over the proposed primacy of the Mediterranean, which could increase the possibility of a German attack in the west by appearing as a tacit French disengagement from Central Europe. Without overtly resisting his Minister's arguments, Gamelin observed that Germany's present military situation did not allow it simultaneously to attack Czechoslovakia and France, although he allowed that the situation could be modified by the expansion of German forces. Adducing his continuing conviction that Germany would turn east before moving against France, he revealed his root fear: 'Moreover, even at present, after having dealt with the Czech and Austrian questions, Germany could be tempted to attack us through Belgium or Switzerland with the support of Italy. We would then have before us the bulk of the German forces.' It was precisely this last possibility which Gamelin combated. He never took his eyes off Germany, and this unswerving gaze made his position the most defensive possible. When he alluded to the interdependence of France's defence and Italian toleration of transports of French troops from North Africa,

[5] SHA, CPDN, 3 November 1937.

implicit in his remarks was the argument that French forays into the Mediterranean would diminish French strength along the Reich's classic avenues of invasion. Thus, while appearing to defer to Daladier's Mediterranean strategy, Gamelin insisted that Germany remain the principal adversary, and he suggested equivocal wording for the CPDN's closing resolution which reserved the sacrosanct war of coalition: 'There are grounds for our eventually being able to pursue as a matter of first urgence the defeat of Italy, while remaining in a position to face an attack from Germany at any moment, and to pin down its forces to the extent necessary in order to allow action by us or our allies in other theatres.'[6]

The logic ultimately most compelling to the General Staff in the face of the eastern crises of 1938–9 was roughed out in a memorandum written by Gamelin's colleague and rival on the EMA, Alphonse Georges, soon after Daladier's Mediterranean presentation to the CPDN. Reasoning from the Italo-German rapprochement and the resulting threat of an unlimited conflict, Georges was concerned to construct a coalition for a world war begun in defence of an eastern ally (Czechoslovakia), but which would soon be extended to multiple theatres, including a primary theatre in the Mediterranean. In this conflict, the last battle, rather than the first, would be the only battle to matter. Georges's memorandum unequivocally advanced the concept of a prolonged war, a concept closely linked to the polemic during the Ethiopian war over British versus Italian support, as well as to the defensive lessons of the Spanish war.[7] Georges assumed both a hostile Italy and an allied Britain, willing to declare war on behalf of the beleaguered Czechs. His resounding emphasis on the last battle, a shorthand for reliance on Britain rather than Italy, suggested that, while Germany moved in the east, France sit behind the Maginot line and rearm with impunity, the better to attract allies. Writing in November 1937, he pre-empted Gamelin's subsequent inaction by advocating 'une attitude d'attente stratégique':

We have then every interest, *from the political point of view*, in not compromising the value and prestige of the French Army by committing the bulk of its strength to early engagements, which it would alone bear the brunt of and which would risk leaving it weakened ... To defeat Germany, it will be necessary to obtain, in addition to the support of England, that of Poland, Roumania, and Yugoslavia. The clarification of these alliances,

[6] Ibid., 8 December 1937.　　　[7] See above, pp. 68–9, 278–9.

the mobilisation and supplying of these armies will require *time* and the certainty of being able to count at the opportune moment on the support of a French army in possession of *all* its means. An immediate and powerful offensive in support of our Czech allies would only have the *symbolic* value of a *costly* gesture.

To mitigate the moral disadvantages of inaction, the note stipulated small, local offensives in the Saar. It framed in effect the conditions for a *drôle de guerre* or phony war over Czechoslovakia before that actually fought over Poland.[8]

Certain that the British would not countenance a world war over Czechoslovakia, Gamelin disengaged himself from the Czechs' fate when Mussolini allowed Hitler to seize Austria in March 1938. The extreme gravity of the crisis opened by the Anschluss provided the theme of two notes by Gamelin.[9] The core of his response was as usual anticipation. In a note of 14 March 1938, foreshadowed by his remarks in the December 1937 CPDN, he wrote that the time approached when Germany could simultaneously carry on a two-front war:

the military potential of Germany has been increased by 7 million Austrians and by ten active Austrian divisions. Germany today has 40 peacetime divisions, which will make 120 divisions in wartime [the EMA calculated that every German division would become three divisions in wartime]; its programme certainly entails 60 peacetime divisions or 180 in wartime. Tomorrow it will be able to envisage mounting a mobilisation of at least 200 divisions, which will permit it effectively to make war on two fronts, and even to revive the idea, if Poland does not commit itself at the beginning, of attacking us, either via Switzerland or via Belgium.

This changed estimate of the Franco-German balance of force imperilled Gamelin's critical calculation – dating from 1933 – that a war in the east would forestall a German onslaught against France itself. Panic-stricken at the Anschluss, which had caught French intelligence off guard, Gamelin wrote on 14 March that a general conflict could break out 'from one moment to the next', the Anschluss having proven the solidity 'at least for the moment' of the Axis.[10] Visibly dubious of their efficacity, he groped for what was at hand in the way of allies – Britain and Poland. As Georges had done

[8] SHA, IN46, Georges Note, 'Réflexions concernant la politique de guerre de la France', 20 November 1937; his italics.   [9] DDF II, 8, no. 432; 9, no. 73.
[10] R. Young, 'French Military Intelligence and Nazi Germany, 1938–1939', in Ernest May (ed.), *Knowing One's Enemies* (Princeton, 1984), p. 287.

in November, he evoked a world war in which Czechoslovakia, like Serbia in 1914–18, submerged by German force, would be revived and enlarged at the war's end, but to very different effect, for he concluded with a plea for rearmament as the only chance of avoiding a conflict.

Although the 29 March note treated Italy and Germany as allies, Gamelin's reflections were not without a vestigial hope that a rapid Italian volte-face might prevent a crisis of sweeping proportions over Czechoslovakia. Writing personally for Daladier, Gamelin sketched the catastrophic consequences of Italian enmity. He prophesied that Italy could push Germany into war, in order to obtain recompense for its behaviour at the Anschluss, and that, in the event of a German operation in Central Europe, Italy could carry on an offensive against France. The profitability of immediately disarming the Italian menace was patent.

Daladier's ministerial dossier contains several such manifestations of the lengthy Italophile agony of the General Staff. The day after the Anschluss, Louis Buisson, the head of the army's strategic studies section, the 3e Bureau, lamented the lapse of the Rome Accords which he exalted as a true alliance with a common plan of operations against the German menace in Central Europe, and accompanying staff accords of unprecedented solidarity. For Buisson, French military prestige had reached its apogee in 1935, when French policy had been based on military cooperation with Belgium and Italy. Frustrated at France's inability to wage offensive operations except with the greatest prudence, Buisson concluded that Germany could only be stopped in Central Europe by recreating the Paris-Rome Axis: 'Whatever the price of our agreement with Rome, it will never be too dear; because irrevocably it will result in the peace of Europe.'[11] Several days later, an officer on Daladier's staff took as his perspective the action necessary (implementation of *couverture*) to prevent Germany, after crushing Czechoslovakia in several days, from turning on France with all its force. If Italy was hostile, the Czech situation would be critical before France could call up all of its forces. Effective direct action on behalf of Czechoslovakia being possible only with Italian neutrality or friendship, the writer urged the obtaining of assurances from Italy, which would enable France

---

[11] SHA, 5N579, 'L'alliance France-Italie c'est du point de vue militaire la paix de l'Europe assurée', 13 March 1938.

to intervene rapidly.[12] Gamelin wrote more neutrally to Daladier the following month, after Daladier's choice of Georges Bonnet as Minister of Foreign Affairs had set his government's course: 'the power of our offensive action [in favour of Czechoslovakia] will depend on whether our forces will be required or not in the Alps and in North Africa according to Italy's attitude'.[13]

Under the impact of Italian acquiescence in the Anschluss and the changed Franco-German balance of force, Gamelin's approach to the Czech problem narrowly defined was increasingly supple. When the Blum Government had issued a 14 March assurance that France would integrally maintain its obligations to Czechoslovakia, Gamelin manoeuvred to prevent unilateral French action, that is, action without any prospect of Italian support, on Czechoslovakia's behalf. His recommendation in his 29 March note of new Czech fortifications outside Bohemia did not exclude a Czech-German solution of the Sudetendeutsch issue, with some measure of territorial revision.

Gamelin sought to ensure that the Czechs' surrender of Bohemia would be a diplomatic, not a military, defeat for France. He drew a sharp line between a diplomatic settlement, and the military disaster brought on by a German 'campagne d'été' in Central Europe, followed directly by an onslaught against France. His subtle pressure was for timely, limited negotiations over Czechoslovakia. But he also warned that a French renunciation in Central Europe which made war redundant for Germany would not modify the baleful consequences for France. Even in the case of what Gamelin called 'une mainmise [allemande] indirecte sur la Tchécoslovaquie' (indirect German control over Czechoslovakia), foreseeable German acquisition of Central European raw materials would allow it to outlast a Franco-British blockade. As Gamelin had long reminded his ministers, time worked for Germany at least as much as for France. Written after reflection on the implications of Italy's acquiescence to the Anschluss, his 29 March note was extremely pessimistic – indeed, its implications for French victory in a prolonged conflict go a long way towards explaining Daladier's celebrated moroseness at Munich.[14]

On 12 September 1938, before the staged Sudetendeutsch revolt

---

[12] SHA, 5N579, "Information du président: la question tchécoslovaque: les forces en présence', 15 March 1938.

[13] Ibid., 'Note du gal. Gamelin', 27 April 1938. Gamelin wrote during the Riom trial, 'I always personally believed that it was possible to try a reversal of alliances with Italy.' FNSP, Papiers Blum, 3BL3 Dr1, p. 23.   [14] DDF II, 9, no. 73.

activated Chamberlain's personal diplomacy, Gamelin personally acted to prepare the way for negotiations which would allow the retention of Czechoslovakia as a strategic piece in the French system. The new Czechoslovakia would be defensively organised, like Belgium, according to an elaborate system of national redoubts, his answer to minority problems within a rump Czech state. It could then play its part *à la Belgique* in a siphoning system to channel the German inundation, while France pursued the policy of retrenchment behind the sea wall of its frontier defences and reliance on the British fleet, especially in the Mediterranean, to which Daladier had been drawn since 1937.[15]

The ensuing debate, ostensibly about the scant possibilities of defending Czechoslovakia, was in fact about protecting France from attack by timely negotiations on the Czech problem. When Gamelin conferred with Daladier at the height of the Czech crisis on 23 September, Italian estrangement gave his reasoning an almost surgical cleanness. He proceeded directly from his antiseptic position in April 1936 to evoke three contemporary hypotheses which, in his view, made French intervention unwarranted: an Italian mobilisation against France; Polish intervention against Czechoslovakia; and a recent deterioration in Franco-Belgian military relations which precluded a French sprint through Belgium to aid Czechoslovakia.[16] French military displays in late September 1938 were calibrated by Gamelin and Léger to reinforce the great power negotiations underway.[17] For the rest, Gamelin effaced himself before what he respectfully termed 'the importance of the air factor to the government's deliberations'.[18] The Soviet air force did not figure in the discussions of mid September 1938 between Daladier and Gamelin. Reliable reports that three to four hundred Soviet planes had overflown Roumania and landed safely in Czechoslovakia in late September (before returning to their home bases at

[15] DDF II, 11, no. 65. Gamelin drew up proposals for territorial cessions to Germany with René Massigli, who presumably acted on the instructions of Alexis Léger. SHA, 7N2522, undated folio, map marked 'Solution Gamelin-Massigli'. Gamelin's delimitation of Czech concessions would have allowed France to withdraw behind the Maginot line, while a truncated Czechoslovakia immolated itself in the defence of France.
[16] FNSP, Papiers Daladier, 2DA1 Dr3, 'Munich', pp. 70, 95–7. In May 1938, when the Czech army had mobilised at the rumour of a German attack, the Belgians had held manoeuvres in Walloon areas to prevent any French incursions into Belgium in support of the Czechs. [17] DDF II, 11, no. 343.
[18] FNSP, Papiers Blum, 3BL3 Dr1, p. 16.

word of the Munich conference) doubtless influenced Gamelin to treat the USSR less dismissively by the close of 1938.[19]

A cogent historical case has been made that a determined French offensive on behalf of Czechoslovakia might have succeeded in September 1938, because the German fortifications in the Rhineland were still incomplete. Gamelin, however, had long since 'completed' the Siegfried line in anticipation. He did not alter his conclusion that Czechoslovakia could not be saved when he learnt before Munich that the Siegfried line was unfinished and guarded by only eight German divisions (as against fifty-six French divisions in the west).[20] To a query from Daladier in early September on the efficacity of direct French intervention on behalf of Czechoslovakia, Gamelin's reply had been scarifying, but, for both men, a foregone conclusion: 'We would take the offensive in battle as soon as possible; but it would present itself initially as a modernised form of the battle of the Somme.'[21] Dismissal of a unilateral French

---

[19] SHA, 7N2525, 'Compte-rendu de la réunion hebdomidaire' (René Massigli), 28 September 1938; earlier reports from French intelligence of Soviet determination to lend air aid to Prague, a possibility steadily discounted by the military on technical grounds, ibid., reports of 14 March, 30 March, 6 July 1938. Informed of the Soviet air presence in Czechoslovakia by a still astonished Daladier several months after Munich, Blum and his Socialist colleague, Jules Moch, took the opportunity to remind him of the error of excluding the Soviets from the long negotiations over Czechoslovakia's fate. Moch, *Rencontres*, p. 255.

[20] W. Deist, *The Wehrmacht and German Rearmament* (London, 1981), pp. 88–9; Adamthwaite, *France*, pp. 226–7, 234; see also the simulation of multilateral military options in 1938 in Murray, *Change*, pp. 217–63.

   Informed of German weakness on the western frontier, the elated head of Czech military intelligence sent word to his French colleague, 'Your regiments can start marching with their bands in front!' F. Moravec, *Master of Spies: the Memoirs of General František Moravec* (London, 1975), pp. 136–7. On Czech strength, see General E. Faucher, 'Some Recollections of Czechoslovakia', *International Affairs*, 18, 1939 and M. Hauner, 'Czechoslovakia as a Military Factor in British Considerations of 1938', *Journal of Strategic Studies* (1978). The modern Czech force had a strength estimated at one-half that of the *Wehrmacht* forces designated for 'Plan Green'. French intelligence received indications of German unpreparedness for a campaign against Czechoslovakia, as did the Berlin Embassy. Schacht was reported as saying that the country was on the brink of ruin. 'Constant messages' from the German General Staff encouraging France to resist Hitler's claims against Czechoslovakia and declaring that the Nazi régime would collapse in case of war were suppressed by François Poncet, who did not report them to Paris because he believed 'that their origins made them suspect and that they might unduly strengthen the hands of the warmongers in France'. SHA, 7N2525, 8 April, 31 August 1938; PRO, FO 800 (Halifax) 311, cited in R. J. Young, *In Command of France* (Cambridge, Mass., 1978), pp. 299–300.

[21] Gamelin, *Servir*, II, p. 345. Such analogies were not confined to the EMA. After Munich, reports reached French military intelligence of the astonishment of the German military at the strength of the surrendered Czech fortifications 'which would have brought about, they say... a new Verdun'. SHA, 7N2525, 19 October 1938. The dissident Czech historian

intervention on the Czechs' behalf had been constant in Gamelin's planning between 1933 and 1938.

Gamelin composed an obituary for Czechoslovakia as an essential piece of France's eastern system in mid October 1938. Italian estrangement and Polish deceit had made impossible a war of coalition in aid of Czechoslovakia, which, reduced by the Munich accords, was no longer capable of fulfilling its role as an obstacle to German expansion in the east. Increasing the estimates of German strength he had made at the Anschluss, Gamelin now regarded the Reich as possessing matchless military potential. It would, he wrote, soon be able to wage war on several fronts at once. The Poles' seizure of Teschen during the Munich crisis convinced him that Poland was in league with an expansionist Germany, henceforth bound to continue its *Drang nach Osten* unimpeded. Gamelin's strategy of Italo-Polish aid in a war over Czechoslovakia – the strategy with which he had anticipated the Rhineland reoccupation – was in shambles. He thus prepared to renounce an eastern counterweight in favour of the strategy advocated by Daladier since 1937, a strategy centred on the Mediterranean and conducted in close alliance with Britain. France, he wrote, should withdraw behind fortifications and conduct war like England behind the Channel. The 'new orientation to military policy', as Gamelin termed it, espoused in the 12 October note makes untenable the view that, while unwilling to fight over Czechoslovakia, he remained unwaveringly attached to the idea of an eastern counterweight. His only constant attachment was to a war elsewhere, as the note demonstrated when it set against the possibility of a lengthy war imposed by an attack on fortified fronts, always an entirely distasteful prospect for Gamelin, the prospect of a large-scale manoeuvre in a distant theatre ('manoeuvre de large envergure sur des théâtres lointains'), in the eastern Mediterranean or colonies. Moving firmly away from Eastern Europe, he extolled *le repli impérial*: France would remain a great power by maintaining the cohesion of its empire in North Africa and the Levant.

For the first time, in a passage in his 12 October disengagement

---

Václav Kural uses the strength of Czechoslovakia's frontier fortifications to argue that penetration in depth by German forces would have been both difficult and slow, thus affording time for French aid in the west to take effect. Kural concludes from this and other military data that the purely military possibility existed to defeat Nazism in 1938. His compelling conclusions are summarised in Karel Bartošek's 'Could We Have Fought? – The "Munich Complex" in Czech Policies and Czech Thinking', in N. Stone and E. Strouhal (eds.), *Czechoslovakia: Crossroads and Crises, 1918–88* (London, 1989), pp. 110–14.

from an eastern front, Gamelin used the celebrated expression 'une guerre de longue durée'. That he remained sceptical of the possibility of besting the German juggernaut in a long war is clear from his acknowledgement in the same note that, as it continued its move eastward, Germany would obtain the wheat and petrol necessary to withstand a Franco-British blockade.[22] The desperation of this strategic schema makes understandable the note's conclusion on the lesson of 1938, a plea for rearmament to enable France to negotiate with Germany from a position of strength. The prospect of a long, costly war in itself induced negotiation. Neville Chamberlain in these weeks used similar language.

Gamelin's veiled renunciation of an eastern counterweight in the aftermath of Munich provoked immediate protest from his colleague on the General Staff, Louis Colson. In a hard hitting response, Colson drew Daladier's attention to the clear defect of a strategy based on the Mediterranean theatre. France's withdrawal from Central Europe in favour of close entente with Britain and defence of its imperial interests would ensure Germany the raw materials enabling it to withstand and possibly win a long war. Unlike Gamelin, Colson refused to write off the Poles, whom he presented as increasingly aware of the German menace. He granted that France had, above all, to remain in close contact with Britain, but argued that the search for an eastern counterweight should remain

---

[22] DDF II, 11, no. 86; as with other pronouncements made by Gamelin on Czechoslovakia, this view flowed naturally from his appreciations at the Anschluss.

The phrase 'la guerre de longue durée' has made its historiographical fortunes in an article of that title by Robert Young (in Adrian Preston (ed.), *General Staffs and Diplomacy before the Second World War* (London, 1978), pp. 41–64). Professor Young identifies the phrase, which also occurs in Daladier's memoirs of the period, as 'a single vehicle which I believe may be useful for any discussion of French diplomacy and military policy...the idea of a long war...served as the driving force behind French military strategy [throughout the 1930s]', pp. 42, 60. The concept itself is problematic. In the mid 1930s, Pétain, the grand arbiter of doctrine, maintained that the next war could only last several months. Gamelin for his part reckoned that the length of the next war would be less important than where the war was fought, and, vitally, that it would be a function of which allies France could mobilise. Singleminded stress on a long war appeared in French military documents only in November 1937, when Georges advocated the equivalent of a phoney war over Czechoslovakia, with British support. When Gamelin adopted the term belatedly in October 1938, he did so in a rather different sense, in conjunction with his provisional renunciation of an eastern front. The important strategic concept for him remained to carry the war as far as possible outside France's frontiers (thus, Middle Eastern and colonial theatres). Moreover, the repellent prospect of a long war led him immediately to evoke negotiations. His uncertainty with regard to France's prospects as the ally of Britain in *une guerre de longue durée* warred with his fear that the Reich would leave France, without Italy at its side, no choice but inundation or negotiation. Cf. above, pp. 68–9.

an axiom of French foreign policy. Under this heading, French rearmament would serve to win allies in the east among states such as Poland, Roumania, Hungary, and Yugoslavia, which still had a choice between independence and servitude to Germany. France, Colson wrote, could not both disinterest itself in their choice and assure its own future.[23]

Gamelin muted his response to Colson's dissent. He transmitted the Colson note to Daladier without substantive comment, except to say that the question was more in the political than the military domain. Alarmed by the strong priority given air rearmament by Daladier in the demoralising weeks after Munich, he was more concerned to stress the army's funding needs. He sounded the tocsin that the situation even for the defence of France itself was grave. Referring again to his prognostications at the Anschluss, he rammed home the message that Germany would soon enjoy such superiority in the east and west that it would be able to prevent France from carrying the war outside of its own territory, this last constituting Gamelin's sole conception of the defence of France.

The cloud of doom through which Gamelin viewed the defence of France meant that he welcomed the emergence of a clear German threat to Poland. Reports of growing Polish resolve to oppose German expansionism in the east influenced him by early December 1938 to write that Europe's only salvation lay in a profound change in Polish, Yugoslav, and Roumanian public opinion, coupled with a renewal of Soviet power and French rearmament. Under the last heading, he defended the army's programme which, as he phrased it, represented the minimum that could be done at that time and would soon be insufficient if France was not to fall under the German yoke.[24] In mid December 1938, an unnamed German military personage informed Paris: 'Before any action against France, Hitler requires that the fate of Poland be settled.' In response, Gamelin returned to the imposing rhetoric of the eastern counterweight:

the whole question is whether France wishes to give up being a great European power and to abandon to Germany hegemony over not only Central Europe, but also Eastern Europe. Without taking into consideration that France itself and its empire will find themselves involved ... if

---

[23] SHA, 5N579, 'Politique de défense jusqu'en août 1939', Colson note, accompanying letter dated 26 October 1938.

[24] Ibid., three Gamelin notes of 26 October, Gamelin note, 3 December; 1N43, Gamelin note, 11 October 1938.

only because of Italy's ambitions. With France, it is human civilisation, that of all the democratic powers, which is at stake.[25]

As the military historian Martin Alexander has observed, Gamelin's enthusiasm was in direct proportion to 'the diminishing likelihood of meeting his paramount responsibility to ensure France's inviolability...'[26] The threat to Poland also rallied Gamelin to language strikingly reminiscent of that used by Georges at the onset of the international crisis over Czechoslovakia in November 1937: 'it will henceforth be a question of a long war ("une guerre de longue durée"), which will settle the fate of the entire world, which will probably be progressively enveloped by it'.[27]

The question commonly asked with regard to France's eastern alliances is: why did France declare war in 1939 over Poland, rather than in 1938 over the more militarily viable Czechoslovakia? The close observer of French policy notices that the differences in

[25] SHA, 5N579, Gamelin notes, 19, 22 December 1938.
[26] M. Alexander, 'Maurice Gamelin', pp. 320–2. Given the state of France's unpreparedness, Gamelin consistently held back from authorising arms cessions to the desperate Poles. In a letter of June 1939 to Daladier, he stressed the ever more imperative demands of French rearmament, SHA, 5N579, 'Pologne', 23 June 1939. This was far from meaning, however, that Gamelin set little store by Polish resistance. He relied on the Soviets to provide the Poles with much needed war material, and in this regard, it is significant that he was entirely prepared to leave the Poles to make all the decisions as to the extent of their cooperation with the Soviets, a situation which emptied of substance Franco-British negotiations with the USSR in summer 1939. As J.-L. Crémieux-Brilhac has argued in a brilliant essay on French policy in 1939, fearful that Germany would attack in the west while France's preparations were incomplete, he sought to ensure that, if war had to come, it should come over Poland. A separate Polish-German accommodation, caused by a Polish backlash against western pressures for Polish-Soviet entente, would only deflect the Germans to the west. Thus, when Gamelin met with the Polish General Kasprzycki in May 1939 to conclude a new military protocol, he made no mention of Polish cooperation with the USSR. Crémieux-Brilhac concludes that Gamelin relied on time and war itself to bring the Poles round to acceptance of Soviet aid. Correspondingly, by waiting until the outbreak of war, he would ensure that it would actually be in the east, that it would set Poland and Germany against each other, and that the embattled Poles themselves would demand Soviet aid. J.-L. Crémieux-Brilhac, 'La France devant l'Allemagne et la guerre' (15. Deutsch-französisches Historikerkolloquium, Bonn, 1978).
[27] SHA, 5N579, 19, 22 December 1938. In a letter to Daladier of 27 December, Gamelin opined that, having moved in the east in order to gain raw materials to prosecute its war against France, Germany would attack either through Switzerland, with Italian cooperation, or through Belgium. SHA, 1N43, 27 December 1938. For his subsequent manipulation of rumours of a German attack through Holland, in order to compel the British to take up a continental commitment (a cause he had methodically pursued since his attempts to draw them into planning for a Belgian theatre in April 1936), see Martin Alexander, 'Les réactions à la menace stratégique allemande en Europe Occidentale: la Grande Bretagne, la Belgique et le "Cas Hollande" (décembre 1938 – février 1939)', *Cahiers d'histoire de la seconde guerre mondiale*, no. 7, 1982. The article does not treat Gamelin's inner conviction from December 1938 that Hitler would move next against Poland.

Gamelin's policy in 1938–9 were more of form than substance: neither over Poland nor Czechoslovakia did Gamelin prepare effective measures to give substantive French aid to the eastern ally in mortal danger.[28] The substantive difference between 1938 and 1939 lies not in the formula compromise over the Sudetenland versus war over Danzig, but in Gamelin's oft-repeated prophecies of increased German strength at the Anschluss versus the reality of increased German force after the Reich's seizure of the remainder of Czechoslovakia in March 1939. As will be recalled, Gamelin believed from March 1938 that the *Wehrmacht* could carry out an east–west shuttle, subduing first Czechoslovakia and then France in rapid order, and he deployed this argument in order not to go to war over Czechoslovakia. Yet actual German war potential did not approach his estimates in spring 1938. It was Hitler's bloodless occupation of Prague (not Vienna) which underpinned subsequent German military victories.[29]

The evolution of the *Blitzkrieg*, initially an improvised form of warfare, against Poland and then against France itself relied significantly on the German seizure in March 1939 of Czech war materials produced by the Škoda works. The German booty, enough to equip some thirty regular divisions of the *Wehrmacht*, included highly prized Avia 534 fighters with French-patented engines. In May and June 1940, one-half the tanks in Rommel's panzer corps were of Czech provenance. It was Rommel's tank corps which set the

[28] See, e.g., the incisive conclusions of Anna Cienciala, 'Poland in British and French Policy in 1939: Determination to Fight – or Avoid War?', *Polish Review*, no. 3, 1989, pp. 223–5.

[29] Using German sources, Murray gives an inventory of the assets, also including raw material supplies and foreign currency holdings, which the *coup de Prague* transferred to the German military machine, *Change*, pp. 290–2. Contemporary French military intelligence reports (SHA, 7N2524, 16 March 1939) provided much of the same information.

The extreme plasticity and selectivity of Gamelin's use of statistics emerges when one sets against the value of these Czech military resources his inflated estimates of German strength after the Anschluss (DDF II, 8, no. 432). Gamelin's projection of a German strength of 120 wartime divisions from the absorption of the Austrian military caused him evident anxiety, but he had equal, if not greater, reason to be worried about Czechoslovakia. Had he been willing to consider Czechoslovakia in the same framework of calculation, he would have found that seizing the Škoda Works and those at Brno would have enabled the arming of some eighty wartime German divisions plus the destruction of forty Czech divisions = 120 divisions. Thus, there were equally important and compelling reasons to help Czechoslovakia. It is particularly revealing of his panic at Mussolini's acceptance of the Anschluss that his estimates of German potential in spring 1938 made no mention of Škoda. Correspondingly, the emergence of a German threat to Poland and Britain's guarantee to Poland several weeks after the *coup de Prague* were providential for Gamelin, given the disaster of the increase in real German force on 15 March 1939.

distance records among panzer divisions in the actual invasion of France.[30]

The German threat to Poland restored to Gamelin a semblance of strategic equilibrium. It offered the unexpected boon of a war in the east after the humiliation of Munich. With the fillip of the British guarantee from March 1939, France would not enter a conflict alone, although the very mixture in Gamelin's response of self-fulfilling prophecy and desire to economise French means ensured that the EMA would never feel itself prepared, as German force visibly accrued in war materials, power, and prestige. Chronic French feelings of unpreparedness made the sophism of Georges' *attente stratégique* as compelling as ever: *la guerre de longue durée* shaded imperceptibly into *la drôle de guerre* or the apparently endless phoney war, and this against an adversary addicted to the tactic of rapid breakthrough. Gamelin informed his British counterpart, Lord Gort, in July 1939: 'We have every interest in the war beginning in the east and becoming a general conflict only little by little. We will thus have the time necessary to put on a war footing all Franco-British forces.'[31] As he had tutored the British at the height of the Czech crisis in September 1938, 'it is necessary to make strategy not only in space but also in time.'[32]

Cynicism was blatant in Gamelin's planning through the spring and summer of 1939. In May 1939, he promised the Poles a bold French relief offensive within three weeks of a German attack.[33] In September, as they reeled under German blows, he gave almost no active aid. He limited French involvement to skirmishes against the Saar sector of the Siegfried line, the action to mitigate the moral ill-effects of inaction advocated by Georges from November 1937. In an undated apologia written after his memoirs, *Servir*, Gamelin excused himself for not attacking the Siegfried line in September 1939: 'And

---

[30] A. Horne, *To Lose a Battle* (Boston, 1969), p. 271. Horne reflects on the structure of the *Wehrmacht* even as late as 1940: 'behind the thinly armored veneer of the superb élite forces of the *Wehrmacht*... the great mass of its divisions were probably less well equipped with the panoply of modern war than either the French or the British'. Ibid., p. 435.

[31] SHA, CSDN, 'Conversations militaires franco-britanniques...du 13 juillet 1939'.

[32] Cited in Le Goyet, *Le mystère*, p. 159.

[33] Crémieux-Brilhac points out that, in May 1939, Gamelin went so far as to promise the Poles that France would enter the war if Poland took up arms 'in case of menace to its vital interests in Danzig', an enticement which infuriated the Foreign Minister Georges Bonnet. Crémieux-Brilhac, 'La France devant l'Allemagne', p. 11.

I had the very clear impression that the order I gave to suspend operations in the Saar was a relief for everyone. We could hope that time would work for us, if we fully utilised it, we and the British.'[34]

The long war which Gamelin projected remained fraught with ambiguity, notably, the ever-present possibility of negotiations with Germany after the conclusion of its pact with the Soviet Union. He acknowledged this in a September 1940 deposition for the Riom trials. His remarks merit citation at length, because they have been used to support the view that he intended to slug out a long war with Germany.[35] In essence, anticipation of negotiations accompanied Gamelin's continuing commitment to Poland in late August 1939, as it had since he first wrote of a long war in October 1938. Once Germany invaded Poland, France had to be seen to mobilise – lest it be taken unawares should negotiations not come off, but also because a mobilisation would enhance its position in negotiations:

I said at the [governmental] meeting of 23 August [1939] that by spring 1940, I would hope that with British support and American material, we would be able to carry on a defensive battle. But I did not conceal that we could only obtain results against Germany at the price of a long war and that it would only be in 1941 or 1942 that we could take the offensive. If none the less I called for a general mobilisation, it was because the military power of Germany was such that we could not, by allowing it to crush Poland, let Germany attack us afterwards, when our own army was not yet mobilised...especially without an industrial mobilisation. *In asking for mobilisation, I did not ask for war; but Germany having already mobilised, we could not pursue negotiations without having ourselves mobilised...*[36]

---

[34] SHA, Fonds Gamelin, Gamelin manuscript, n.d., 'Les causes de nos revers en 1940'. John Mearsheimer remarks, '[The British] accepted the logic of [Gamelin's] policy, although they found its implications distasteful.' After the fall of Poland, in December 1939, the British Command concluded: 'the French have no intention of carrying out an offensive for years, if at all'. John J. Mearsheimer, *Conventional Deterrence* (Ithaca, 1983), pp. 82–9.

[35] R. J. Young, 'La Guerre de Longue Durée', p. 61, n. 10.

[36] FNSP, Papiers Daladier, 4DA24 Dr5, Gamelin deposition for the Riom trials, 28 September 1940; my italics. In the more polished memorandum which he prepared in December 1940 for the trials, Gamelin turned in the wind: 'If only in order to talk and make the other side show its hand, it was necessary for us to proceed without delay with our concentration and with launching our war industries. The military chief who did not say so would have been criminal. Moreover, in this respect, Daladier was as much in a hurry as I. I did not know in detail the efforts made by M. Georges Bonnet and M. Daladier to maintain peace; I had at that point too many pressing concerns in my own domain. I know that both ardently desired their success...Personally, I did not cease protesting against England's haste in wishing to declare war. If only from the military point of view, we had every interest in gaining time. However, had not the die already been cast?' FNSP, Papiers Blum, 3BL3 Dr1, p. 18. For Daladier's conditional acceptance of negotiations on 1 September 1939, as the French Government decreed mobilisation, and Gamelin's pressures to delay a declaration of war, Cienciala, 'Poland', and Adamthwaite, *France*, pp. 346–51.

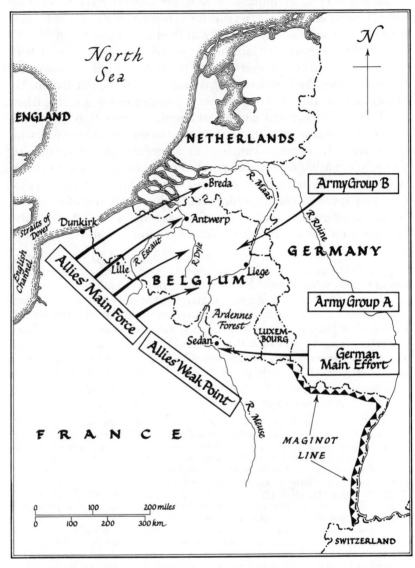

Map 2   The German attack on France and the allied response, May 1940

So Gamelin was divided between apprehension of the German attack, which would usher in a long war, and hopes of negotiation and was thus strategically not committed to the consequences of the former. While he was sceptical of a long war before the conclusion of the Nazi-Soviet pact, it is likely that his position in late August 1939 was also affected by increasingly vehement messages from the French Embassy in Berlin, now headed by Robert Coulondre, that France must hold firm ('Tenir, tenir, tenir'), that Hitler's martial resolve would give way to a willingness to negotiate.[37] In Paris Gamelin and Léger allegedly entertained a desperate mystique with regard to French mobilisation, Gamelin telling the incredulous future historian of the German Army, Benoist-Méchin, that, once France mobilised, the German war effort would crumple.

In mid September 1939, at the first word of *Wehrmacht* shuttles from east to west with the success of the *Blitzkrieg* in the east, Gamelin clung to the vestiges of his strategy for a war elsewhere.[38] In one breath he castigated the Belgians for the fall of Poland and announced his next strategic move:

And among them all, it's the Belgians who are the villains. They are unthinking, short-sighted mediocrities... in large part to blame for Poland's obliteration; they have considerably handicapped Franco-British action when they could have helped in numerous ways... Belgium must bear a heavy responsibility – and she will pay for it by serving as the powers' battlefield.[39]

Gamelin was relieved when the arrival of autumn rains delayed the German onslaught in the west. He had been dismayed by the prospect of an early battle, in which unseasoned French troops would face crack German forces. Senior French officers, particularly

[37] Coulondre's messages might have been effective in autumn 1938 (cf. above, p. 288, n. 20); by 1939, they were tragically misplaced.

[38] Gamelin and Schweisguth had hoped that the German Army would be mired for months in a Polish campaign, but the rain and fog during the projected invasion period of Czechoslovakia in autumn 1938 was not repeated in September 1939. On 18 September, only two days after the completion of France's general mobilisation, French intelligence detected the arrival at the western front of the first German veteran units of the Polish campaign. Gamelin wrote off the Poles as early as a 9 September staff meeting, when he gave instructions that the French press should not extol the resistance of 'Poland, which, we do not hide it, is done for' ('la Pologne, qui, nous ne le cachons pas, est foutue'). He then spoke of Germany turning against France with all its force. For these and the following references to Gamelin in wartime, I am again indebted to Martin Alexander.

[39] Gamelin to Paul Reynaud, October 1939, cited in an unpublished lecture on the fall of France by Martin Alexander.

Gamelin, were deeply pessimistic at times about the effects of German attack at any point, given the combat experience which German troops had gained in Poland. But, while the German military rooted out the operational flaws revealed by the Polish campaign, complacency overcame Gamelin and his colleagues with the advance of winter.[40] In Martin Alexander's image, 'On the western front, the ground froze, the troops froze, and it seemed as if in a military hibernation the commander's thinking froze also.' For years dismissive of the rigours of operational planning, Gamelin complained even before Poland fell: 'The military operations are really as nothing; what's so hard to endure is the government, the politicians, and their cliques.' He became bitingly critical of Daladier and, from March 1940, was distracted by his own political concerns as he fought for his future amid rumours of Paul Reynaud's intention to dismiss him.

THE FALL OF FRANCE

The German inundation came in May 1940. Despite highly adverse political circumstances and in the perennial hope of economising on French blood, Gamelin dispatched the cream of the French army to northern Belgium and Holland, while the Germans broke through in the south, through the Ardennes. The Breda Variant – his sprint to southern Holland to stem the German flood – was intended to anchor the battle deep in Belgian territory.[41] Crucial reserves, including tank units designated to repulse a German onslaught, were shifted northwards into Belgium and Holland, stripping forces originally situated within reach of the critical Ardennes hinge. Gamelin continued to transfer tank divisions to the north even as German tank units appeared on the Meuse.[42]

The pivotal Breda issue concerns the use of the strategic reserve, which from 1936 Gamelin had sought to redefine as a specialised

---

[40] On the strenuous self-correction of the German High Command after the Polish campaign, Murray, *Change*, pp. 338–40.

[41] Gamelin presided over a military meeting on 5 November 1939 which concluded that an allied intervention in Holland would 'inevitably provoke' an enemy riposte in Belgium. J. Minart, *P.C. Vincennes, Secteur 4* (Paris, 1945), p. 93. It is often said that Gamelin was drawn to the Breda Variant in order to prevent a German conquest of the Low Countries, from which an assault on Britain might be launched. Minart adds that the positioning of the advance guard of French troops in Holland was meant to discourage British evacuation in case of military reversal. Ibid., p. 152.

[42] Minart, *P.C. Vincennes*, pp. 92–3; Don Alexander, 'Repercussions of the Breda Variant', *French Historical Studies*, spring 1974.

force for a combined operation in Belgium and Holland.[43] He wrote in September 1939 that the strategic reserve should be employed very close to the front, whose location would be determined by the rapidity with which the Germans could move through neutral territory.[44] It followed that he would race to their encounter as far into neutral territory as the circumstances permitted. This was all the more likely as his notion of counter-attack called for a forward line behind which a series of strong points would disrupt and canalise the German assault. The alternative in French military planning in 1939, the so-called Escaut Plan which many historians have viewed as a more viable option, would have situated the battle very close to the industrial centre of Lille, with the system of strong points reaching back farther on to French soil, the very situation Gamelin was determined to avoid. In the context of the evolution of Gamelin's mechanised doctrine, the Breda Variant was neither new nor a contradiction in his strategy.

In his seminal article, 'Repercussions of the Breda Variant', Don Alexander attempts to separate Breda from the Dyle manoeuvre, the French advance into Belgium, which he considers justifiable because it spared northern France from invasion. He argues that the disaster of Breda lay not in carrying the war outside French territory, but in the fact that to execute it Gamelin stripped his strategic reserves on French soil before he ascertained the direction of the main German attack. The original proximity of the strategic reserves to the point of German breakthrough is tantalising, but the area behind the Ardennes, located roughly at the centre of the French defensive system, was merely a staging ground for the reserve which Gamelin long intended to dispatch either to the Low Countries or to Switzerland. Nor did he commit his entire reserve to the Breda Variant, despite being taken in by the 'matador's cloak', the action of German armies in Belgium and Holland to distract attention from the Ardennes. Once he sent the 7th Army to Breda, he maintained a large force behind the Maginot line to protect against an Italo-German eruption through Switzerland outflanking the line. When the significance of the Ardennes became all but inescapable, Goebbels threatened to invade Switzerland in order to persuade Gamelin that the attack at Sedan might not be the main attack after all, and to deter him from transferring troops from the Maginot line

---

[43] See above, pp. 77–88.   [44] Gamelin, *Servir*, I, p. 246.

to stop the German advance. These various German attempts at disorientation were wildly successful.[45]

Gamelin's reticence about Breda, his hesitation in bringing it forward as soon as the war broke out in September 1939 appear to have been related to the very difficulties which necessitated its incorporation in his planning. Once temporary progress was made in establishing liaison with the Belgians in November 1939, he hastened to unveil Breda and did not deviate from it afterwards. As Don Alexander comments, by spring 1940 Breda had become an *idée fixe* for Gamelin. His entire strategic conception since 1936 having been to carry the war outside French territory, he counted on improvising a forward defence in the Low Countries with French troops acting as liaison between the Dutch and Belgians who had failed to establish liaison between themselves. The liaison role was thus central to the reserves' function for Gamelin who by 1940 threw caution to the winds in his alacrity to join what would in effect have been a battle of encounter, had the critical mass of the German army been present in southern Holland for the encounter.[46]

Paul Reynaud's papers contain a typescript of notes taken in May 1940 by Paul de Villelume, the liaison officer between the Quai d'Orsay and the Ministry of War, and like Reynaud, an enemy of Gamelin. Remarks by Gamelin on 12 May 1940 reveal the *idée fixe* quality of his response to the unfolding 'matador's cloak' in the north. Villelume voiced to Gamelin his disquiet at the campaign in Belgium and Holland: 'Everything is happening as though the Germans are inviting us to penetrate more and more massively into Belgium. The indulgence of their aviation towards our troops has no other explanation. The trap is evident.' Gamelin is recorded as replying: 'It is possible that enemy aviation cannot meet all of its tasks...Perhaps it hasn't enough planes to attack the French columns. It bombards the Belgian columns and the rail road stations.' Villelume countered: 'If the Belgian columns are the only ones being attacked, perhaps it is because they are the only ones who

---

[45] Horne, *To Lose a Battle*, pp. 198–9, 345, 399, 440, 470; see also Minart, *P.C. Vincennes*, p. 80, n. 2. On the threat of German invasion of Switzerland, which caused general panic in the Swiss border population, DGFP, D, 10, nos. 153, 319, 337.

[46] D. Alexander, 'Repercussions', pp. 483–4. On the ominous British failure in early 1939 to arrange workable liaison with the Dutch and Belgians, Martin Alexander's 'Les réactions à la menace stratégique allemande' is instructive. The British failure did not faze Gamelin, who relied on a conflict to galvanise a united allied effort in the west, if not in aid of Poland then in self-defence. This reliance was yet another element underpinning his planning for a battle of encounter in the Low Countries.

are retreating. If the Germans wanted to prevent us from advancing, they would consider it more urgent to stop our divisions as they approached their objectives than to drop bombs on distant train stations.' Without trying to respond to Villelume's arguments, Gamelin answered: 'When we took the decision to enter Belgium, we accepted all the risks of the enterprise.'[47] This tendency to make strategy on the basis of what suited the allies, of what best matched allied preconceptions, had long characterised his planning for an eastern front.

By May 1940, nothing remained but to plan to fight in alliance with Britain on French soil, but this Gamelin had planned never to do. It still amazes that the fall of France came about not from lack of weapons, nor until after Dunkirk from an insuperable lack of men, but from a virtual absence of planning for a German breakthrough on French soil. This fact resists explanation until placed in the context of Gamelin's allied calculations from 1933 and his long-term attachment to a cut-price conflict on the peripheries. These were the unifying strands in a strategy which, more than any other single factor, accounts for the armistice of June 1940. By always attempting to fight the war elsewhere, Gamelin in effect made it impossible to fight at all.

Reflections on the Franco-German Armistice, June 1940

From that bitter summer of 1940, two texts. The prose of the German preamble to the conditions of the Armistice of 22 June 1940 is inflated and seductive: 'After an heroic resistance, France, in a unique series of bloody battles, has been vanquished and has collapsed. Thus, Germany does not propose to give to... the negotiations for an armistice the character of an affront with regard to such a brave adversary.'[48] The second text is from the great medievalist, Marc Bloch, who was executed as a *résistant* by the Germans in 1944. Bloch wrote in rage immediately after the defeat, which he had witnessed as a serving officer:

[47] AN, Papiers Paul Reynaud, 'Notes prises par le lt.-col. Villelume...avril–mai 1940', 12 May 1940.

[48] Cited in Anne Brassié, *Robert Brasillach ou encore un instant de bonheur* (Paris, 1987), p. 216. The Paris archives contain, to the author's knowledge, no official fatality figures for the 1940 campaign. A confidential note submitted by Gamelin to Premier Reynaud during the decisive days of the German breakthrough concluded: 'the loss of men is slight, but...a high percentage of our units of manoeuvre and general reserve is disorganised and in large part, unusable'. AN, Papiers Paul Reynaud, Annex II, Gamelin to Minister of National Defence, 18 May 1940.

The generation to which I belong has a bad conscience. It is true that we emerged from the last war desperately tired...That is our excuse. But I have long since ceased to believe that it can wash us clean of guilt...Since that moment when the weapons which we held with too indeterminate a grasp fell from our hands, the future of our country and our civilisation has become the stake in a struggle of which we, for the most part, are only the rather humiliated spectators...I cannot tell when the hour will sound when...we can once more control our own destiny...My only hope and I make no bones about it is that when the moment comes we shall have enough blood left to shed, even though it be the blood of those who are dear to us (I say nothing of my own, to which I attach no importance). For there can be no salvation when there is not some sacrifice, and no national liberty in the fullest sense unless we have ourselves worked to bring it about.[49]

This chapter has explored some of the strategic reasons for the French rout, which for Marc Bloch constituted the real opprobrium of defeat, and which, in their initial occupation of France, the Germans tried to camouflage for political reasons vividly illustrated by Bloch's early spirit of resistance. It has done so by pursuing a theme which characterised French strategy in the years before the armistice, planning for a war of coalition in Central Europe and Belgium, a war predicated on the blood of others. Its theme, in a single phrase, has been the search for a cut-price war on the peripheries. Placing the eastern alliances in their neglected, military context elucidates the consistency in French strategy from the Gamelin-Syrový conversations on the days Hitler came to power until Gamelin's dash to Breda in southern Holland, the miscalculation which precipitated the French demand for an armistice in mid June 1940.

This strategy derived its impetus from Gamelin's lengthy expectation of a German reoccupation of the Rhineland. He sought to parry a reoccupation by an anticipatory strategy which would replace French resistance to a reoccupation, resistance which he believed would end in stalemate on the Franco-German frontier, in what he subsequently called 'une bataille de la Somme modernisée', and which would ensure Germany's movement eastward after it fortified the zone. Like his determination in 1939–40 to carry the war into Belgium, Gamelin's penchant for a war in the east rested on the attraction of a war of extended fronts. The Maginot line, which

[49] Bloch, *L'étrange défaite*, pp. 187, 190–1 (original edition); quotations are taken from *Strange Defeat*, trans. Gerard Hopkins (Oxford, 1949), pp. 171, 174–5. For Bloch's more conventional views of the war before the German attack on France, see Carole Fink, *Marc Bloch: A Life in History* (Cambridge, 1989), pp. 208, 211.

comforted politicians such as Daladier, served this strategy by providing, in Gamelin's phrase, 'an element of suppleness' in the deployment of forces for a war outside of France's frontiers, a war preferably in the east, but, if circumstances dictated, in that tattered remnant of allied cartography, Belgium.

Nothing could be more rational, indeed more self-evident for a commander, than the wish that the enemy's first blow fall elsewhere. But the defensiveness of Gamelin's attachment to the eastern front was psychologically ruinous. Fed by immobilising feelings of unpreparedness, the nature of Gamelin's attachment to the eastern theatre dictated his departure from the sound strategic principle of the two-front war, although he continued nominally to lay claim to it through the eve of the Polish campaign. Relentless anticipation of crises, as Henry Dutailly has pointed out, led to the postponement of action on the grounds of unpreparedness and the inchoate state of the anti-German coalition.[50] The *drôle de guerre* afforded only a more subtle variation on this theme. The cynicism of Gamelin's strategy was laid bare by its exploitation of allied circumstance. Italian complicity in the Anschluss having already dramatically undercut his allegiance to a two-front war, by convincing him that German strength would henceforth enable it to carry on war simultaneously on two fronts, entente with Britain over Poland reduced to vanishing point his allegiance to a two-front war. British aid could do little to facilitate even limited French action on behalf of Poland. But the core of Gamelin's attachment to the eastern allies emerges only when one remembers that, at its chimerical height, the Italian entente served his need to avoid the impression that France contemplated a war on its own soil. And present from the creation of Gamelin's strategy, the logic of negotiations only increased with time. The disarmament conference, fiscal cuts, and above all, a diplomacy avid for arms limitation having supplied the original context for the construction of his strategy, Gamelin afterwards subordinated rearmament to strategy, and this in a way which transcended the simple fitting of means to ends. Thus, this study contends that strategy, far more than the flaws of French rearmament, was key to the military events leading to the armistice.

Marc Bloch repeatedly returns to a single point, the General Staff's failure to improvise an in-depth resistance on French soil

---

[50] Dutailly, *Les problèmes de l'armée*, pp. 70, 113, 118.

after the German breakthrough on the Meuse. This, in his view, transformed the French campaign to rout, when victory might still have been possible.[51] The Germans, real kill-joys for strategy, he wrote, did not do what was expected of them, but the fault was not that the General Staff had not sufficiently anticipated their actions. If anything, its forecasts had been almost too detailed. The trouble was that these covered a limited number of eventualities ('Dieu sait que nous l'avions assez fignolée, notre "manoeuvre Dyle"!'). The EMA expected events to conform to its own excessive faith in spaces of manoeuvre, to its own calculations. When the Germans refused to play the game according to these rules, it was at a loss as to how to respond.[52] These passages in Bloch recall the frustrations experienced by higher ranking officers, like Paul de Villelume, with direct access to a Gamelin fixated on carrying the war outside of France into Belgium, and so rectifying French misunderstanding of the German war plan in 1914.

In unforgettable pages on the General Staff's misuse of history ('histoire comprise à rebours'), Bloch reflected on the process whereby it founded strategy on an almost scientific amalgam of lessons extracted from the laboratory of the First World War.[53] On the kind of primacy which Gamelin gave to strategy, as well as on the problem of the rectification of illusion in the flux of time, the novelist Marcel Proust, a shrewd and impassioned observer of military events in the course of the First World War, had this to say:

[51] Bloch, *L'étrange défaite*, pp. 58, 62, 128–30.
[52] Ibid., pp. 135–6. In an apologia written for Daladier and Reynaud at the height of the Battle for France, Gamelin turned on his own troops, censuring them for indiscipline and failure of morale. He blamed their putative pacifism and criticism of authority, in one passage, writing: 'In battle there were too many weaknesses [in evidence], which allowed the enemy to exploit local successes, to outflank the most brave, to wipe out, at the level of application, the Command's concepts and knowledge.' AN, Papiers Reynaud, Gamelin to the Minister of Defence, 18 May 1940. Bloch, writing two months later, provided an apt retort: 'In their hearts, [the military commanders] were only too ready to despair of the country they had been called upon to defend, and of the people who furnished the soldiers they commanded.' Bloch, *L'étrange défaite*, p. 144; *Strange Defeat*, Hopkins trans., p. 125. For Gamelin's long-standing discomfort in the presence of his troops, Minart, *P.C. Vincennes*, p. 74.
[53] Bloch, *L'étrange défaite*, pp. 136–42. He added ruefully, while not finding it excuse enough, that the EMA had had four years in the course of that first conflict to rectify its errors; Gamelin and his colleagues in 1940 faced a German army moving so rapidly that adaptation to the hard facts had to be accomplished in only a few weeks. His explanation of the visceral and moral effect of recollections of combat in the First World War on the aged French Command in 1940 (ibid., pp. 140–1) is an anatomy of memory worthy of Proust.

there is a side of war which is human, which is lived like a love affair or an intense hatred, and which can be recounted like a novel. So that if someone goes about saying that strategy is a science, he understands nothing about war, because war is not strategic... Even if one supposes that war is scientific, still it would be necessary to describe it... from illusions, from beliefs that are only rectified bit by bit, much as Dostoevsky would recount a life.[54]

Perhaps the largest question the student of military history may ask, the question which draws on the widest range of military, societal, diplomatic, demographic, and psychological factors is: What really constitutes defeat and victory for a given military organisation? Arguably, the armistice of 1940 represented for many members of the French General Staff something less than complete defeat. Demanded not by Gamelin but by his successor – although as Marc Bloch wrote, there was no change in strategic response with Weygand's eleventh hour reappearance – the timing of the armistice served the two purposes for which Gamelin's strategy had been invented: it ensured that there would be no prolonged conflict on French soil, and no repetition of the bloodletting of 1914–18.[55]

From the defeat of 1870, French political discourse had been obsessed with decadence. By the 1930s, in a society polarised by economic crisis and international political divisions, the rhetoric of decadence deeply influenced decision-making. In particular, the officer class as a group came to loathe the Front populaire and easily equated it with what for the army was the nation's irrevocable descent into defeat.[56] In our parlance, the language of decadence and decline diverted policy-makers from creating and adapting effective defensive strategies, from accomplishing a genuine transition to continental, if not yet global, interdependence among allies. In the aftermath of the 1940 armistice, the Germans took pains to

[54] Marcel Proust, *A la Recherche du Temps Perdu*, III, Editions de la Pléiade (Paris, 1973), pp. 982–3.

[55] Those who would believe that Gamelin was proved right by the relatively low casualty rate of the French during the 1939–45 conflict forget the enormous and enduring trauma of their civil war. I owe this insight to Philip Bankwitz.

[56] On the transition in 1938 from the Front populaire to the Daladier Government, a government 'free of socialist allegiance and soon opposed to Communism', Gamelin asked rhetorically in his Riom memorandum: 'In the realm of foreign policy... was not the damage already done in such a way that it could not be repaired?' FNSP, Papiers Blum, 3BL3 Dr1, p. 14. Cf. Bloch's view that the 'decadence' which the military projected on to the French people was essential to military acceptance of the armistice. Bloch, *L'étrange défaite*, pp. 144, 186–7. Of course for the military, the Front populaire epitomised that decadence.

impress upon the demoralised French officer corps that, given the Franco-German balance of power since 1870, the armistice might even be said to represent an ineluctable fate dealt by a vastly superior military machine. The history of the eastern alliances and the French military's allied calculations suggest otherwise. Ultimately, the blood of others was not a viable solution to the historical problem of confronting Germany with a two-front war.

Léon Blum and Czechoslovakia in 1938

SUMMARY: THE ROLE OF IDEOLOGY IN FRENCH POLICY, 1936–7

In an unpublished manuscript on the defeat in 1940, General Schweisguth juxtaposed the German-Soviet pact, which enabled Germany, after a rapid campaign in Poland, to bring all its weight to bear in the west, with the formation of the Axis, whose significance he analysed thus: 'The change in Italy's attitude in 1936 deprived France and England of any possibility of action in the countries situated to the east of the Rome-Berlin Axis, which cut Europe in two from the Mediterranean to the Baltic.'[1] French military estimates of Soviet duplicity were such that the Nazi-Soviet accord could have shocked few on the General Staff, but, for Schweisguth and his colleagues, the Italo-German entente of 1936–7 was the painful growth which neutralised French power.

The November 1937 Hossbach memorandum, his celebrated disquisition on future geo-political solutions, suggests the importance to Hitler of Italy's being diverted elsewhere. In 1936, during the Ethiopian war, Hitler had struck in the Rhineland; in 1937–8, when Italy, overextended in Spain, diverted its concerns to the Mediterranean, he projected his moves against Austria and Czechoslovakia.[2] Hitler grasped that Italy was the nerve centre of Gamelin's planning to counter German expansionism: thus the tone of unshakeable conviction in his insistence to his querulous generals that France and Britain would not fight.

Blum's year as Premier brought the real disintegration of France's

[1] Schw., SC4 Dr8, 'Etude sur la défaite de 1940', pp. 10–11.
[2] DGFP, D, I, no. 19. A May 1938 directive from Hitler to the *Wehrmacht* flatly stated that Italy's alignment with Germany would deter France from unleashing a general war on behalf of Czechoslovakia. Ibid., no. 221.

external position, a disintegration which was the necessary obverse of Hitler's diplomatic revolution in Europe. By June 1937, the policy of collective negotiations with Italy and the Soviet Union, intended to revivify France's bilateral ties with Poland and Czechoslovakia, was in tatters. The Soviet Union had been dismissed from European politics, and Italy had slighted the defence of Austria, in order to consolidate a new power bloc with the connivance of France's former client state, Yugoslavia. Of the other geographical imperatives in French policy, reliance on Belgium had been stripped of a juridical basis and reduced to the vagaries of personal relations between Gamelin and the Belgian military; while Poland, to which the EMA looked to defend Czechoslovakia, saw in its neighbour's demise one of its principal hopes of salvation. Refused accommodation by Berlin, Czechoslovakia was isolated within the Petite Entente and internationally suspect on account of its treaty with the Soviet Union, a treaty which would be activated only by French involvement.

Any summing-up of this study's central portion on the Front populaire must assess the role of ideology in the French abandonment of Czechoslovakia. In June 1936, the pivots of the policy inaugurated by the April 1934 note – Italy and the USSR – were seen as antithetical for the first time. The 26 June meeting of the CPDN defined the choice to be made for the defence of Czechoslovakia as between an Italo-Polish front and a Soviet military agreement. The pressures within the new government for a Soviet military agreement came primarily from Pierre Cot, and they had a novel aspect, the leverage provided by Communist participation in the Front populaire coalition. Conservative fear of the spontaneous strikes of May–June 1936 and the Ministry of Defence's fears of Communist agitation in the army, fears which dated from the formation of the Front populaire's electoral alliance, heightened these domestic aspects of the internal struggle for control of the government's policy. The domestic constraints the General Staff experienced under Blum were quite different from those of preceding governments. Not only was there Pierre Cot's zealous Russophilia, but the Front populaire departed from the deflationary policies of the past to begin serious rearmament, with defence expenditures exceeding the military's original estimates. Civilian-military relations, however, were scarred by the government's attempts to implement a major arms programme alongside social reform, and by what the EMA regarded as outright Comintern sabotage of arms production. In external terms, the military and many diplomats blamed the Front populaire for what they considered the government's lamentable performance *vis-à-vis* allies, notably Italy. This was imputed to ideological blindness and cavalier disregard of the geographic realities on which a land-based strategy should be based. The General Staff's unwavering opposition to Soviet staff talks, and the related allied ambiguities it allowed to subsist during and after the Rambouillet arms negotiations with Poland ensured that it would not generate a new strategy, despite the strong commitment of the Front populaire to national rearmament. The ideological decomposition of Gamelin's strategy for a war of coalition predicated on Italy, together with the military's acute anxiety about the launching of rearmament in the corrosive circumstances of 1936–7, – this conjunction was central to the Riom debate, which pitted rearmament against strategy in a series of recriminations over political versus military responsibility for the 1940 defeat, including the false allegation that the Blum Government emptied French arsenals to arm the Spanish Republic.

The Spanish war, which left no part of French policy untouched, immeasurably exacerbated this entire complex of fears. Spain transformed French relations with Italy and the USSR, while it gave Hitler free range for a crusade against Bolshevism which besmirched France itself. For the General Staff, the German anti-Bolshevik campaign prepared the benevolent neutralities and complicities *vis-à-vis* states such as Belgium, Poland, and Italy indispensable to German action against Czechoslovakia, the point at which 'the Reich's desire for pan-Germanist expansion coincides with its anti-Communist ideal'.[3] The German anti-Bolshevik campaign was all the more effective for being viciously seconded by the right-wing French weeklies. Marc Bloch recalled that, after Belgium repudiated its alliance with France, a Belgian friend had lamented the incalculable harm done by the excesses of these weeklies, tireless in their proclamations to wide Belgian as well as French audiences that Front populaire France was rotten to the core. The deadly effectiveness of the German campaign in so far as many French officers were concerned was inseparable from their own distrust of Blum's Government.[4]

---

[3] SHA, 7N2522, 2e Bureau, 'Note au sujet de la possibilité d'un conflit en Europe', n.d.
[4] Bloch remarks that so reactionary were the newspapers strewn about his own officers' mess in 1939, *Le Temps* might have been taken to represent the political views of the extreme left. Bloch, *L'étrange défaite*, pp. 184–5.

The EMA assumed that Blum, known for his domestic anti-fascism, would be exclusively partisan in the matter of dealings with Mussolini. In fact, Blum tried from June 1936 to distance his government from questions involving Italian internal affairs. His initial position *vis-à-vis* Italy, which did not markedly diverge from that of his predecessors, was resolutely non-ideological. The exact timing of the collapse of the Blum Government's hopes for entente with Italy – the fiasco over returning the Italian delegation to Geneva – is noteworthy: September 1936, not from early Italian involvement in the Spanish war, but from the period in which the German anti-Bolshevik crusade became diplomatically effective in Rome. The choice for Blum, when it came, was imposed by Mussolini in ideological terms, an Italian entente dependent on Blum's acceptance of a Francoist régime in Spain.

Until summer 1936, Italy had represented the allied option involving for France the greatest number of immediate advantages, and equally importantly, the least number of choices. During the brief, untroubled period of Franco-Italian relations before the onset of the wars over Ethiopia and Spain, French external conceptions – military, diplomatic, and economic – had been all of one piece in their reliance on Italy to restore France's Central European ties. The military and diplomatic consequences of the April 1934 note were matched by projects for Central European economic federation, based on the merger of the Italian-sponsored Rome Protocol and the French-sponsored Petite Entente. A long-term consequence of this economic deference to Italy was that Italian and Czech commerce cancelled each other out – to Germany's benefit – in the sensitive Yugoslav market.

Of the permanent servants of the state, the EMA was the most consistently Italophile. It transposed the dangerous ideological problem on to the plane of peace and war, with damaging implications for the defence of Czechoslovakia. Thus, in December 1936, Gamelin and Daladier agreed that the Italian entente meant peace, whereas a Soviet alliance implicitly meant war, and war in the west. This mentality pre-dated the Spanish Civil War, as is shown by the relative values already lent the phrase 'encirclement of Germany' by the EMA in June 1936: if realised with Italy, giving France the largest possibilities of manoeuvre; if realised with a Soviet military alliance, providing Hitler with a motive for aggression.[5]

---

[5] Schw., 1SC2 Dr9, 25 June 1936.

The Spanish war then caught Paris in an ideological cul-de-sac in which German and Soviet pressures amplified each other. It was lashed by Soviet rumours of immediate German attack in the west, as part of the Soviet campaign for a military pact; the Soviets combined these rumours with threats of unrestricted Comintern action in France. Soviet pressures on French internal and external policies grew heavier in 1937, but from autumn 1936 the EMA saw Soviet overtures for a military pact as manipulation to bring about a Franco-German war. For its part, wary of the Soviet underside of the Franco-Petite Entente negotiations, the Quai d'Orsay warned Moscow of the spread of a psychosis, generated by fear of Central European Front populaires (or *Frentes populars*), and tending to neutralise the formation of a coalition in defence of Czechoslovakia.[6] Coulondre's warning in November 1936 against a 'paralysis of the cooperation of pacific powers' also showed the persistence of the Quai d'Orsay's hope of being able to negotiate with Germany from a position of strength.

The EMA's stance was similarly constant: avoidance of any course which would bring a German attack in the west. Its unrequited attachment to Italy deepened as the Spanish conflict intensified its revulsion at the USSR and its wariness of Soviet designs. Notwithstanding the Quai d'Orsay's consternation at the Italian *volte-face* and continuing military fears after the Rambouillet accords of a Polish-German bloc, Schweisguth in 1936–7 lectures at the 'Collège des Hautes Etudes de Défense Nationale' treated Italy and Poland as volatile but indispensable elements of victory. His talk of geographical realities, itself an expression of the EMA's fixation on a war of extended fronts, served to refute any possibility of direct French action on behalf of Czechoslovakia. Schweisguth dismissed arguments, such as Victor de Lacroix's, that France's position as a great power depended on its resistance to German predations in Czechoslovakia, with redoubled insistence that only Italy could remedy the dilemmas of French impotence in Central Europe.

The preceding pages have examined Blum's year in power in relation to Barthou's policy towards Italy and the USSR; the ways in which this policy came apart in 1936–7; the importance of ideology, internally and externally, to this disintegration, and its

---

[6] Cf. the statement after Munich by a Czech commentator which traced the 'main cause of our national defeat' to the fact that 'a counter-revolution against the social revolution is sweeping through Europe', a counter-revolution which overwhelmed Czechoslovakia. Jan Slávik, cited in Bartošek, 'Could We Have Fought?', p. 105.

implications for the problem of defending Czechoslovakia. The ultimate French response to the Czechs' plight, as the Yugoslav Minister in Paris caustically observed in the summer of 1937, depended on what Paris was prepared to say not in Prague, but in Berlin.[7] Pragmatically speaking, it rested on Paris's estimate of the likelihood of reaching an acceptable settlement over the Sudeten-deutsch question, and, to this estimate, Paris's long-term desires for a general settlement with Germany were highly relevant. Since Barthou's day, Paris had sought multilateral regional pacts with Germany, to which arms limitation and some form of German-Soviet non-aggression undertaking were capital. Blum in 1936, in this as in other respects, followed in the footsteps of his predecessors. For the continuities in Blum's policy, it is revealing to compare a conversation in Warsaw between Laval and Göring in May 1935 with Blum's August 1936 conversation in Paris with Schacht.

Laval's remarks to Göring at Piłsudski's funeral did not cover colonial or financial settlements, as Blum's were to do a year later, but proceeding in his fashion from Barthou's diplomacy, Laval both pressed Göring for a multilateral agreement on Austria, and sought to transform the Franco-Soviet pact into a general non-aggression pact. Laval's line in May 1935 was collectivist. He rejected Göring's overtures for a bilateral Franco-German entente by arguing for German inclusion in European-wide security arrangements: 'We make these pacts because in our view, peace can only exist if it exists in all regions of Europe... But you must understand, since we want peace, that we cannot want it with you alone; *you must also want to make peace with the other states.*'[8]

The primordial element in Laval's approach to Germany, arms limitation, appeared starkly in the November 1935 meeting of the *Haut Comité militaire*, when he argued that, given German re-armament, neglect of direct conversations would be imprudent. Whereas Laval's conversation with Göring had been unplanned, Schacht's visit to Paris, which followed another escalation in the German military buildup, had a very specific context: the French reading of the German economic conjuncture, and hopes that the French devaluation of September 1936 would lead to an international economic conference and a disarmament settlement. As did Laval, Blum insisted on the interdependent nature of

[7] DDF II, 6, no. 141.
[8] MAE, Papiers Rochat, 'Pologne', Laval-Göring conversation, 18 May 1935; italics in the original.

peace, although he defended with more ardour the importance of the Soviet tie and the necessity of a German-Soviet non-aggression undertaking. And, like Laval, although less fatalistically, Blum saw the issue of arms limitation as central. His talk of a colonial settlement was part of an ambitious plan to restore the German economy to a peacetime footing. More integrated financially and politically than Laval's desultory talk with Göring, Blum's conversation with Schacht sought to lift the German commercial mortgage in Central Europe, as well as to obtain security guarantees for France's allies.

Alongside the policy of non-intervention in Spain, Blum's willingness to meet with Schacht has been perhaps the most criticised aspect of his external policy, and with reason. In addition, Blum is often faulted for talking with Hitler rather than Mussolini. With both Berlin and Rome, Blum's position was non-ideological, as he took pains to impress upon Hjalmar Schacht. His personal fault, then, was to underestimate the supreme importance of ideology, while overestimating the power of rationality. But it is also true that, in 1936–7, he set greater store by détente with Germany than by Italy's friendship. In reductionist terms, Germany was the greater threat to peace. Another historical criticism has been Blum's lingering attraction to arms limitation. While serious French rearmament began under his first government, it was a two-edged sword, indispensable to armed resistance, but also to the position constantly sought by French diplomacy, negotiation from a position of strength. The challenge, as he came to see it, was to construct a non-ideological, ethical foreign policy which would strive to keep the peace while accepting the real risk of war.[9] A *Bildungsroman* of Blum in power emerges when one juxtaposes his disillusionment with Schacht's second voyage to Paris in May 1937, with his decision in the same month to order discreet staff talks with the USSR. Blum's

---

[9] The language of ethics as applied to foreign policy was in this period even more morally ambiguous than ordinarily, as aggressors and arch-appeasers also spoke of rights and dealt, selectively, in victimisation – in this case, the right of national self-determination and the 'victimisation' of the Sudetendeutsch at the hands of Czech bureaucrats. Such talk served to cloud rather than clarify underlying power political issues, by obscuring the extent to which facile moralists in fact sympathised with the 'lost overdog', the invasive Nazi protectors of the Sudetendeutsch minority. This was brutally used by Hitler to bring the Czech state to its knees. For examples of the misappropriation of such language in Great Britain, which for a time generally discredited its use, Martin Gilbert, *The Roots of Appeasement* (London, 1966); on the philosophical difficulties of such language in public life, see Václav Havel's speech on receiving the 1989 Friedenpreis des Deutschen Buchandels, 'Words on Words', *The New York Review of Books*, 18 January 1990.

decision signified a willingness to contemplate a war against Hitler, a war likely to be fought over Czechoslovakia.

The break in this string of direct Franco-German contacts came in November 1937, during conversations between Bonnet, Chautemps, and Papen. While lamenting Blum's failure with Schacht, Bonnet made remarks which outwardly resembled Blum's, notably on the desire for a general settlement, as well as German colonial demands, transatlanticism, and the need to reintegrate Germany into the world economy. But Bonnet sought a very different sort of German undertaking in the east: the pacific, tolerable extension of German influence in Austria and Czechoslovakia, as long as German aims were limited, and there were no surprises.

Two months earlier, while in Prague at the funeral of the founder of the inter-war Czech state, Thomas Masaryk, Blum had been sounded on the eventuality of German action on the Spanish model in aid of Henlein's Sudetendeutsch. He had then reiterated the position maintained by his government in 1937, that German intervention would be a *casus foederis*, while indicating that he could only speak personally. The Germans lost no time in obtaining more satisfying semi-official assurances, Franz von Papen arriving in Paris in November. In his confidential interchanges with Chautemps and Bonnet, conversations to which Blum was a stranger, there was no mention of the USSR, while Franco's imminent victory in Spain was described as a relief.[10]

EPILOGUE: LÉON BLUM AND CZECHOSLOVAKIA, 1938

In the last years of the Spanish and Czechoslovak republics, between 1937 and 1939, perceptions of the Czech problem were moulded by analogies between the two states engulfed by Fascist violence and intimidation. For many in French ruling circles, as Delbos's remarks at the opening of the preceding chapter demonstrate, the indelible marking of the Czech crisis with a Spanish imprint shaped the diplomatic perceptions which led to Munich in September 1938. Blum rejected the drift of such comparisons between Czechoslovakia and Spain. In the light of his acceptance of the increased risk of war, he wanted to see important distinctions between Czechoslovakia and Spain. As he recalled in 1947:

[10] In the way of assurances on French internal unrest, a subject which had also exercised Blum, Chautemps's were strongly authoritarian: 'The Army would shoot'. DGFP, D, 1, no. 22, 63.

[Spain and Czechoslovakia]...were very difficult to compare with each other, or to weigh in relation to each other. Both in different forms and under different aspects posed in reality the same problem, but to hold out in the Czechoslovak affair, we could count on the cohesion of French opinion and on the support of the majority of the European powers which we had always been unable to realise in the Spanish affair.[11]

The direction of Blum's efforts in 1938 was determined by this dual agenda: the fostering of national consensus around the Czech issue and of an Anglo-French-Soviet front.

On 12 March 1938, Hitler bloodlessly invaded his Austrian homeland. The Czechs received word of the Anschluss without illusion. The correspondent of one of several Alsatian-based intelligence organisations in Prague reported that the usually voluble Beneš, on hearing an account of events in Vienna, had put down the receiver without a word. The most 'dynamic' elements of opinion, the correspondent continued, considered that it was henceforth necessary to make immediate contact with Berlin, and to organise the modifications to internal and external Czech policy which the German government would be bound to suggest. The Central European horror began: as a first satisfaction to the Reich, the Czech frontier was closed to Austrian refugees.[12]

At the Anschluss, France found itself without a government. Blum immediately attempted to form a supra-ideological government, ranging from the Right Nationalists to the Communists, 'appropriate to the circumstances' in Central Europe. Before reluctant members of the profoundly pacifist national council of the SFIO and before parliamentary deputies previously opposed to the Front populaire, his pleas for a coalition of national unity were characterised by the dualism which defined his position on Czechoslovakia in 1938. To ensure national unity, he undertook to do all that could be done to save the peace, but his insistence on

---

[11] *CE Témoignages*, I, p. 255. Blum's post-war remarks would have been influenced by knowledge of Soviet overflight of Roumania during the Munich crisis, as well as of the British tandem with France in late September 1938. His views on the cohesion of French political opinion, however, reflect his consistent misreading of Daladier's policies, see below, p. 318, n. 18.

[12] SHA, 7N2522, 'Institut d'études européennes de Strasbourg', 12 March 1938. The push for some accommodation with Berlin supported by Hodža and the Agrarians after the Anschluss exemplifies the 'policy of bio-social survival' which led the same circles to opt for cooperation with Germany after Munich. The phrase is that of the Czech writer Vojtěch Kořán, cited in Bartošek, 'Could We Have Fought?', pp. 105, 109.

Communist participation was explicitly justified in terms of the requirements of national rearmament and the eventuality of war.

Paul Reynaud attempted to persuade those who worried about Communist participation in such a government: 'It is not Stalin who enters Vienna today, who will menace Prague tomorrow, it is Hitler.' A speech by Pierre-Etienne Flandin, however, doomed Blum's project and vindicated the prediction made to Papen by various politicians of the Right in November 1937: a government of national union could only be achieved in France in case of a direct threat to its own borders. Behind the French Right's prediction to Papen was a more widespread view, pernicious but difficult to combat. Yvon Delbos, the former Foreign Minister, lobbied against Blum's plan, telling deputies that 'the Communists, frightened by their defeat in Spain, and the Jews, hunted down everywhere, are searching for salvation in a world war'.[13]

After offering to step down in favour of a broader national government, Blum formed a brief second government (13 March–8 April 1938). Virtually its first external act was to publicise its assurance to the Czech Minister in Paris that France would maintain 'effectively, immediately and fully all its obligations towards Czechoslovakia by a treaty known to all'.[14] The transmission of these assurances to London resulted in a predictable response: what would France do for Czechoslovakia? To answer this question, Blum and Paul-Boncour, his new Foreign Minister, assembled the CPDN.

The 15 March 1938 CPDN is commonly regarded as the epitome of the futility of foreign policy deliberations under the Third Republic. The topics of discussion were Czechoslovakia and Spain. Paul-Boncour opened the meeting by explaining the recent interchange with London. A discussion, abbreviated in the military transcript, ensued on the strategic repercussions of the Anschluss and a greater German troop commitment in Spain. Linkage of Czechoslovakia and Spain in this discussion arose from a question posed by Blum as to the effects of increased German involvement in Spain on any French action on behalf of Czechoslovakia. The Minister of Defence, Daladier, a late arrival, then delivered a set piece on the indefensibility of Czechoslovakia. Without any apparent link (according to the official transcript), discussion then passed on to Spain. Its underlying assumption was Franco's victory, as was

---

[13] Colton, *Léon Blum*, pp. 292–7; John Sherwood, *Georges Mandel and the Third Republic* (Palo Alto, 1970), p. 204; Paul Reynaud, *Mémoires*, vol. 2, *Envers and contre tous* (Paris, 1963), p. 196.   [14] DDF II, 8, no. 432, note 1.

shown when Paul-Boncour asked about the consequences of Franco's total success and his collusion with Germany and Italy. Blum, for whom it was emotionally punishing to watch the Spanish Republic go down in defeat, asked what could be done for the Loyalists. The line of his questioning concentrated on the problem of foreign intervention, only to conclude wearily that the Spanish situation had reached a point at which Franco no longer needed foreign military aid. His conclusion on Czechoslovakia was to ask the British to bring their good offices to bear on Belgium, to facilitate a French offensive on behalf of the Czechs, and on Roumania, to enable the Soviets to aid Czechoslovakia. Blum, who welcomed Litvinov's subsequent proposal for an international conference on Czechoslovakia, repeatedly alluded in the meeting to the Soviet factor. Gamelin systematically dismissed these allusions to Soviet aid. Gamelin then joined Daladier and Léger in closing ranks to prevent further unilateral declarations of support for Czechoslovakia. Franco's imminent victory in Spain frightened the three into believing that France, encircled on the Rhine, Alps, and Pyrenees, could not afford the two-front war for Czechoslovakia vital to its own security. Hitler's gamble in the Spanish war – that German action against Czechoslovakia depended on France's absorption in the complications of the Spanish situation – had succeeded.[15] Léger's *mot d'ordre* on Spain was to be binding for Czechoslovakia as well: 'for us it can only be a question of reaction and not of initiative'.

Outside the constraints of the CPDN, Blum and Paul-Boncour worked to resuscitate France's moribund relations with Italy. Under political pressure to fill the post of ambassador to Rome vacant since his first government, Blum's desire to reopen channels with Italy also had a clear Central European referent, in the EMA's position after the Anschluss that effective, direct action on behalf of Czechoslovakia would only be possible with Italian neutrality or friendship. Blum's willingness to negotiate with Italy at this juncture suggests not only inner knowledge that the cause of the Spanish Republic was lost, but awareness that Czechoslovakia would henceforth be uppermost in his calculations.[16]

Blum's second attempt within the month to confront the Central

---

[15] Ibid., no. 446; Paul-Boncour, *Entre deux guerres*, III, pp. 86–93. Cf. François-Poncet's December 1936 account of the close attention which the Germans were paying to events in Spain: 'For the Reich to risk a military operation in Czechoslovakia, it is important that France not have free hands. [Germany] hopes that General Franco will increasingly occupy and absorb it.' MAE, 717, 8 December 1936.

[16] Paul-Boncour, *Entre deux guerres*, III, pp. 70–6.

European crisis failed in short order. To underwrite its commitment to Czechoslovakia, the second Blum Government projected a major rearmament programme more ambitious in scope than that which it had launched in September 1936. Blum acknowledged:

a kind of tragic irony that a nation devoted to peace and human progress is compelled to strain and concentrate all its resources for a gigantic military effort. We have not wanted this; our thoughts have turned away from it with aversion and with horror... But we shall prove that free peoples can rise to... their duties... We shall proceed in such a way that... in the very midst of this painful task... the work of social solidarity and human fraternity shall be continued...[17]

His second government fell when the Senate denied Blum powers to pursue all-out rearmament underpinned by financing organised on a Keynesian basis.

Czechoslovakia remained an abiding concern for Blum once he was out of office after April 1938. In a June speech at Royan to the SFIO congress, he expressed approval of Daladier's search for a Czech settlement, which settlement, in Blum's view, would involve a modest degree of cultural autonomy for the Sudetendeutsch. His approval of Daladier's Czech policy was heavily coloured by concern that France not find itself without a government as at the Anschluss. At Royan, Blum applauded Daladier's firmness during the 21 May crisis when the Czechs had partially mobilised at rumours of a German buildup on their frontier, and right into September 1938, he acted in 'loyal opposition', conferring with Daladier on the Czech crisis.[18] At the same time, Blum's evocations at Royan and elsewhere of the Franco-Soviet treaty functioned as shorthand for commitment to the ultimate defence of Czechoslovakia. He reiterated the position he had held since May 1937: the primary diplomatic task of the French Government was to mediate between London and Moscow. Despite powerful emotional remnants of his

[17] L. Blum, Populaire, 5 April 1938.
[18] Blum later confessed puzzlement at Daladier's almost aggressive post-war assumption of responsibility for Munich. He told the 1947 parliamentary commission that, to his knowledge, Daladier's attitude did not correspond to reality, Daladier having been infinitely less munichois than he boasted. With Mandel as well as with Blum, Daladier concealed the profound ambivalence with regard to Czechoslovakia which had shown itself with the British in April 1937. Blum's perception of him as prepared to go to war for Czechoslovakia directly influenced his acceptance of Daladier's refusal to summon the Chambre des Députés in early September 1938. (Blum confided to a British Labour leader at the time that parliamentary speeches by Flandin and Caillaux might weaken rather than strengthen the will of the government.) CE Témoignages I, p. 255; Georges Wormser, Georges Mandel (Paris, 1967), pp. 220–1; Adamthwaite, France, p. 127.

conditional pacifism, Blum had pointed words on the perils of pacifism: 'I know very well that to see the idea of collective security through to the very end is to accept a risk of war. But I say, and I say this as a man whom one will call "Blum the warmonger"... that to avoid war, it is necessary, at certain times, to accept running the risk of it.'[19]

The acute phase of the Czech crisis opened with the Sudeten-deutsch uprising of 12–13 September, which was promptly quelled by the Czech Army. Blum praised Daladier's avoidance of a French mobilisation in mid September. His reluctance to see France mobilise before Germany became involved reflected an irrepressible hope that a generalised conflict might be averted. Timely and calibrated use of Czech force might not only avoid a deepening of the crisis, as was widely believed to have happened during the 21 May episode. It might also increase the chance of a viable Czech-German agreement.

The following days were striated by tragic internal divisions in Czechoslovakia. Spurred by Chamberlain's pilgrimage to Berchtes-gaden, Beneš indeed followed the declaration of martial law on Henlein's insurrection with a peace initiative delivered by Jaromír Nečas, a Social Democrat in his government, to Blum. On the eve of the Franco-British summit on Hitler's Berchtesgaden demands, Blum agreed to give Daladier a map sent by Beneš via Nečas. Beneš's map indicated not an undefined willingness to offer concessions, but the final limits of territorial concessions he was prepared to make. The purpose of the Nečas mission was the drawing of a line beyond which the Czechs should not be subjected to further Franco-British pressure, beyond which France would maintain its engagements in an act of self-preserving altruism, by carrying on a two-front war against Germany. When French concessions in London instead went beyond the boundaries of the map brought by Nečas, French pressures on Prague reopened splits within the Czech Government and the Czech military. These splits mirrored those in France.[20]

---

[19] *L'oeuvre*, IV-2, p. 151.

[20] These splits included not only ideological divides and the question of the centuries' old Czech-German symbiosis, issues particularly to influence the Agrarians under Milan Hodža, but also a history and cultural tradition which tended to compromise rather than to take up arms, a desire always to avert bloodshed as against what appeared to many Czechs in 1938 a categorical imperative to resist. These complex psychological factors, amounting to a struggle for identity in the Czech case, are explored in a brilliantly suggestive essay by Karel Bartošek, 'Could We Have Fought? – The "Munich Complex"

Actuated in part by old fears that Beneš would turn to the Soviets, Premier Hodža requested an ultimatum from Bonnet. Only allied pressures, he argued, would enable Prague to bow to the inevitable and accept the Anglo-French plan which completely disregarded the limits of Beneš's concessions.[21]

At this moment, surely one of the most painful in Franco-Czech relations between 1918 and 1938, Blum was again drawn in. Caught off guard by Hodža's appeal to Paris and in shock at the delivery of the allied ultimata, Beneš turned to Nečas and Hubert Ripka, who urged opposition to the Franco-British proposals. According to Ripka: 'Convinced that we would be able by ourselves to contain the German attack for several weeks, I hoped that public opinion in France and Great Britain would rise up against the policy of appeasement and push the governments to come to the aid of our small country.' At 3 a.m. on 21 September, Ripka and Nečas telephoned Oreste Rosenfeld of *Le Populaire* and asked him on behalf of Beneš to approach Blum and Edouard Herriot. The two senior opposition statesmen were to be told that Czechoslovakia could hold out militarily for a fortnight. Could the Czechs hope that after two weeks of battle, French opinion would change and rally to their cause? Rosenfeld saw little hope of persuading President Lebrun and the Daladier Government to rescind the ultimatum; he also was painfully aware that the government's lead would be followed by the strongly pacifist portion of the SFIO inspired by Paul Faure. He telephoned Blum, whose response indicated what both men already knew. The Czechs could not be guaranteed so rapid a change in France and her government. Rosenfeld transmitted this message early on 21 September.

Hubert Ripka in his contemporary study of Munich deplored the 'passivity' of Blum and Herriot in the face of the allied ultimata to Prague, which Ripka and Beneš had hoped would stir cabinet revolts in France and Britain. Winston Churchill, who visited Paris later on 21 September to meet with Paul Reynaud and Georges Mandel, the

in Czech Policies and Czech Thinking'. The ultimate stake for the Czechs in 1938, Bartošek's essay suggests, was the missed opportunity to play an active part in shaping their own destiny, a formulation which echoes Marc Bloch on 1940: 'Since that moment when the weapons which we held with too indeterminate a grasp fell from our hands, the future of our country and our civilisation has become the stake in a struggle of which we, for the most part, are only the rather humiliated spectators. ...'

[21] For the lengths to which Hodža was reportedly prepared to go in avoiding any aid from the Soviets, see above, p. 239; for General Syrový's extreme reluctance to allow Soviet troops on Czech soil, J. W. Wheeler-Bennett, *Knaves*, pp. 138, 153.

hard-line ministers in Daladier's cabinet, urged them not to resign. Their resignations, Churchill argued, would not alter the course of events, while they would deprive the Daladier Government of its most resolute men. Churchill shared the desire of Mandel and Reynaud for Czech resistance, on which he believed all else depended, but he did not advocate governmental crises in the democracies as a means to ensure this resistance. The leader of a party itself divided, Blum shared the view that the defence of Czechoslovakia could not be sustained by democracies pulverised by political division.[22]

As the crisis wore on, Blum's response in a series of articles in *Le Populaire* was an eddy of conflicting emotion.[23] While the Munich Conference met, Blum, despite the exclusion of the Czechs, dramatically expressed relief at the continuance of negotiations: 'The crime against humanity would be precisely to break off negotiations or to make them impossible.'[24] In an important speech before the SFIO Council several weeks after Munich, Blum did not repudiate this sense of deliverance at the maintenance of peace, from a desire to claim kinship with the most human aspects of the national experience, as well as from concern for party unity.

Knowledge of the terms of Munich led Blum to reiterate the mixture of relief and shame which he had originally expressed in an editorial of 20 September voicing indignation at the prospect of a settlement imposed on Prague. In the legislative debate on Munich, he cast his vote as a *munichois*, in an attempt he later recognised as misbegotten to maintain the SFIO's fragmented unity. The parliamentary statement Blum read on the party's behalf again

---

[22] L. Blum, *Populaire*, 23 September 1938; *CE Témoignages* I, p. 256; *Munich 1938: Revue des études slaves*, LII, 1–2, 1979, pp. 132–40; Colton, *Léon Blum*, pp. 314–16; Henri Noguères, *Munich* (London, 1965), pp. 141–57; Hubert Ripka, *Munich: Before and After* (London, 1939), pp. 189–90 and *Le Coup de Prague* (Paris, 1949), pp. 3–4.

[23] Colton's account, *Léon Blum*, pp. 316–19 is admirably balanced; see also Jacques Bariéty's more critical essay, 'Léon Blum', pp. 52–5. Colton and Bariéty have pointed out that the relevant volume of *L'oeuvre de Léon Blum* is diminished by its omission of the full range of Blum's response to the September negotiations. However, it should also be noted that, in the course of 1938, no French newspaper had devoted more extensive coverage to Czechoslovakia than *Le Populaire*. Blum had gone to great lengths to educate his readers about the power-political issues behind the Czech crisis: for example, several articles from *Lidové Noviny* by Hubert Ripka appeared in translation in their entirety in *Le Populaire*.

[24] Having earlier warned against exclusion of the Czechs as intolerable, Blum on 29 September regretted their and the Soviets' initial exclusion at Munich, but argued that discussions could be enlarged in time to include them. L. Blum, *Populaire*, 29 September 1938.

brought out conflicting sentiments of relief and shame, while attempting to reconcile the SFIO's attachment to peace with resolve to struggle for a just cause.

Only in his 8 November speech to the SFIO Council did Blum refer to his personal conviction that he would not have allowed himself to be carried by circumstances to the point of disowning France's obligations.[25] With the advantage of greater hindsight, as has been seen, a cogent historical case can be made that, given the Germans' unpreparedness for *Blitzkrieg* before their seizure of Škoda in March 1939, a determined offensive in the west on behalf of Czechoslovakia might ultimately have succeeded. In speaking as he did to the SFIO Council, perhaps Blum had his involvement in the original Nečas mission in mind. His consistent sympathy for Czechoslovakia, as well as those qualities – fidelity and a radically educable perception – which characterised his long career allow the speculation that had a French Government supported Beneš's diplomacy of only limited concessions, Blum might have counteracted the powerful current of circumstance to urge a declaration of war for Czechoslovakia.

In the months which followed, Blum publicly lingered over the mistakes of Munich, the better to undertake a strenuous policy of educating the SFIO to the exigencies of imminent war. Privately, there was no more sombre time for him in the inter-war period than March 1939, the German invasion of Prague and the fall of Madrid. Blum's 'pédagogie politique', with its stress on a Grand Alliance on the 1914 model, brought him increasingly close to Winston Churchill, who had eloquently opposed Munich in the House of Commons, while it painfully estranged him from the pacifist wing of the SFIO.[26]

For the some ten remaining years of Léon Blum's life, during their respective imprisonments, exiles and beyond, Hubert Ripka and his Alsatian-born wife, Noémi, held Blum in great personal esteem. In Noémi Ripka's view, despite his faults, Blum was more sympathetic to Czechoslovakia than any other French politician. There was not any lack of goodwill and 'certainly never incomprehension' on his part. At the beginning of the Spanish war, Hubert Ripka had been dismayed at the way in which the prospect of a European war dulled

[25] L. Blum, *Populaire*, 8 November 1938.
[26] Colton, *Léon Blum*, pp. 317–25; *A l'échelle humaine* in *L'oeuvre*, vol. V (Paris, 1955), pp. 455–6; conversation with Renée Robert Blum, 22 July 1987.

Blum's responses. Ripka feared that the War of the Spanish Obsession would divert France from Central Europe and, as he rightly saw, the essential condition of French security, presenting Germany with the danger of a war fought on two fronts. It has been suggested here that the intervening two years and the cruel disappointments of non-intervention sharpened Blum's perceptions of the high stakes involved in international negotiations and led him to growing, if incomplete, acceptance of the risk of war. This sharpening of perception accounts for his highly charged response to the events surrounding Munich.[27]

The Czechoslovak democracy was the most culturally liberal state in Central Europe, and the only ally of France with a modern, combat-ready army and the industrial strength to replenish it. In the midst of the negotiations whose aim was to avoid war, Blum, in a phrase which characteristically used the first person singular, described the mixture of national elation and shamed rush of negotiation as 'lâche soulagement', craven relief. The phrase, the most famous he ever wrote in *Le Populaire*, was more apt than his readers then or since have realised. Blum took it from François Mauriac's novel, *Le noeud de vipères*, where it signifies the craven acceptance of the death of another in the knowledge that one's own death is imminent.[28] As he had recognised in an earlier editorial in *Le Populaire* on 9 September:

For the fall of Czechoslovakia or even its definitive vassalisation is equivalent to the absorption of Central and South-eastern Europe by the German Reich. It is not France's grandeur or status as a great power which would then be menaced – I have not learned to make use of such formulas – but its security and its liberty.[29]

[27] Conversation with Noémi Hubert Ripka, 5 February 1979.
[28] L. Blum, *Populaire*, 20 September 1938; F. Mauriac, *Le noeud de vipères* (Paris, 1932), pp. 237–8. The textual identification is the present author's.
[29] L. Blum, *Populaire*, 9 September 1938.

Bibliography

PRIMARY SOURCES

UNPUBLISHED

French Archives

Archives de l'Assemblée Nationale
    Commission des Affaires étrangères:
    15th Legislature, 1932–6
    16th Legislature, 1936–40
Archives Nationales de France
    Papiers Joseph Paul-Boncour
    Papiers Paul Reynaud
    Papiers Général Victor-Henri Schweisguth
Bibliothèque de documentation internationale contemporaine
    Papiers Lucien Lamoureux
Bibliothèque Nationale
    Papiers Pierre-Etienne Flandin
    Papiers Marcel Déat
Fondation Nationale des Sciences Politiques
    Papiers Léon Blum
    Papiers Edouard Daladier
Ministère des Affaires étrangères
    Dossiers of 1934–5 being assembled for publication in Documents
    diplomatiques français
    Dossiers, 1934–5:
    Société des nations 770, 806
    Pologne
    Roumanie
    Tchécoslovaquie
    Yougoslavie
    Série B: Relations commerciales
    1937 Exposition
    Importations en France
    Série C: Relations commerciales
    Pologne
    Tchécoslovaquie

Série Z: Allemagne 1930–40
Papiers André Tardieu
Papiers Fouques-Duparc, 1940
Série papiers d'agents:
  Alexis Léger
  René Massigli
  Léon Noël
  André d'Ormesson
  Charles Rochat
Ministère des Finances
  Direction du Mouvement général des Fonds, 1935–7
  Dossiers, 1932–7:
    Tchécoslovaquie
    Yougoslavie
  Dévaluation du franc, 1936
  Balance commerciale française, 1934–8
  Allemagne
  Clearing franco-allemand (SICAP)
  Italie
Service historique de l'armée de l'air
  Fonds 'Collaboration avec les pays étrangers', 1932–9:
    Italie
    Pologne
    Roumanie
    Tchécoslovaquie
    Yougoslavie
  Rapport Loizeau: Manoeuvres en l'URSS 1935
Service historique de l'armée de terre
  Cabinet du ministre
  Comité permanent de la Défense nationale
  Conseil supérieur de la Défense nationale
  Conseil supérieur de la Guerre
  Haut Comité militaire
  Etat-Major de l'Armée, 2e Bureau
  Attachés militaires, 1935–7:
    Pologne
    Roumanie
    Tchécoslovaquie
    Yougoslavie
  Fonds Jean Fabry
  Fonds Gamelin, 1935–9
  EM Georges
  Politique de défense jusqu'en août 1939
  Armée française du Rhin 1923–30
  Mobilisation

British Archives

Churchill College, Cambridge
 Eric Phipps Papers
Private Collections
 Privately printed diaries of Thomas Jones
 (courtesy of Tristan Lloyd Jones)
Public Records Office, London
 FO 371, Foreign Office General Correspondence 1935–7:
  Czechoslovakia
  France
  Italy
  Poland
  Roumania
  USSR
  Yugoslavia
 FO 954, Anthony Eden Papers
 CAB 23, Cabinet Minutes and Conclusions
 CAB 24, Cabinet Memoranda

American Archives

National Archives, Washington DC
 Captured Czechoslovak documents in T-120
Hoover Institution
 Nicolas Titulesco Papers

Interviews and Correspondence

Armand Bérard, Ambassadeur de France: Member of Cabinet du ministre, M.A.e., under Yvon Delbos, June 1936–June 1937.
Hubert Beuve-Méry: Correspondent of *Le Temps* and of the Comité alsacien d'études et d'information in Prague; Professor, Institut français de Prague.
Renée Blum: Daughter-in-law of Léon Blum; wife of Robert Blum, emissary of Léon Blum to Belgrade, December 1936.
Etienne de Crouy-Chanel: Private Secretary of Alexis Léger, 1932–9.
Jacques Daridan: Secretary, French Legation in Prague, 1936–8.
Roger Glachant: Member of successive Cabinets du ministres, M.A.e., under Herriot, Paul-Boncour, Daladier, Barthou, Laval and Flandin, 1932–6.
Jean Laloy: Attaché, Consulate in Tallinn, 1937; in Moscow, 1940.
Renée Maly: Private Secretary of Léon Noël and Victor de Lacroix, Ministers of France in Prague, 1934–8.
René Massigli, Ambassadeur de France: Assistant Director for Political and Commercial Affairs, M.A.e., 1933–7; Director, 1937–8.
Pierre Mendès France: Sous-Secrétaire, Ministère des Finances, Second Léon Blum Government, 1938.

Jules Moch: Secrétaire-Général, Présidence du Conseil, June 1936–June 1937.

Léon Noël, Ambassadeur de France: Director of Laval's Cabinet du Ministre, 1931; Minister in Prague, 1932–5; brought back from the field as special diplomatic counsellor to the government and Secrétaire-Général, Présidence du Conseil, January-April 1935; Ambassador to Poland, 1935–9.

Jean Pasquier: Correspondent of *Le Petit Parisien* in Prague; Professor, Institut français de Prague.

Noémi Ripka: Professor, Institut français de Prague; wife of Hubert Ripka, correspondent for *Lidové noviny* and emissary of Beneš.

Marie Lacroix-Rist: Daughter of Victor de Lacroix, the last French Minister in Prague before the war.

Noël Rist: Son of Charles Rist, Governor of the Banque de France, financial advisor to numerous governments.

Henry Rollet: Representative of the Banque franco-polonaise in Poland.

Louise Weiss: Director, *L'Europe Nouvelle*.

PUBLISHED

Documentary Collections

Documents diplomatiques belges, 1920–1940, 5 vols., Commission royale d'histoire, Brussels, 1964–6.

Documents diplomatiques français, 1st Series (1932–5); 2nd Series (1936–9), edited under the direction of P. Renouvin, J.-B. Duroselle and M. Baumont for the Commission de publication des documents relatifs aux origines de la guerre 1939–45, Imprimerie nationale, 1963 *et seq.*

Documents on British Foreign Policy 1919–1939, 2nd Series (1930–7); 3rd Series (1938–9), edited under the direction of E. L. Woodward and R. Butler, HMSO, 1946 *et seq.*

Documents on German Foreign Policy, 1918–45, Series C, (1933–7), HMSO, 1957 *et seq.*

Europäische Politik, 1933–39, im Spiegel der Prager Akten, edited by Fritz Berber, Essen, 1941.

Les événements survenus en France de 1933 à 1945. Rapport présenté par M. Charles Serre, Député au nom de la Commission d'enquête parlementaire, 2 vols.; Témoinages et documents recueillis par la Commission d'enquête parlementaire, 9 vols., Presses universitaires de France, 1947–52.

Foreign Relations of the United States. Diplomatic papers. 1936, vol. I; 1937, vol. I; Government Printing Office, Washington DC, 1953, 1954.

Situazione politica nel 1935, *Francia*, St. Antony's Papers, St. Antony's College, Oxford.

Sovetsko-frantsuzskie otnocheniia, 1941–1945, Moscow, 1959.

The Struggle of the USSR for Collective Security in Europe during 1933–5, *International Affairs*, nos. 6, 7, 8, 10, Moscow, 1963.

Reference Works, Yearbooks

Annuaire diplomatique et consulaire de la République française, volumes for 1919–39, Imprimerie nationale.
Jolly, Jean: *Dictionnaire des parlementaires français 1889–1940*, 6 vols., Presses universitaires de France, 1960–77.
Tableau général du Commerce et de la Navigation, vols. for 1935–7, Imprimerie nationale.
Toynbee, Arnold J.: *Survey of International Affairs* 1920–3 *et seq.*, British Institute of International Affairs, Oxford University Press, 1925–53.

Le Populaire de Paris

BOOKS AND ARTICLES

Note: All works written in French are published in Paris, and all those written in English are published in London unless otherwise stated.

Adamthwaite, Anthony: *France and the Coming of the Second World War*, 1977.
The Making of the Second World War, 1979.
The Lost Peace: International Relations in Europe 1918–1939, 1980.
Alexander, Donald: 'Repercussions of the Breda Variant, (May 1940)', *French Historical Studies*, Spring 1974.
Alexander, M. S. and Graham, H. (eds.): *The French and Spanish Popular Fronts*, Cambridge, 1989.
Alexander, M. S.: 'Les réactions à la menace stratégique allemande en Europe occidentale: la Grande-Bretagne, la Belgique et le "Cas Hollande" (décembre 1938–février 1939)', *Cahiers d'histoire de la seconde querre mondiale*, no. 7, 1982.
'Soldiers and socialists the French officer corps and leftist government, 1935–7', in M. S. Alexander and H. Graham (eds.), *The French and Spanish Popular Fronts*, Cambridge, 1989.
Aloisi, Baron Pompeo: *Journal, 25 juillet 1932–14 juin 1936*, trans. Maurice Vaussard, ed. Mario Toscano, 1957.
Amaury, Philippe: *Les deux premières expériences d'un 'Ministère de l'information' en France*, 1969.
Aron, Raymond: *Mémoires*, 1983.
Artaud, Denise: *La question des dettes interalliées et la reconstruction de l'Europe 1917–1929*, Lille, 1978.
Audry, Colette: *Léon Blum ou la politique du juste: essai*, 1955.
Bankwitz, Philip Charles Farwell: *Maxime Weygand and Civil-Military Relations in Modern France*, Cambridge, Mass., 1967.
Bariéty, Jacques: 'Léon Blum et l'Allemagne', in *Les relations franco-allemandes 1933–1939*, 1976.
Les relations franco-allemandes après la première guerre mondiale, 1977.
'La France et le problème de l'Anschluss mars 1936–mars 1938',

Deutschland und Frankreich 1936–9, 15. Deutsch-französisches Historikerkolloquium, Bonn, 1978.

Barré, Jean-Luc: *Le seigneur-chat: Philippe Berthelot 1866–1934*, 1988.

Barros, James: *Betrayal from Within: Joseph Avenol, Secretary-General of the League of Nations, 1933–1940*, New Haven, 1969.

Bartošek, Karel: 'Could We Have Fought? – The "Munich Complex" in Czech Policies and Czech Thinking', in Norman Stone and Eduard Strouhal (eds.), *Czechoslovakia: Crossroads and Crises, 1918–88*, 1989.

Beaud, Claud: 'Schneider et l'union européenne industrielle et financière au lendemain de la première guerre mondiale', Colloque de Nanterre, 1977.

Beck, Jósef: *Dernier rapport*, Neuchâtel, 1951.

Bédarida, François: 'La "gouvernante anglaise"', in René Rémond and Janine Bourdin (eds.), *Edouard Daladier chef du gouvernement*, 1977.

Beneš, Edouard: *The Memoirs of Dr. Beneš*, 1954.

Bérard, Armand: *Au temps du danger allemand*, 1976.

Bernard, Philippe: *La fin d'un monde 1914–1929*, 1975.

Beuve-Méry, Hubert: *Réflexions politiques 1932–1951*, 1951.

Birnbaum, P.: *Un mythe politique: 'la République juive'*, 1988.

Bloch, Marc: *L'étrange défaite*, 1946.

Strange Defeat, trans. Gerard Hopkins, Oxford, 1949.

Blum, Léon: *Du mariage*, 1907.

Souvenirs sur l'affaire, 1935.

L'histoire jugera, Montreal, 1943.

L'oeuvre de Léon Blum, vols. IV, parts 1 and 2; V, ed. Robert Blum, 1955, 1964–5.

Bodin, Louis and Touchard, Jean: *Front populaire 1936*, 1985.

Bonnefous, Edouard: *Histoire politique de la Troisième République*, vols. V (1930–6), VI (1936–8), 1962, 1965.

Bonnet, Georges: *The Quai d'Orsay*, 1965.

Vingt ans de vie politique 1918–38: de Clemenceau à Daladier, 1969.

Dans la tourmente 1938–1948, 1971.

Bouffotot, Patrice: 'Le haut commandement français et l'alliance franco – soviétique (1933–39)', Congrès international d'histoire militaire et d'études de Défense nationale, Montpellier, 1981.

Boyce, Robert and Robertson, E. M. (eds.): *Paths to War*, 1989.

Brassié, Anne: *Robert Brasillach ou encore un instant de bonheur*, 1987.

Bullitt, Orville H. (ed.): *For the President, Personal and Secret*, Boston, 1972.

Bury, J. P. T.: *France: the Insecure Peace*, 1972.

Butterworth, Susan Bindoff: 'Daladier and the Munich Crisis: a Reappraisal', *JCH*, IX, 3, July 1974.

Cairns, J. C.: 'Along the Road Back to France, 1940', *American Historical Review*, LIV, 3, 1959.

Cameron, Elizabeth: 'Alexis Saint-Léger Léger', in Gordon A. Craig and Felix Gilbert (eds.), *The Diplomats*, vol. II, New York, 1974.

Carlton, David: 'Eden, Blum and the Origins of Non-Intervention', *JCH*, VI, 3, 1971.

Carmi, Ozer: *La Grande Bretagne et la Petite Entente*, Geneva, 1972.

Carr, E. H.: *Twilight of the Comintern 1930–1935*, New York, 1982.

Challener, Richard: 'The French Foreign Office: the Era of Philippe Berthelot', in Gordon A. Craig and Felix Gilbert (eds.), *The Diplomats*, vol. I, New York, 1974.

Chambrun, Charles de: *Traditions et souvenirs*, 1952.

Chastenet, Jacques: *Histoire de la Troisième République: Déclin de la Troisième 1931–1938*, 1962.

Quatre fois vingt ans, 1974.

Chauvel, Jean: *Commentaire: de Vienne à Alger 1938–1944*, 1971.

Churchill, Winston S.: *The Second World War: the Gathering Storm*, Boston, 1948.

Ciano, Galeazzo: *Ciano's Diplomatic Papers*, ed. Malcolm Muggeridge, 1948.

Cienciala, Anna: 'The Significance of the Declaration of Non-Aggression of January 26, 1934 in Polish-German and International Relations: a Reappraisal', *East European Quarterly*, I, 1, 1967.

Poland and the Western Powers, 1968.

'Poland in British and French Policy in 1939: Determination to Fight or Avoid War?', *The Polish Review*, no. 3, 1989.

Claudel, Paul: *Oeuvres en prose*, 1965.

Colton, Joel: *Léon Blum: Humanist in Politics*, New York, 1966.

Colvin, Ian: *Vansittart in Office: the Origins of World War II*, 1965.

Conquest, Robert: *The Great Terror*, New York, 1968.

Conquet, Alfred: *Auprès du maréchal Pétain*, 1970.

Constant, Monique: 'L'accord commercial franco-allemand du 10 juillet 1937', *Revue d'histoire diplomatique*, nos. 1–2, 1984.

Cot, Pierre: *Le procès de la République*, New York, 1944.

Coulondre, Robert: *De Staline à Hitler: Souvenir de deux ambassades 1936–1939*, 1950.

Craig, Gordon A. and George, A.G.: *Force and Statecraft: Diplomatic Problems of Our Time*, Oxford, 1983.

Germany 1866–1945, Oxford, 1978.

and Gilbert, Felix (eds.): *The Diplomats 1919–1939*, vols. I and II, New York, 1974.

Crémieux-Brilhac, J.-L.: 'La France devant l'Allemagne et la guerre', Deutschland und Frankreich 1936–1939, 15. Deutsch-französisches Historikerkolloquium, Bonn, 1978.

Dallek, Robert: *Franklin D. Roosevelt and American Foreign Policy 1932–1945*, New York, 1979.

Dampierre, Robert de: 'Dix années de politique française à Rome', *RDM*, I, 1 November 1953; II, 15 November 1953.

'Une entente italo-yougoslave (mars 1937)', *RDM*, 1 September 1955.

Daridan, Jean: *Le chemin de la défaite*, 1980.

Debicki, Roman: 'The Remilitarization of the Rhineland and Its Impact on the Franco-Polish Alliance', *Polish Review*, XIV, 4, 1969.

Deist, Wilhelm: *The Wehrmacht and German Rearmament*, 1981.

Delmas, Col. J.: 'Les exercices du Conseil supérieur de la Guerre 1936–7 et 1937–8', *Revue historique des armées*, no. 4, 1979.

Dhers, Pierre: 'Du 7 mars 1936 à l'Ile d'Yeu', *RHDGM*, no. 5, January 1952.

Doise, Jean and Vaïsse, Maurice: *Diplomatie et outil militaire*, 1987.

Domaniewski, Wieslaw: 'Umowa w Rambouillet', *Zeszytg historyczne*, no. 47, 1979.

Doughty, R. A.: *The Seeds of Disaster: the Development of French Army Doctrine 1919–1939*, Hamden, Conn., 1985.

Dreifort, John: *Yvon Delbos at the Quai d'Orsay*, Kansas, 1973.

'The French Popular Front and the Franco-Soviet Pact 1936–37: a Dilemma in Foreign Policy', *JCH*, XI, 2 and 3, 1976.

Dubief, Henri: *Le déclin de la IIIe République 1929–1938*, 1976.

Duroselle, Jean-Baptiste: 'France and the Crisis of March 1936', in E. Acomb and Marvin Brown (eds.), *French Society and Culture Since the Old Régime*, New York, 1966.

La décadence 1932–1939, 1979.

Dutailly, Lt. Col. Henry: *Les problèmes de l'armée de terre française (1935–1939)*, 1980.

Edouard Daladier chef de gouvernement, 1977.

Emmerson, J. T.: *The Rhineland Crisis: 7 March 1936*, 1977.

Erickson, John: *The Soviet High Command*, 1962.

Fabry, Jean: *De la Place de la Concorde au Cours de l'intendance*, 1942.

Faucher, Gen. Eugène: 'Some Recollections of Czechoslovakia', *International Affairs*, XVIII, May–June 1939.

Fink, Carole: *Marc Bloch: A Life in History*, 1989.

Flandin, Pierre-Etienne: *Politique française 1919–1940*, 1947.

Frank, Pierre: *Histoire de l'Internationale communiste*, 1981.

Frankenstein, Robert: 'A propos des aspects financiers du réarmement français, 1935–39', *RDGM*, no. 102, April 1976.

Le prix du réarmement français (1935–1939), 1982.

Freymond, Jacques: *Le IIIe Reich et la réorganisation économique de l'Europe 1940–1942*, Leiden/Geneva, 1974.

Fridenson, Patrick with Lecuir, Jean: *La France et la Grande Bretagne face aux problèmes aériens 1935–mai 1940*, 1976.

Friedländer, Saul: *Reflets du Nazisme*, 1982.

Gamelin, Maurice: *Servir: le prologue du drame 1930–août 1939*, 3 vols., 1946.

Gasiorowski, Zygmunt J.: 'Did Piłsudski Attempt to Initiate a Preventive War in 1933?', *JMH*, XXVII, 2, June 1955.

Gehl, Jürgen: *Austria, Germany and the Anschluss*, Oxford, 1963.

Gellhorn, Martha: *A Stricken Field*, 1986.

Giradoux, Jean: *Bella*, 1926.

Girault, René: 'Les relations internationales et l'exercice du pouvoir pendant le Front populaire, juin 1936 – juin 1937', *Cahiers Léon Blum*, no. 1, May 1977.

'Léon Blum, la dévaluation de 1936 et la conduite de la politique extérieure de la France', Colloque de Nanterre, 1977.

'L'influence de la situation économique française sur la politique extérieure de la France 1936–1939', Anglo-German Historical Conference, Cumberland Lodge, 1980.

Goldman, Aaron L.: 'Sir Robert Vansittart's Search for Italian Co-operation against Hitler, 1933–1936', *JCH*, IX, 3, July 1974.

Gorce, Paul de la: *The French Army: A Military and Political History*, trans. K. Douglas, 1963.

Grant Duff, Shiela: *The Parting of Ways*, 1981.

Grisoni, Dominique and Hertzog, Gilles: *Les brigades de la mer*, 1979.

Guariglia, R.: *Ricordi 1922–1946*, 1950.

Gunsberg, J. A.: *Divided and Conquered: the French High Command and the Defeat of the West, 1940*, Westport, Conn., 1979.

Harvey, John: *The Diplomatic Diaries of Oliver Harvey 1937–1940*, 1970.

Haslam, Jonathan: 'The Soviet Union and the Czechoslovakian Crisis of 1938', *JCH*, XIV, 3, July 1979.

The Soviet Union and the Struggle for Collective Security in Europe, 1933–1939, 1984.

Hauner, Milan: 'Czechoslovakia as a Military Factor in British Considerations of 1938', *Journal of Strategic Studies*, II, September 1978.

'Military Budgets and the Armaments Industry', in M. C. Kaser and E. A. Radice (eds.), *The Economic History of Eastern Europe 1919–1975*, vol. II, Oxford, 1986.

Herriot, Edouard: *Jadis*, vol. II, 1952.

Hildebrand, Klaus: *The Foreign Policy of the Third Reich*, Berkeley, 1973.

Hodža, F. Milan: *Federation in Central Europe: Reflections and Reminiscences*, 1942.

Hoisington, William A. Jr: 'The Struggle for Economic Influence in Southeastern Europe: the French Failure in Roumania, 1940', *JMH*, XLIII, 3, September 1971.

Hoptner, J. B.: 'Yugoslavia as Neutralist: 1937', *Journal of Central European Affairs*, XVI, July 1956.

Yugoslavia in Crisis, 1934–1941, New York, 1962.

Horne, Alistair: *To Lose a Battle*, Boston, 1969.

Howard, Michael: *The Continental Commitment*, 1972.

Hughes, Judith M.: *To the Maginot Line: the Politics of French military preparation in the 1920s*, Cambridge, Mass., 1971.

Jackson, Julian: *The Popular Front in France: defending democracy*, Cambridge, 1988.

Jacobson, Jon: *Locarno Diplomacy: Germany and the West 1925–1929*, Princeton, 1972.

'Strategies of French Foreign Policy after World War I,' *JMH*, LV, 1, March 1983.

Jedlicka, L.: *Ein Heer Im Schatten der Parteien: die militärpolitische Lage Osterreichs*, Graz, 1955.

Jędrzejewicz, Wacław: 'The Polish Plan for a "Preventive war" against Germany in 1933', *Polish Review*, XI, 1, 1966.

Johnson, Douglas: 'Léon Blum and the Popular Front', *History*, no. 55, June 1970.

Joll, James: 'Léon Blum: the Intellectual in Politics', in *Three Intellectuals in Politics*, New York, 1960.

'The Front Populaire after Thirty Years', *JCH*, I, 2, 1966.

Europe since 1870, 1973.

Jones, F. C.: *Japan's New World Order in East Asia*, 1954.

Jordan, W. M.: *Great Britain, France and the German Problem 1918–1939*, 1971.

Kaegi, Walter: 'The Crisis in Military Historiography', *Armed Forces and Society*, VII, 2, 1981.

Kaiser, David E.: *Economic Diplomacy and the Origins of the Second World War, Germany, Britain, France and Eastern Europe 1930–1939*, Princeton, 1980.

Kaser, M. C. and Radice, E. A. (eds.): *The Economic History of Eastern Europe 1919–1975*, vol. 1, *Economic Structure and Performance Between the Wars*, vol. 2, *Interwar Policy, the War and Reconstruction*, Oxford, 1985, 1986.

Kennedy, Paul: *The Rise and Fall of the Great Powers*, New York, 1987.

Kieft, David: *Belgium's Return to Neutrality*, Oxford, 1972.

Kiszling, Rudolf: *Die Kroaten: der Schicksalsweg eines Südslawenvolkes*, Graz, 1956.

Knapp, W. F.: 'The Rhineland Crisis of March 1936', in James Joll (ed.), *The Decline of the Third Republic*, St. Antony's Papers, no. 5, 1955.

France: Partial Eclipse, 1972.

Knox, MacGregor: *Mussolini Unleashed 1939–1941*, Cambridge, 1982.

Komjathy, Anthony: *The Crises of France's East Central European Diplomacy 1933–1938*, Boulder, Colo., 1976.

Kupferman, F.: *Pierre Laval*, 1976.

Lacouture, Jean: *Léon Blum*, 1977.

Lagardelle, Hubert: *Mission à Rome*, 1955.

Larmour, Peter J.: *The French Radical Party in the 1930s*, Palo Alto, 1964.

Laroche, Jules: *La Pologne de Piłsudski: Souvenirs d'une Ambassade 1926–1935*, 1953.

Au Quai d'Orsay avec Briand et Poincaré 1913–1926, 1957.

Laval, Pierre: *Le procès Laval: compte-rendu sténographique*, 1946.

Lee, Bradford: 'Strategy, arms and the collapse of France, 1933–1940', in R. B. T. Langhorne (ed.), *Diplomacy and Intelligence during the Second World War*, Cambridge, 1985.

Le Goyet, Pierre: *Le mystère Gamelin*, 1976.

Léon Blum chef de gouvernement 1936–1937, 1967.

Leslie, R. F., A. Polonsky, J. Liechanowski and Z. A. Pelcyznski (eds.): *The History of Poland Since 1863*, Cambridge, 1980.

Liebling, A. J.: *The Road Back to Paris*, New York, 1988.

Lipski, Jósef: *Diplomat in Berlin 1933–1939*, Wacław Jędrzjewicz (ed.), New York, 1968.

Loizeau, General Lucien: 'Une mission militaire en URSS', *RDM*, 15 September 1955.

Łukasiewicz, Juliusz: *Diplomat in Paris 1936–1939*, Wacław Jędrzjewicz (ed.), New York, 1970.

Lungu, Dov: *Romania and the Great Powers 1933–1940*, Durham, NC, 1989.

Macartney, C. A. and Palmer, A. W.: *Independent Eastern Europe*, 1962.

MacDonald, C. A.: 'Britain, France and the April Crisis of 1939', *European Studies*, II, 2, April 1972.

'Economic Appeasement and the German "Moderates" 1937–1939: an Introductory Essay', *Past and Present*, no. 36, August 1972.

McDougall, Walter: *France's Rhineland Diplomacy 1914–1924*, Princeton, 1978.

'Political Economy versus National Sovereignty: French Structures for German Economic Integration after Versailles', *JMH*, LI, 1, March 1979.

Maier, Charles: *Recasting Bourgeois Europe*, Princeton, 1975.

'The Truth About the Treaties?', *JMH*, LI, 1, March 1979.

Malino, Frances and Wasserstein, Bernard (eds.): *The Jews in Modern France*, Hanover, NH, 1985.

Marès, Antoine: 'La faillite des relations franco-tchécoslovaques: la mission militaire française à Prague (1926–1939)', *RHDGM*, 111, July 1978.

Marguerat, Philippe: 'L'Allemagne et la Roumanie à l'automne 1938: économie et diplomatie', *Relations internationales*, no. 1, May 1974.

Le IIIe Reich et le pétrole roumain 1938–1940, Leiden, 1977.

Marks, Sally: 'Reparations Reconsidered', *Central European History*, II, 1969.

The Illusion of Peace: International Relations in Europe 1918–1933, 1976.

'The myths of reparations', *Central European History*, II, 1978.

Marseilles, J.: 'Le commerce entre la France et son empire colonial dans les années trente', Colloque de Nanterre, 1977.

Martel, Gordon (ed.): *The Origins of the Second World War Reconsidered*, Boston, 1986.

Mauriac, François: *Le noeud de vipères*, 1932.

Mearsheimer, John: *Conventional Deterrence*, Ithaca, NY, 1983.

Medlicott, W. N.: 'Britain and Germany: the Search for Agreement 1930–1937', Creighton Lecture in History 1968, Athlone Press, University of London, 1969.

Meisner, Maurice and Murphey, Rhoads (eds.): *The Mozartian Historian: Essays on the Works of Joseph Levenson*, Berkeley, 1976.

Mendès France, Pierre: *La vérité guidait leurs pas*, 1976.

Micaud, Charles A.: *The French Right and Nazi Germany 1933–1939*, New York, 1964.

Michel, Bernard: 'La Petite Entente et les crises internationales des années 1930', *RHDGM*, no. 77, January 1970.

Michel, Henri: *Le procès de Riom*, 1979.

Milza, Pierre: 'Le voyage de Pierre Laval à Rome en janvier 1935', in J.-B.

Duroselle and Enrico Serra (eds.), *Italia e Francia dal 1919 al 1939*, Instituto per gli Studi di Politica Internazionale, Milan, 1981.

Minart, Jacques: *P. C. Vincennes, Secteur 4*, 1945.

Moch, Jules: *Rencontres avec Léon Blum*, 1970.

Le front populaire, grande espérance, 1971.

Une si longue vie, 1976.

Morand, Paul: *Journal d'un attaché d'ambassade*, 1963.

Moravec, General František: *Master of Spies*, 1975.

Munich 1938: Mythes et Réalités, Revue des études slaves, LII, fascicule 1–2, Institut national d'études slaves, 1979.

Murray, Williamson: *The Change in the European Balance of Power, 1938–1939*, Princeton, 1984.

Néré, Jacques: *The Foreign Policy of France*, 1975.

Noël, Léon: *L'agression allemande contre la Pologne*, 1946.

Les illusions de Stresa: l'Italie abandonnée à Hitler, 1975.

La guerre de '39 a commencé quatre ans plus tôt, 1979.

La Tchécoslovaquie d'avant Munich, Institut d'études slaves, 1982.

La Pologne entre deux mondes, 1984.

Noguères, Henri: *Munich*, 1965.

Oprea, I. M.: *Nicolae Titulesco's Diplomatic Activity*, Bucharest, 1968.

Ormesson, Wladimir d': *France*, trans. J. Lewis May, 1939.

Les vraies confidences, 1962.

Paillat, Claude: *Le désastre de 1940*, 1983.

Parker, R. A. C.: 'The First Capitulation: France and the Rhineland Crisis of 1936', *World Politics*, VII, April 1956.

'Great Britain, France and the Ethiopian Crisis 1935–36', *EHR*, LXXXIX, 351, April 1974.

Paul-Boncour, Joseph: *Entre deux guerres*, 3 vols., 1945–7.

Paulhan, Jean (ed.): *Honneur à St. John-Perse: hommages et témoinages littéraires suivis d'une documentation sur Alexis Léger diplomate*, 1965.

Pedroncini, Guy: 'La stratégie française et l'Italie de 1932 à 1939', in J.-B. Duroselle and Enrico Serra (eds.), *Italie e Francia dal 1919 al 1939*, Instituto per gli Studi di Politica Internazionale, Milan, 1981.

Pertinax, pseudonym of Geraud, André: *The Gravediggers of France: Gamelin, Daladier, Reynaud, Pétain, and Laval – Military Defeat, Armistice, Counter-revolution*, New York, 1944.

Pétain, Maréchal Philippe: *Procès du maréchal Pétain*, compte rendu officiel in extenso des audiences de la Haute Cour de Justice, 1976.

Pétrement, Simone: *La vie de Simone Weil*, 2 vols., 1973.

Piétri, François: 'Souvenir de Barthou', *RDM*, 1 March 1961.

Planté, Louis: *Un grand seigneur de la politique: Anatole de Monzie 1875–1947*, 1955.

Polonsky, A. B.: *Politics in Independent Poland 1921–1939*, Oxford, 1972.

Posen, Barry: *The Sources of Military Doctrine*, Ithaca, 1984.

Preston, Adrian (ed.): *General Staffs and Diplomacy before the Second World War*, 1978.

Proust, Marcel: *A la recherche du temps perdu*, vol. III, 1973.

Pryor, Zora: 'Czechoslovak Economic Development in the Interwar Period', in S. Mamatey and R. Luža (eds.), *A History of the Czechoslovak Republic*, Princeton, 1973.

Puaux, Gabriel: *Mort et transfiguration de l'Autriche*, 1966.

Radice, E. A.: 'General Characteristics of the Region between the Wars', in M. C. Kaser and E. A. Radice (eds.), *The Economic History of Eastern Europe 1919–1975*, vol. I, Oxford, 1985.

Radice, Lisanne: *Prelude to Appeasement: East Central European Diplomacy in the Early 1930s*, New York, 1981.

Raupach, Hans: 'The Impact of the Great Depression in Eastern Europe', *JCH*, IV, 4, October 1969.

Les relations franco-allemandes 1933–1939, 1976.

Les relations franco-britanniques 1935–1939, 1975.

Les relations militaires franco-belges mars 1936–10 mai 1940, 1968.

Renouvin, Pierre: 'La politique extérieure de la France de 1933 à 1939: progrès et lacunes de l'information historique', in *Bulletin de la classe des lettres et des sciences morales et politiques*, 5th Series, XLIX, Académie royale de Belgique, 1963.

Histoire des relations internationales: les crises du XXe siècle, vol. VII (1914–29), vol. VIII (1929–45), 1958, 1969.

Reussner, André: *Les conversations franco-britanniques d'Etat-major 1935–39*, 1969.

Reynaud, Paul: *La France a sauvé l'Europe*, 2 vols., 1947.

Au coeur de la mêlée, 1951.

Ripka, Hubert: *Munich: Before and After*, 1939.

Le Coup de Prague, 1949.

Robertson, E. M.: *Hitler's Pre-War Policy and Military Plans*, 1963.

(ed.): *The Origins of the Second World War*, 1971.

Mussolini as Empire-Builder: Europe and Africa 1932–1936, 1977.

'Hitler and Sanctions: Mussolini and the Rhineland', *European Studies Review*, VI, 4, October 1977.

Rollet, Henry: 'Deux mythes des relations franco-polonaises entre les deux guerres', *Revue d'histoire diplomatique*, nos. 3–4, July–December 1982.

La Pologne au XXe siècle, 1984.

Rostow, Nicolas: *Anglo-French Relations 1934–36*, 1984.

Rothschild, Joseph: *East Central Europe between the Two World Wars*, Seattle, 1974.

Rothstein, Robert: *Alliances and Small Powers*, New York, 1968.

Rutych, N.: 'L'affaire du maréchal Toukhatchevsky', *RDM*, 15 April 1961.

Sakwa, George: 'The "Renewal" of the Franco-Polish Alliance in 1936 and the Rambouillet Agreement', *Polish Review*, XVI, 2, 1971.

'The Franco-Polish Alliance and the Remilitarisation of the Rhineland', *Historical Journal*, XVI, 1, 1973.

Sauvy, Alfred and Hirsch, Anita: *Histoire économique de la France entre les deux guerres*, 4 vols., 1965–1975.

Sauvy, Alfred: 'The economic crisis of the 1930s in France', *JCH*, IV, 4, October 1969.

Schellenberg, Walter: *The Schellenberg Memoirs*, Louis Hagen (ed.), 1956.

Scherer, André: 'Le problème des "mains libres" à l'est', *RHDGM*, no. 32, October 1958.

Schroeder, Hans-Jürgen: 'Les relations économiques franco-allemandes de 1936 à 1939', Deutschland und Frankreich 1936–1939, 15. Deutsch-französisches Historikerkolloquium, Bonn, 1978.

Schroeder, Paul: 'The 19th Century International System: Changes in the Structure', *World Politics*, XXXIX, October 1986.

Schuker, Stephen: *The End of French Predominance in Europe: The Finance Crisis of 1924 and the Adoption of the Dawes Plan*, Chapel Hill, NC, 1976.

'France and the Remilitarization of the Rhineland 1936', *French Historical Studies*, spring 1986.

Scott, W. E.: *Alliance against Hitler*, Durham, NC, 1962.

Seton-Watson, Christopher: 'The Anglo-Italian Gentlemen's Agreement', Anglo-German Historical Conference, Cumberland Lodge, 1980.

Seton-Watson, Hugh: *Eastern Europe Between the Wars*, Cambridge, 1945.

Sherwood, John: *Georges Mandel and the Third Republic*, Palo Alto, 1970.

Shorrock, William I.: 'The Jouvenal Mission to Rome and the Origins of the Laval-Mussolini Accords 1933–1935', *The Historian*, XLV, 1982.

From Ally to Enemy: the Enigma of Fascist Italy in French Diplomacy, 1920–1940, Kent, Ohio, 1988.

Soucy, Robert J.: 'The Nature of Fascism in France', *JCH*, I, 1, 1966.

Soutou, Georges-Henri: 'Problèmes concernant le rétablissement des relations économiques franco-allemandes après la première guerre mondiale', *Francia*, II, 1974.

'Die deutschen Reparationen und das Seydoux-Projekt 1920–21', *Vierteljahrshefte für Zeitgeschichte*, XXIII, 1975.

'L'impérialisme du pauvre', *Relations internationales*, VII, 1976.

'L'alliance franco-polonaise (1925–1933) ou comment s'en débarrasser?', *Revue d'histoire diplomatique*, nos. 2, 3, 4, 1981.

Stone, Glyn: 'The European Great Powers and the Spanish Civil War, 1936–1939', in R. Boyce and E. M. Robertson (eds.), *Paths to War*, 1989.

Stone, Norman and Strouhal, Eduard (eds.): *Czechoslovakia: Crossroads and Crises, 1918–1988*, 1989.

Suarez, Georges: *Briand, sa vie, son oeuvre*, 1941.

Szembek, Comte Jean: *Journal 1933–1939*, 1952.

Taylor, A. J. P.: *The Origins of the Second World War*, New York, 1983.

A Personal History, 1983.

Taylor, Telford: *Munich: the Price of Peace*, New York, 1980.

Teichova, Alice: *An Economic Background to Munich: International Business and Czechoslovakia 1918–1938*, Cambridge, 1974.

'Industry', in M. C. Kaser and E. A. Radice (eds.), *The Economic History of Eastern Europe 1919–1975*, vol. I, Oxford, 1985.

Tournoux, General Paul-Emile: *Défense des frontières: haut commandement et gouvernement 1919–1939*, 1960.

Trachtenberg, Marc: 'Reparations at the Paris Peace Conference', *JMH*, LI, 1, March 1979.
Reparation in World Politics: France and European Diplomacy 1916–1923, New York, 1980.

Vago, Bela: 'Popular Front in the Balkans: Failure in Hungary and Roumania', *JCH*, III, 1970.

Vaïsse, Maurice: *Sécurité d'abord: la politique française en matière de désarmement*, 1981.
'La mission de Jouvenal à Rome', in J.-B. Duroselle and Enrico Serra (eds.), *Italia e Francia dal 1919 al 1939*, Instituto per gli Studi di Politica Internazionale, Milan, 1981.
'Les militaires français et l'alliance franco-soviétique au cours des années 1930', Colloque forces armées et systèmes d'alliances, Montpellier, September 1981.

Vichniac, Marc: *Léon Blum*, 1937.

Wall, Irwin M.: 'Socialists and Bureaucrats: the Blum Government and the French Administration of 1936–37', *International Review of Social History*, 1979.

Wandycz, Piotr: *France and her Eastern Allies 1919–1925*, Minneapolis, 1962.
'The Foreign Policy of Edvard Beneš, 1918–1938', in S. Mamatey and R. Luža (eds.), *A History of the Czechoslovak Republic*, Princeton, 1973.
'La Pologne face à la politique locarnienne de Briand', *Revue d'histoire diplomatique*, nos. 2, 3, 4, 1981.
'The Little Entente Sixty Years Later', *Slavonic and East European Review*, 4, 1981.
The Twilight of France's Eastern Alliances, 1926–1936, Princeton, 1988.

Warner, Geoffrey: *Pierre Laval and the Eclipse of France*, 1968.

Watt, D. C.: 'The Anglo-German Naval Agreement of 1935: an Interim Judgement', *JMH*, XXVIII, 2, June 1956.
'The Secret Laval-Mussolini Agreement of 1935 on Ethiopia', *Middle East Journal*, XV, 1, 1961.
'German plans for the reoccupation of the Rhineland: a Note', *JCH*, I, 4, October 1966.
Too Serious a Business: European Armed Forces and the Approach of the Second World War, 1975.
How War Came, New York, 1989.

Weber, Eugen: 'The Men of the Archangel', *JCH*, I, 1966.

Weinberg, David: *A Community on Trial: the Jews of Paris in the 1930s*, Chicago, 1977.

Weinberg, Gerhard: 'The Secret Hitler-Beneš Negotiations in 1936–37', *Journal of Central European History*, XIX, 4, January 1960.
The Foreign Policy of Hitler's Germany, I, 1933–6, II, 1937–9, Chicago, 1970, 1980.

Weiss, Louise: *Mémoires d'une Européenne: Combats pour l'Europe 1919–1934*, 1969.

Mémoires d'une Européenne: Combats pour les femmes 1934–1939, 1970.
Werth, Alexander: *Twilight of France 1933–1940*, 1942.
Weygand, Jacques: *Weygand, mon père*, 1970.
Wheeler-Bennett, John: *Munich: Prelude to Tragedy*, 1948.
Knaves, Fools and Heroes: Europe Between the Wars, 1974.
Wiskemann, Elizabeth: *The Rome-Berlin Axis*, 1966.
The Europe I Saw, 1968.
Fascism in Italy: Its Development and Influence, 1969.
Young, Robert: 'The Strategic Dream: French air doctrine in the interwar period', *JCH*, IX, 4, October 1974.
'Le Haut Commandement français au moment de Munich', *Revue d'histoire moderne et contemporaine*, January-March 1977.
In Command of France, Cambridge, Mass., 1978.
'La Guerre de Longue Durée', in Adrian Preston (ed.), *General Staffs and Diplomacy before the Second World War*, 1978.
'*L'Attaque Brusquée* and Its Use as Myth in Interwar France', *Historical Reflections*, VIII, 1, 1981.
'French Military Intelligence and Nazi Germany, 1938–1939', in E. May (ed.), *Knowing One's Enemies*, Princeton, 1984.
'Soldiers and Diplomats: the French Embassy and Franco-Italian Relations 1935–6', *Journal of Strategic Studies*, VII, 1984.
'French Military Intelligence and the Franco-Italian Alliance, 1933–1939', *Historical Journal*, XXVIII, 1, 1985.

UNPUBLISHED MANUSCRIPTS AND THESES

Adamthwaite, A. P.: 'The Franco-German Declaration of 6 December 1938'.
Alexander, Martin S.: 'Anglo-French Relations, Strategy in France and Belgium, and B.E.F. Deployment, September 1939–May 1940'.
'Architects of French Rearmament: A Reappraisal of Edouard Daladier and Maurice Gamelin in French War Preparation'.
'Maurice Gamelin and the Defence of France: French Military Policy, the U.K. Land Contribution and Strategy Towards Germany, 1935–1939'. Unpublished D. Phil. thesis, University of Oxford, 1982.
'The French Catastrophe of 1940: Forty Six Years Later', the 1986 Mead Lecture, Trinity College, Connecticut, 1986.
Parker, R.A.C.: 'Dr Schacht and the British: the Repercussions of Schacht's Visit to Paris in August 1936'.
Passmore, K.J.: 'The Failure of France and Italy to Conclude a Military Alliance'. Unpublished M.A. Thesis, University of London, 1972.
Young, Robert J.: 'Louis Barthou, Portrait Intime'.

Index